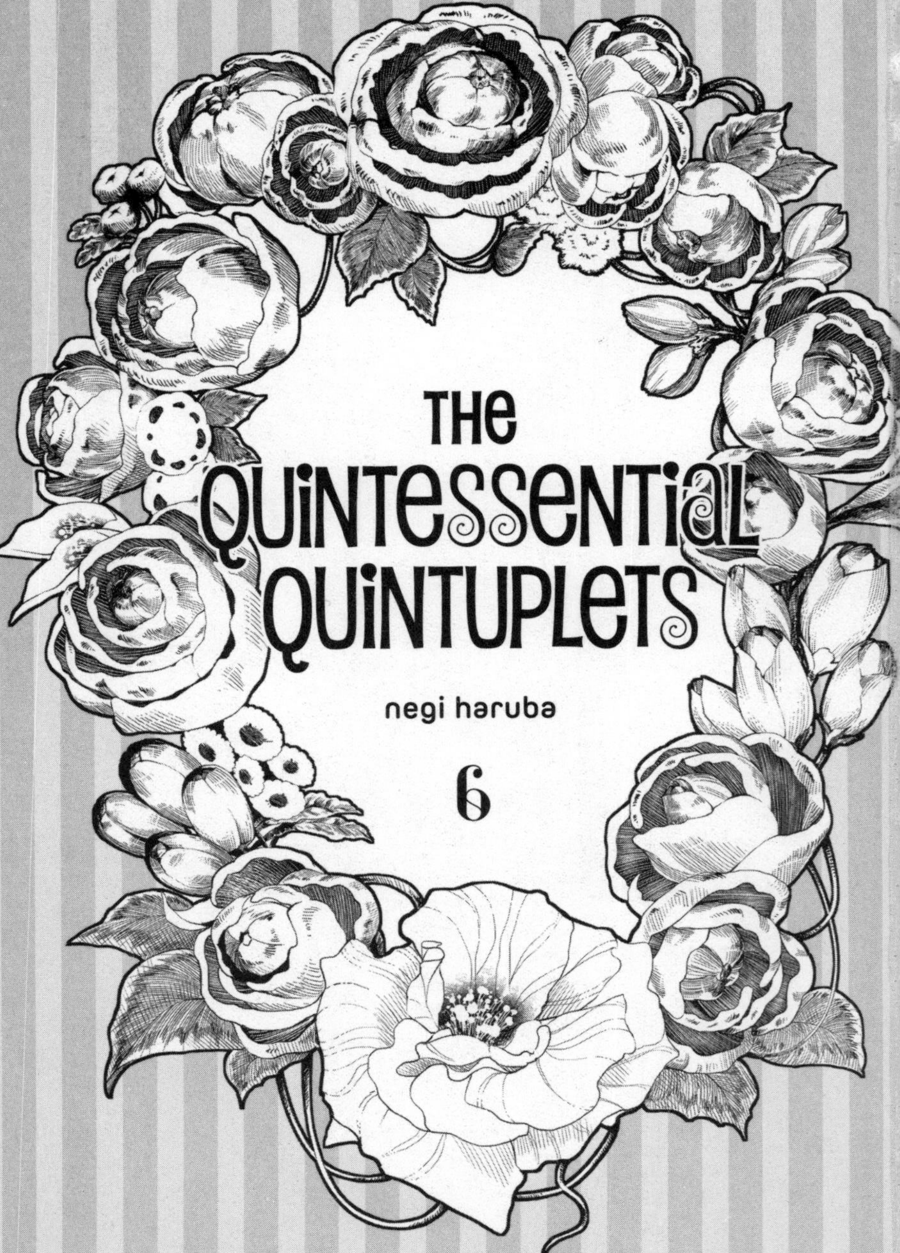

# THE QUINTESSENTIAL QUINTUPLETS

negi haruba

6

Character intros

# HIS FUTURE BRIDE IS ONE OF THE QUINTS!!

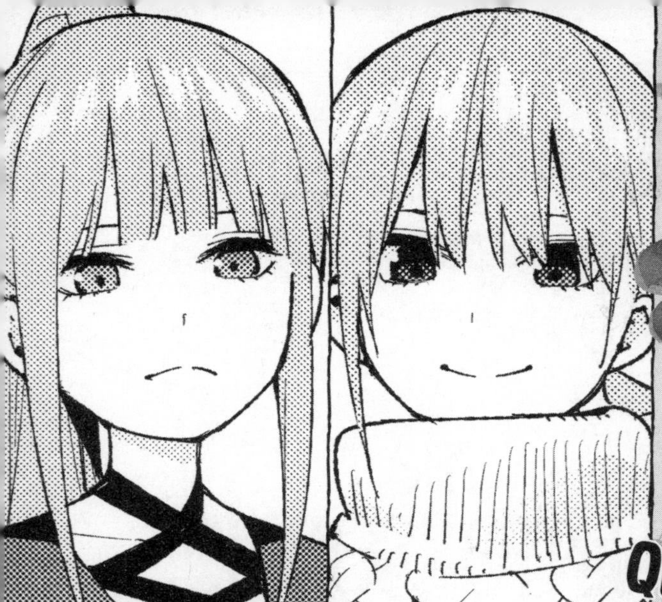

**ICHIKA NAKANO**

THE ELDEST SISTER. SHE'S BEEN SO BUSY WITH WORK AND STUDYING LATELY THAT SHE'S ONLY BEEN GETTING EIGHT HOURS OF SLEEP A NIGHT. DOESN'T LIKE TO EAT SHIITAKES.

**NINO NAKANO**

THE SECOND SISTER. WHEN SHE OVERSLEEPS, SHE APPLIES HER MAKEUP IN THE ELEVATOR AS IT TRAVELS DOWN 30 FLOORS. DOESN'T LIKE TO EAT PICKLED THINGS.

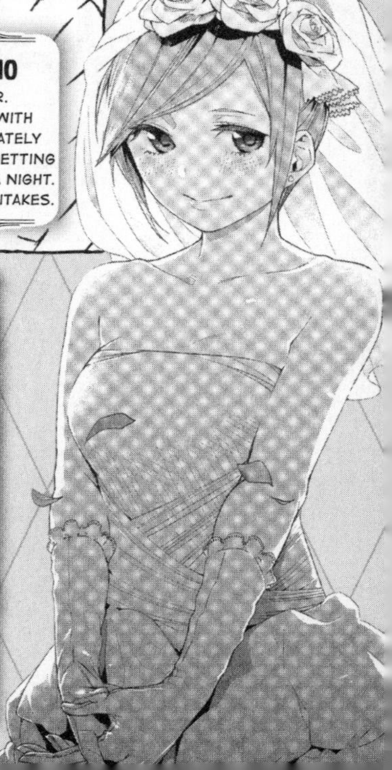

## Quints Memo

- ★ Hate to Study: If you try to teach them anything, they run.
- ★ Potential Flunkers: Their score on Futaro's quiz was 100 points...between the five of them.
- ☆ On the Verge of Flunking: Had to change schools to avoid flunking out.
- ★ Very Idiosyncratic: The five sisters each have their own intense quirks, so dealing with them won't be easy.

...Guide the five of them to graduation!!

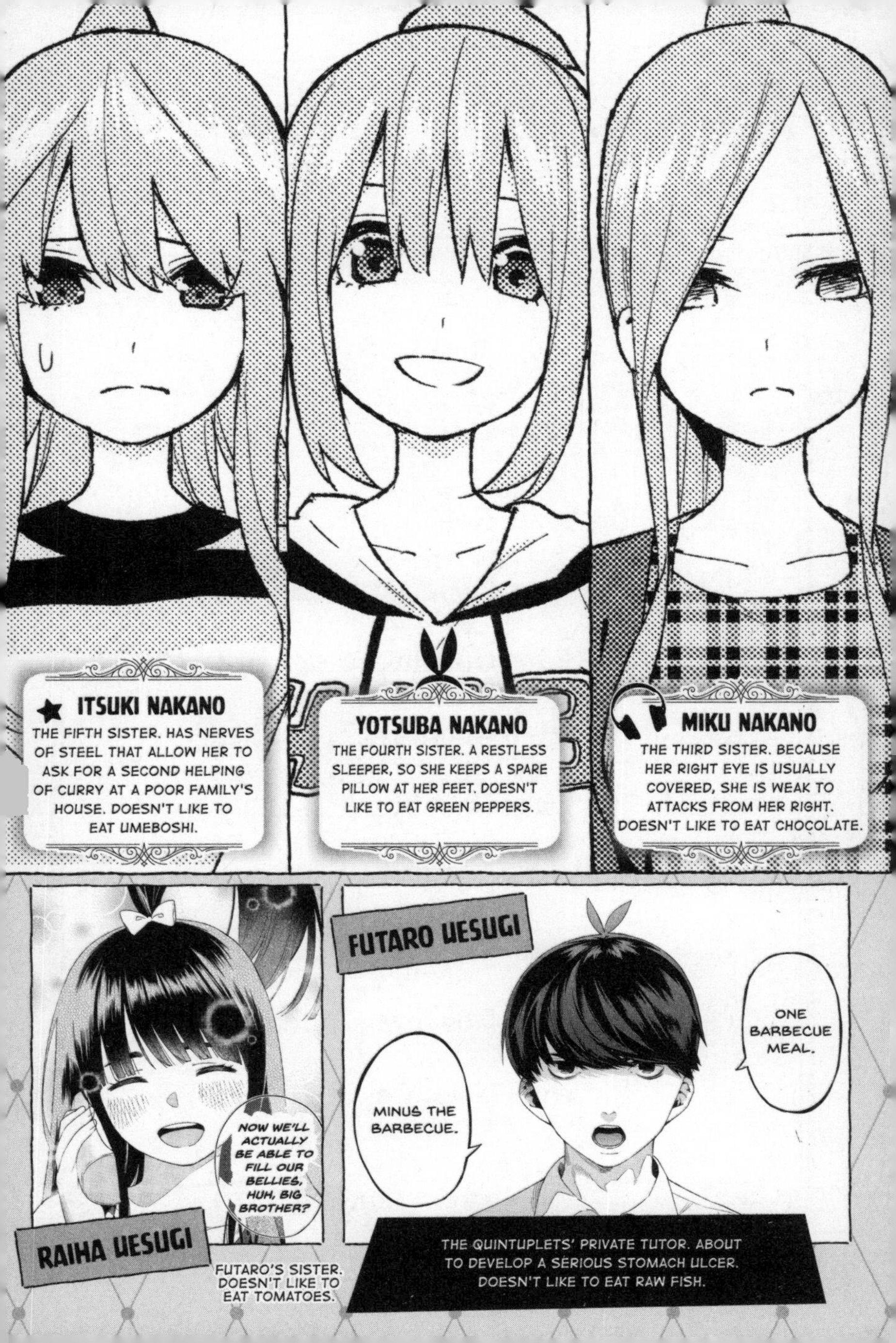
MIKU NAKANO
THE THIRD SISTER. BECAUSE HER RIGHT EYE IS USUALLY COVERED, SHE IS WEAK TO ATTACKS FROM HER RIGHT. DOESN'T LIKE TO EAT CHOCOLATE.
YOTSUBA NAKANO
THE FOURTH SISTER. A RESTLESS SLEEPER, SO SHE KEEPS A SPARE PILLOW AT HER FEET. DOESN'T LIKE TO EAT GREEN PEPPERS.
ITSUKI NAKANO
THE FIFTH SISTER. HAS NERVES OF STEEL THAT ALLOW HER TO ASK FOR A SECOND HELPING OF CURRY AT A POOR FAMILY'S HOUSE. DOESN'T LIKE TO EAT UMEBOSHI.
FUTARO UESUGI
ONE BARBECUE MEAL.
MINUS THE BARBECUE.
THE QUINTUPLETS' PRIVATE TUTOR. ABOUT TO DEVELOP A SERIOUS STOMACH ULCER. DOESN'T LIKE TO EAT RAW FISH.
NOW WE'LL ACTUALLY BE ABLE TO FILL OUR BELLIES, HUH, BIG BROTHER?
RAIHA UESUGI
FUTARO'S SISTER. DOESN'T LIKE TO EAT TOMATOES.

# CONTENTS

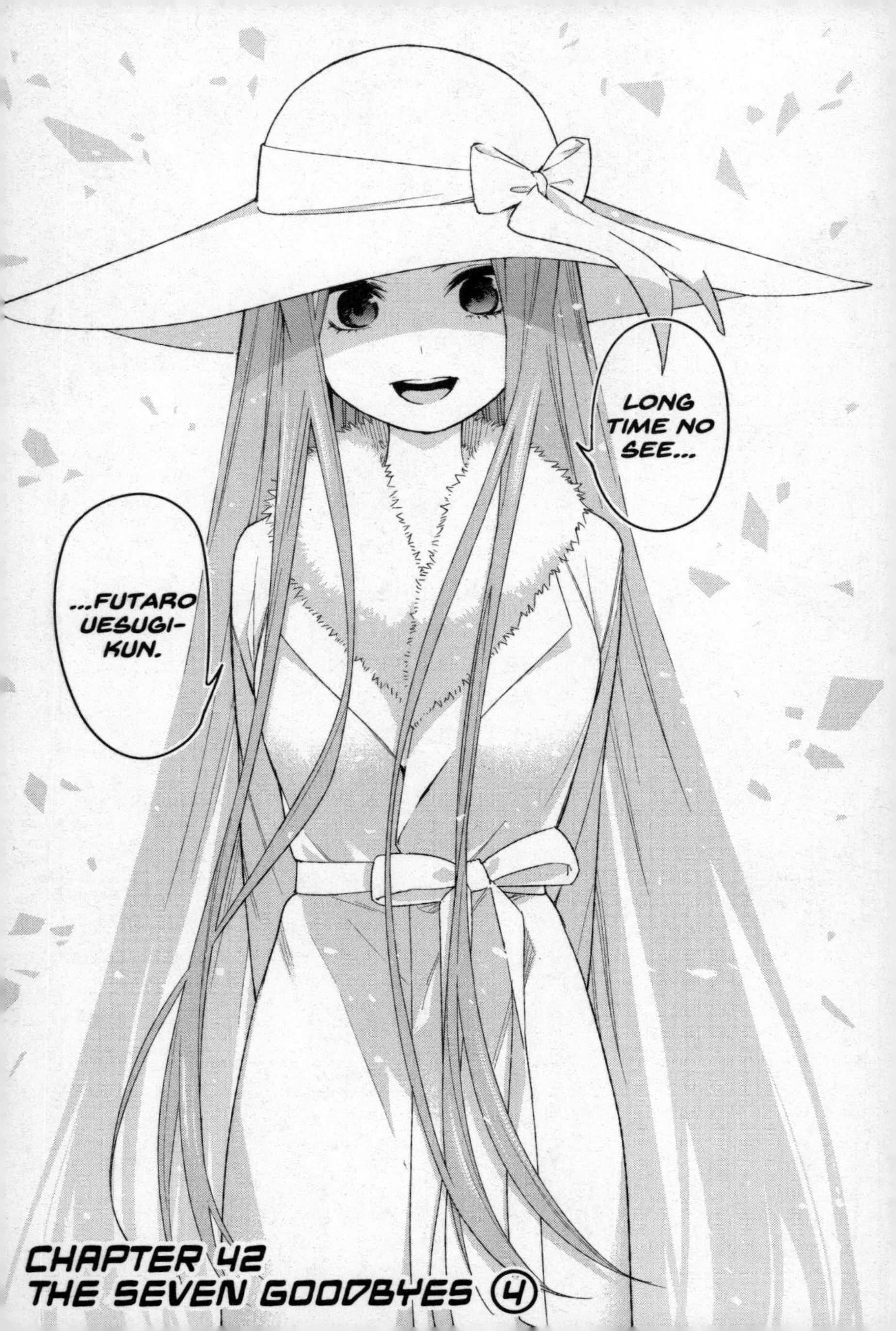
LONG TIME NO SEE...
...FUTARO UESUGI-KUN.

# CHAPTER 42
# THE SEVEN GOODBYES ④

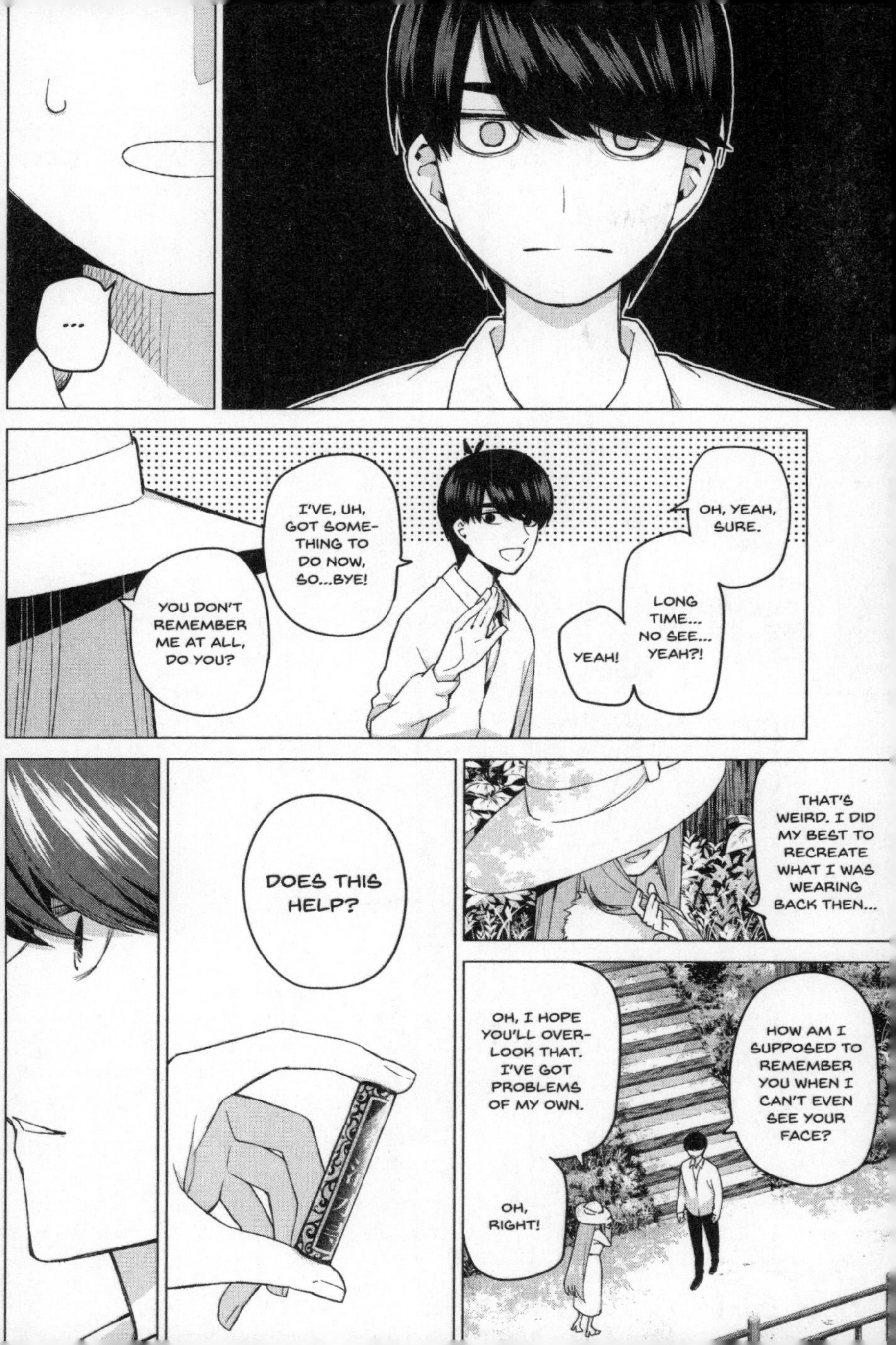
...
OH, YEAH, SURE.
LONG TIME... NO SEE... YEAH?!
YEAH!
I'VE, UH, GOT SOME-THING TO DO NOW, SO...BYE!
YOU DON'T REMEMBER ME AT ALL, DO YOU?
THAT'S WEIRD. I DID MY BEST TO RECREATE WHAT I WAS WEARING BACK THEN...
HOW AM I SUPPOSED TO REMEMBER YOU WHEN I CAN'T EVEN SEE YOUR FACE?
OH, I HOPE YOU'LL OVER-LOOK THAT. I'VE GOT PROBLEMS OF MY OWN.
OH, RIGHT!
DOES THIS HELP?

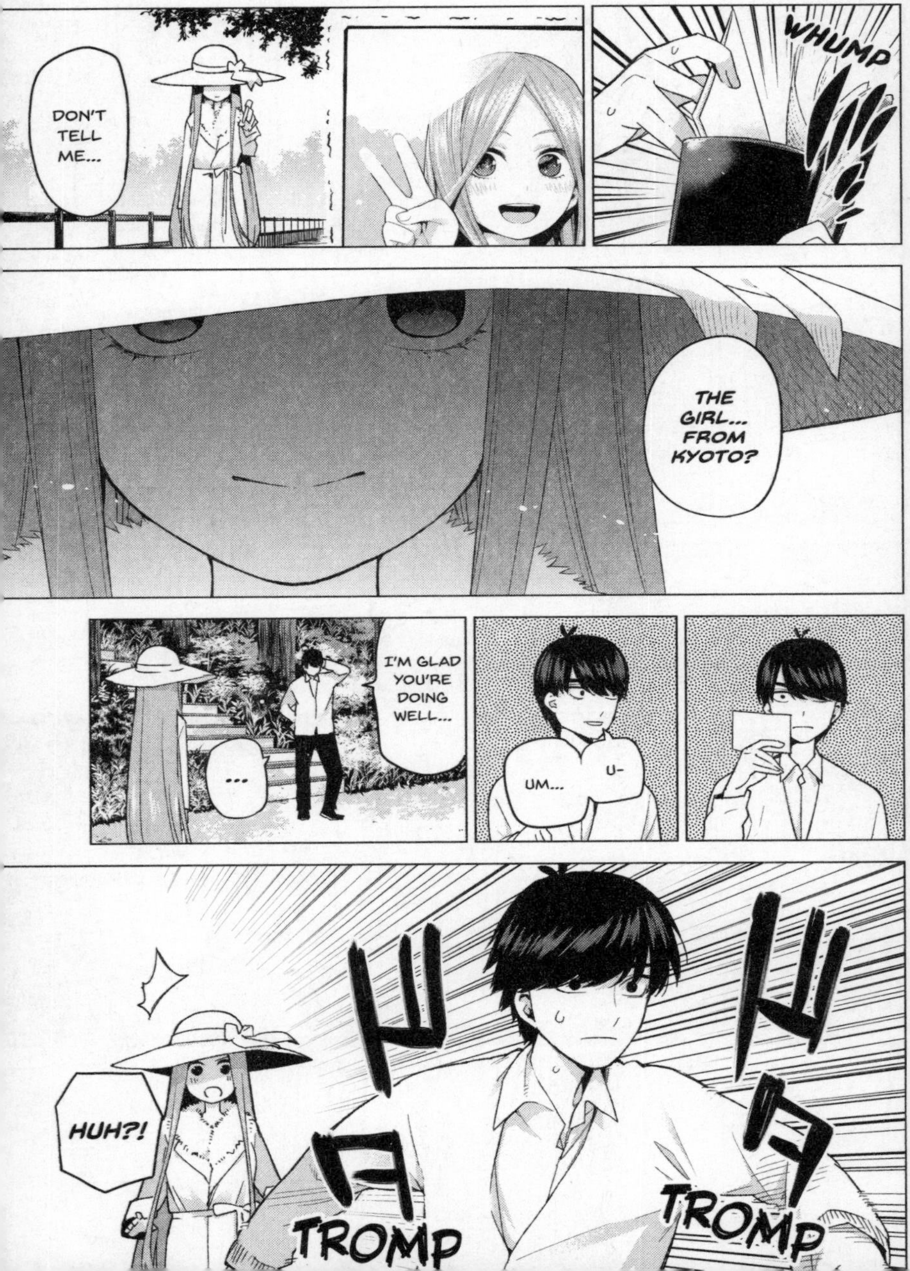
WHUMP
DON'T TELL ME...
THE GIRL... FROM KYOTO?
U-
UM...
I'M GLAD YOU'RE DOING WELL...
...
ドタ
TROMP
HUH?!
ドタ
TROMP

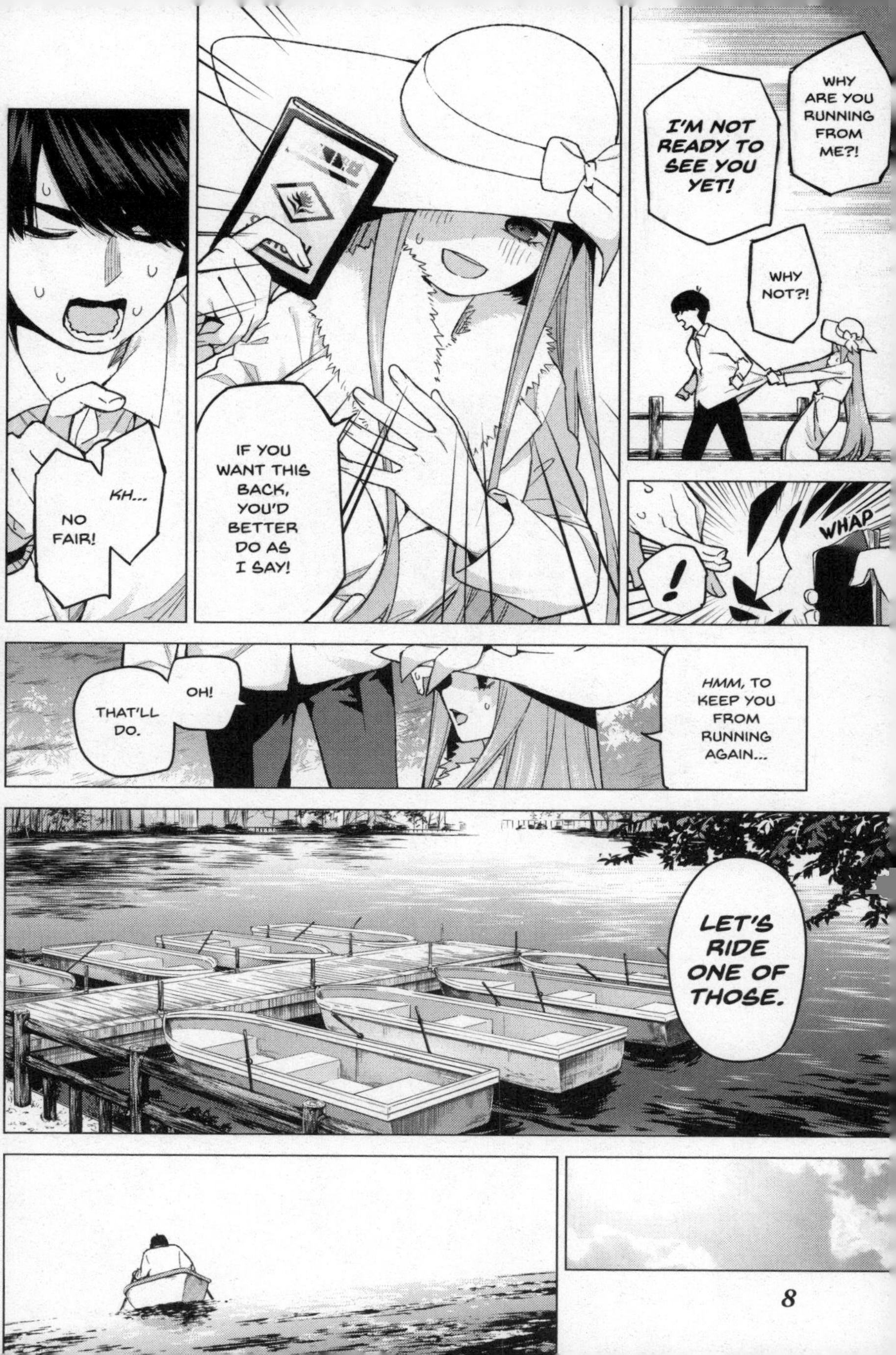
WHY ARE YOU RUNNING FROM ME?!
I'M NOT READY TO SEE YOU YET!
WHY NOT?!
WHAP
!
IF YOU WANT THIS BACK, YOU'D BETTER DO AS I SAY!
KH...
NO FAIR!
HMM, TO KEEP YOU FROM RUNNING AGAIN...
OH!
THAT'LL DO.
LET'S RIDE ONE OF THOSE.

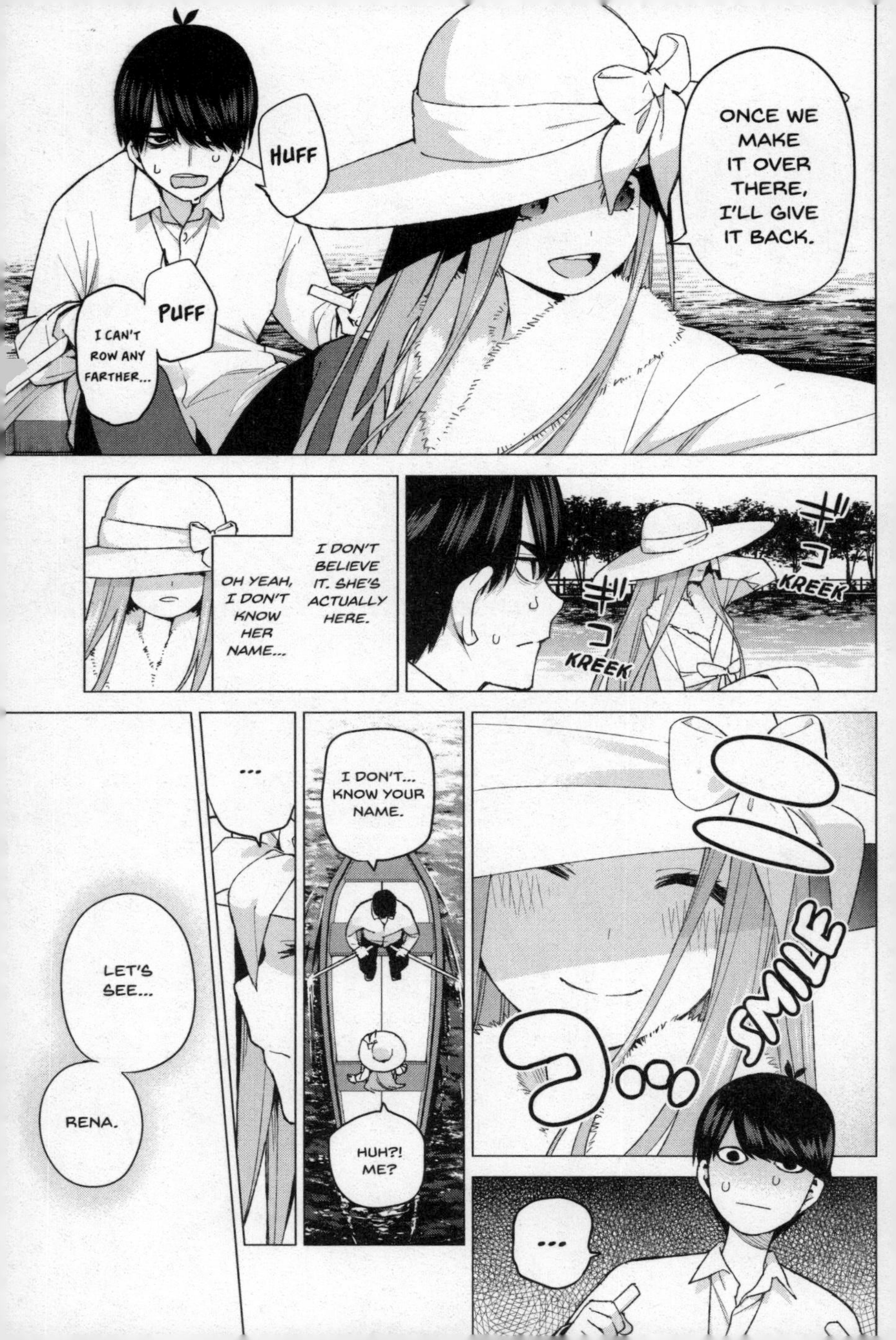
ONCE WE MAKE IT OVER THERE, I'LL GIVE IT BACK.
HUFF
PUFF
I CAN'T ROW ANY FARTHER...
ギコ
KREEK
ギコ
KREEK
I DON'T BELIEVE IT. SHE'S ACTUALLY HERE.
OH YEAH, I DON'T KNOW HER NAME...
SMILE
...
I DON'T... KNOW YOUR NAME.
HUH?! ME?
...
LET'S SEE...
RENA.

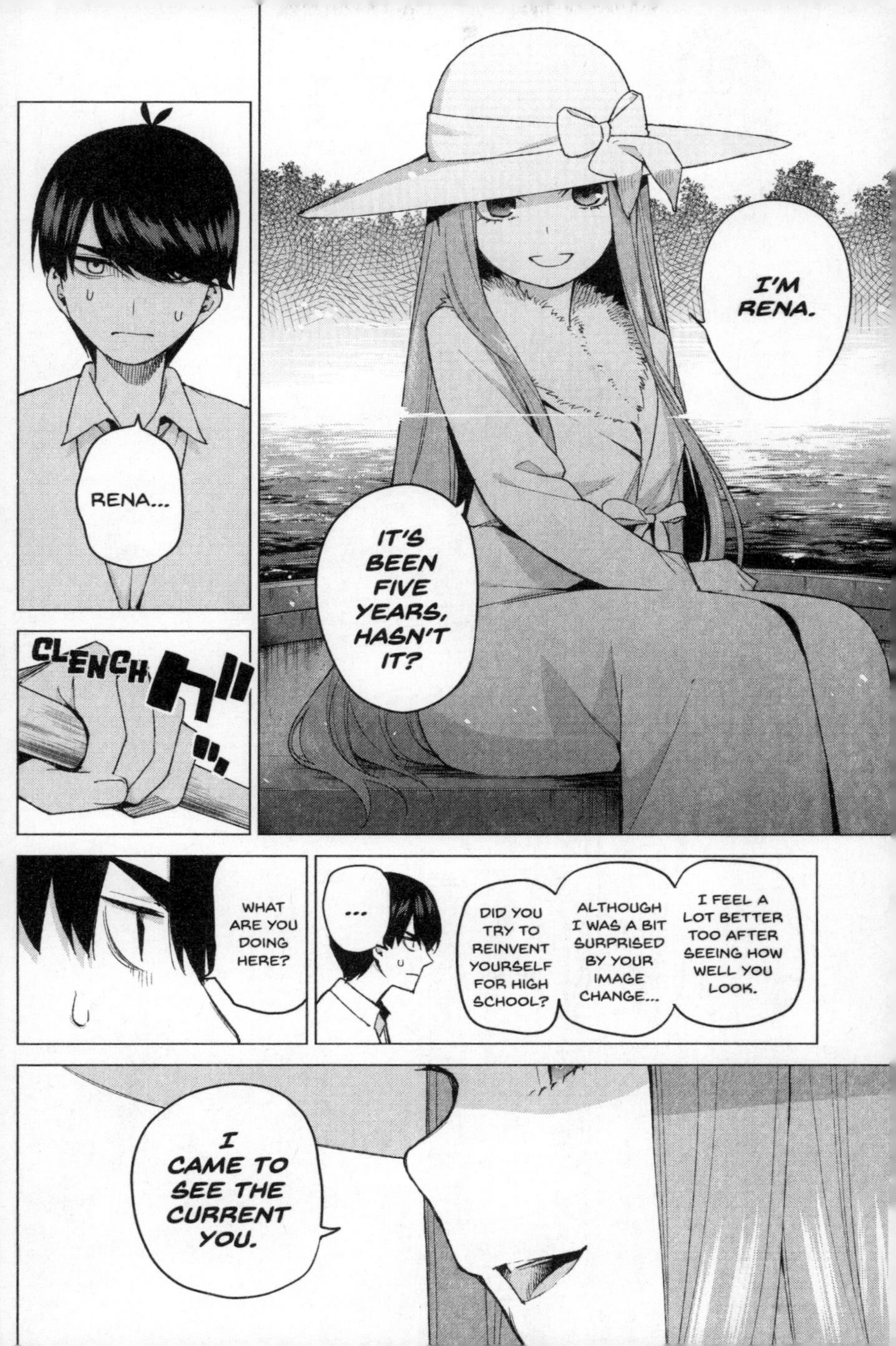
I'M RENA.
IT'S BEEN FIVE YEARS, HASN'T IT?
RENA...
CLENCH
I FEEL A LOT BETTER TOO AFTER SEEING HOW WELL YOU LOOK.
ALTHOUGH I WAS A BIT SURPRISED BY YOUR IMAGE CHANGE...
DID YOU TRY TO REINVENT YOURSELF FOR HIGH SCHOOL?
...
WHAT ARE YOU DOING HERE?
I CAME TO SEE THE CURRENT YOU.

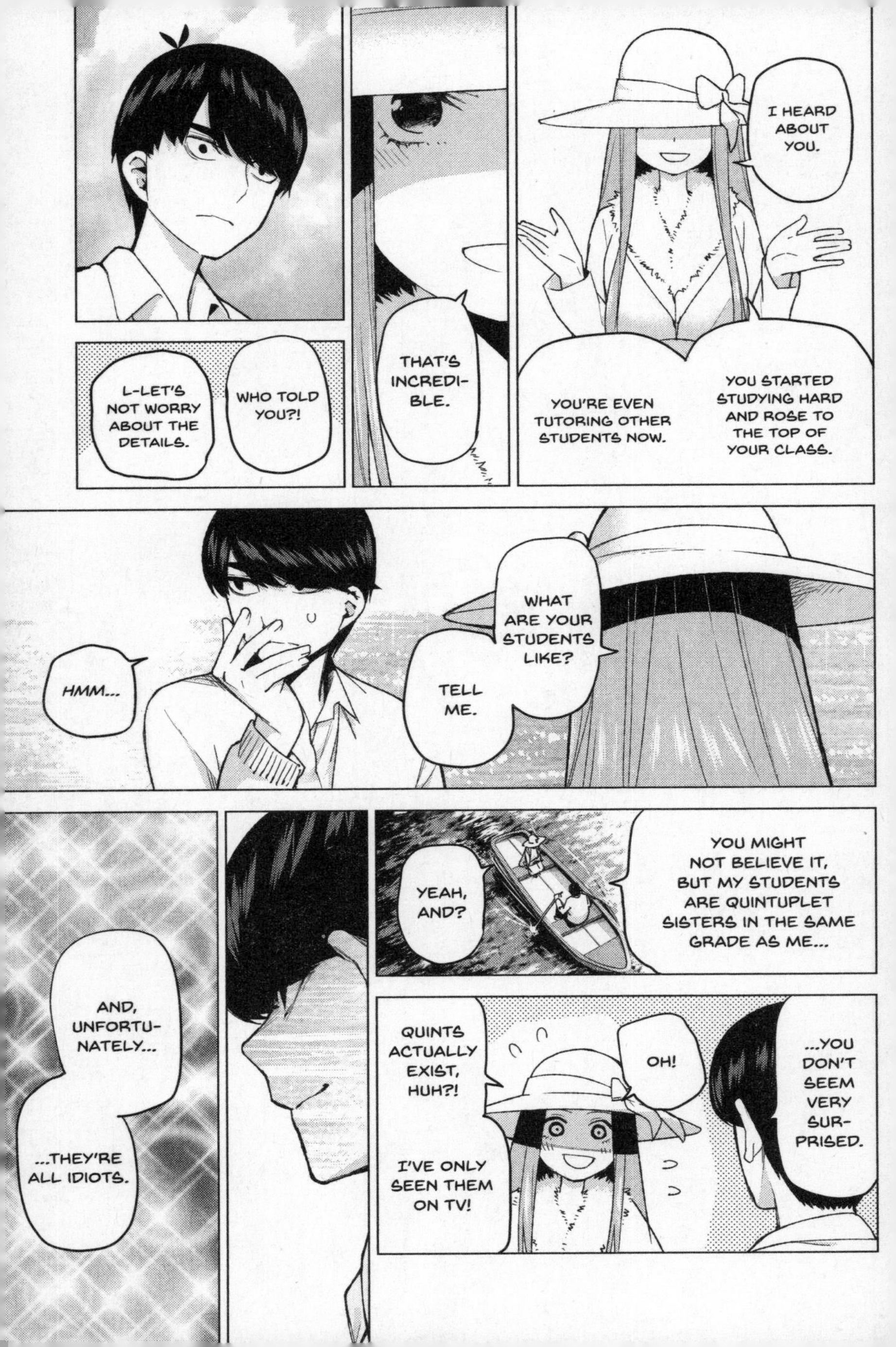
I HEARD ABOUT YOU.
YOU STARTED STUDYING HARD AND ROSE TO THE TOP OF YOUR CLASS.
YOU'RE EVEN TUTORING OTHER STUDENTS NOW.
THAT'S INCREDI-BLE.
WHO TOLD YOU?!
L-LET'S NOT WORRY ABOUT THE DETAILS.
WHAT ARE YOUR STUDENTS LIKE?
TELL ME.
HMM...
YOU MIGHT NOT BELIEVE IT, BUT MY STUDENTS ARE QUINTUPLET SISTERS IN THE SAME GRADE AS ME...
YEAH, AND?
...YOU DON'T SEEM VERY SUR-PRISED.
OH!
QUINTS ACTUALLY EXIST, HUH?!
I'VE ONLY SEEN THEM ON TV!
AND, UNFORTU-NATELY...
...THEY'RE ALL IDIOTS.

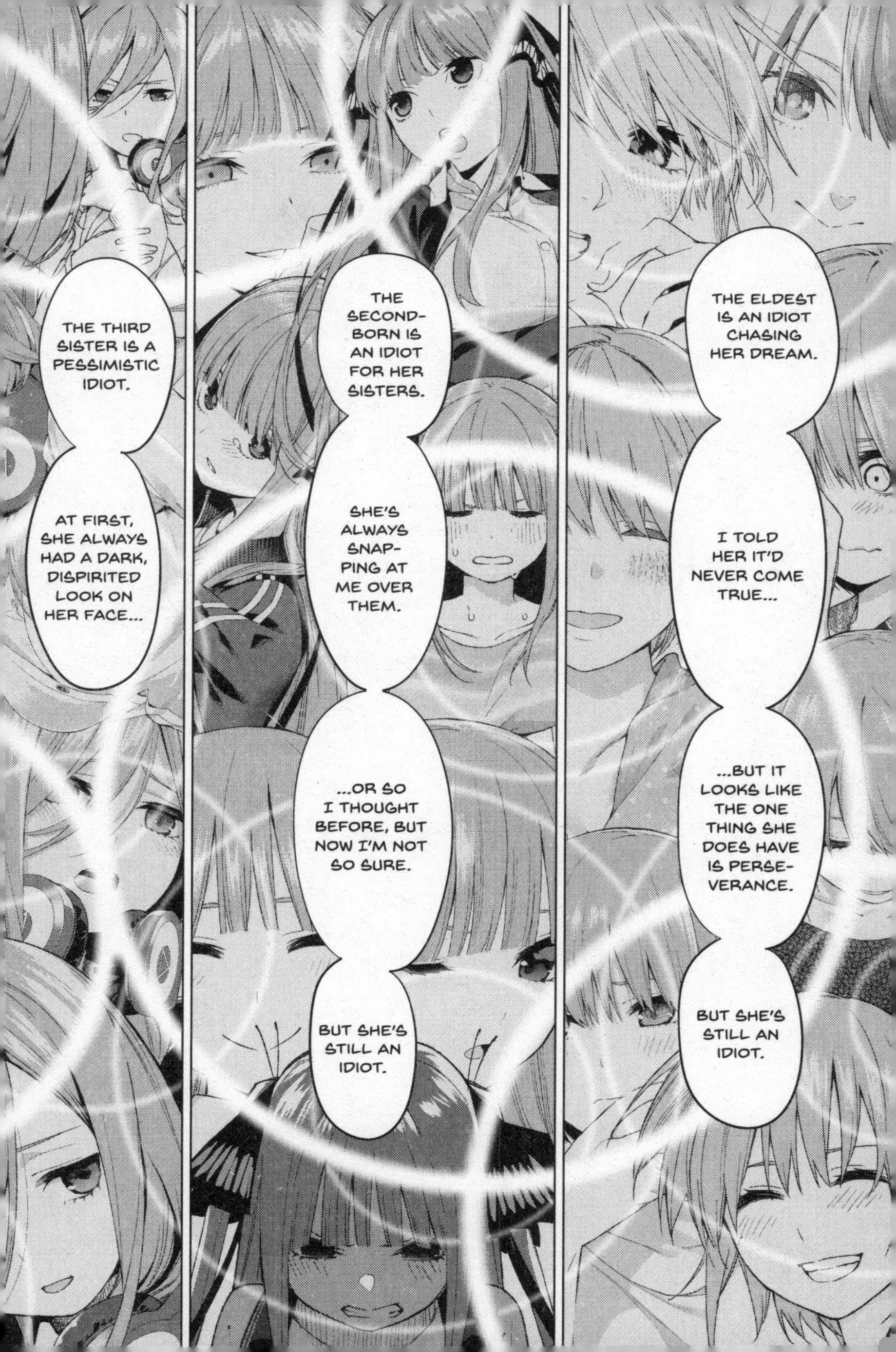
THE ELDEST IS AN IDIOT CHASING HER DREAM.
I TOLD HER IT'D NEVER COME TRUE...
...BUT IT LOOKS LIKE THE ONE THING SHE DOES HAVE IS PERSEVERANCE.
BUT SHE'S STILL AN IDIOT.
THE SECOND-BORN IS AN IDIOT FOR HER SISTERS.
SHE'S ALWAYS SNAPPING AT ME OVER THEM.
...OR SO I THOUGHT BEFORE, BUT NOW I'M NOT SO SURE.
BUT SHE'S STILL AN IDIOT.
THE THIRD SISTER IS A PESSIMISTIC IDIOT.
AT FIRST, SHE ALWAYS HAD A DARK, DISPIRITED LOOK ON HER FACE...

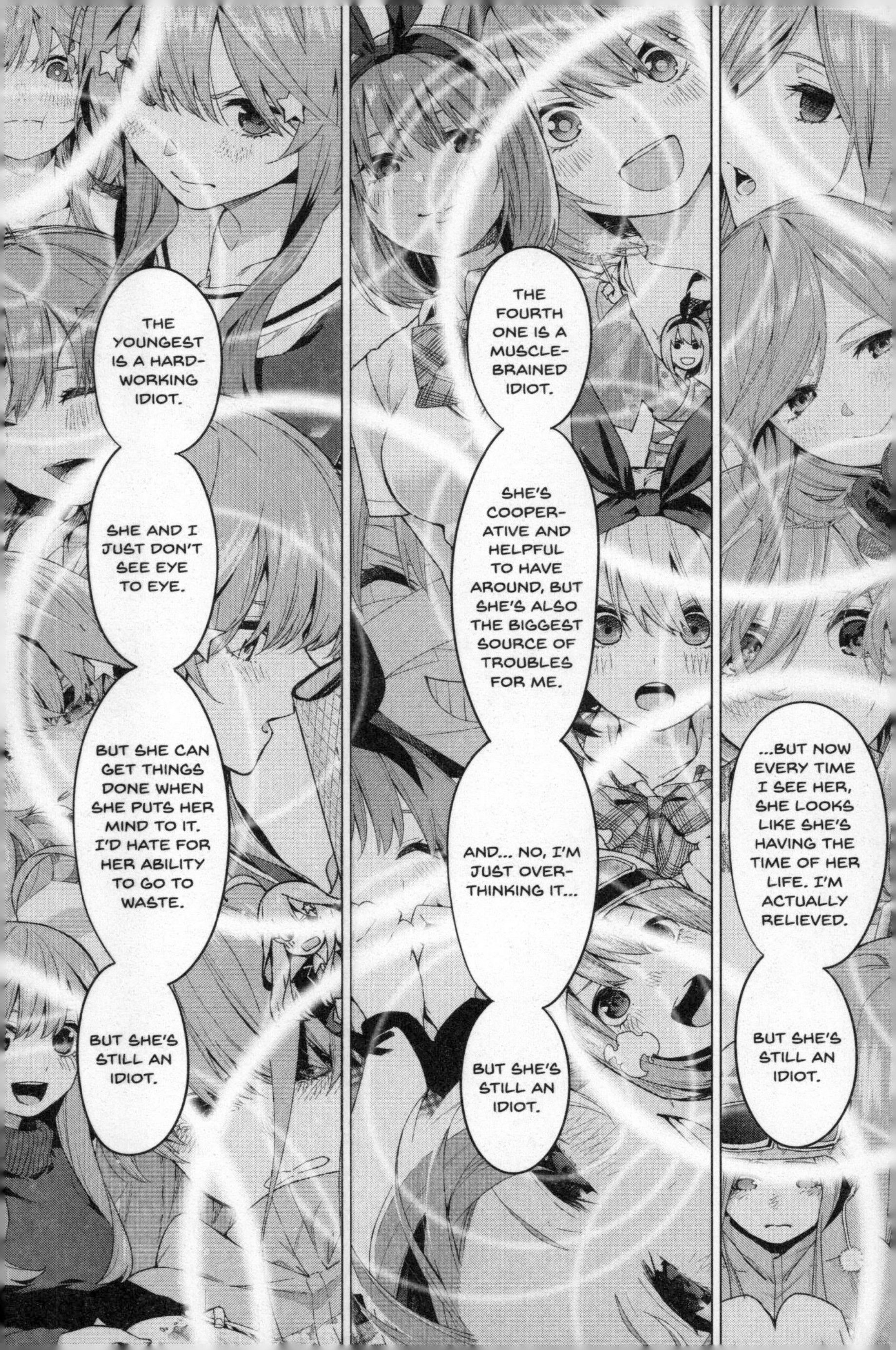
...BUT NOW EVERY TIME I SEE HER, SHE LOOKS LIKE SHE'S HAVING THE TIME OF HER LIFE. I'M ACTUALLY RELIEVED.
BUT SHE'S STILL AN IDIOT.
THE FOURTH ONE IS A MUSCLE-BRAINED IDIOT.
SHE'S COOPERATIVE AND HELPFUL TO HAVE AROUND, BUT SHE'S ALSO THE BIGGEST SOURCE OF TROUBLES FOR ME.
AND... NO, I'M JUST OVER-THINKING IT...
BUT SHE'S STILL AN IDIOT.
THE YOUNGEST IS A HARD-WORKING IDIOT.
SHE AND I JUST DON'T SEE EYE TO EYE.
BUT SHE CAN GET THINGS DONE WHEN SHE PUTS HER MIND TO IT. I'D HATE FOR HER ABILITY TO GO TO WASTE.
BUT SHE'S STILL AN IDIOT.

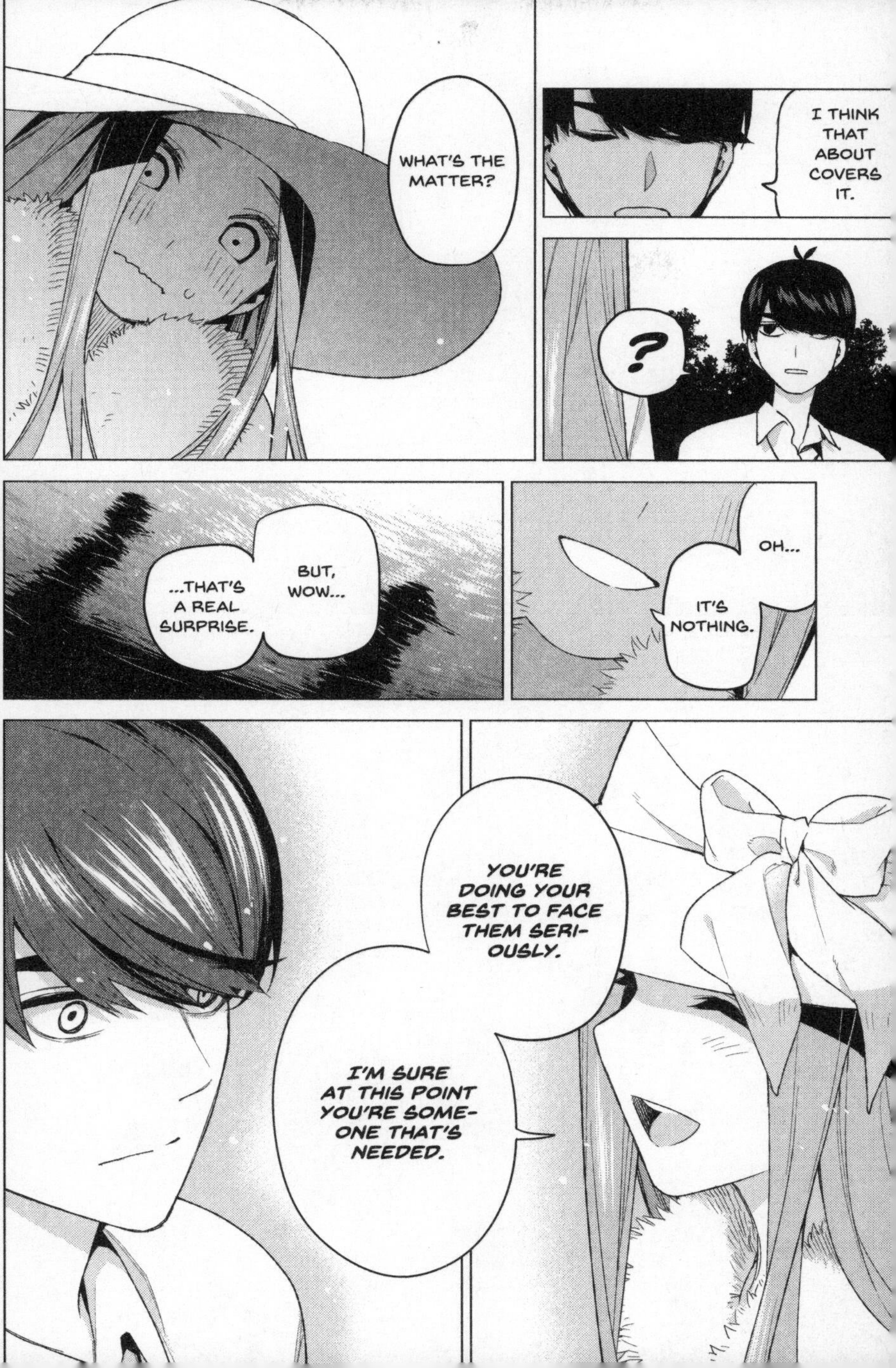
I THINK THAT ABOUT COVERS IT.
?
WHAT'S THE MATTER?
OH...
IT'S NOTHING.
BUT, WOW...
...THAT'S A REAL SURPRISE.
YOU'RE DOING YOUR BEST TO FACE THEM SERI-OUSLY.
I'M SURE AT THIS POINT YOU'RE SOME-ONE THAT'S NEEDED.

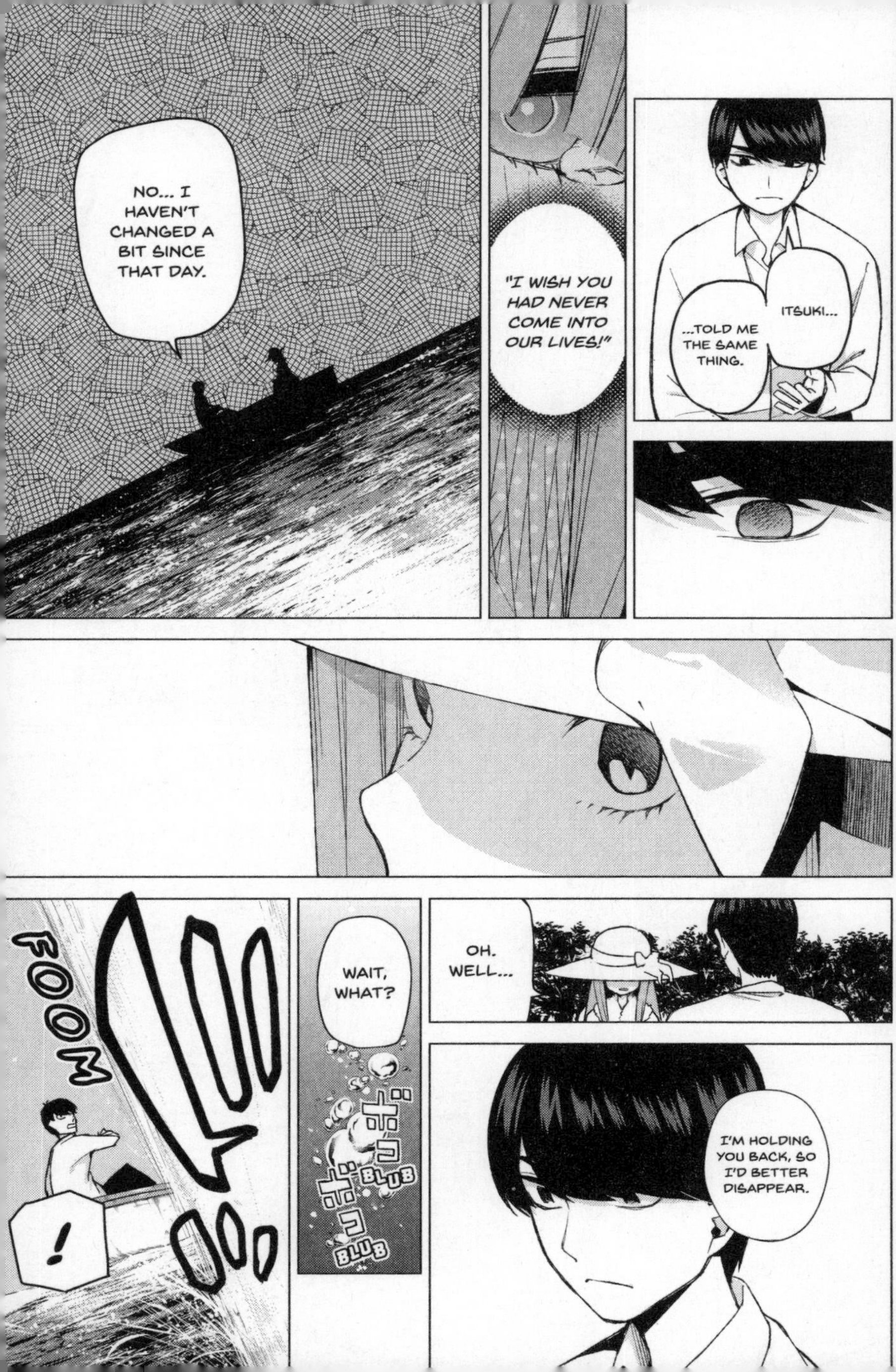
ITSUKI...
...TOLD ME THE SAME THING.
"I WISH YOU HAD NEVER COME INTO OUR LIVES!"
NO... I HAVEN'T CHANGED A BIT SINCE THAT DAY.
OH. WELL...
I'M HOLDING YOU BACK, SO I'D BETTER DISAPPEAR.
WAIT, WHAT?
BLUB
BLUB
FOOM
!

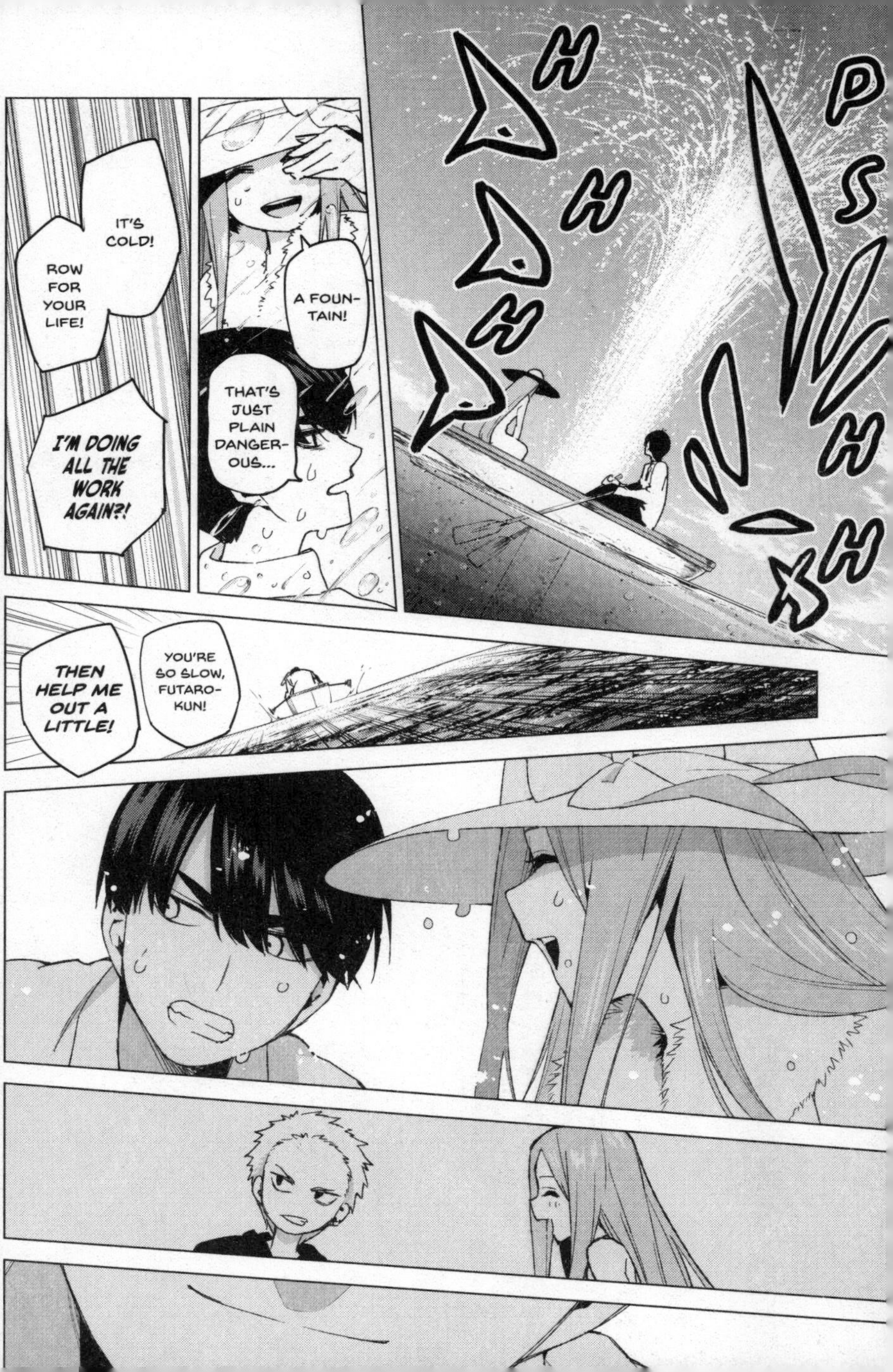
A FOUN-TAIN!
THAT'S JUST PLAIN DANGER-OUS...
IT'S COLD!
ROW FOR YOUR LIFE!
I'M DOING ALL THE WORK AGAIN?!
YOU'RE SO SLOW, FUTARO-KUN!
THEN HELP ME OUT A LITTLE!

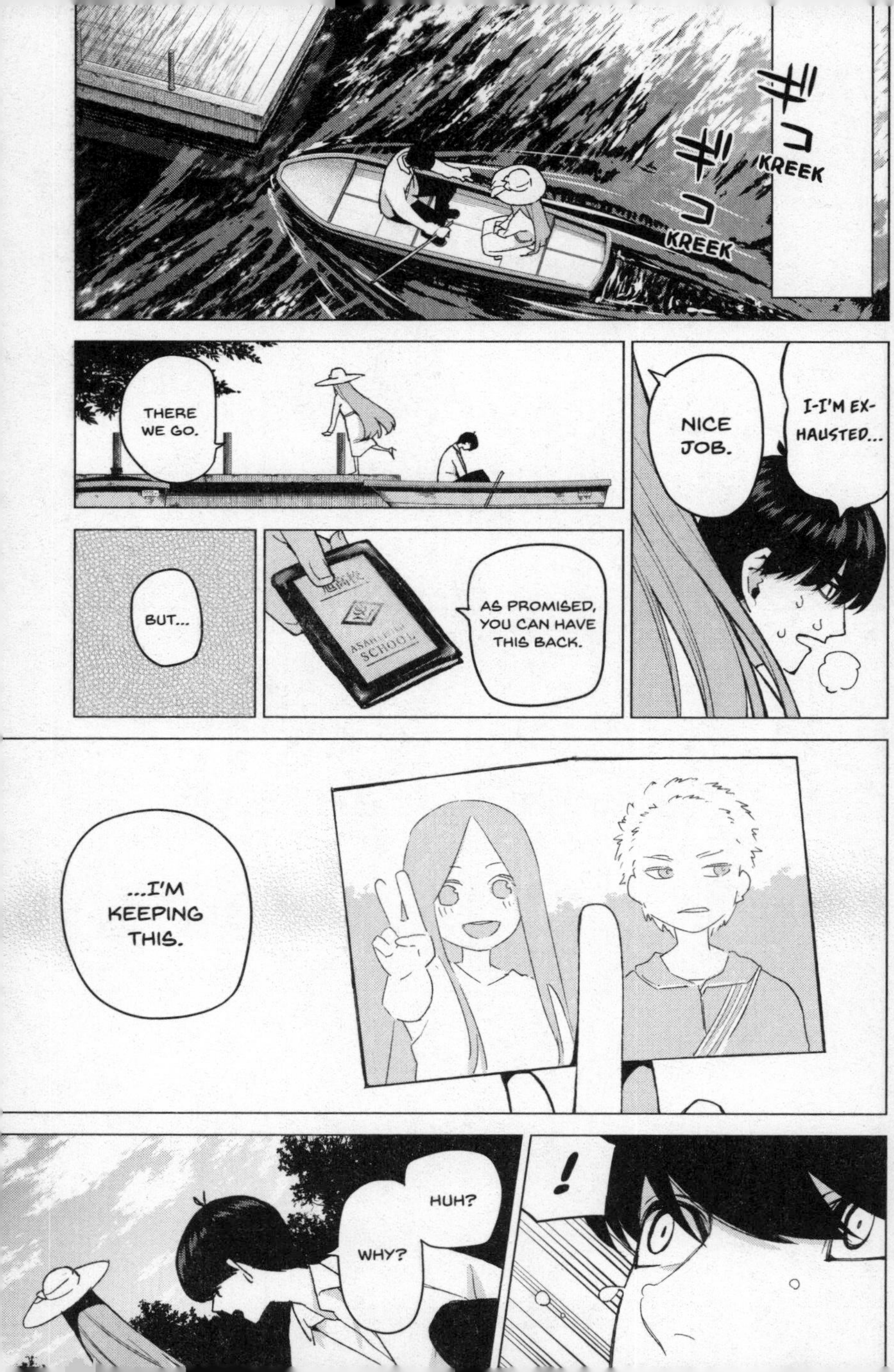
ギコ
KREEK
ギコ
KREEK
I-I'M EX-HAUSTED...
NICE JOB.
THERE WE GO.
AS PROMISED, YOU CAN HAVE THIS BACK.
BUT...
...I'M KEEPING THIS.
!
HUH?
WHY?

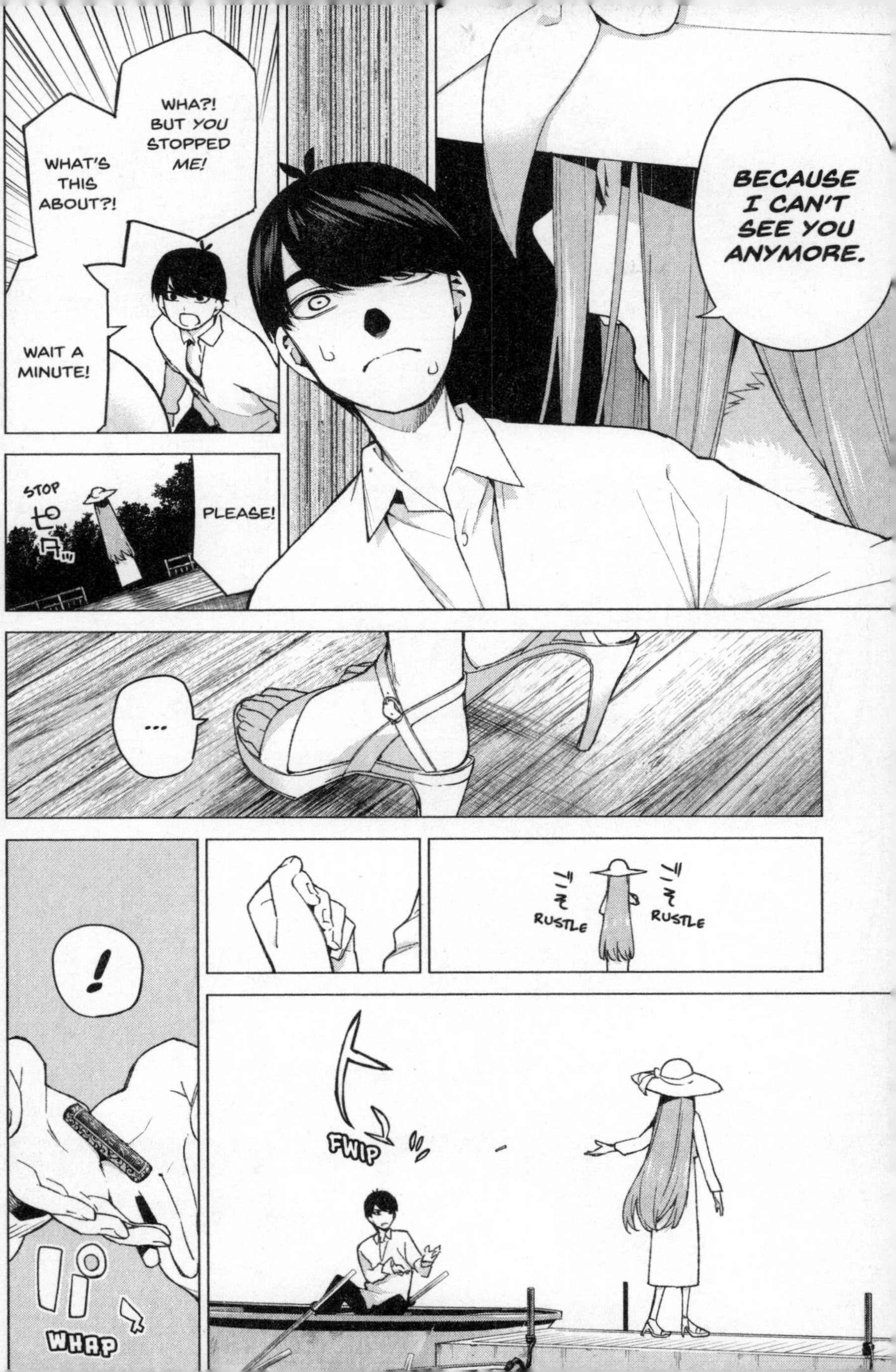
BECAUSE I CAN'T SEE YOU ANYMORE.
WHA?! BUT YOU STOPPED ME!
WHAT'S THIS ABOUT?!
WAIT A MINUTE!
PLEASE!
STOP
...
RUSTLE
RUSTLE
FWIP
!
WHAP

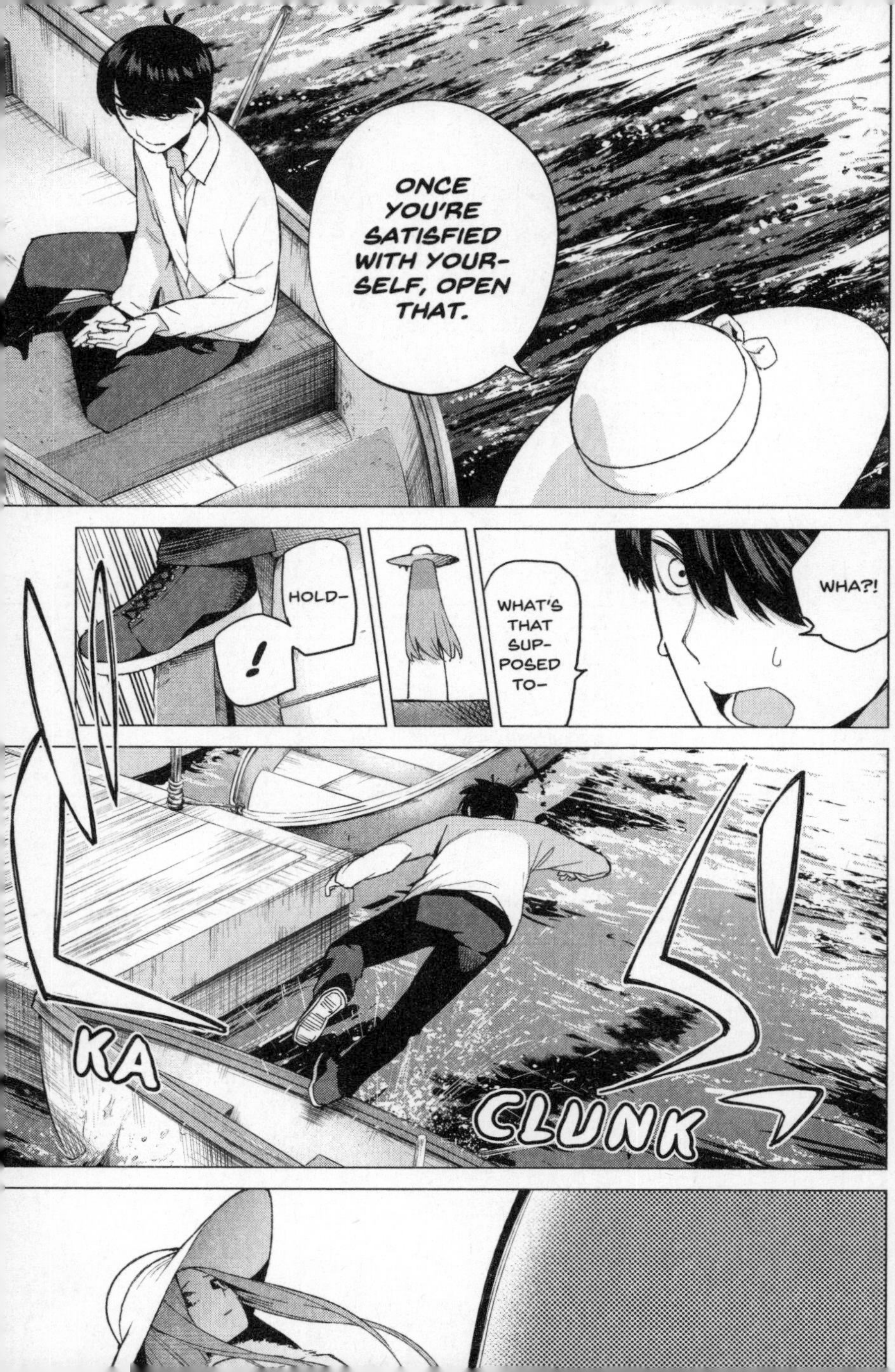
ONCE YOU'RE SATISFIED WITH YOUR-SELF, OPEN THAT.
WHA?!
WHAT'S THAT SUP-POSED TO-
HOLD-
!
KA
CLUNK

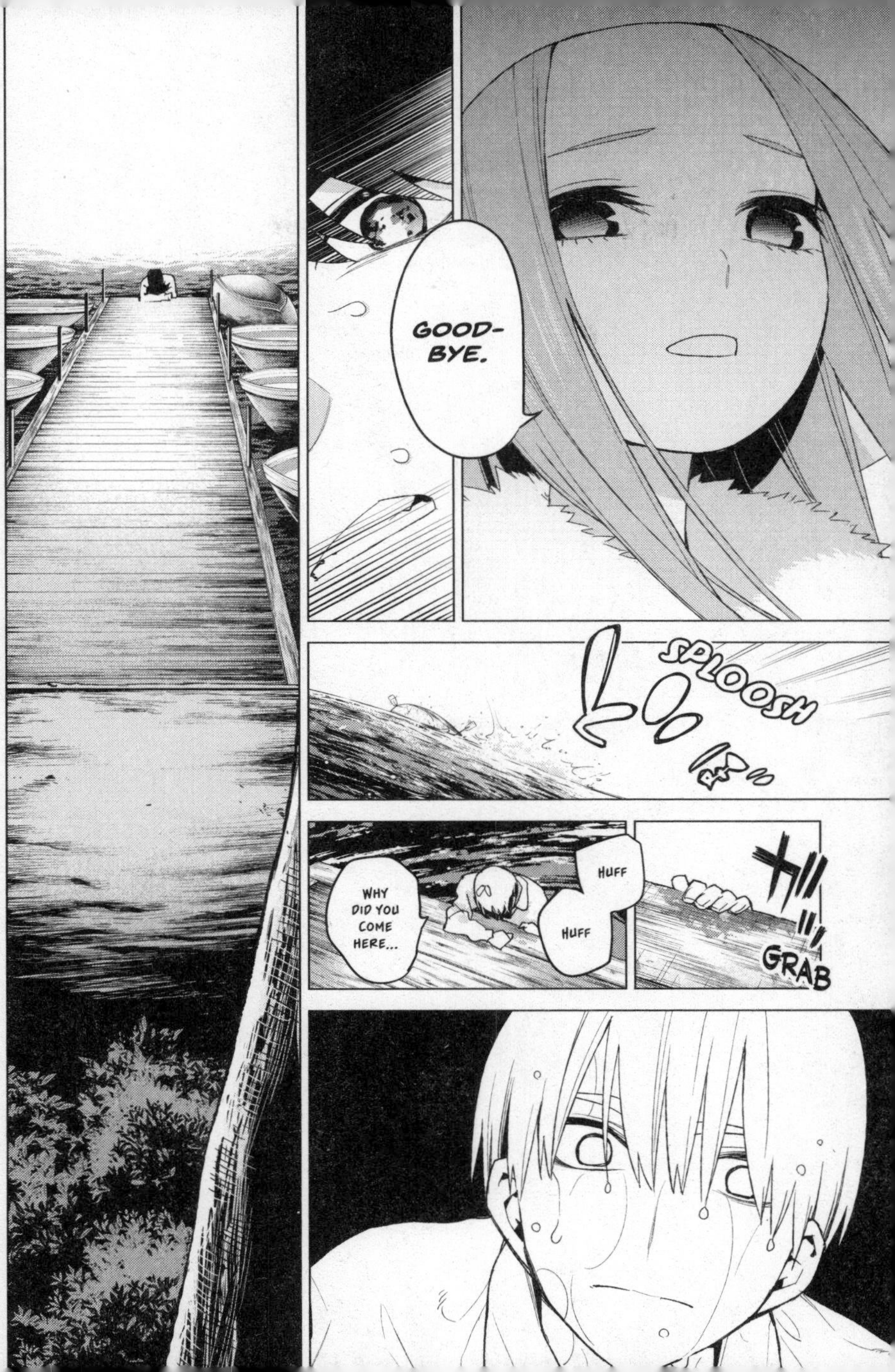
GOOD-BYE.
SPLOOSH
GRAB
HUFF
HUFF
WHY DID YOU COME HERE...

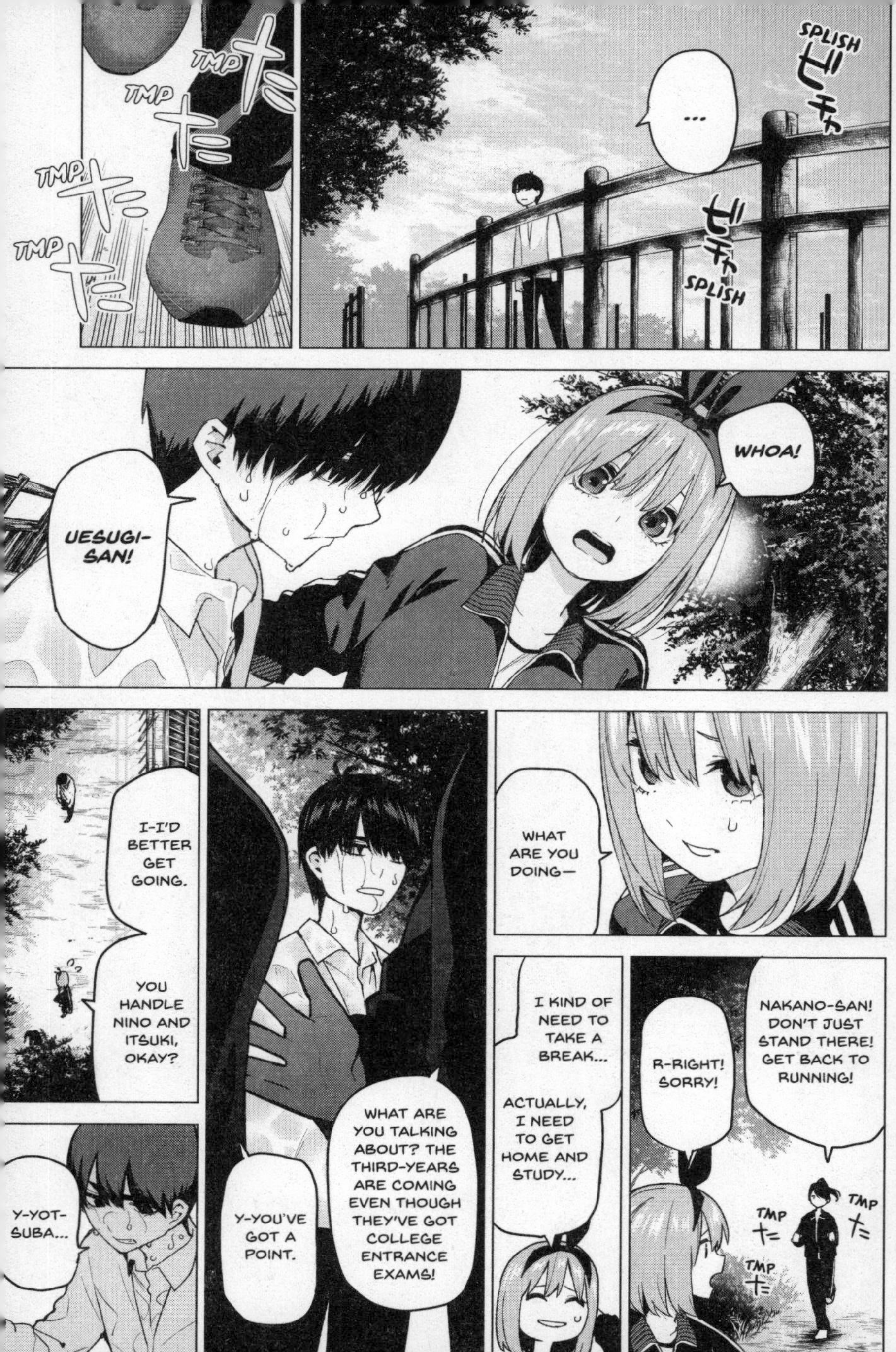
SPLISH
ビチャ
...
ビチャ
SPLISH
TMP
TMP
TMP
TMP
WHOA!
UESUGI-SAN!
WHAT ARE YOU DOING—
NAKANO-SAN! DON'T JUST STAND THERE! GET BACK TO RUNNING!
R-RIGHT! SORRY!
TMP
TMP
TMP
I KIND OF NEED TO TAKE A BREAK...
ACTUALLY, I NEED TO GET HOME AND STUDY...
WHAT ARE YOU TALKING ABOUT? THE THIRD-YEARS ARE COMING EVEN THOUGH THEY'VE GOT COLLEGE ENTRANCE EXAMS!
Y-YOU'VE GOT A POINT.
I-I'D BETTER GET GOING.
YOU HANDLE NINO AND ITSUKI, OKAY?
Y-YOTSUBA...

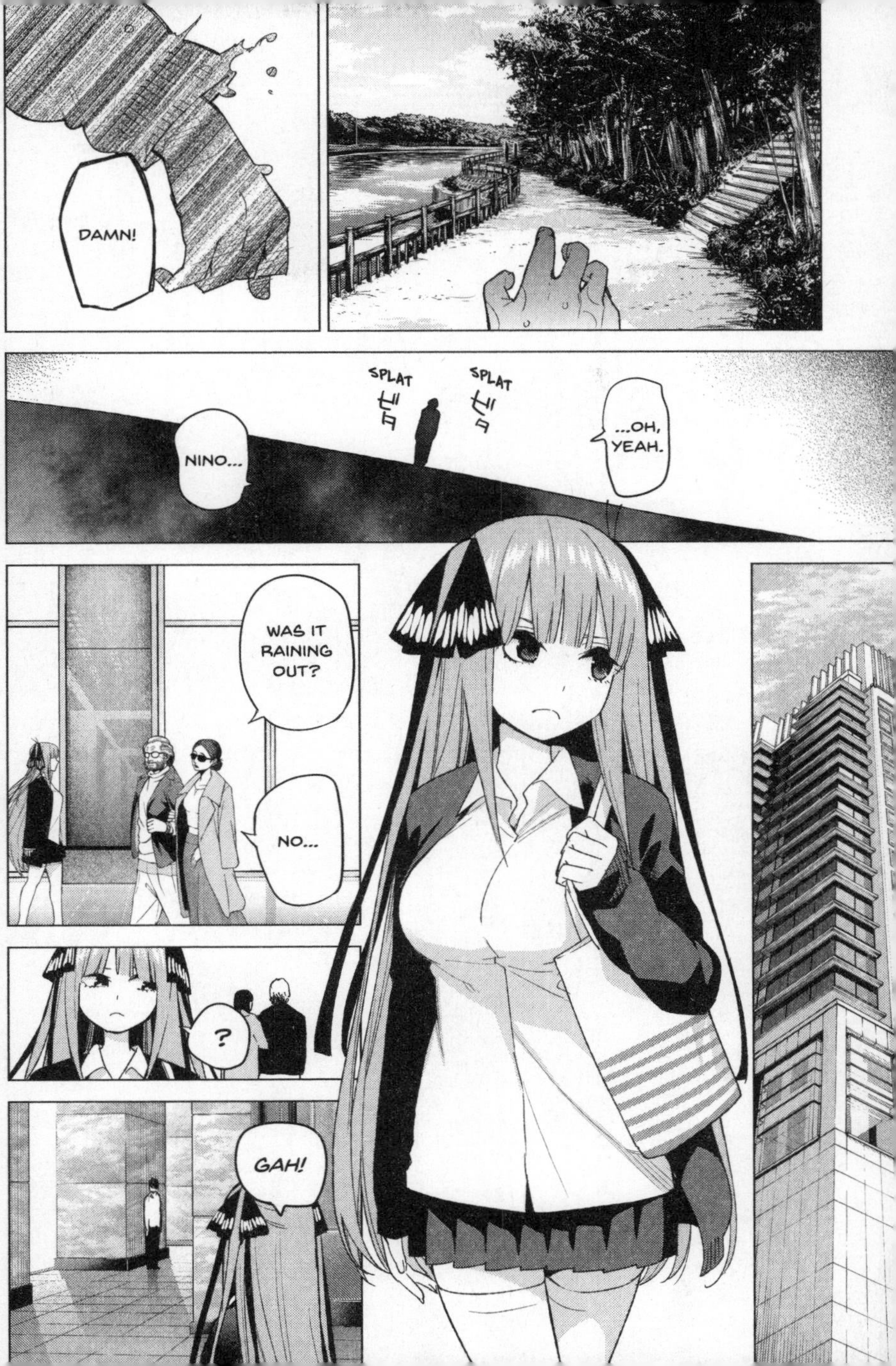
DAMN!
...OH, YEAH.
SPLAT
SPLAT
NINO...
WAS IT RAINING OUT?
NO...
?
GAH!

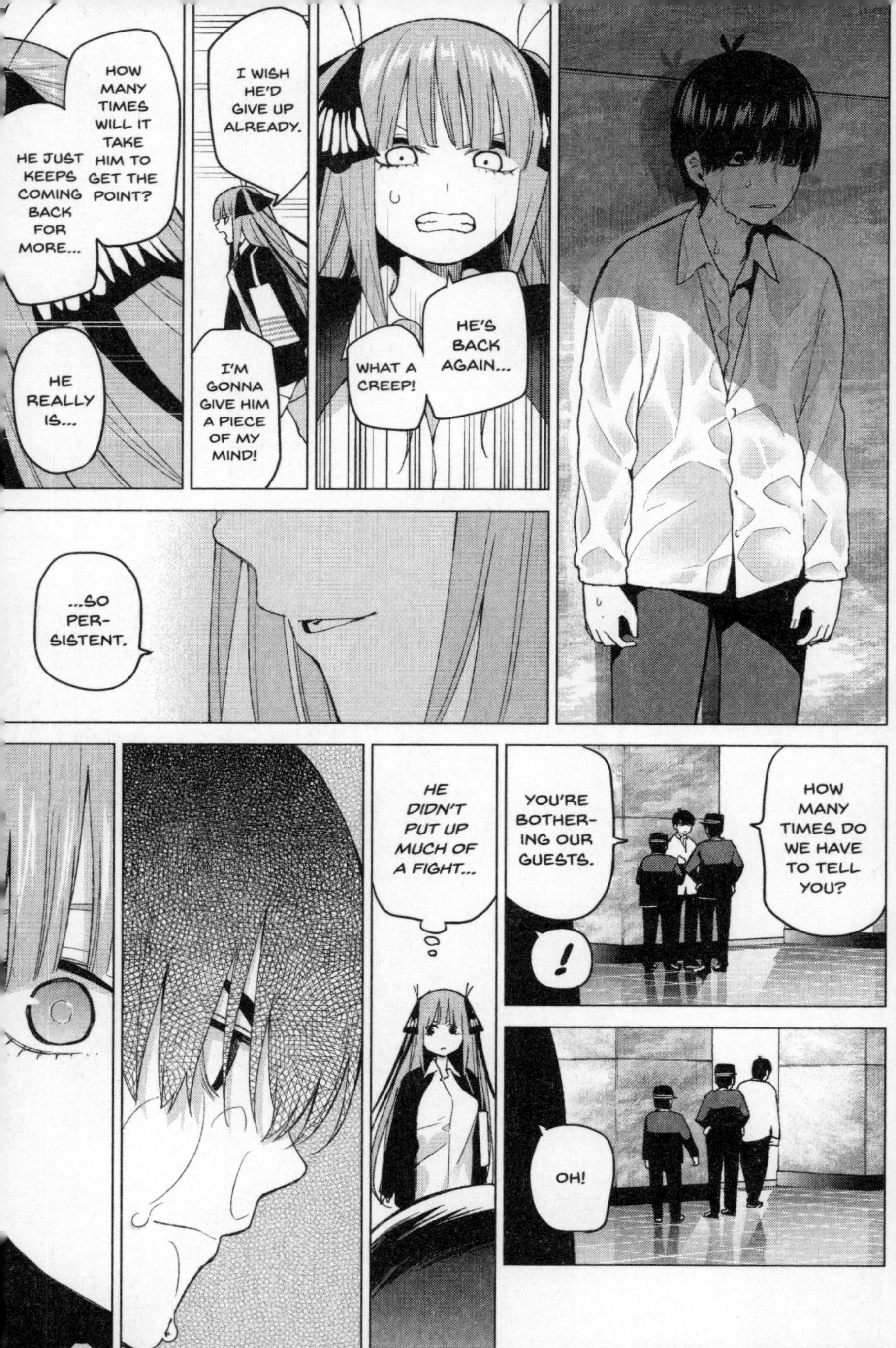
HE'S BACK AGAIN...
WHAT A CREEP!
I WISH HE'D GIVE UP ALREADY.
I'M GONNA GIVE HIM A PIECE OF MY MIND!
HOW MANY TIMES WILL IT TAKE HIM TO GET THE POINT?
HE JUST KEEPS COMING BACK FOR MORE...
HE REALLY IS...
...SO PERSISTENT.
HOW MANY TIMES DO WE HAVE TO TELL YOU?
YOU'RE BOTHERING OUR GUESTS.
!
OH!
HE DIDN'T PUT UP MUCH OF A FIGHT...

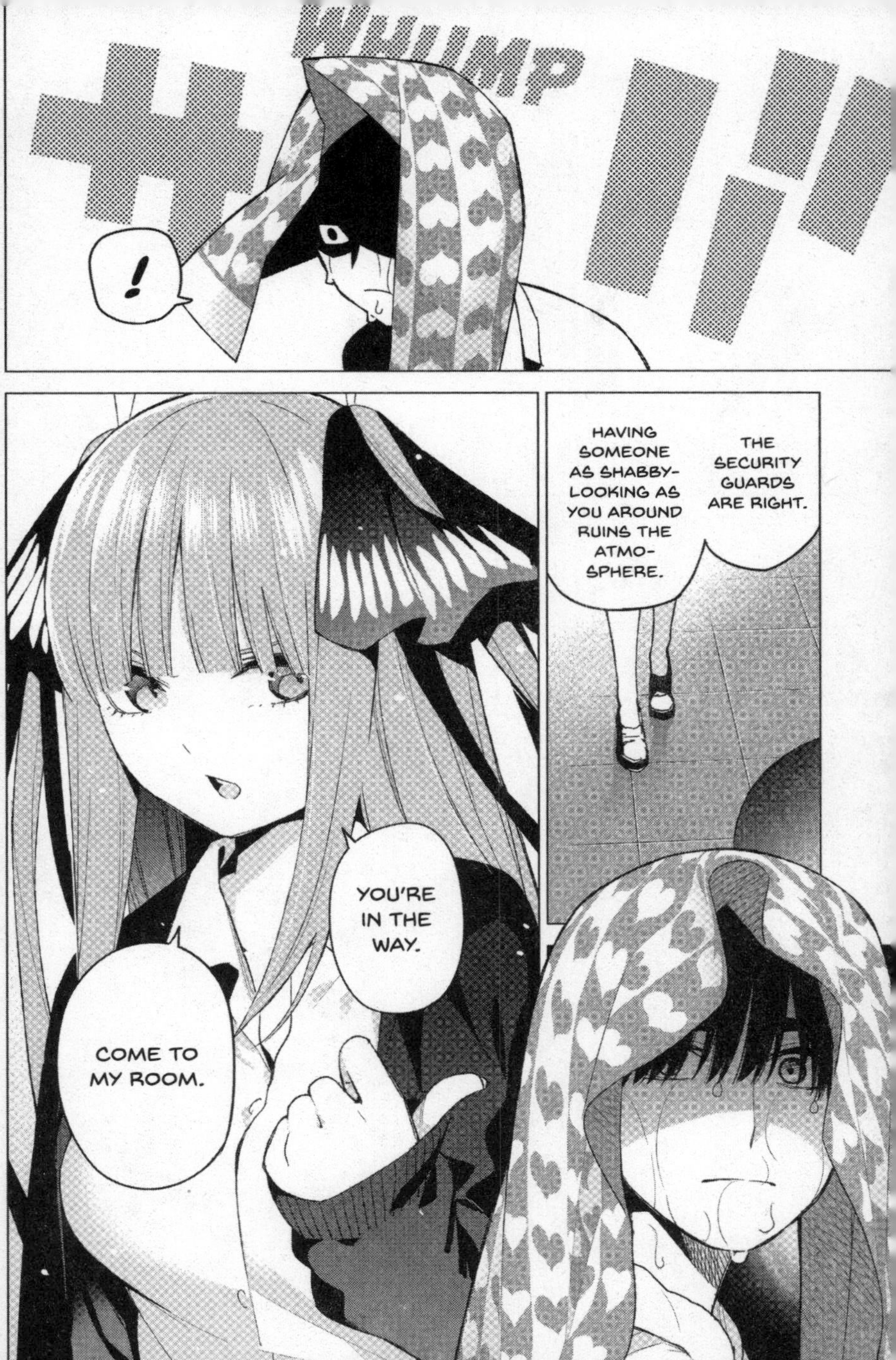
WHUMP
!
THE SECURITY GUARDS ARE RIGHT.
HAVING SOMEONE AS SHABBY-LOOKING AS YOU AROUND RUINS THE ATMO-SPHERE.
YOU'RE IN THE WAY.
COME TO MY ROOM.

## CHAPTER 43
## THE SEVEN GOODBYES ⑤

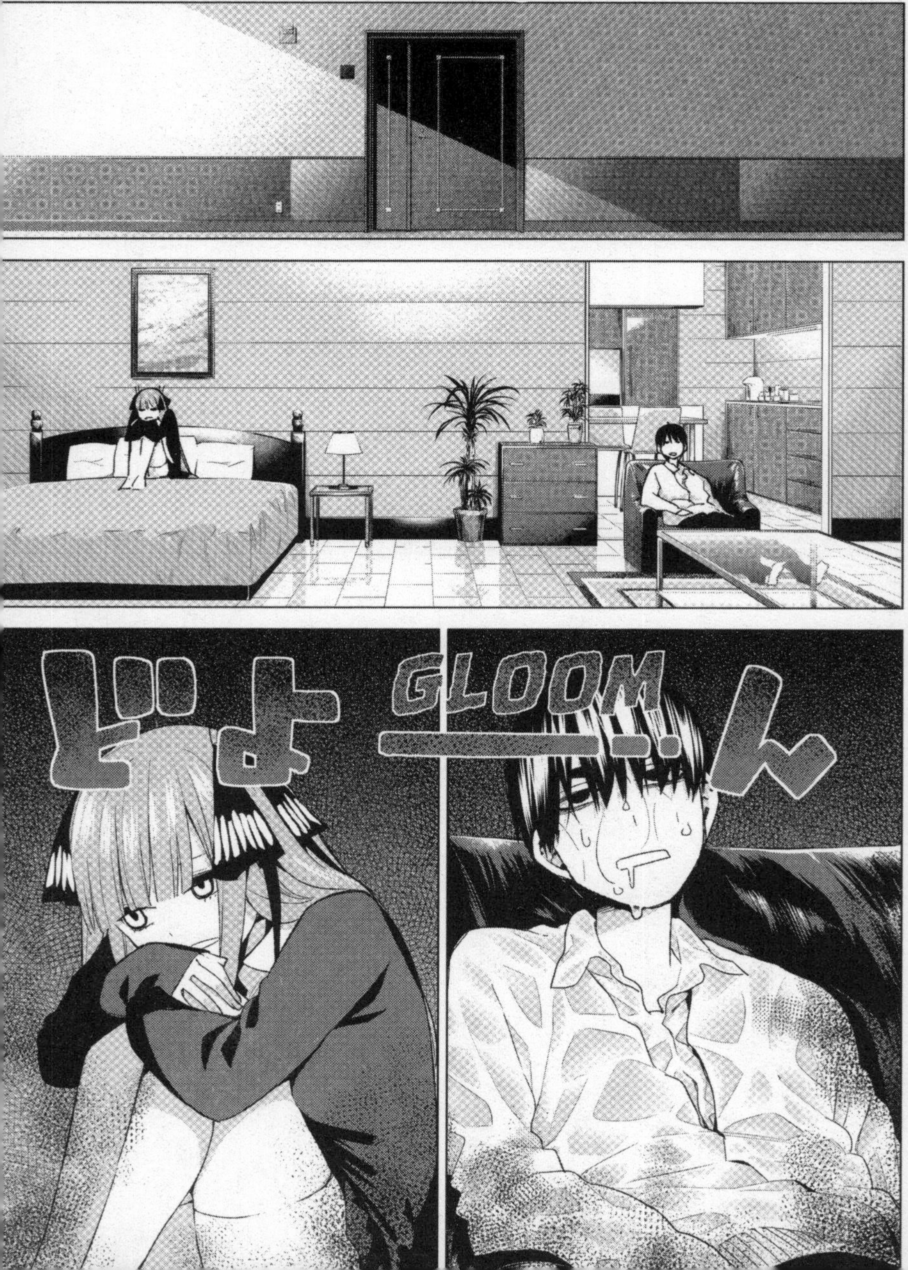
どよーん
GLOOM

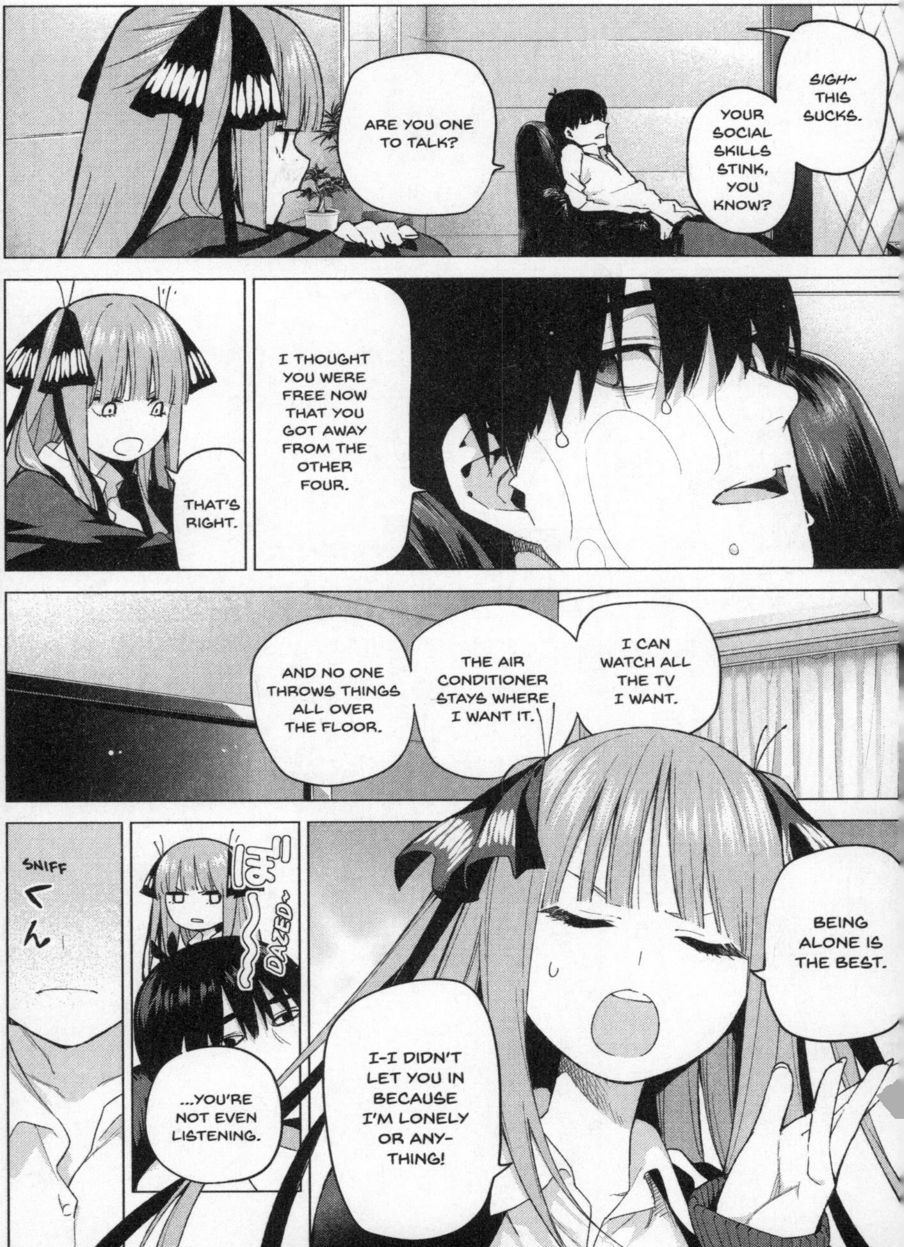
SIGH~ THIS SUCKS.
YOUR SOCIAL SKILLS STINK, YOU KNOW?
ARE YOU ONE TO TALK?
I THOUGHT YOU WERE FREE NOW THAT YOU GOT AWAY FROM THE OTHER FOUR.
THAT'S RIGHT.
I CAN WATCH ALL THE TV I WANT.
THE AIR CONDITIONER STAYS WHERE I WANT IT.
AND NO ONE THROWS THINGS ALL OVER THE FLOOR.
BEING ALONE IS THE BEST.
I-I DIDN'T LET YOU IN BECAUSE I'M LONELY OR ANY-THING!
DAZED~
...YOU'RE NOT EVEN LISTENING.
SNIFF

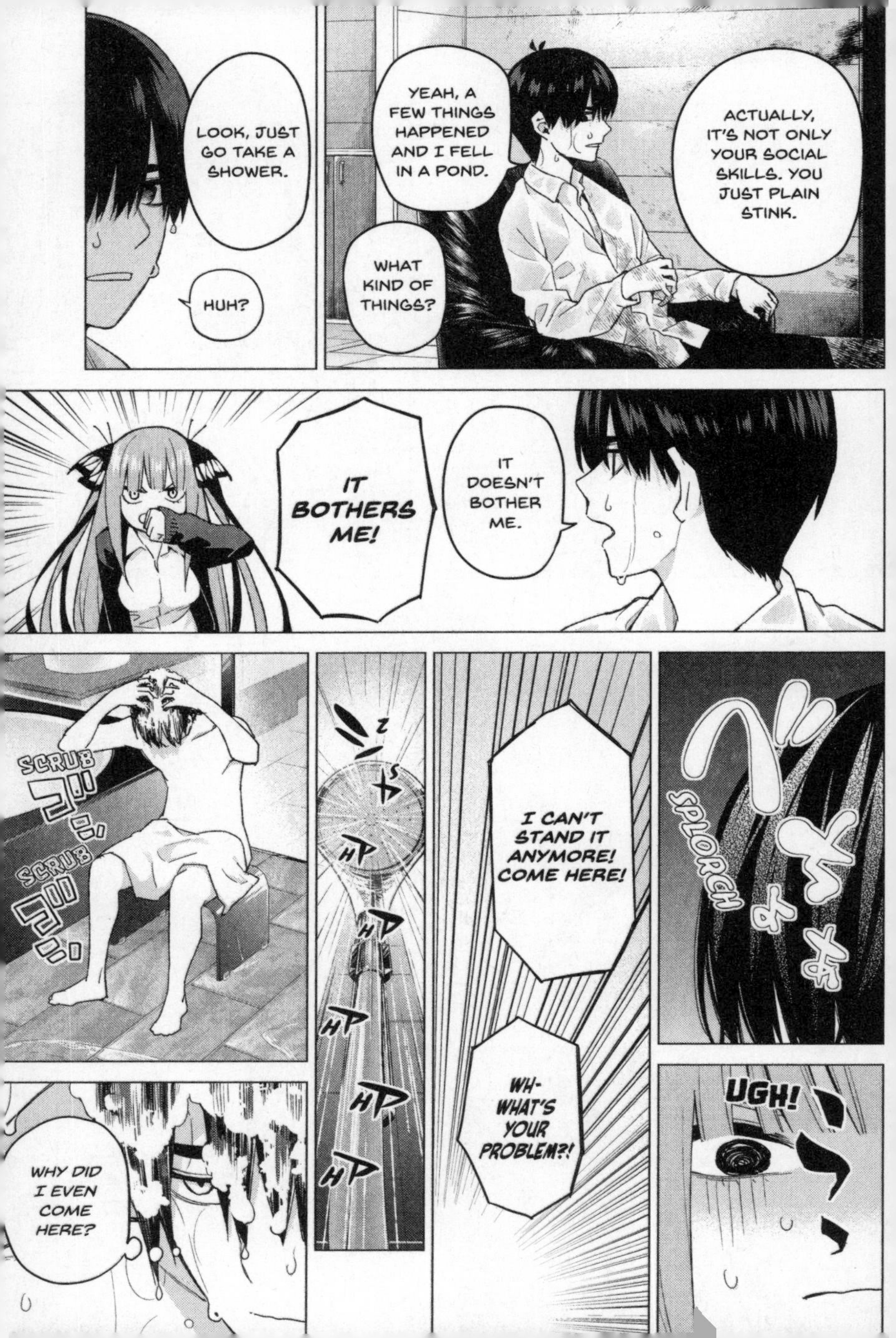
ACTUALLY, IT'S NOT ONLY YOUR SOCIAL SKILLS. YOU JUST PLAIN STINK.
YEAH, A FEW THINGS HAPPENED AND I FELL IN A POND.
WHAT KIND OF THINGS?
LOOK, JUST GO TAKE A SHOWER.
HUH?
IT DOESN'T BOTHER ME.
IT BOTHERS ME!
SPLORCH
I CAN'T STAND IT ANYMORE! COME HERE!
WH- WHAT'S YOUR PROBLEM?!
SCRUB
SCRUB
UGH!
WHY DID I EVEN COME HERE?

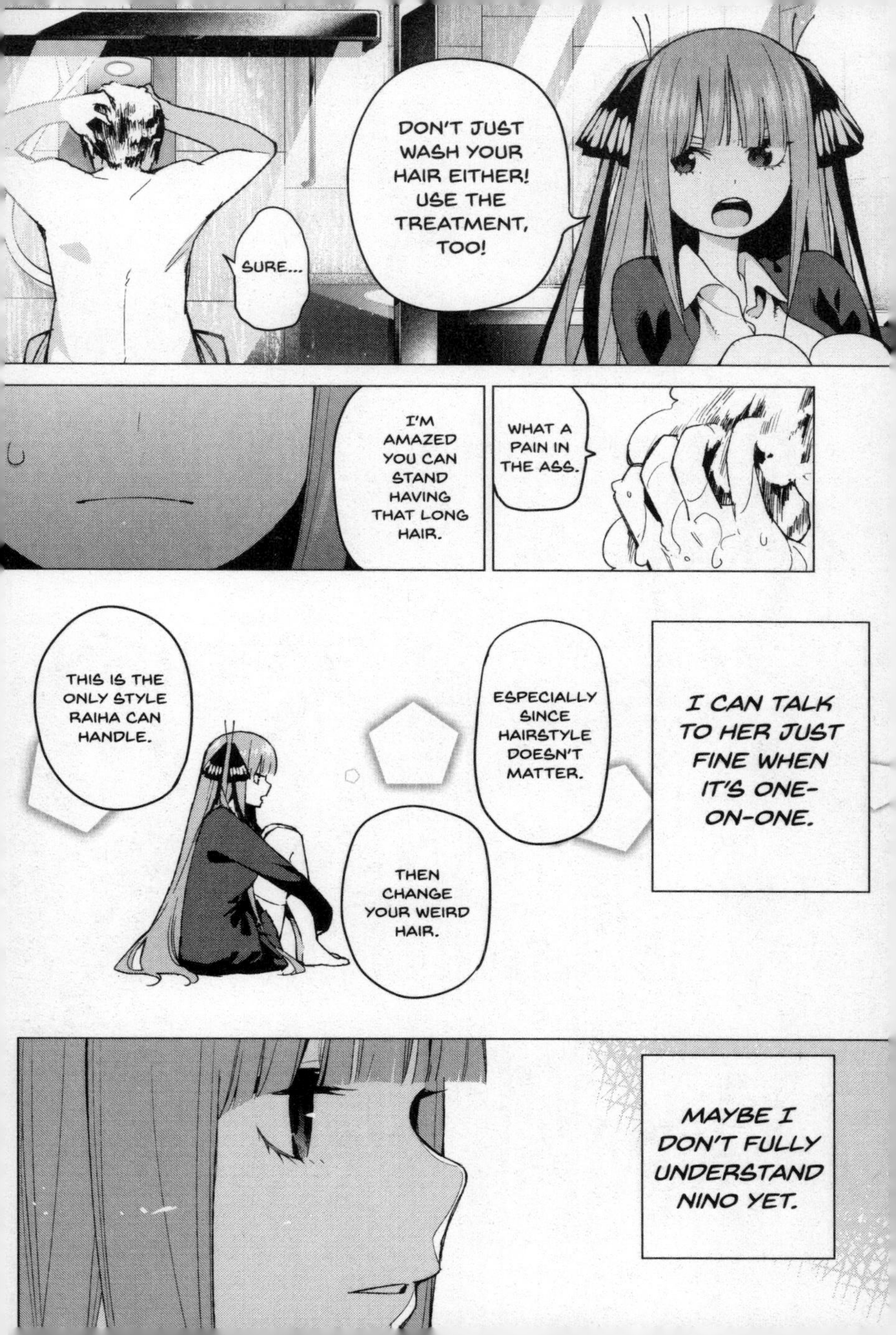
DON'T JUST WASH YOUR HAIR EITHER! USE THE TREATMENT, TOO!
SURE...
WHAT A PAIN IN THE ASS.
I'M AMAZED YOU CAN STAND HAVING THAT LONG HAIR.
I CAN TALK TO HER JUST FINE WHEN IT'S ONE-ON-ONE.
ESPECIALLY SINCE HAIRSTYLE DOESN'T MATTER.
THIS IS THE ONLY STYLE RAIHA CAN HANDLE.
THEN CHANGE YOUR WEIRD HAIR.
MAYBE I DON'T FULLY UNDERSTAND NINO YET.

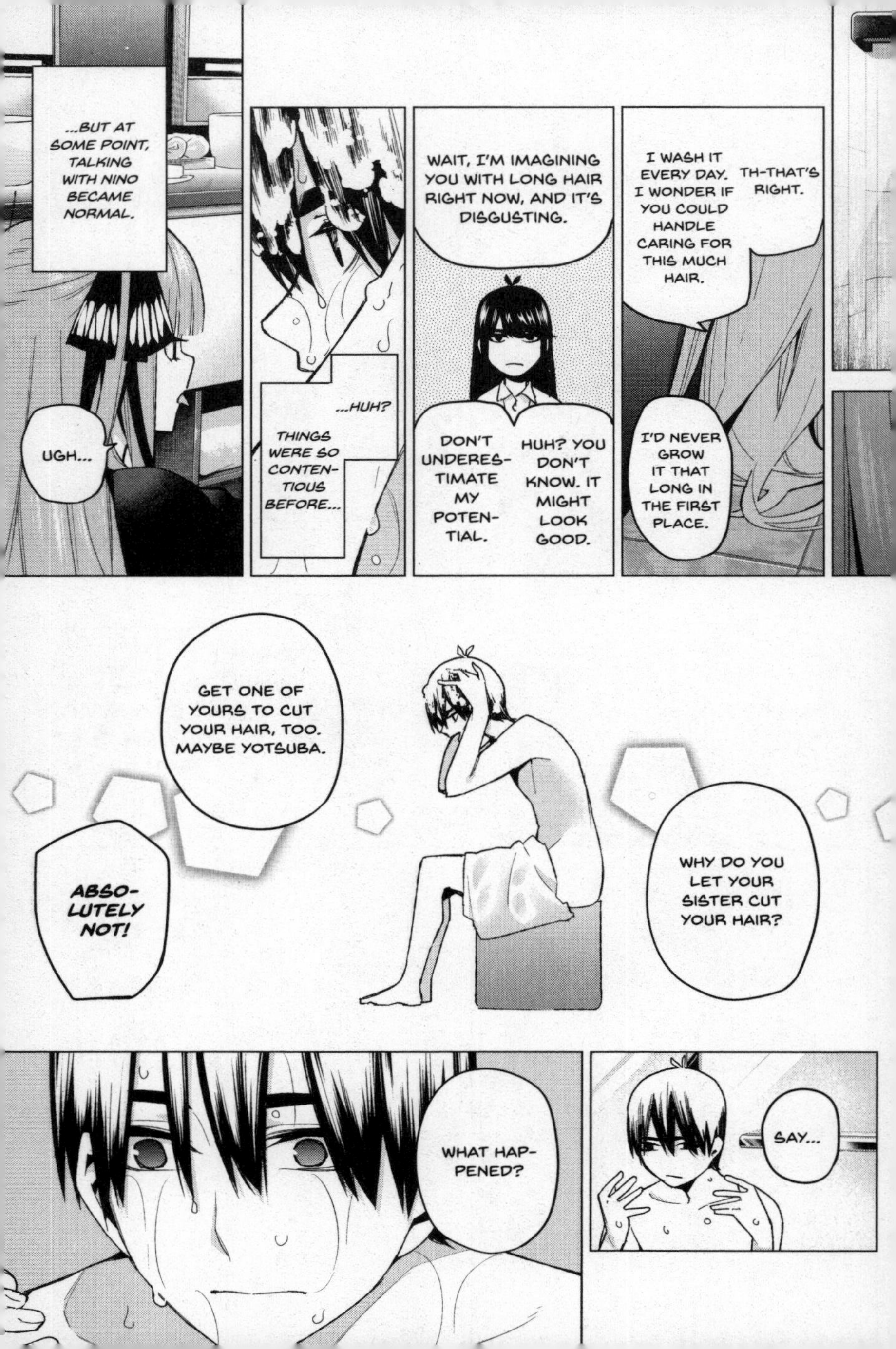
TH-THAT'S RIGHT.
I WASH IT EVERY DAY. I WONDER IF YOU COULD HANDLE CARING FOR THIS MUCH HAIR.
I'D NEVER GROW IT THAT LONG IN THE FIRST PLACE.
WAIT, I'M IMAGINING YOU WITH LONG HAIR RIGHT NOW, AND IT'S DISGUSTING.
HUH? YOU DON'T KNOW. IT MIGHT LOOK GOOD.
DON'T UNDERES-TIMATE MY POTEN-TIAL.
...HUH?
THINGS WERE SO CONTEN-TIOUS BEFORE...
...BUT AT SOME POINT, TALKING WITH NINO BECAME NORMAL.
UGH...
WHY DO YOU LET YOUR SISTER CUT YOUR HAIR?
GET ONE OF YOURS TO CUT YOUR HAIR, TOO. MAYBE YOTSUBA.
ABSO-LUTELY NOT!
SAY...
WHAT HAP-PENED?

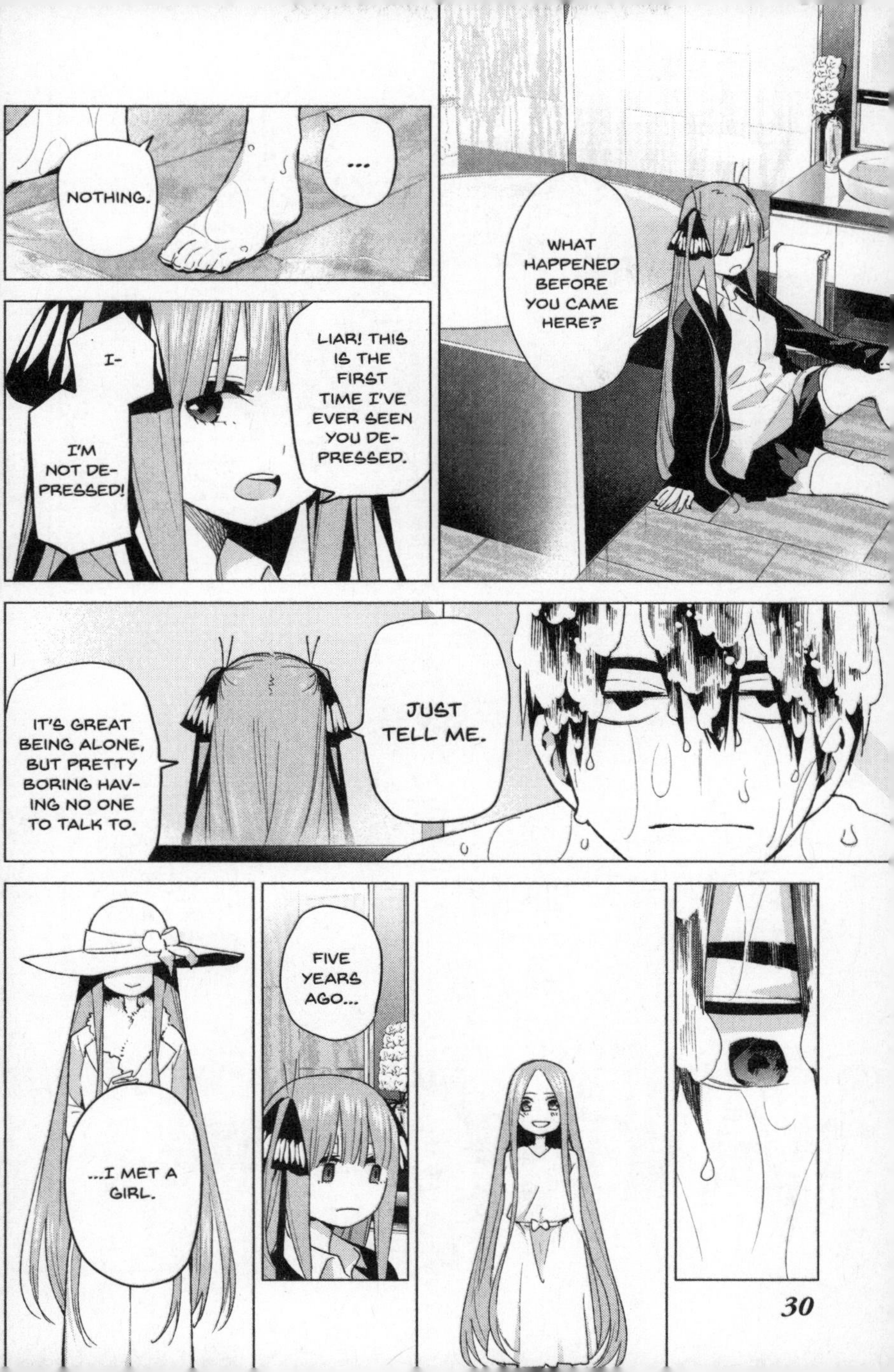
WHAT HAPPENED BEFORE YOU CAME HERE?
...
NOTHING.
LIAR! THIS IS THE FIRST TIME I'VE EVER SEEN YOU DE-PRESSED.
I-
I'M NOT DE-PRESSED!
JUST TELL ME.
IT'S GREAT BEING ALONE, BUT PRETTY BORING HAV-ING NO ONE TO TALK TO.
FIVE YEARS AGO...
...I MET A GIRL.

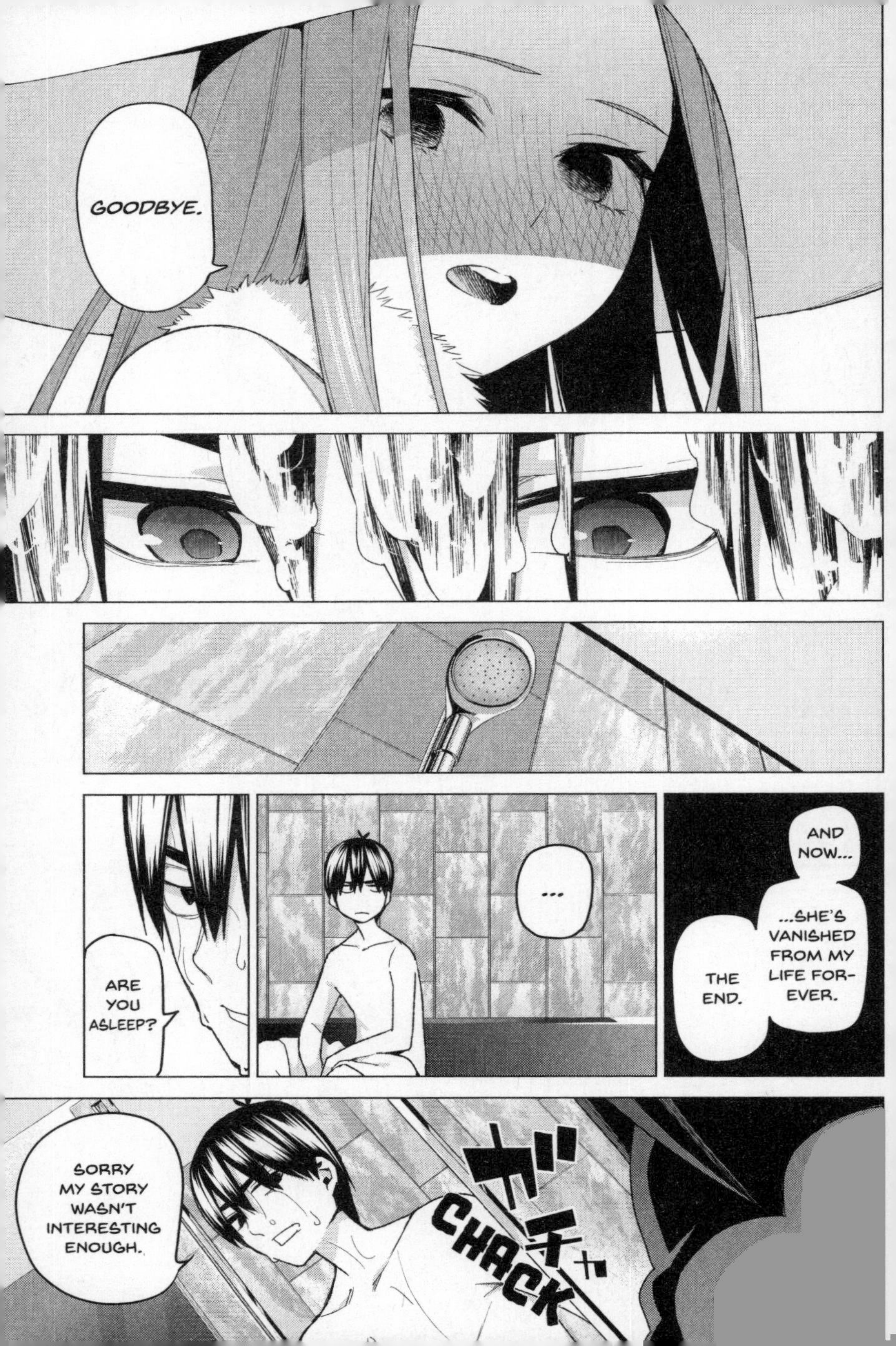
GOODBYE.
AND NOW...
...SHE'S VANISHED FROM MY LIFE FOR-EVER.
THE END.
...
ARE YOU ASLEEP?
CHACK
SORRY MY STORY WASN'T INTERESTING ENOUGH.

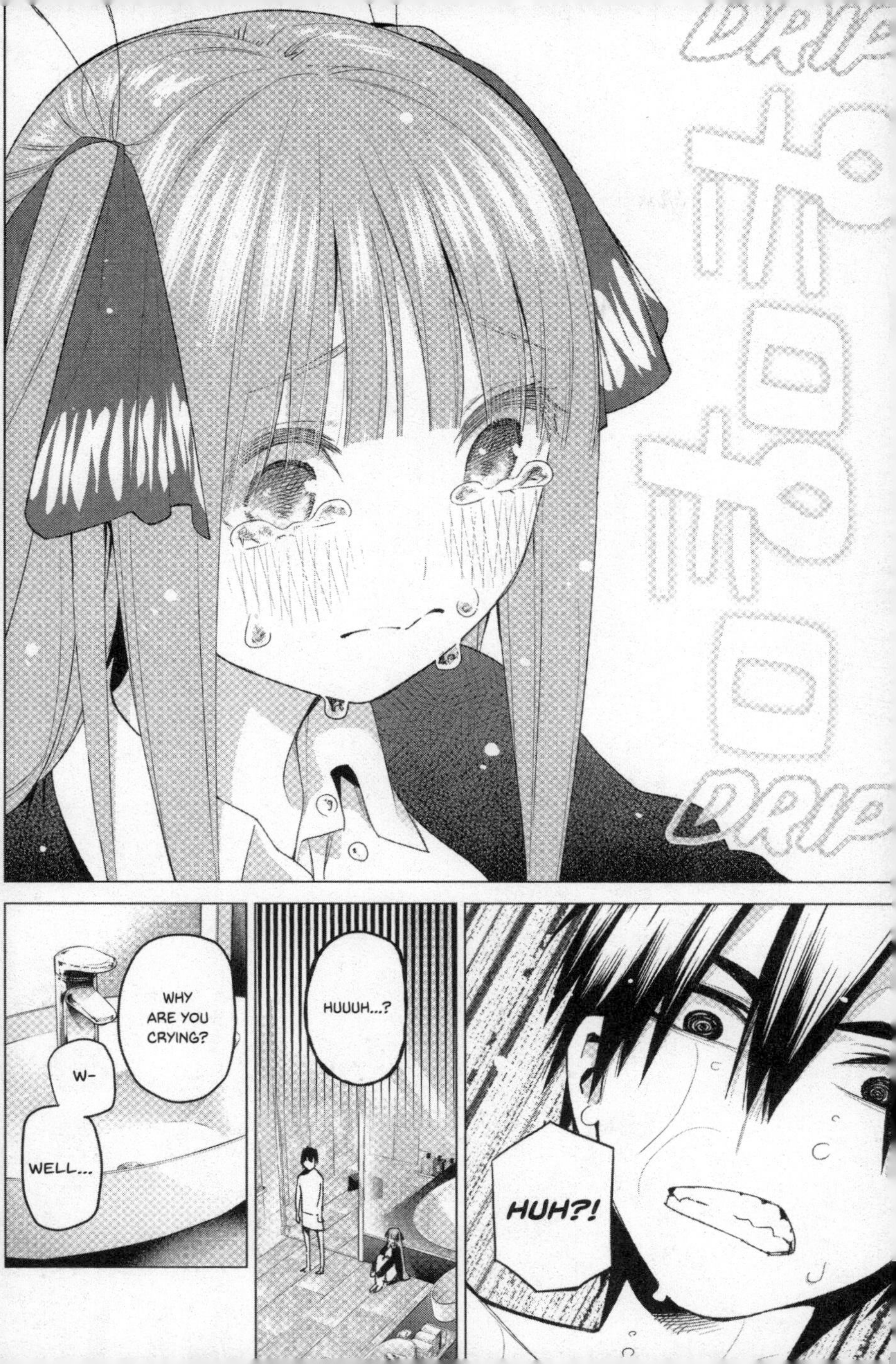
DRIP
DRIP
HUH?!
HUUUH...?
WHY ARE YOU CRYING?
W-
WELL...

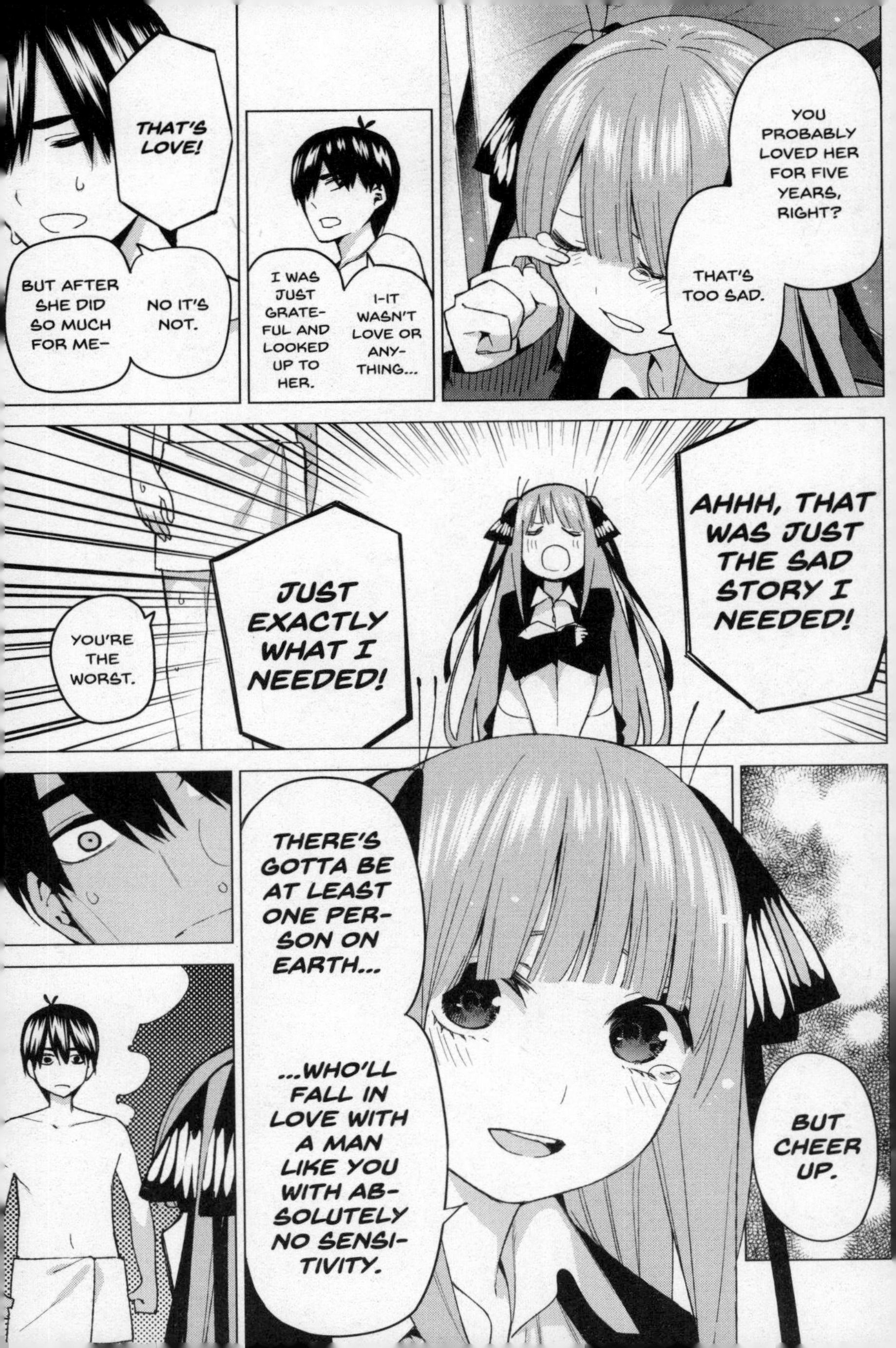
YOU PROBABLY LOVED HER FOR FIVE YEARS, RIGHT?
THAT'S TOO SAD.
I-IT WASN'T LOVE OR ANYTHING...
I WAS JUST GRATEFUL AND LOOKED UP TO HER.
THAT'S LOVE!
NO IT'S NOT.
BUT AFTER SHE DID SO MUCH FOR ME—
AHHH, THAT WAS JUST THE SAD STORY I NEEDED!
JUST EXACTLY WHAT I NEEDED!
YOU'RE THE WORST.
BUT CHEER UP.
THERE'S GOTTA BE AT LEAST ONE PERSON ON EARTH...
...WHO'LL FALL IN LOVE WITH A MAN LIKE YOU WITH ABSOLUTELY NO SENSITIVITY.

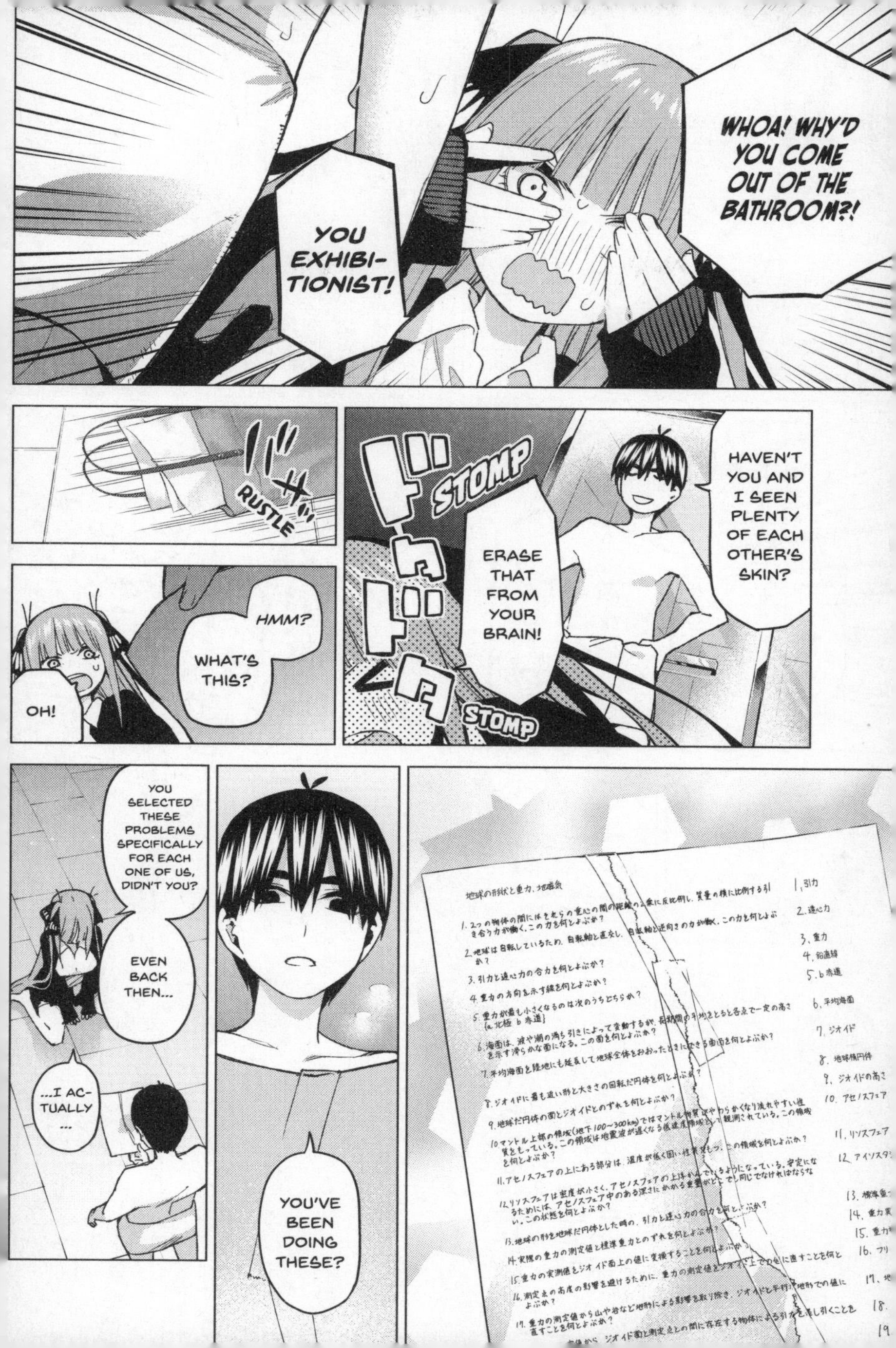
WHOA! WHY'D YOU COME OUT OF THE BATHROOM?!
YOU EXHIBITIONIST!
HAVEN'T YOU AND I SEEN PLENTY OF EACH OTHER'S SKIN?
STOMP
ERASE THAT FROM YOUR BRAIN!
STOMP
RUSTLE
HMM?
WHAT'S THIS?
OH!
YOU'VE BEEN DOING THESE?
YOU SELECTED THESE PROBLEMS SPECIFICALLY FOR EACH ONE OF US, DIDN'T YOU?
EVEN BACK THEN...
...I ACTUALLY...

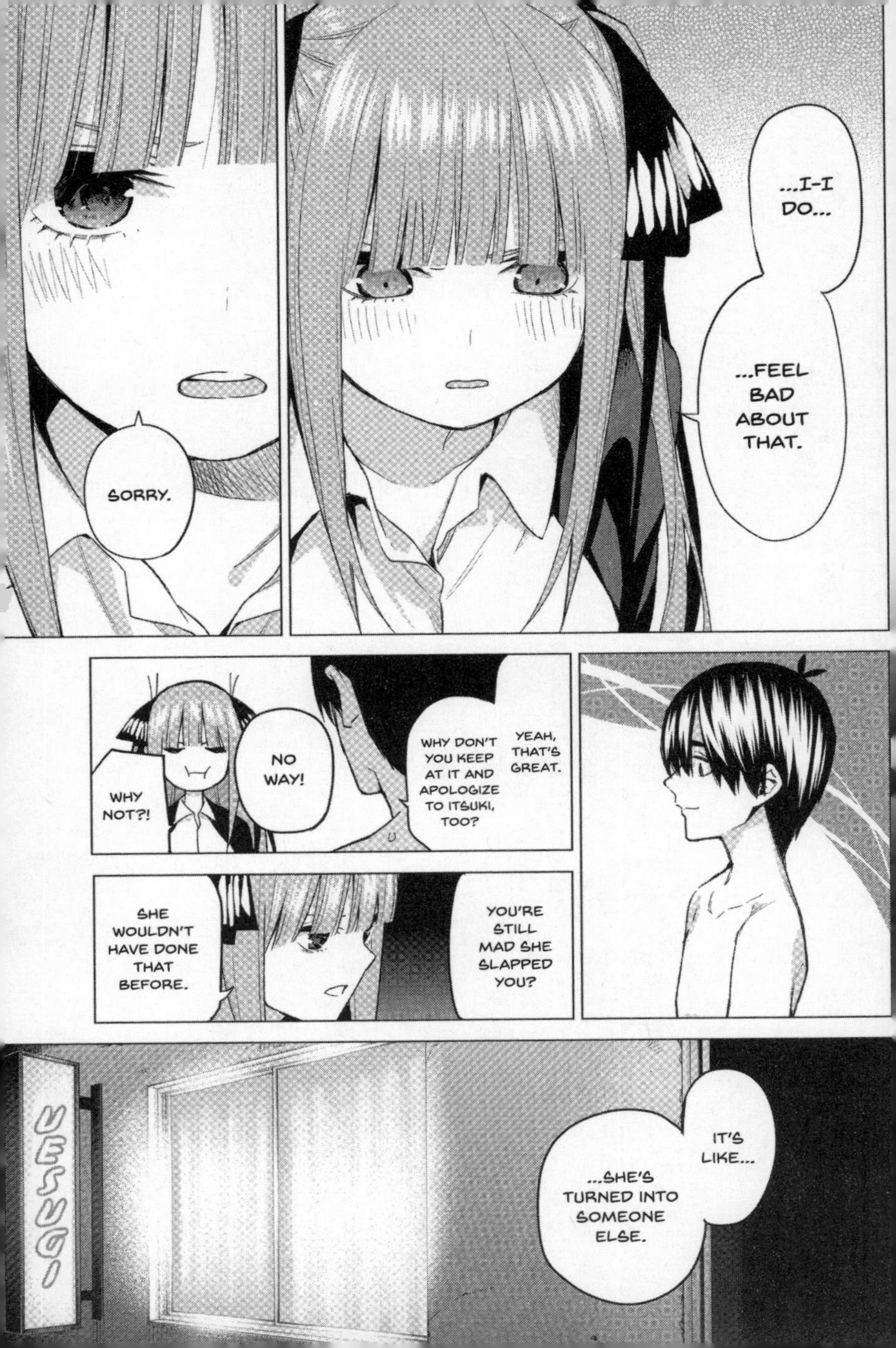
...I-I DO...
...FEEL BAD ABOUT THAT.
SORRY.
YEAH, THAT'S GREAT.
WHY DON'T YOU KEEP AT IT AND APOLOGIZE TO ITSUKI, TOO?
NO WAY!
WHY NOT?!
YOU'RE STILL MAD SHE SLAPPED YOU?
SHE WOULDN'T HAVE DONE THAT BEFORE.
UESUGI
IT'S LIKE...
...SHE'S TURNED INTO SOMEONE ELSE.

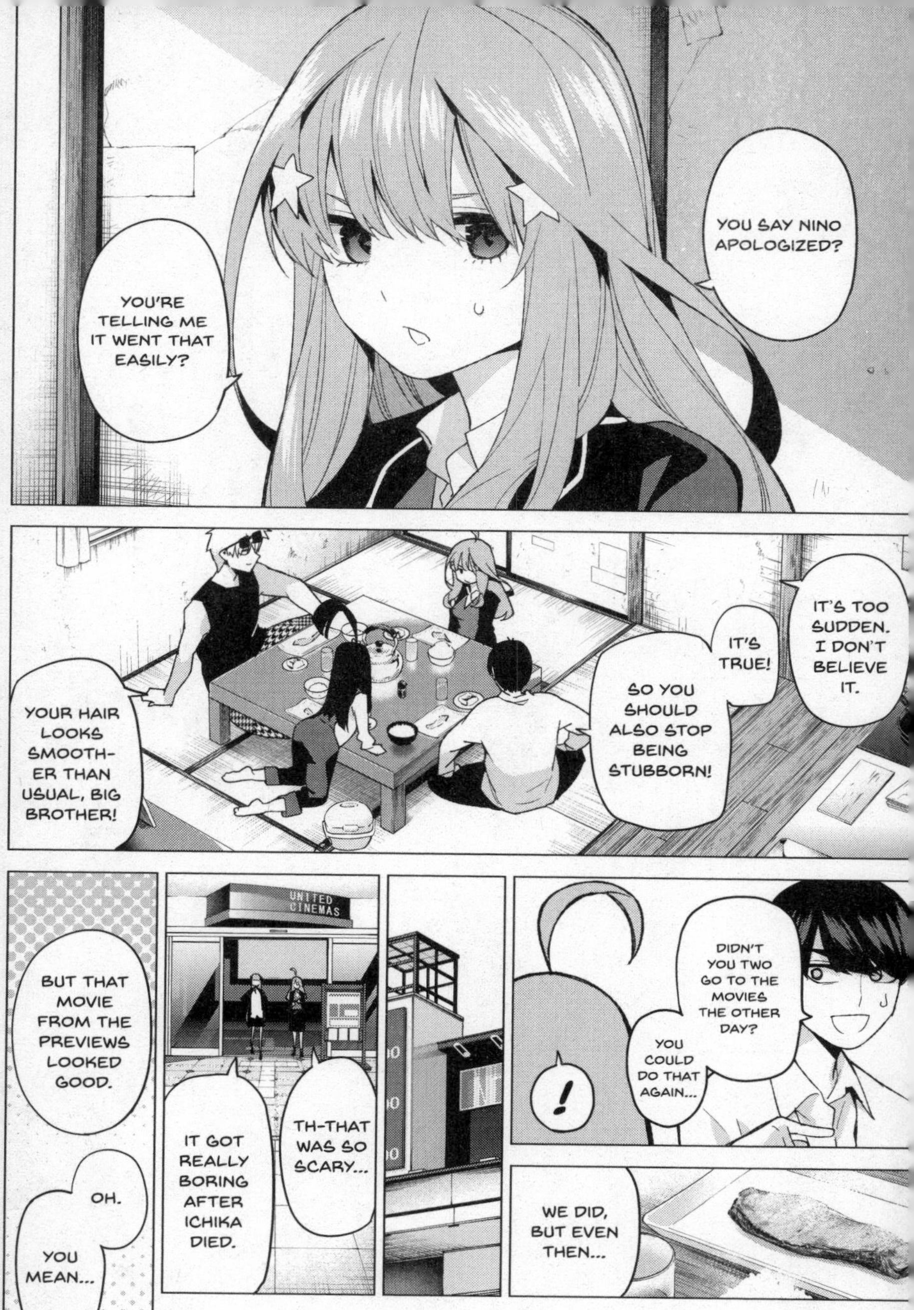
YOU SAY NINO APOLOGIZED?
YOU'RE TELLING ME IT WENT THAT EASILY?
IT'S TOO SUDDEN. I DON'T BELIEVE IT.
IT'S TRUE!
SO YOU SHOULD ALSO STOP BEING STUBBORN!
YOUR HAIR LOOKS SMOOTH-ER THAN USUAL, BIG BROTHER!
DIDN'T YOU TWO GO TO THE MOVIES THE OTHER DAY?
YOU COULD DO THAT AGAIN...
!
WE DID, BUT EVEN THEN...
UNITED CINEMAS
TH-THAT WAS SO SCARY...
IT GOT REALLY BORING AFTER ICHIKA DIED.
BUT THAT MOVIE FROM THE PREVIEWS LOOKED GOOD.
OH.
YOU MEAN...

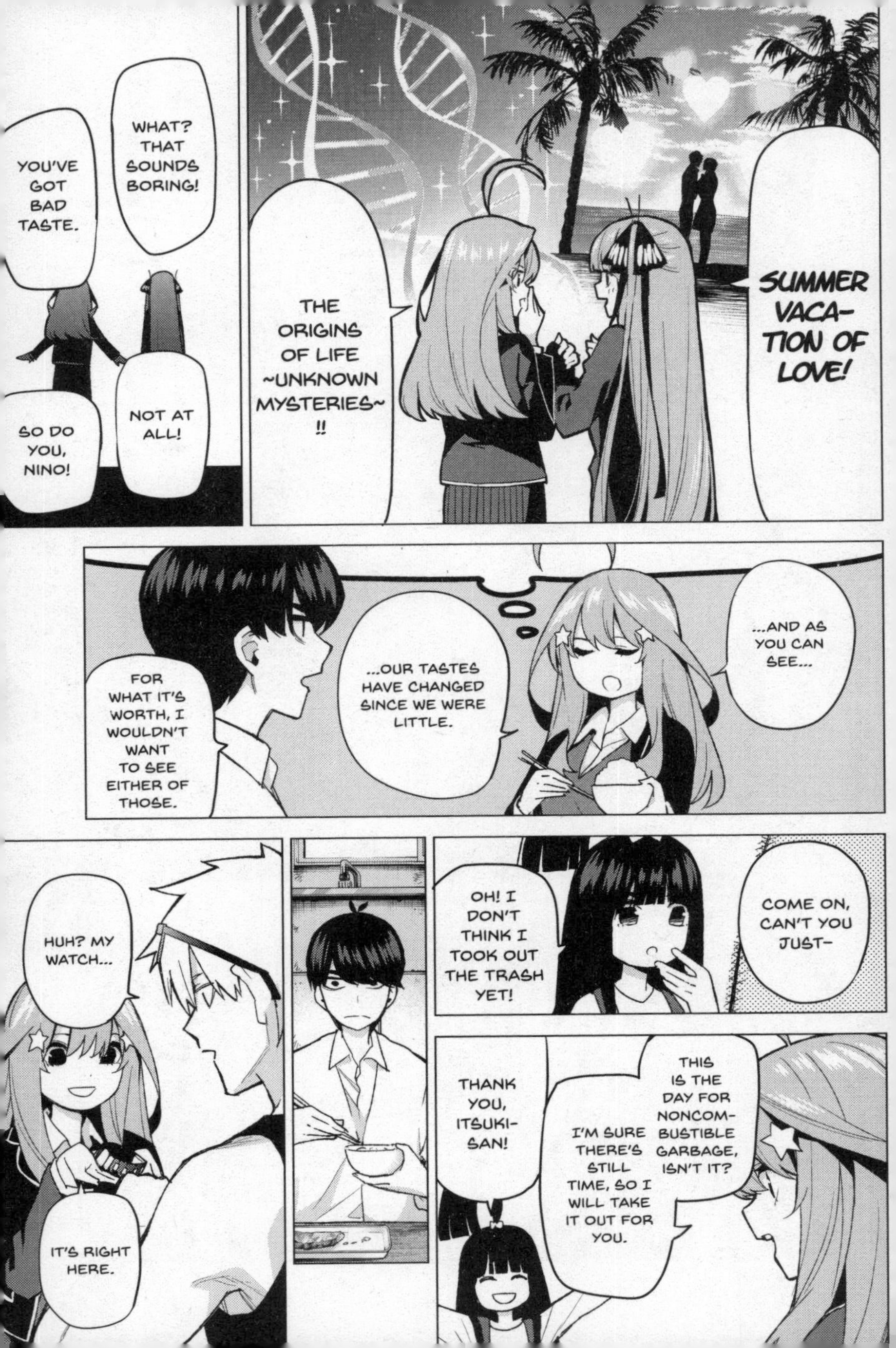
SUMMER VACATION OF LOVE!
THE ORIGINS OF LIFE ~UNKNOWN MYSTERIES~ !!
WHAT? THAT SOUNDS BORING!
YOU'VE GOT BAD TASTE.
NOT AT ALL!
SO DO YOU, NINO!
...AND AS YOU CAN SEE...
...OUR TASTES HAVE CHANGED SINCE WE WERE LITTLE.
FOR WHAT IT'S WORTH, I WOULDN'T WANT TO SEE EITHER OF THOSE.
COME ON, CAN'T YOU JUST-
OH! I DON'T THINK I TOOK OUT THE TRASH YET!
THIS IS THE DAY FOR NONCOMBUSTIBLE GARBAGE, ISN'T IT?
I'M SURE THERE'S STILL TIME, SO I WILL TAKE IT OUT FOR YOU.
THANK YOU, ITSUKI-SAN!
HUH? MY WATCH...
IT'S RIGHT HERE.

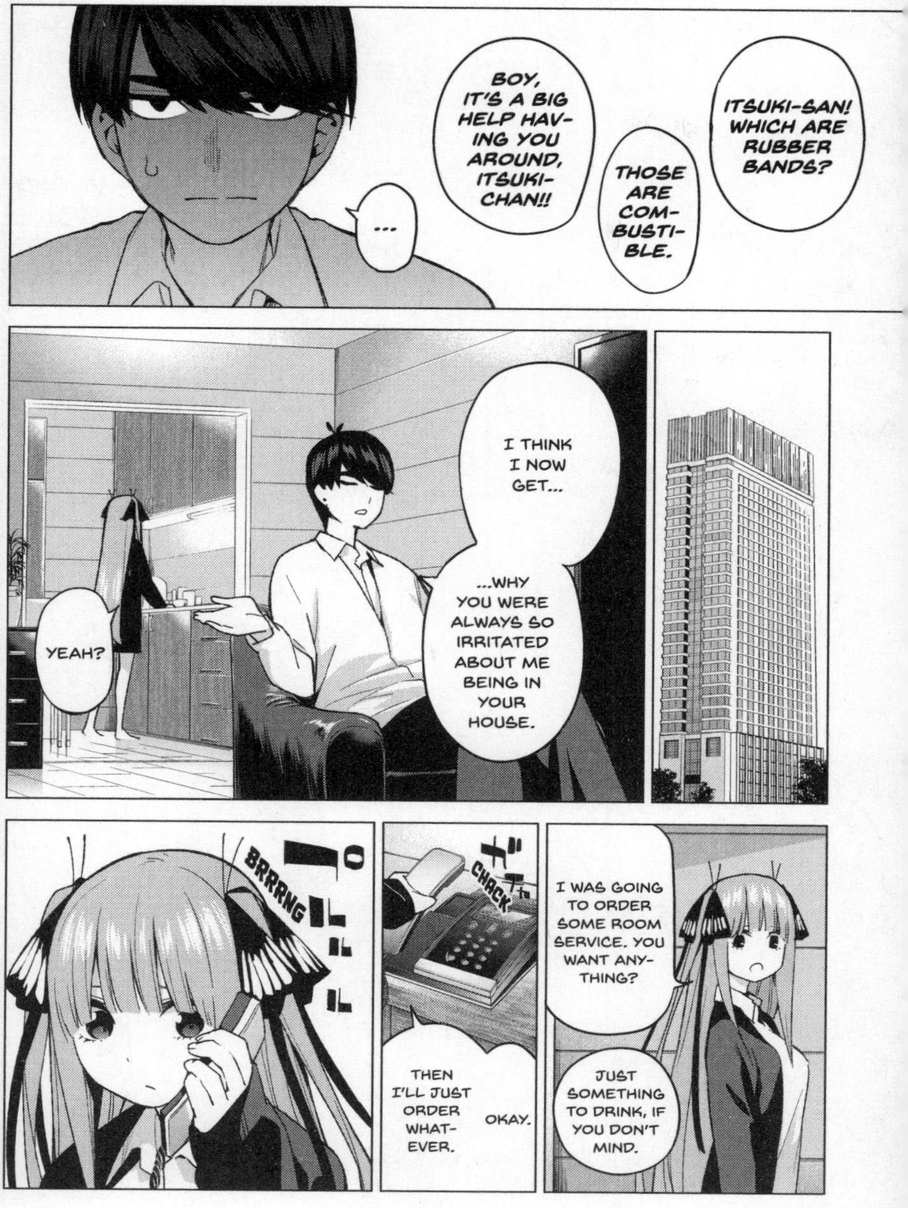
ITSUKI-SAN! WHICH ARE RUBBER BANDS?
THOSE ARE COMBUSTIBLE.
BOY, IT'S A BIG HELP HAVING YOU AROUND, ITSUKI-CHAN!!
...
I THINK I NOW GET...
...WHY YOU WERE ALWAYS SO IRRITATED ABOUT ME BEING IN YOUR HOUSE.
YEAH?
I WAS GOING TO ORDER SOME ROOM SERVICE. YOU WANT ANYTHING?
JUST SOMETHING TO DRINK, IF YOU DON'T MIND.
CHACK
OKAY.
THEN I'LL JUST ORDER WHATEVER.
BRRRNG

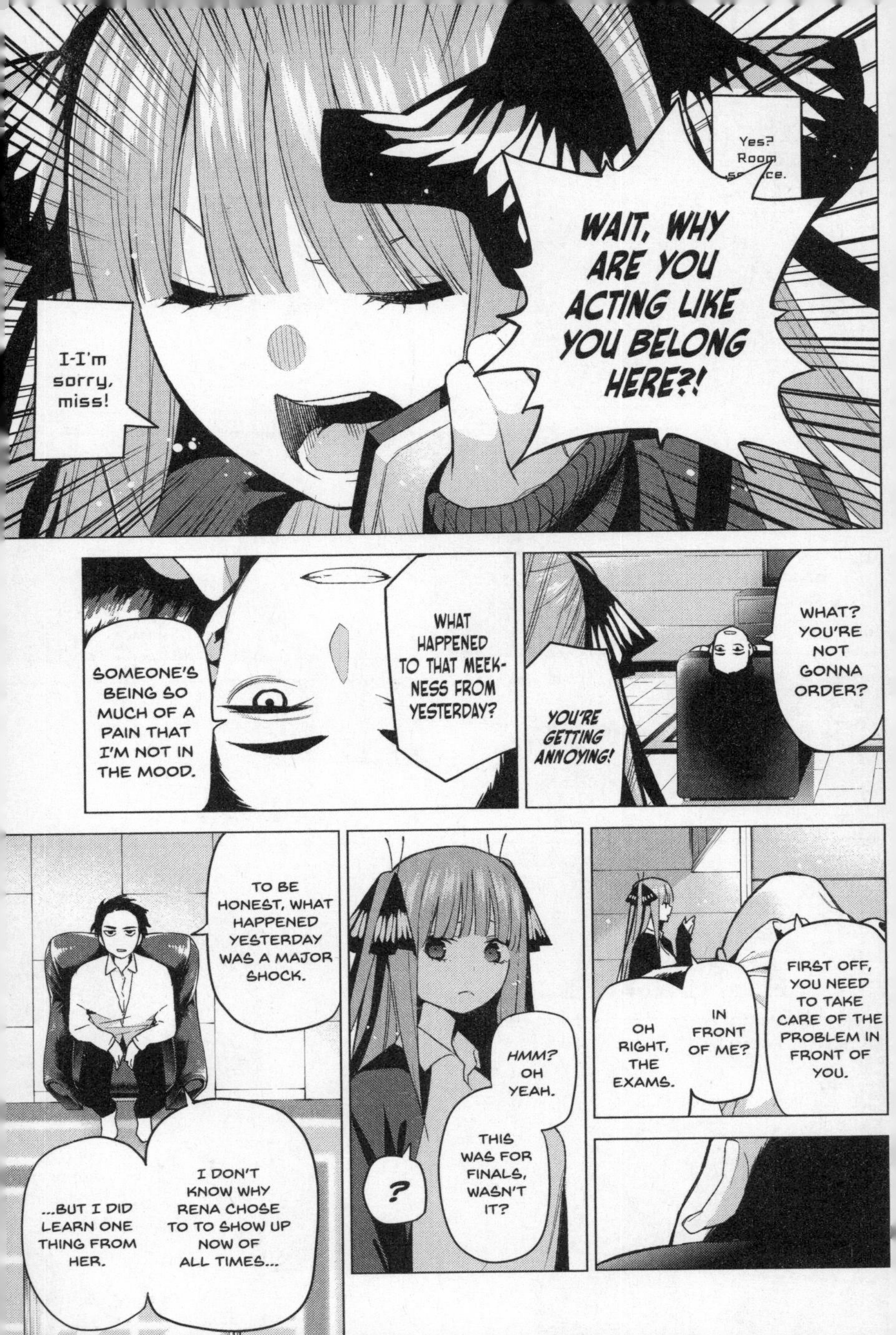
Yes? Room
WAIT, WHY ARE YOU ACTING LIKE YOU BELONG HERE?!
I-I'm sorry, miss!
WHAT? YOU'RE NOT GONNA ORDER?
YOU'RE GETTING ANNOYING!
WHAT HAPPENED TO THAT MEEK-NESS FROM YESTERDAY?
SOMEONE'S BEING SO MUCH OF A PAIN THAT I'M NOT IN THE MOOD.
FIRST OFF, YOU NEED TO TAKE CARE OF THE PROBLEM IN FRONT OF YOU.
IN FRONT OF ME?
OH RIGHT, THE EXAMS.
HMM? OH YEAH.
THIS WAS FOR FINALS, WASN'T IT?
?
TO BE HONEST, WHAT HAPPENED YESTERDAY WAS A MAJOR SHOCK.
I DON'T KNOW WHY RENA CHOSE TO TO SHOW UP NOW OF ALL TIMES...
...BUT I DID LEARN ONE THING FROM HER.

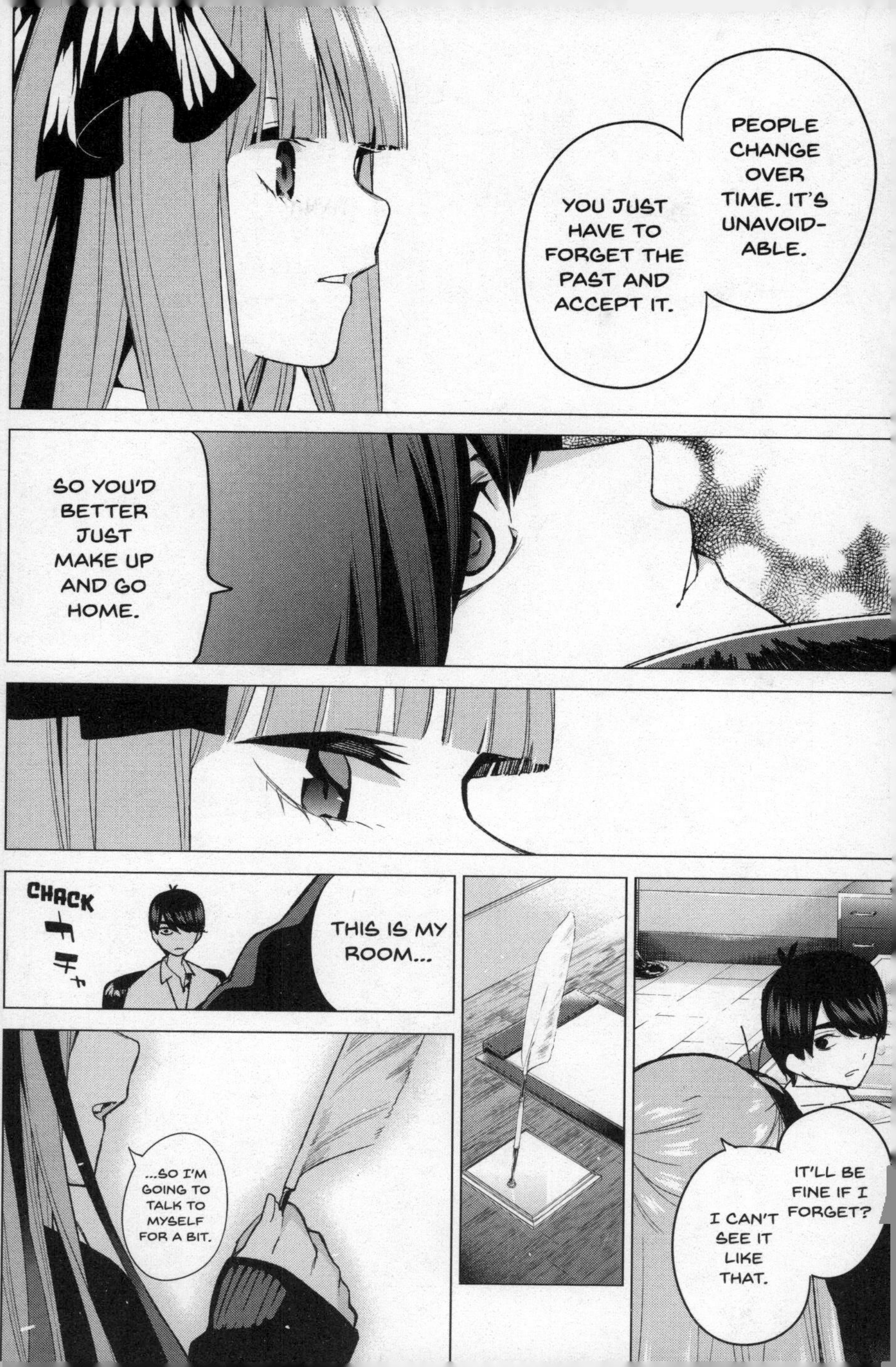
PEOPLE CHANGE OVER TIME. IT'S UNAVOID-ABLE.
YOU JUST HAVE TO FORGET THE PAST AND ACCEPT IT.
SO YOU'D BETTER JUST MAKE UP AND GO HOME.
IT'LL BE FINE IF I FORGET?
I CAN'T SEE IT LIKE THAT.
CHACK
THIS IS MY ROOM...
...SO I'M GOING TO TALK TO MYSELF FOR A BIT.

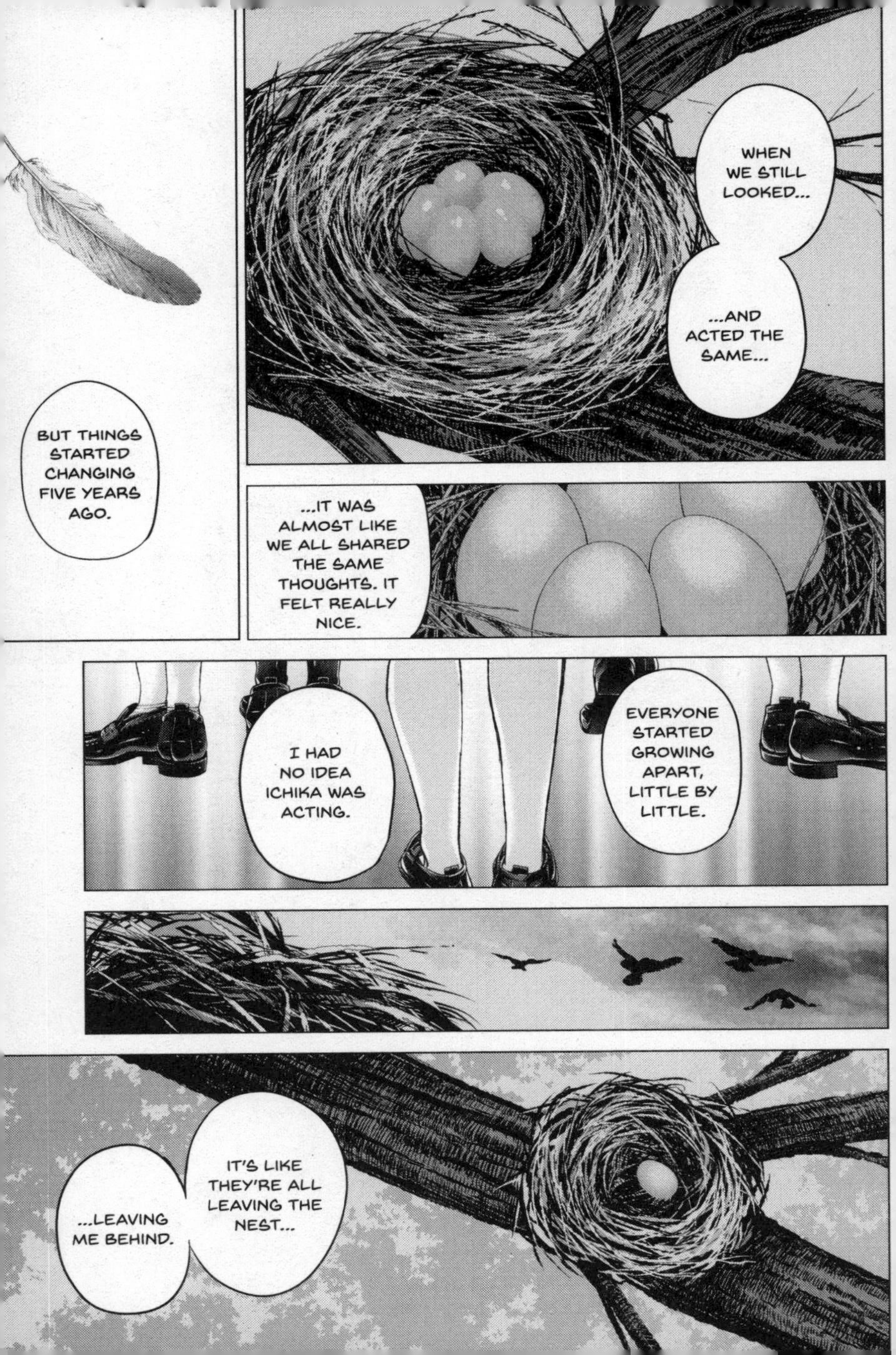
WHEN WE STILL LOOKED...
...AND ACTED THE SAME...
...IT WAS ALMOST LIKE WE ALL SHARED THE SAME THOUGHTS. IT FELT REALLY NICE.
BUT THINGS STARTED CHANGING FIVE YEARS AGO.
EVERYONE STARTED GROWING APART, LITTLE BY LITTLE.
I HAD NO IDEA ICHIKA WAS ACTING.
IT'S LIKE THEY'RE ALL LEAVING THE NEST...
...LEAVING ME BEHIND.

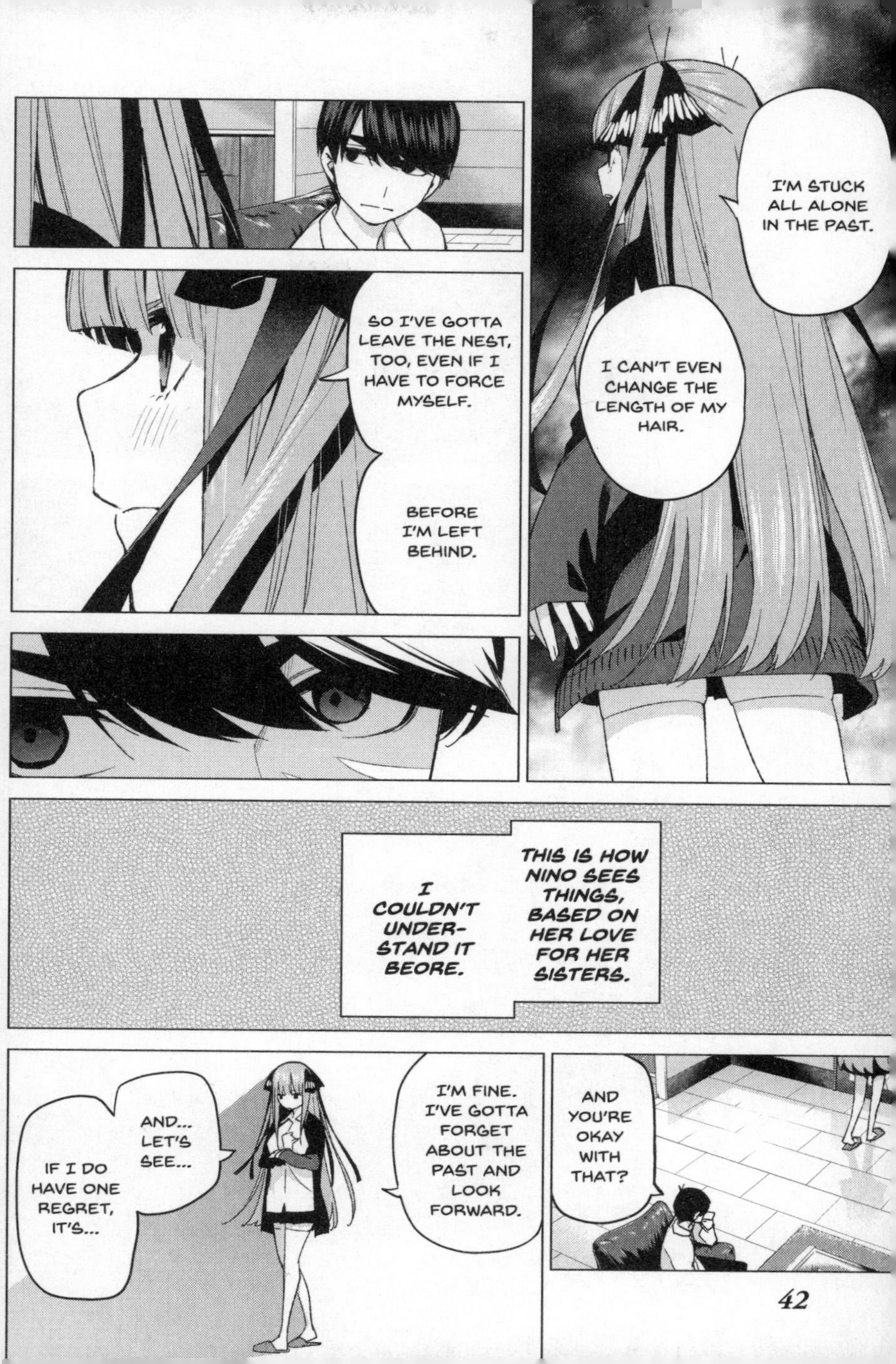
I'M STUCK ALL ALONE IN THE PAST.
I CAN'T EVEN CHANGE THE LENGTH OF MY HAIR.
SO I'VE GOTTA LEAVE THE NEST, TOO, EVEN IF I HAVE TO FORCE MYSELF.
BEFORE I'M LEFT BEHIND.
THIS IS HOW NINO SEES THINGS, BASED ON HER LOVE FOR HER SISTERS.
I COULDN'T UNDER-STAND IT BEORE.
AND YOU'RE OKAY WITH THAT?
I'M FINE. I'VE GOTTA FORGET ABOUT THE PAST AND LOOK FORWARD.
AND... LET'S SEE...
IF I DO HAVE ONE REGRET, IT'S...

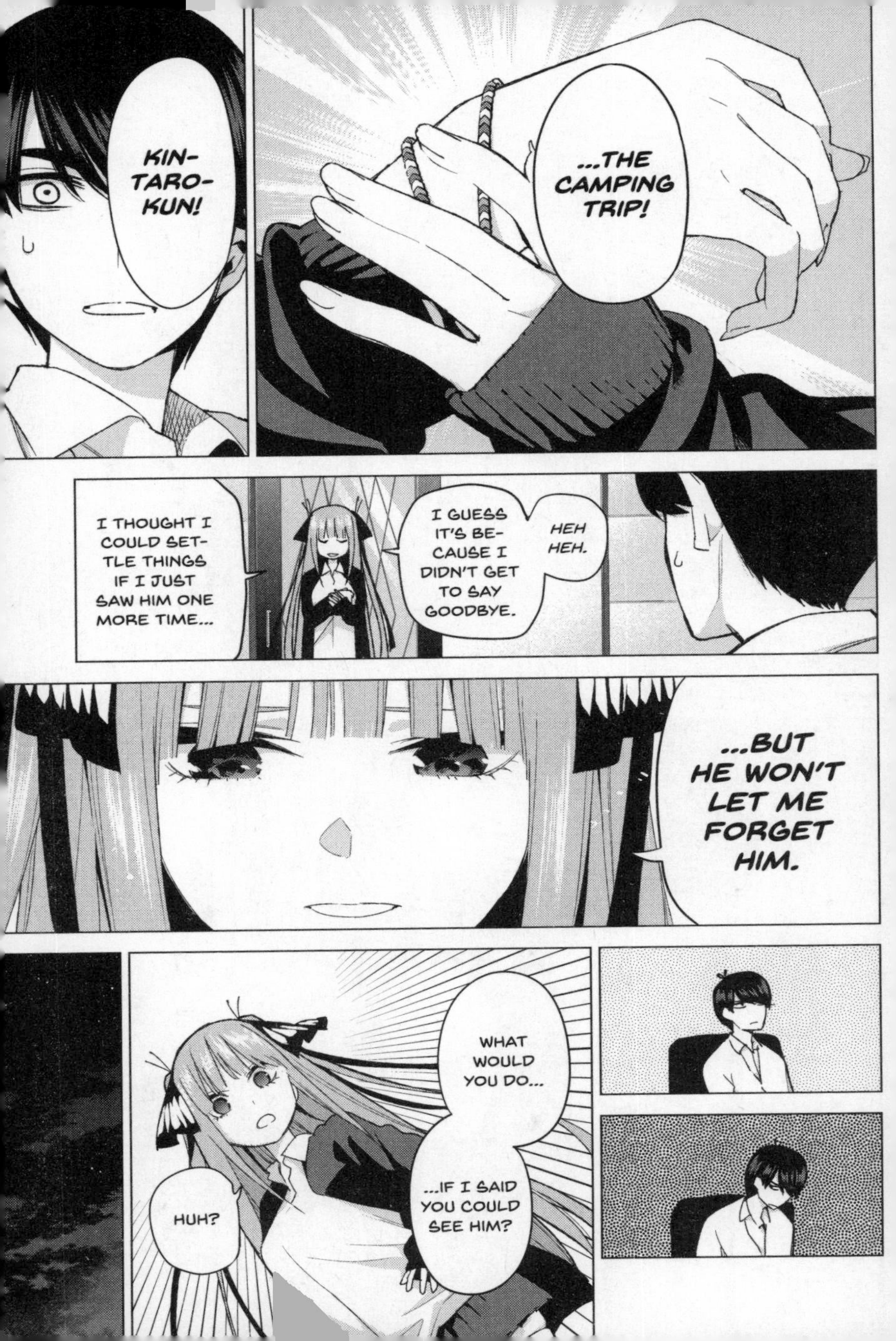
...THE CAMPING TRIP!
KIN-TARO-KUN!
HEH HEH.
I GUESS IT'S BE-CAUSE I DIDN'T GET TO SAY GOODBYE.
I THOUGHT I COULD SET-TLE THINGS IF I JUST SAW HIM ONE MORE TIME...
...BUT HE WON'T LET ME FORGET HIM.
WHAT WOULD YOU DO...
...IF I SAID YOU COULD SEE HIM?
HUH?

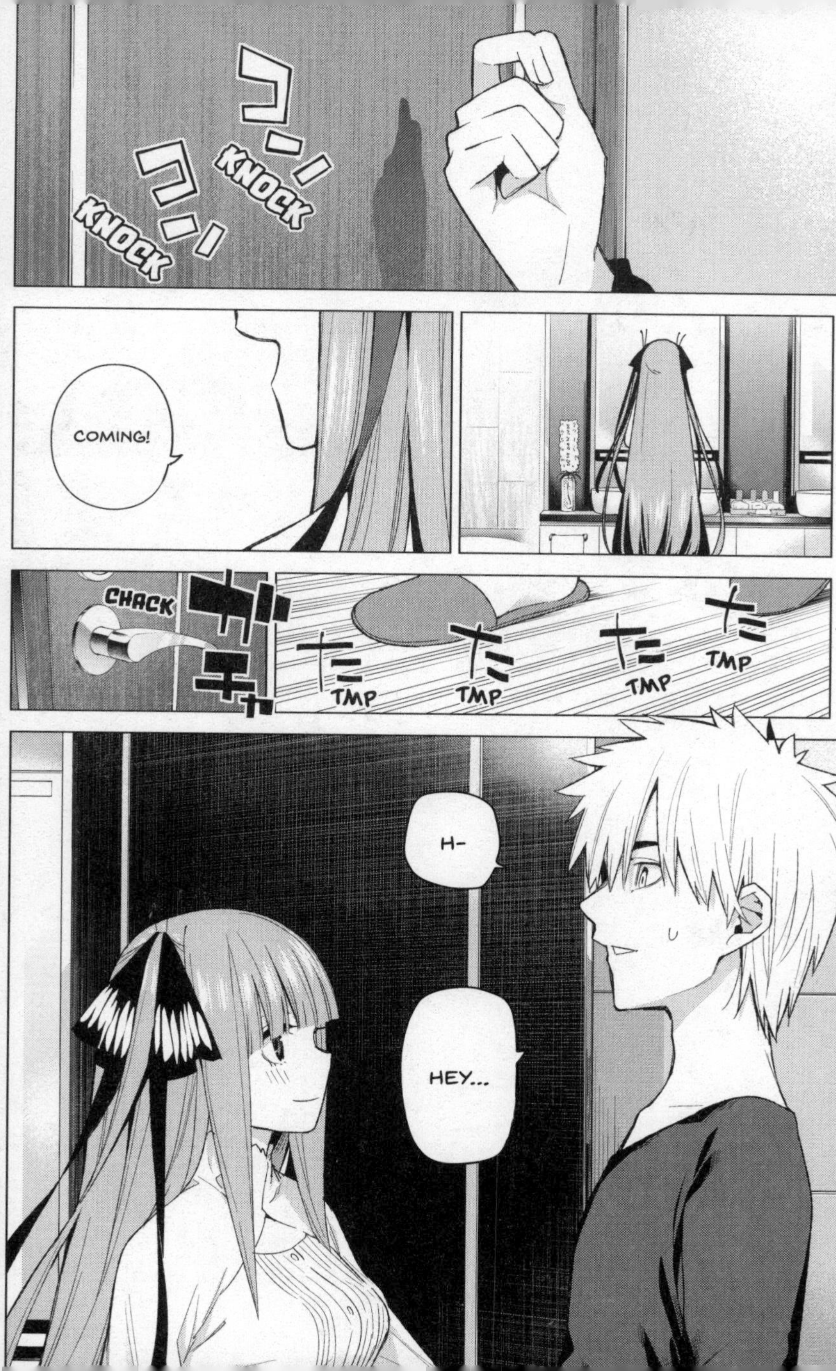
KNOCK
KNOCK
COMING!
TMP
TMP
TMP
TMP
CHACK
H-
HEY...

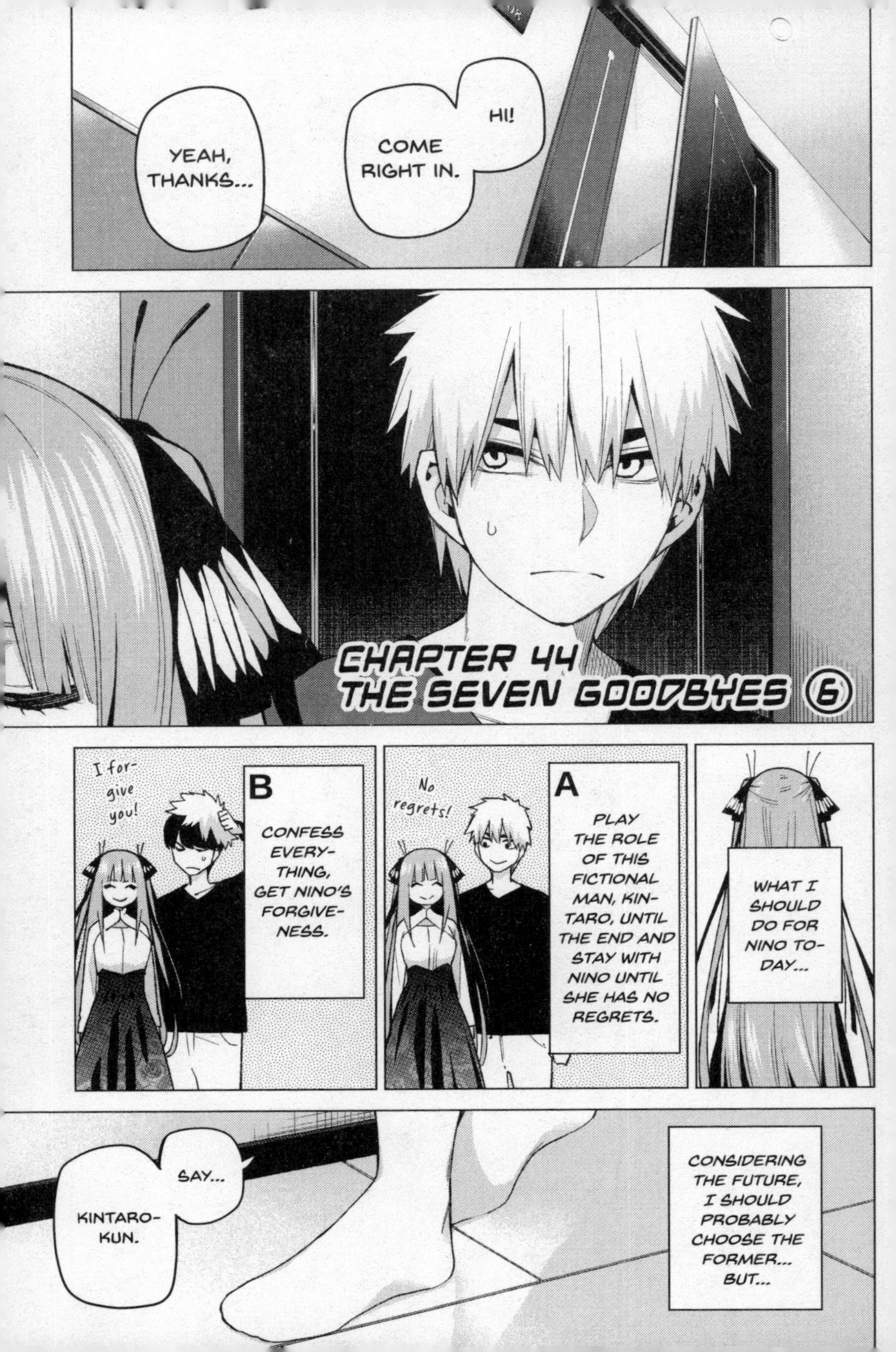

HI!
COME RIGHT IN.
YEAH, THANKS...
CHAPTER 44
THE SEVEN GOODBYES ⑥
WHAT I SHOULD DO FOR NINO TODAY...
A
PLAY THE ROLE OF THIS FICTIONAL MAN, KINTARO, UNTIL THE END AND STAY WITH NINO UNTIL SHE HAS NO REGRETS.
No regrets!
B
CONFESS EVERYTHING, GET NINO'S FORGIVENESS.
I forgive you!
CONSIDERING THE FUTURE, I SHOULD PROBABLY CHOOSE THE FORMER... BUT...
SAY...
KINTARO-KUN.

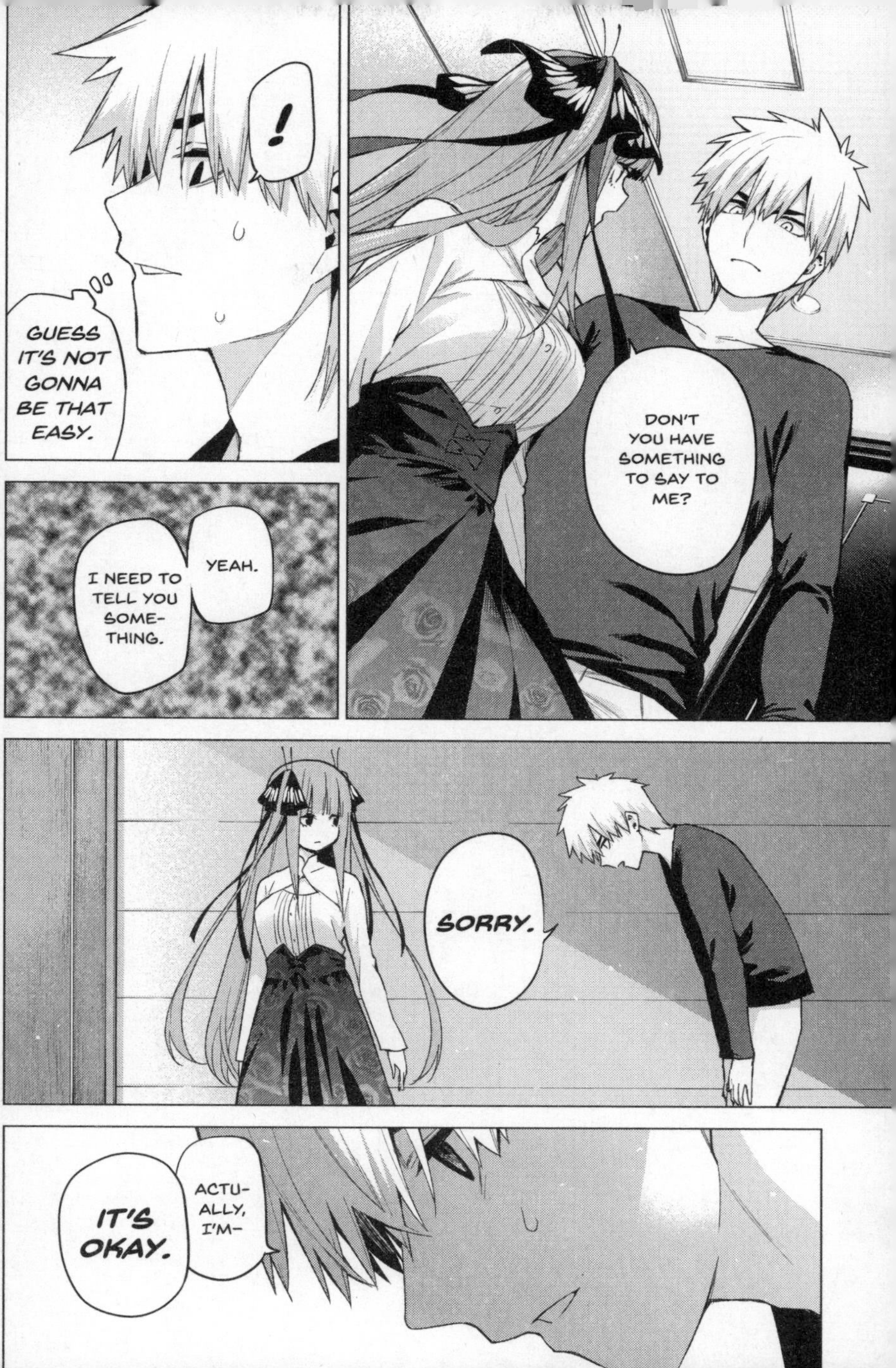
DON'T YOU HAVE SOMETHING TO SAY TO ME?
!
GUESS IT'S NOT GONNA BE THAT EASY.
YEAH.
I NEED TO TELL YOU SOME-THING.
SORRY.
ACTU-ALLY, I'M—
IT'S OKAY.

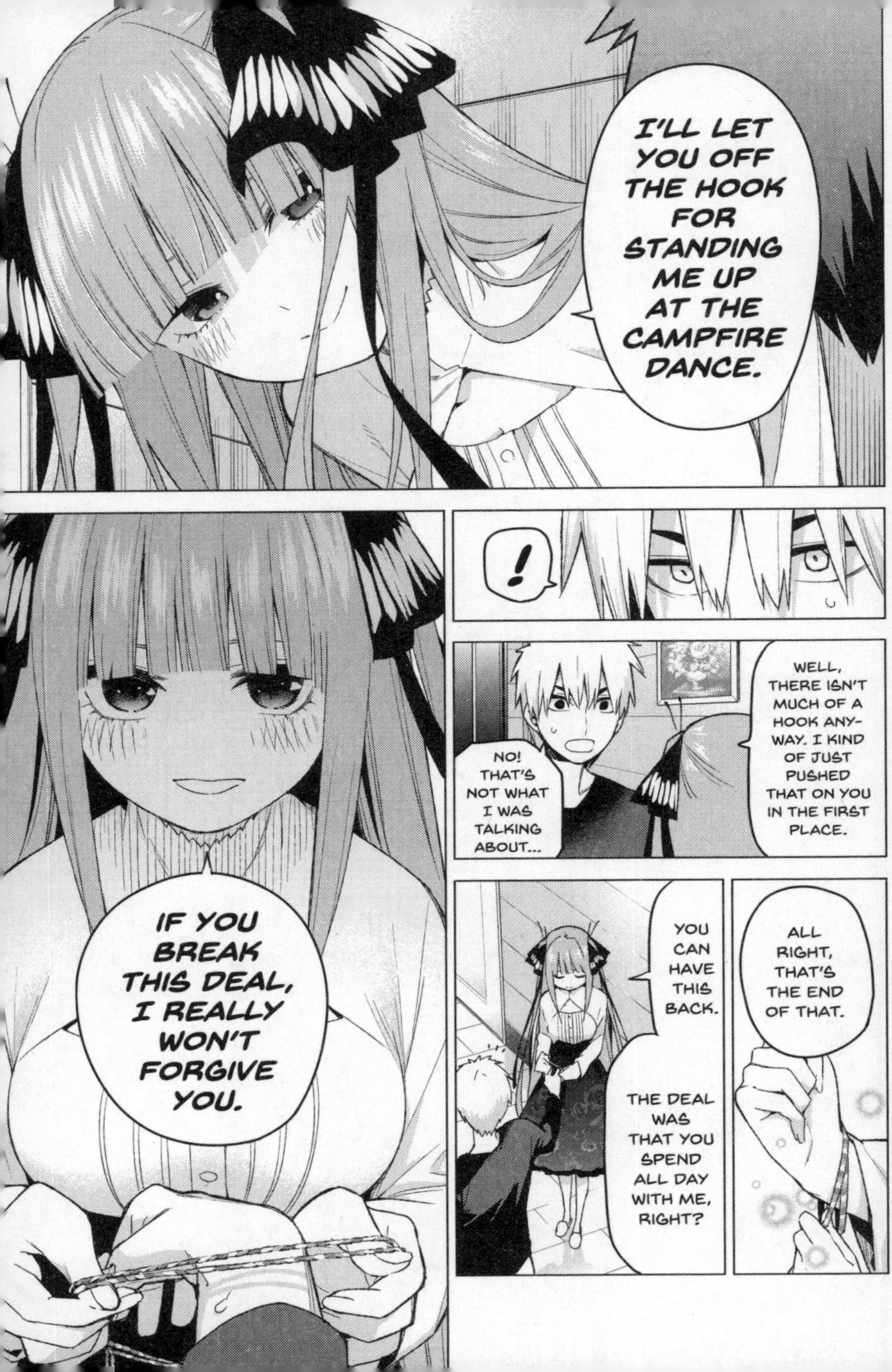
I'LL LET YOU OFF THE HOOK FOR STANDING ME UP AT THE CAMPFIRE DANCE.
!
WELL, THERE ISN'T MUCH OF A HOOK ANY-WAY. I KIND OF JUST PUSHED THAT ON YOU IN THE FIRST PLACE.
NO! THAT'S NOT WHAT I WAS TALKING ABOUT...
ALL RIGHT, THAT'S THE END OF THAT.
YOU CAN HAVE THIS BACK.
THE DEAL WAS THAT YOU SPEND ALL DAY WITH ME, RIGHT?
IF YOU BREAK THIS DEAL, I REALLY WON'T FORGIVE YOU.

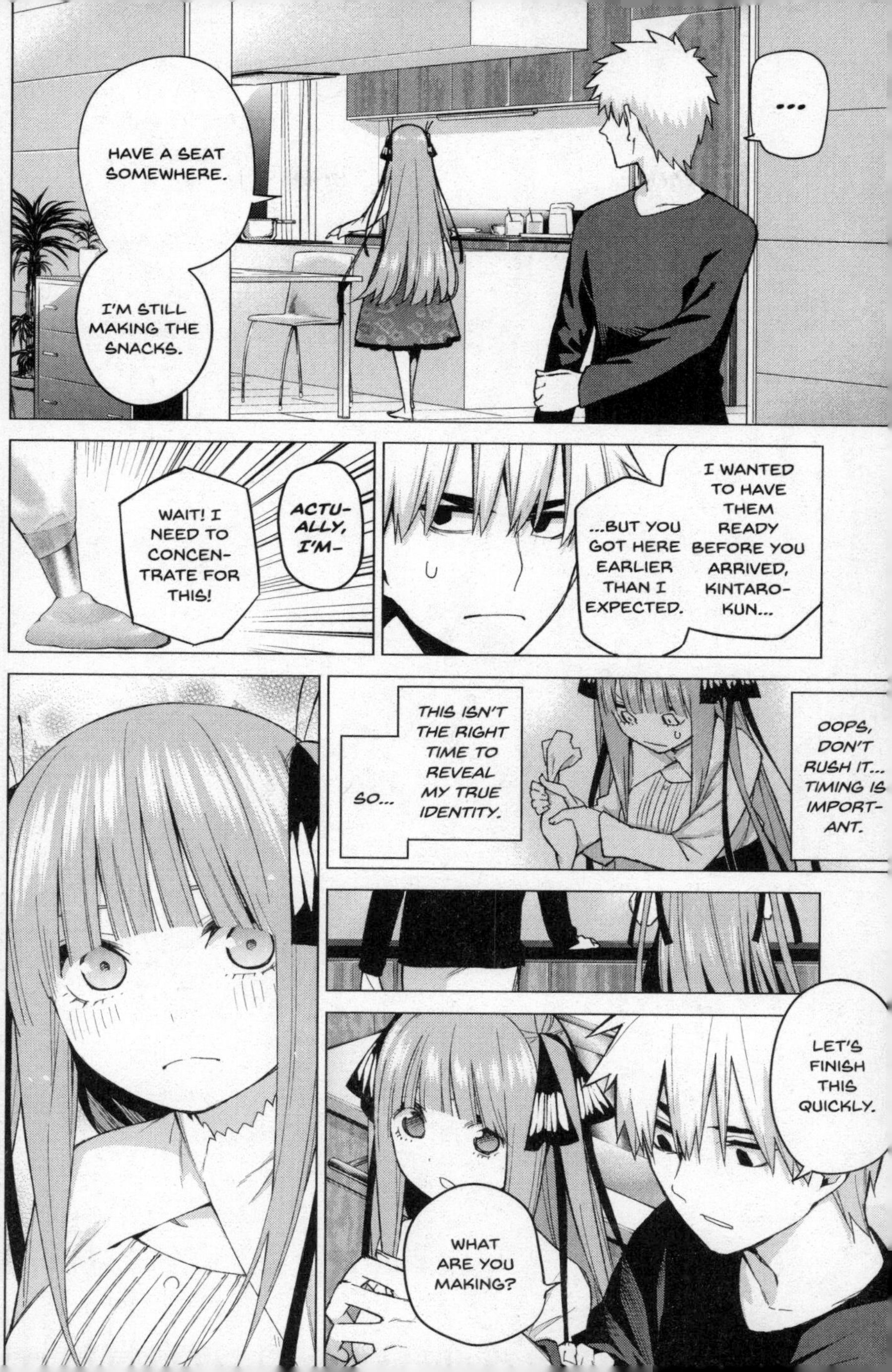
...
HAVE A SEAT SOMEWHERE.
I'M STILL MAKING THE SNACKS.
I WANTED TO HAVE THEM READY BEFORE YOU ARRIVED, KINTARO-KUN...
...BUT YOU GOT HERE EARLIER THAN I EXPECTED.
ACTU-ALLY, I'M-
WAIT! I NEED TO CONCEN-TRATE FOR THIS!
OOPS, DON'T RUSH IT... TIMING IS IMPORT-ANT.
THIS ISN'T THE RIGHT TIME TO REVEAL MY TRUE IDENTITY.
SO...
LET'S FINISH THIS QUICKLY.
WHAT ARE YOU MAKING?

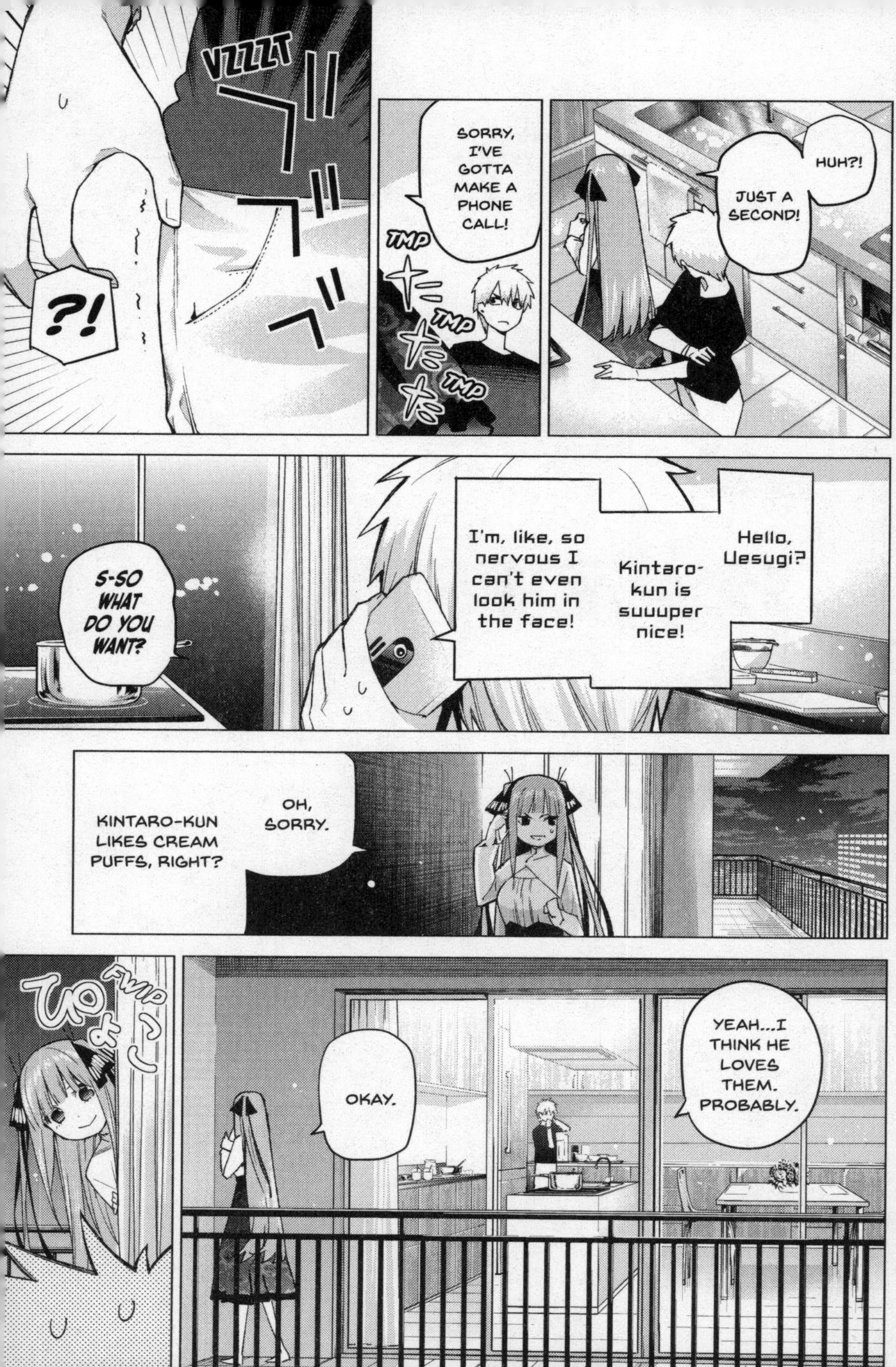
HUH?!
JUST A SECOND!
SORRY, I'VE GOTTA MAKE A PHONE CALL!
TMP
TMP
TMP
VZZZT
?!
Hello, Uesugi?
Kintaro-kun is suuuper nice!
I'm, like, so nervous I can't even look him in the face!
S-SO WHAT DO YOU WANT?
OH, SORRY.
KINTARO-KUN LIKES CREAM PUFFS, RIGHT?
YEAH...I THINK HE LOVES THEM. PROBABLY.
OKAY.
FWIP

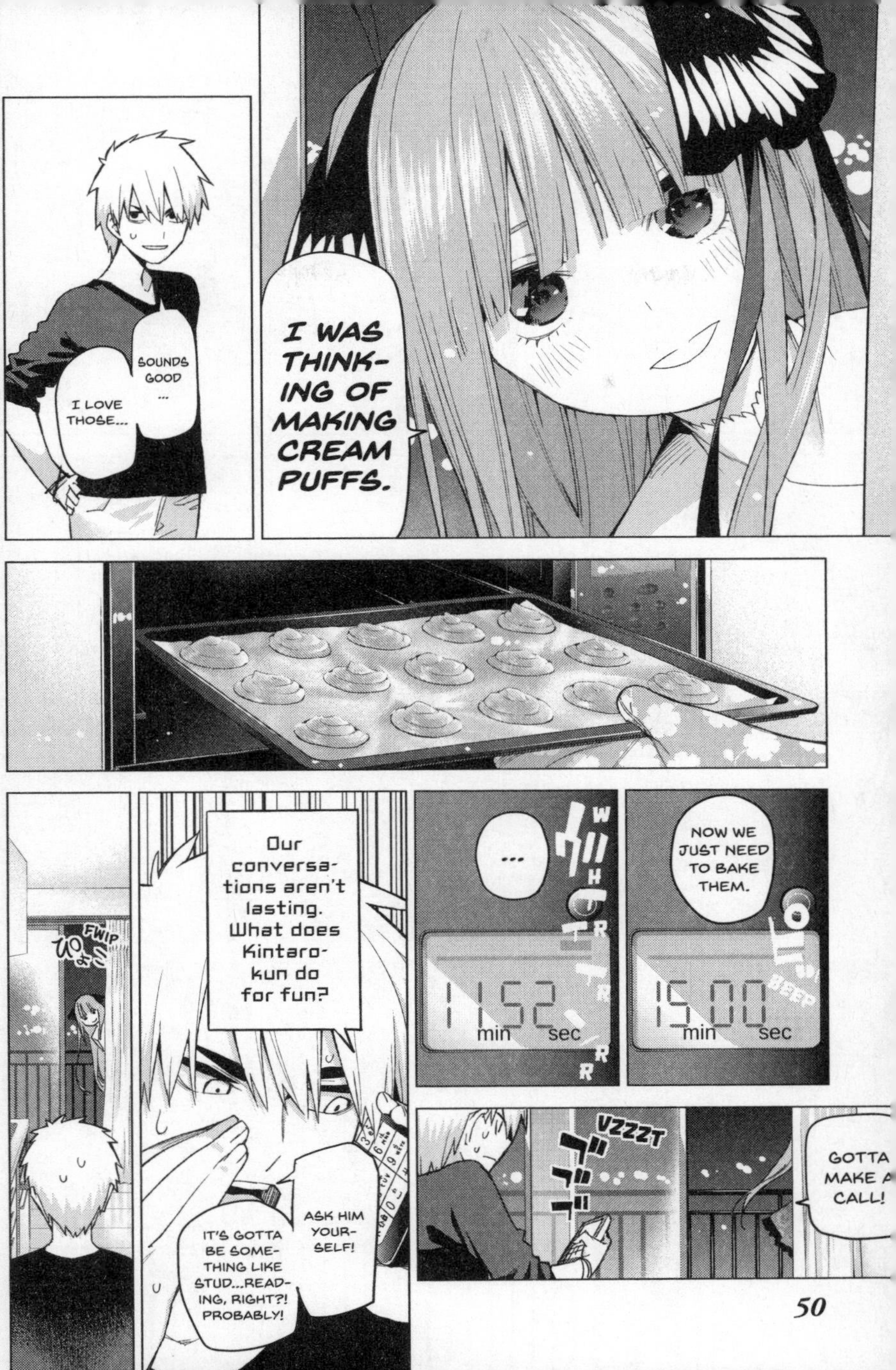
I WAS THINKING OF MAKING CREAM PUFFS.
SOUNDS GOOD ...
I LOVE THOSE...
NOW WE JUST NEED TO BAKE THEM.
BEEP
15 00 min sec
...
WHIRRR
11 52 min sec
VZZZT
GOTTA MAKE A CALL!
Our conversations aren't lasting. What does Kintaro-kun do for fun?
ASK HIM YOURSELF!
IT'S GOTTA BE SOMETHING LIKE STUD...READING, RIGHT?! PROBABLY!
FWIP

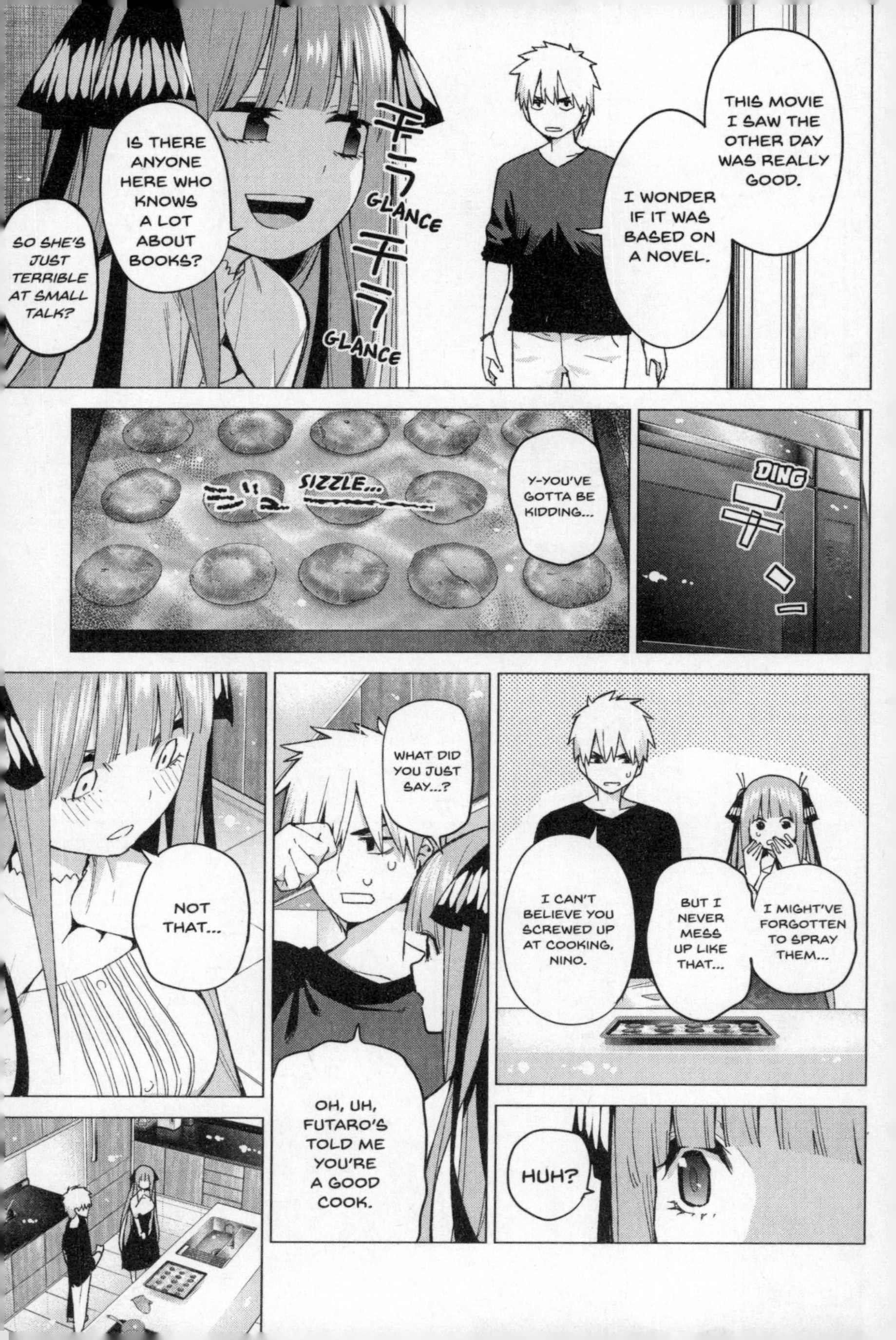
THIS MOVIE I SAW THE OTHER DAY WAS REALLY GOOD.
I WONDER IF IT WAS BASED ON A NOVEL.
IS THERE ANYONE HERE WHO KNOWS A LOT ABOUT BOOKS?
GLANCE
GLANCE
SO SHE'S JUST TERRIBLE AT SMALL TALK?
DING
Y-YOU'VE GOTTA BE KIDDING...
SIZZLE...
I MIGHT'VE FORGOTTEN TO SPRAY THEM...
BUT I NEVER MESS UP LIKE THAT...
I CAN'T BELIEVE YOU SCREWED UP AT COOKING, NINO.
HUH?
WHAT DID YOU JUST SAY...?
OH, UH, FUTARO'S TOLD ME YOU'RE A GOOD COOK.
NOT THAT...

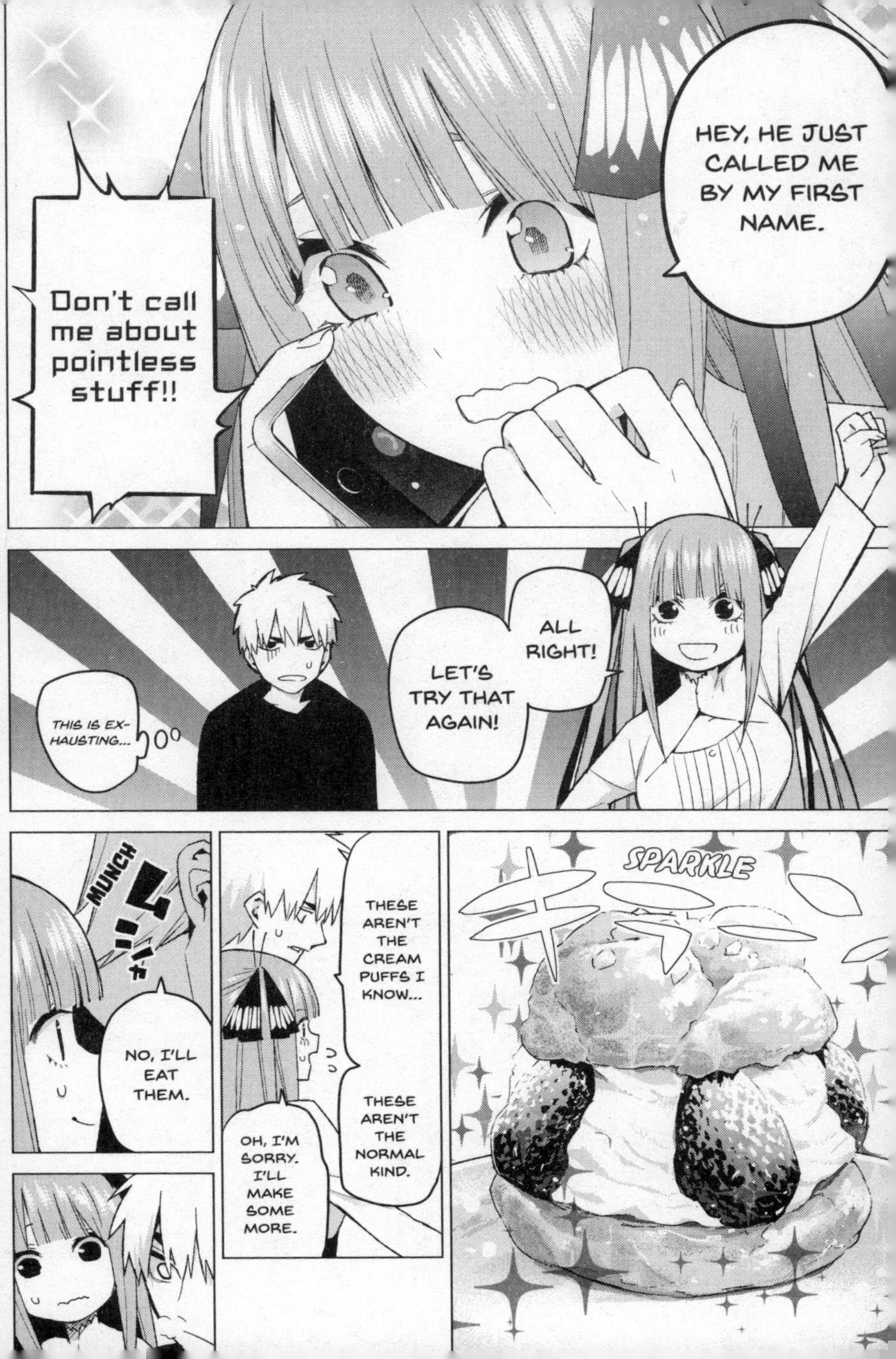
HEY, HE JUST CALLED ME BY MY FIRST NAME.
Don't call me about pointless stuff!!
ALL RIGHT!
LET'S TRY THAT AGAIN!
THIS IS EX-HAUSTING...
SPARKLE
THESE AREN'T THE CREAM PUFFS I KNOW...
THESE AREN'T THE NORMAL KIND.
OH, I'M SORRY. I'LL MAKE SOME MORE.
MUNCH
NO, I'LL EAT THEM.

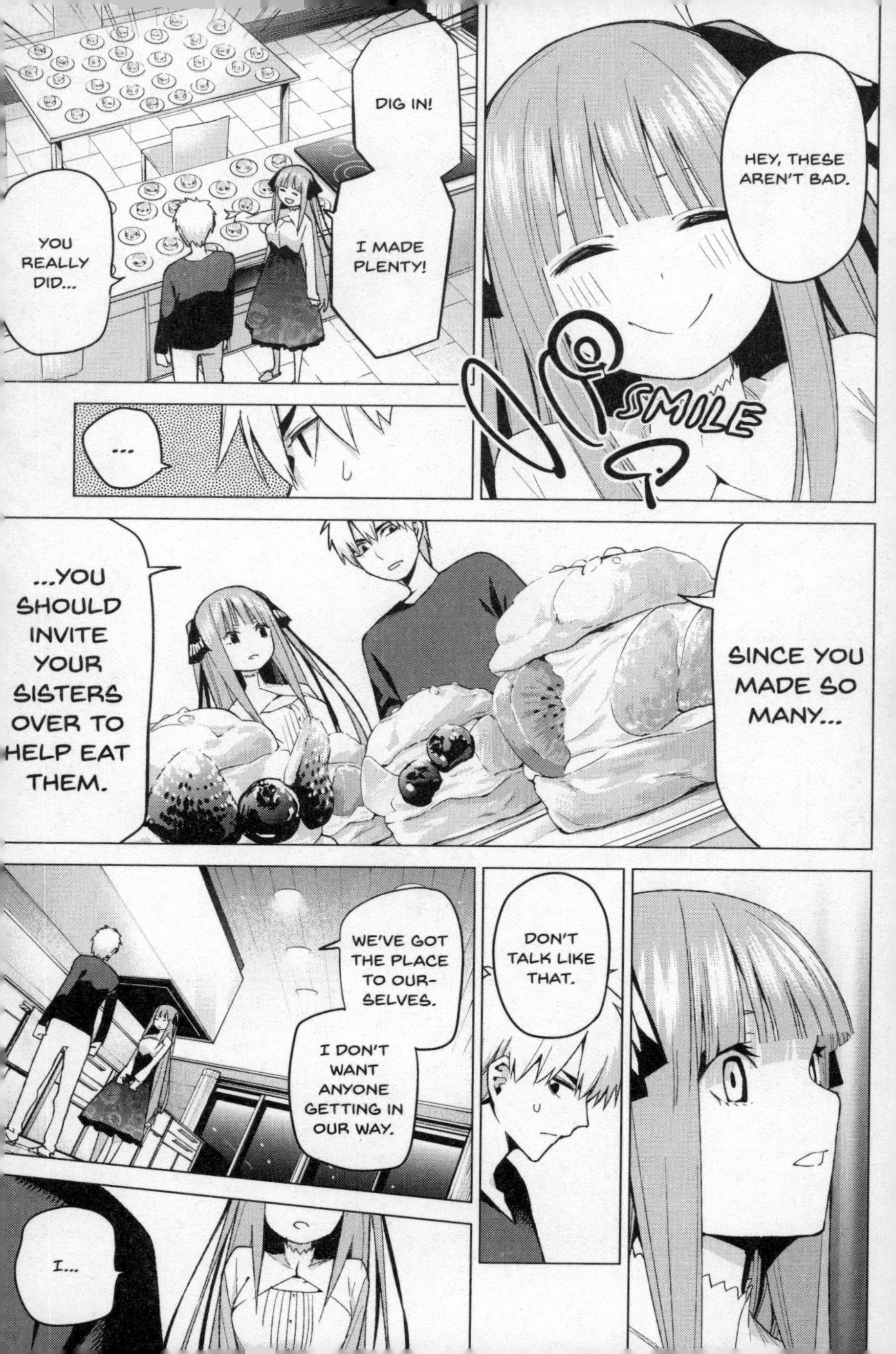
HEY, THESE AREN'T BAD.
SMILE
DIG IN!
I MADE PLENTY!
YOU REALLY DID...
...
SINCE YOU MADE SO MANY...
...YOU SHOULD INVITE YOUR SISTERS OVER TO HELP EAT THEM.
DON'T TALK LIKE THAT.
WE'VE GOT THE PLACE TO OUR-SELVES.
I DON'T WANT ANYONE GETTING IN OUR WAY.
I...

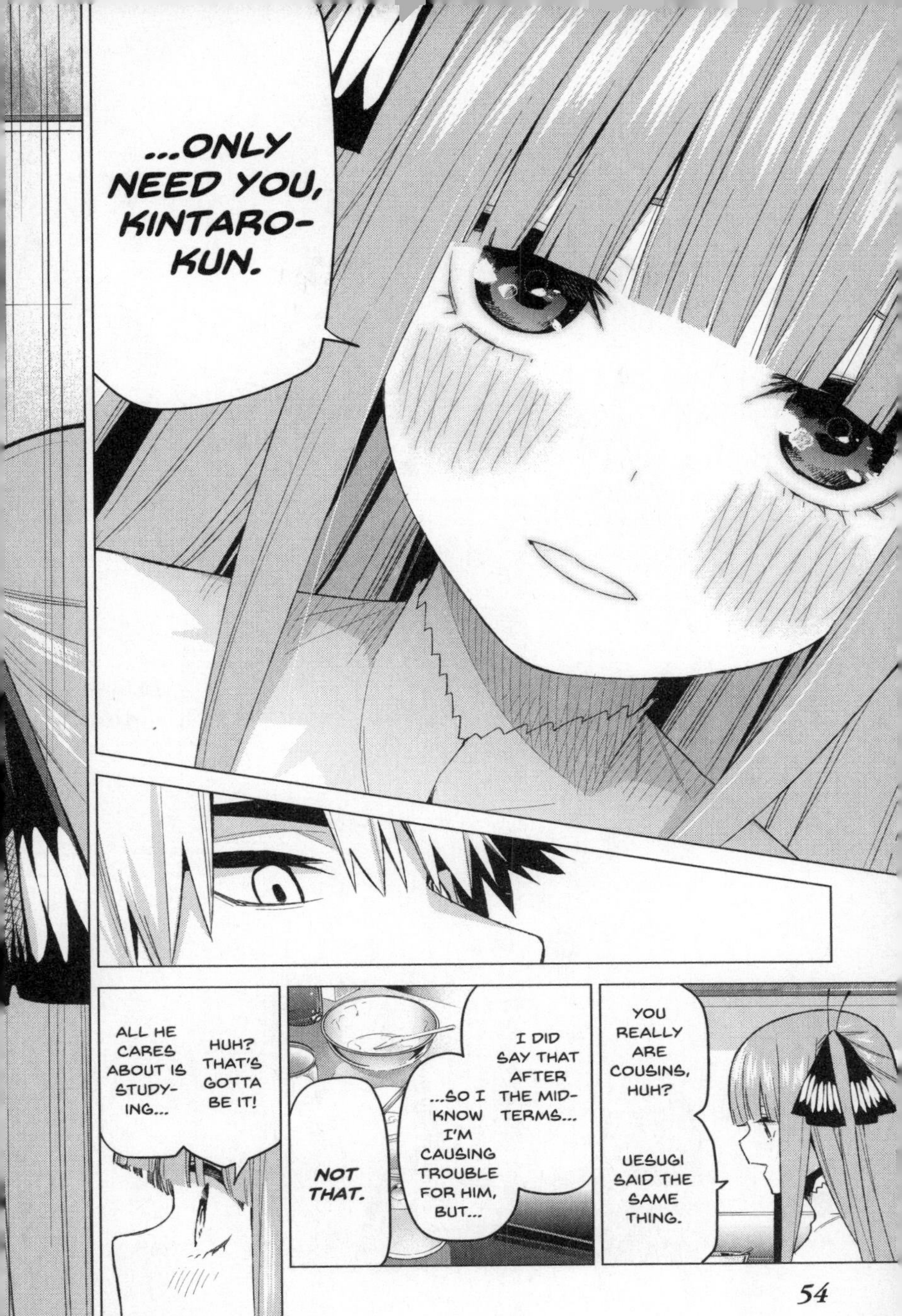
...ONLY NEED YOU, KINTARO-KUN.
YOU REALLY ARE COUSINS, HUH?
UESUGI SAID THE SAME THING.
I DID SAY THAT AFTER THE MID-TERMS...
...SO I KNOW I'M CAUSING TROUBLE FOR HIM, BUT...
NOT THAT.
HUH? THAT'S GOTTA BE IT!
ALL HE CARES ABOUT IS STUDY-ING...

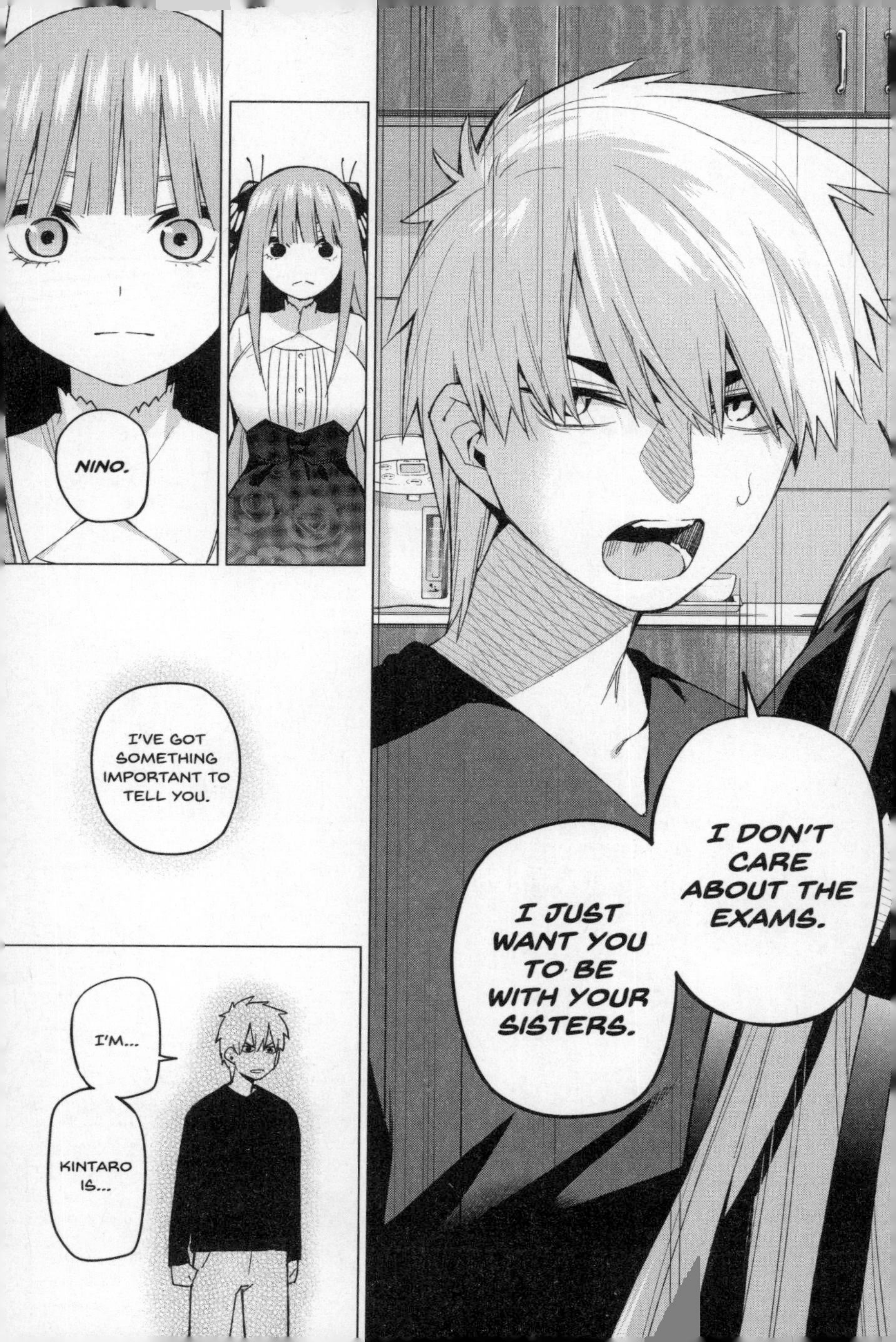
I DON'T CARE ABOUT THE EXAMS.
I JUST WANT YOU TO BE WITH YOUR SISTERS.
NINO.
I'VE GOT SOMETHING IMPORTANT TO TELL YOU.
I'M...
KINTARO IS...

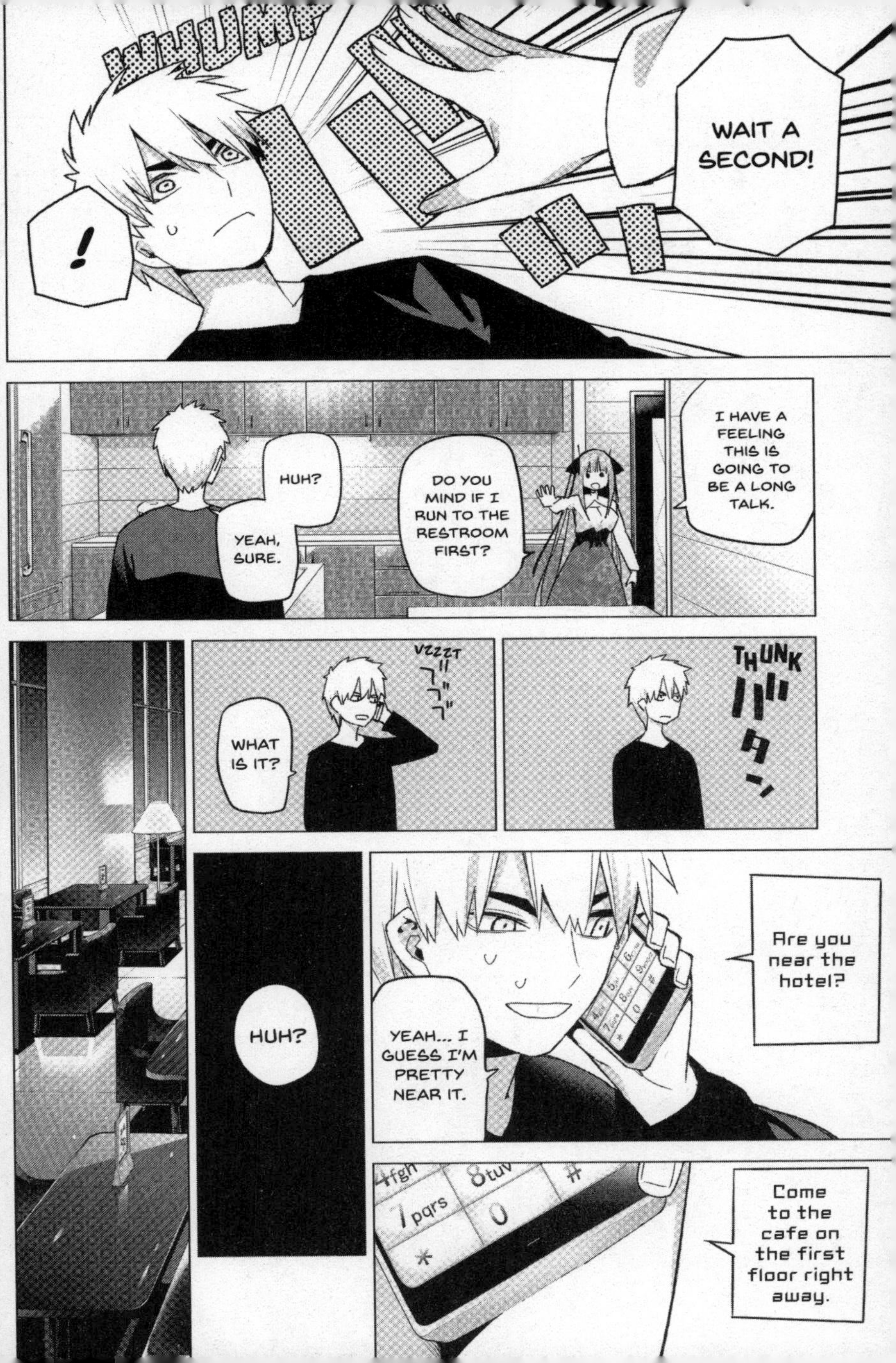
WHUMP
WAIT A SECOND!
!
I HAVE A FEELING THIS IS GOING TO BE A LONG TALK.
DO YOU MIND IF I RUN TO THE RESTROOM FIRST?
HUH?
YEAH, SURE.
THUNK
VZZZT
WHAT IS IT?
Are you near the hotel?
YEAH... I GUESS I'M PRETTY NEAR IT.
HUH?
Come to the cafe on the first floor right away.

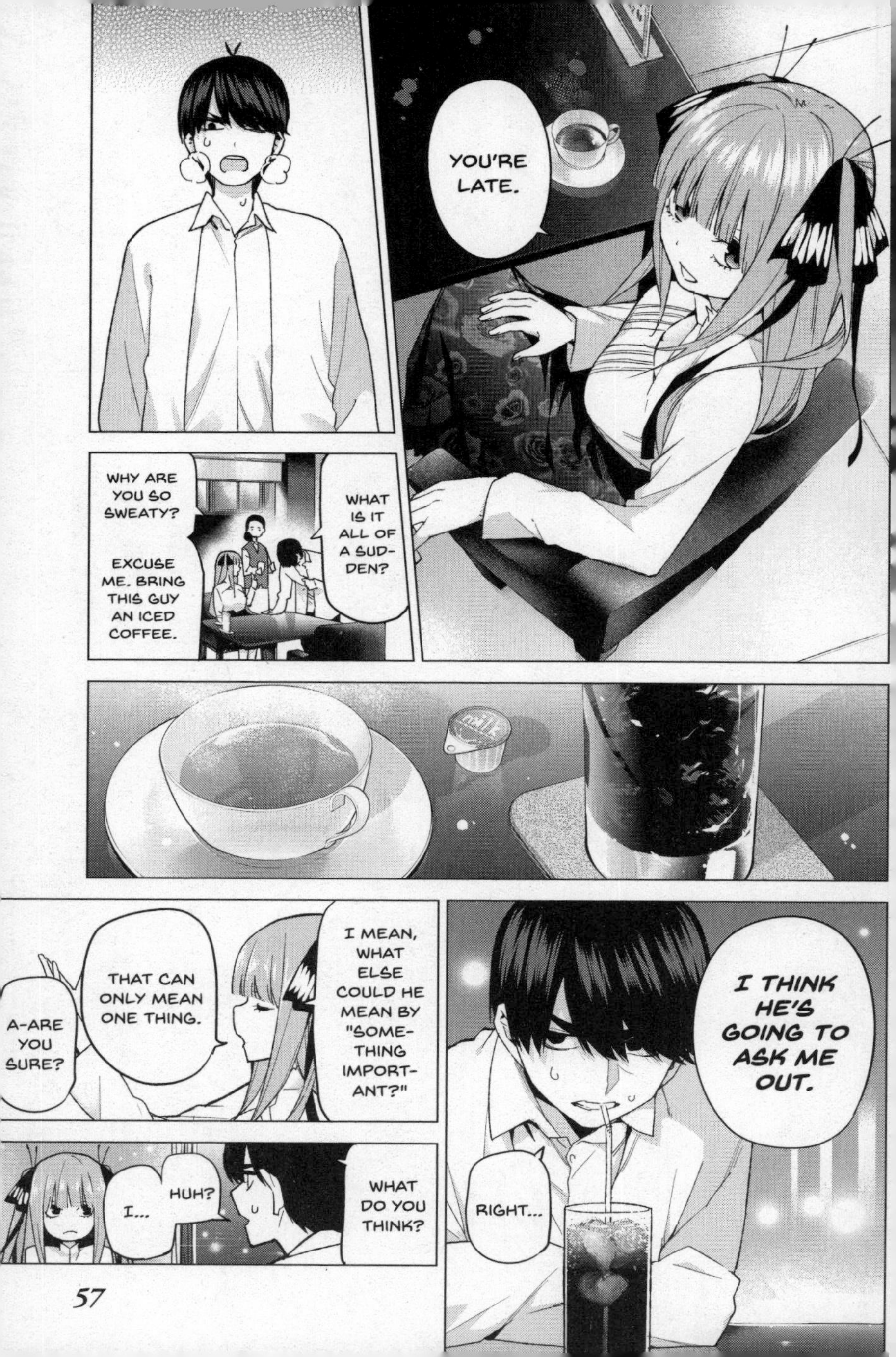
YOU'RE LATE.
WHY ARE YOU SO SWEATY?
WHAT IS IT ALL OF A SUDDEN?
EXCUSE ME. BRING THIS GUY AN ICED COFFEE.
I THINK HE'S GOING TO ASK ME OUT.
RIGHT...
I MEAN, WHAT ELSE COULD HE MEAN BY "SOMETHING IMPORTANT?"
THAT CAN ONLY MEAN ONE THING.
A-ARE YOU SURE?
WHAT DO YOU THINK?
HUH?
I...

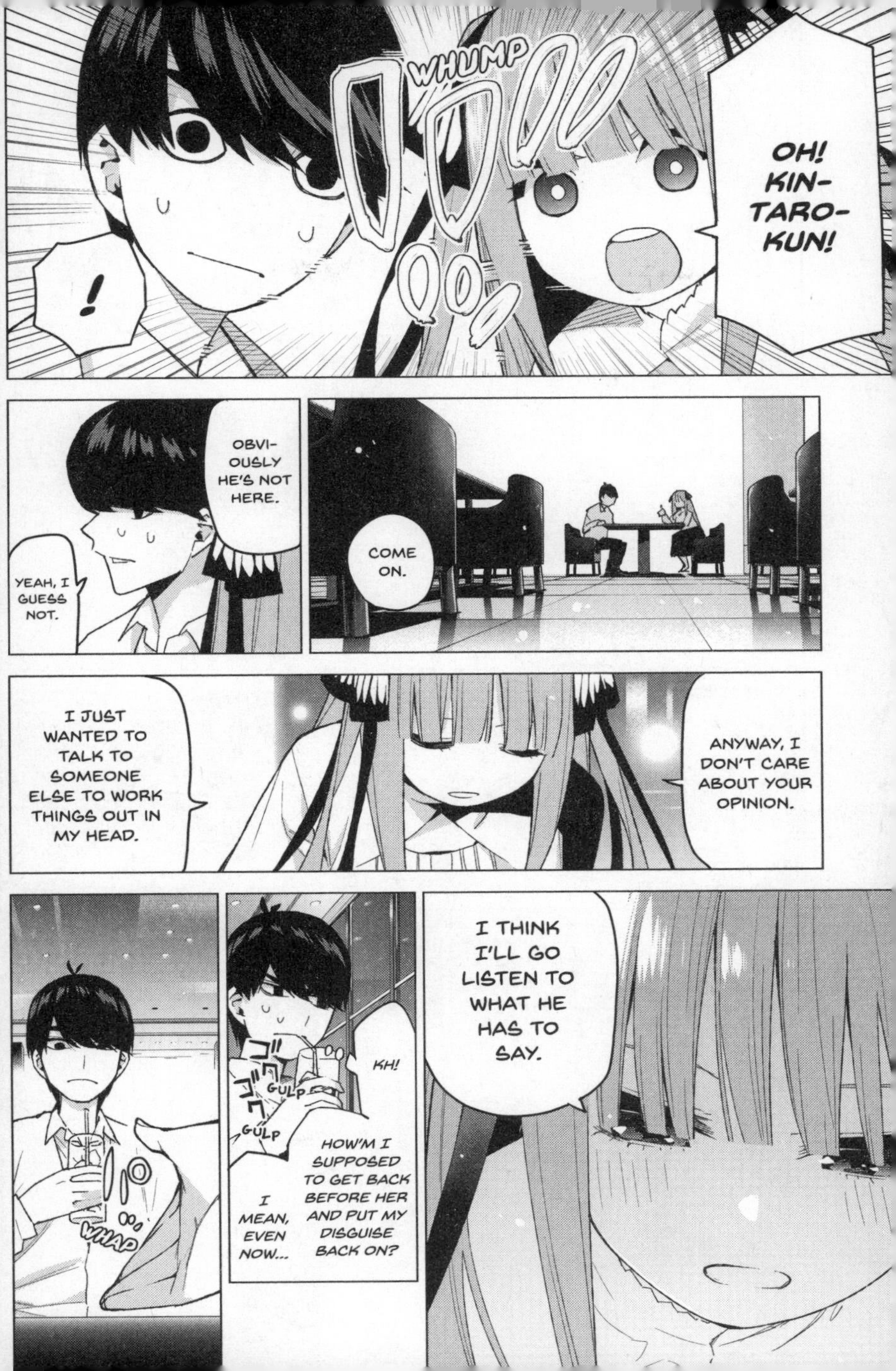
OH! KIN-TARO-KUN!
WHUMP
!
COME ON.
OBVIOUSLY HE'S NOT HERE.
YEAH, I GUESS NOT.
ANYWAY, I DON'T CARE ABOUT YOUR OPINION.
I JUST WANTED TO TALK TO SOMEONE ELSE TO WORK THINGS OUT IN MY HEAD.
I THINK I'LL GO LISTEN TO WHAT HE HAS TO SAY.
KH!
GULP
GULP
HOW'M I SUPPOSED TO GET BACK BEFORE HER AND PUT MY DISGUISE BACK ON?
I MEAN, EVEN NOW...
WHAP

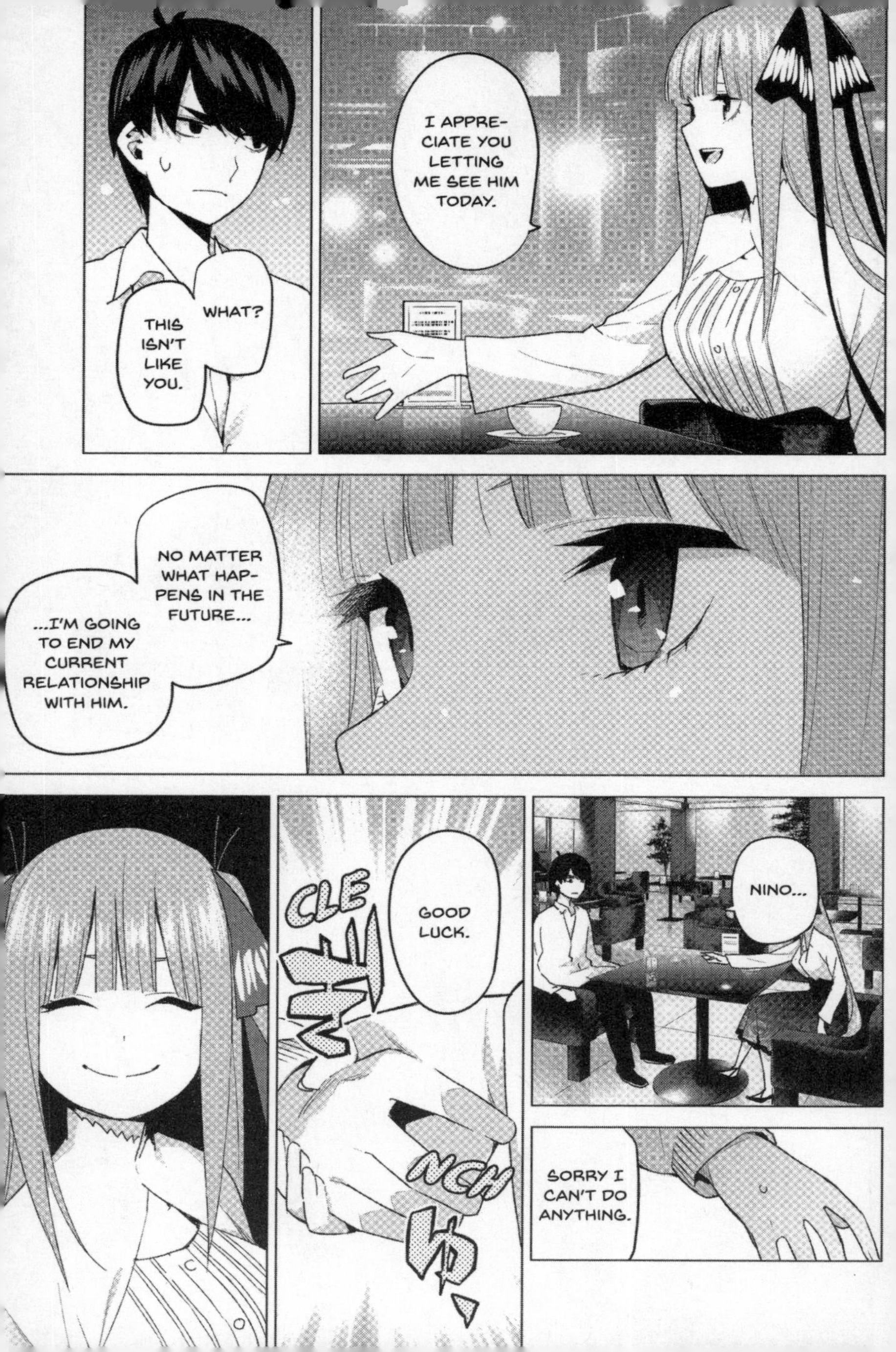

I APPRECIATE YOU LETTING ME SEE HIM TODAY.
WHAT? THIS ISN'T LIKE YOU.
NO MATTER WHAT HAPPENS IN THE FUTURE...
...I'M GOING TO END MY CURRENT RELATIONSHIP WITH HIM.
NINO...
SORRY I CAN'T DO ANYTHING.
GOOD LUCK.
CLE
NCH

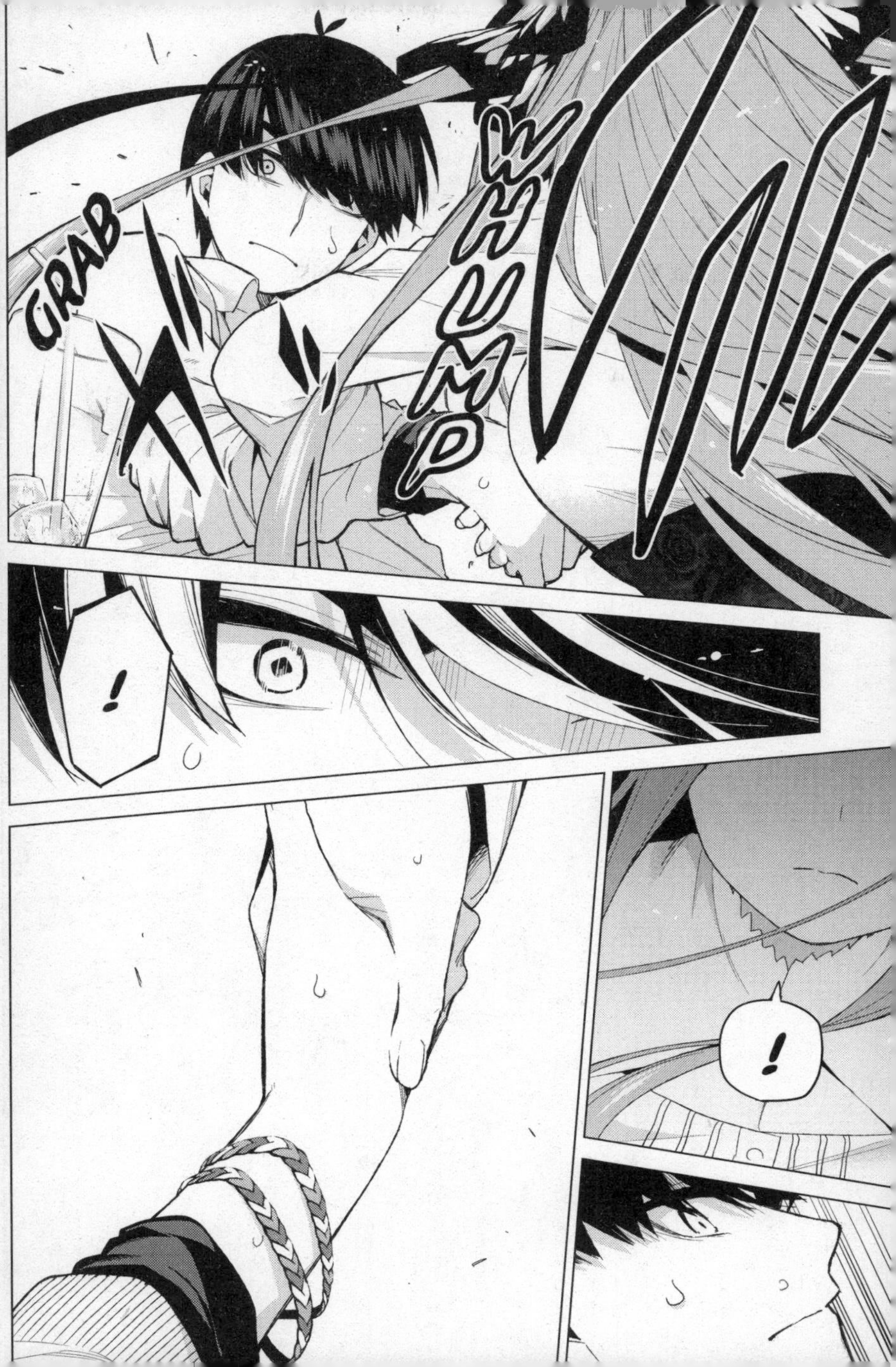
WHUMP
GRAB
!
!

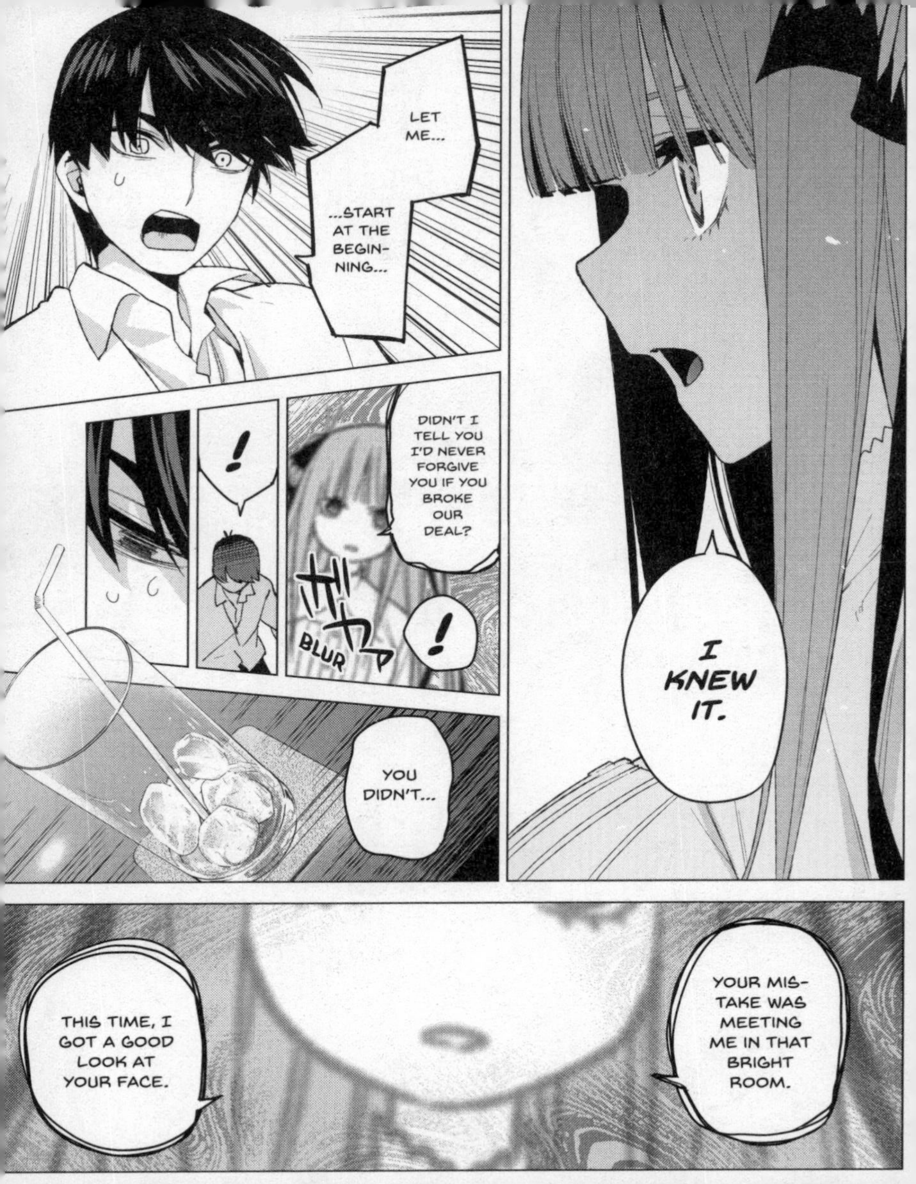
I KNEW IT.
LET ME...
...START AT THE BEGIN-NING...
DIDN'T I TELL YOU I'D NEVER FORGIVE YOU IF YOU BROKE OUR DEAL?
!
BLUR
!
YOU DIDN'T...
YOUR MIS-TAKE WAS MEETING ME IN THAT BRIGHT ROOM.
THIS TIME, I GOT A GOOD LOOK AT YOUR FACE.

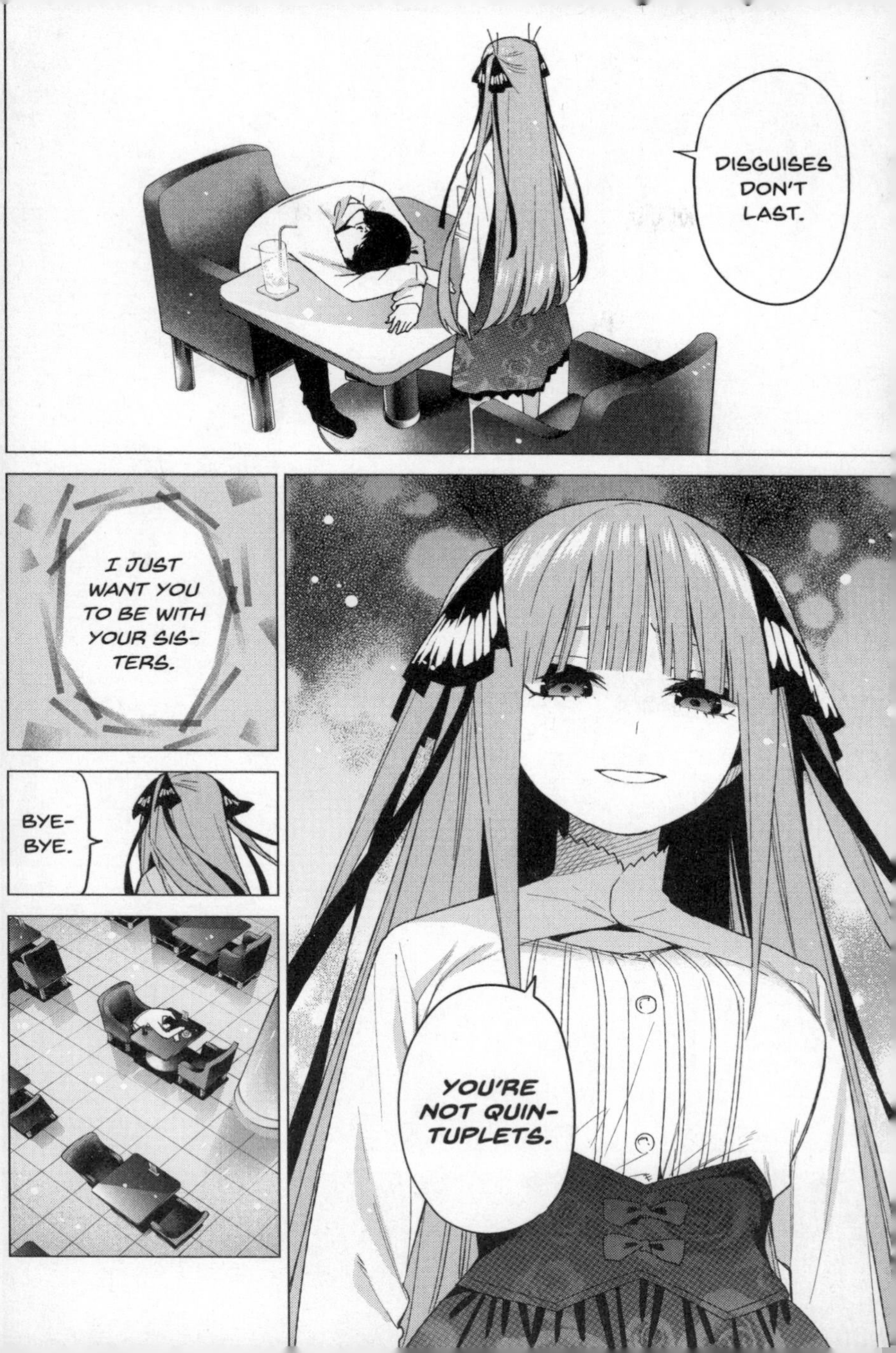
DISGUISES DON'T LAST.
YOU'RE NOT QUIN-TUPLETS.
I JUST WANT YOU TO BE WITH YOUR SIS-TERS.
BYE-BYE.

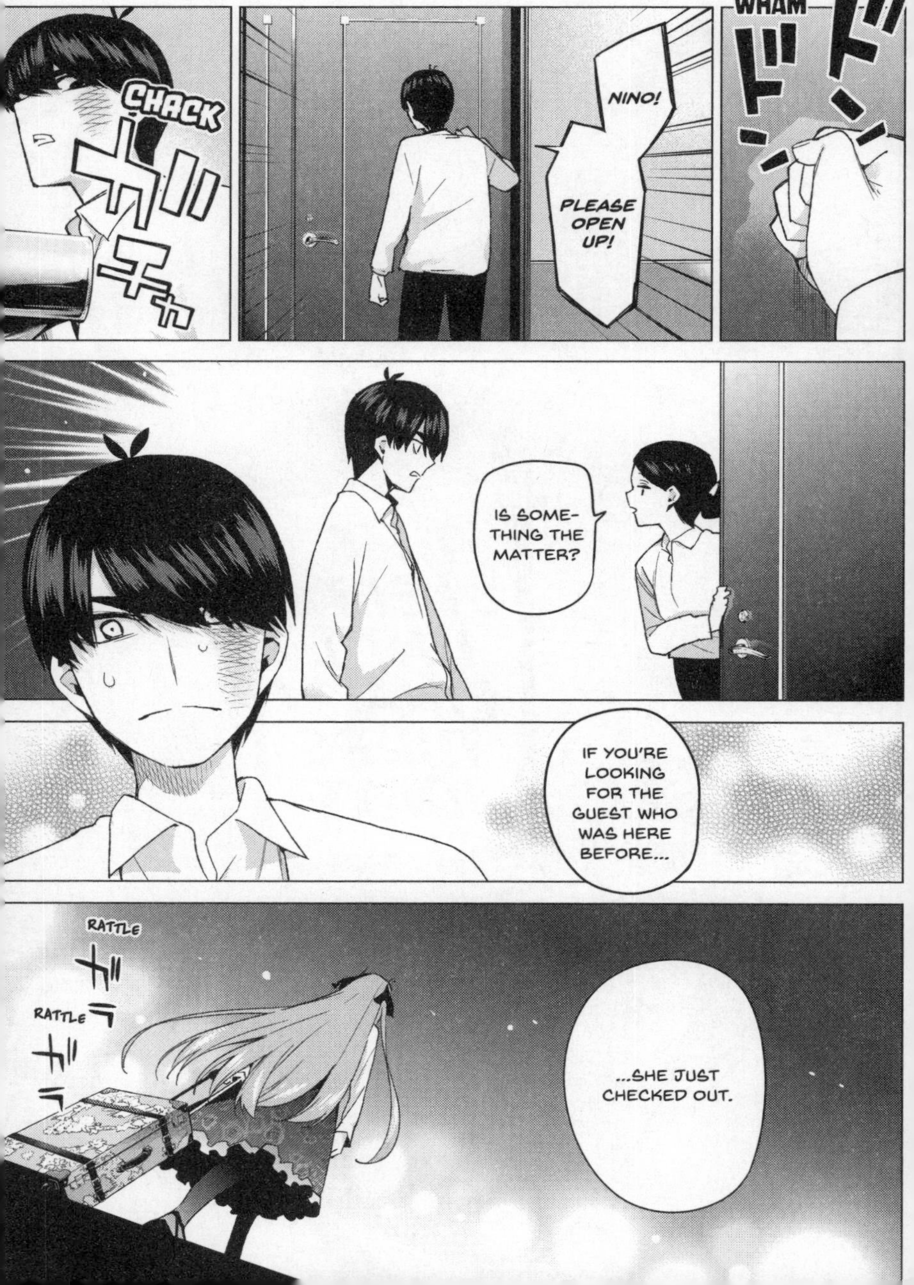
WHAM
WHAM
NINO!
PLEASE OPEN UP!
CHACK
IS SOME-THING THE MATTER?
IF YOU'RE LOOKING FOR THE GUEST WHO WAS HERE BEFORE...
...SHE JUST CHECKED OUT.
RATTLE
RATTLE

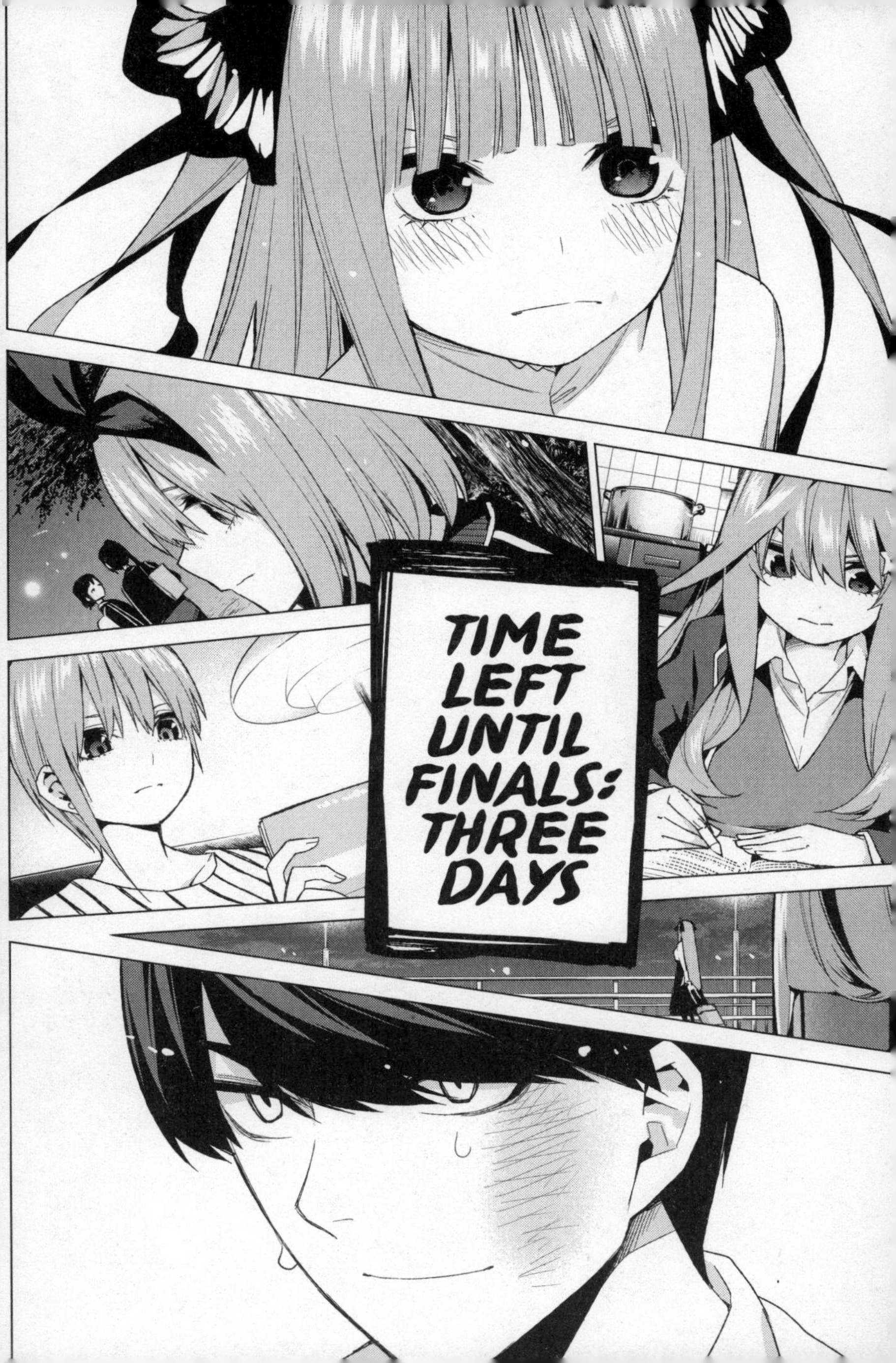
TIME LEFT UNTIL FINALS: THREE DAYS

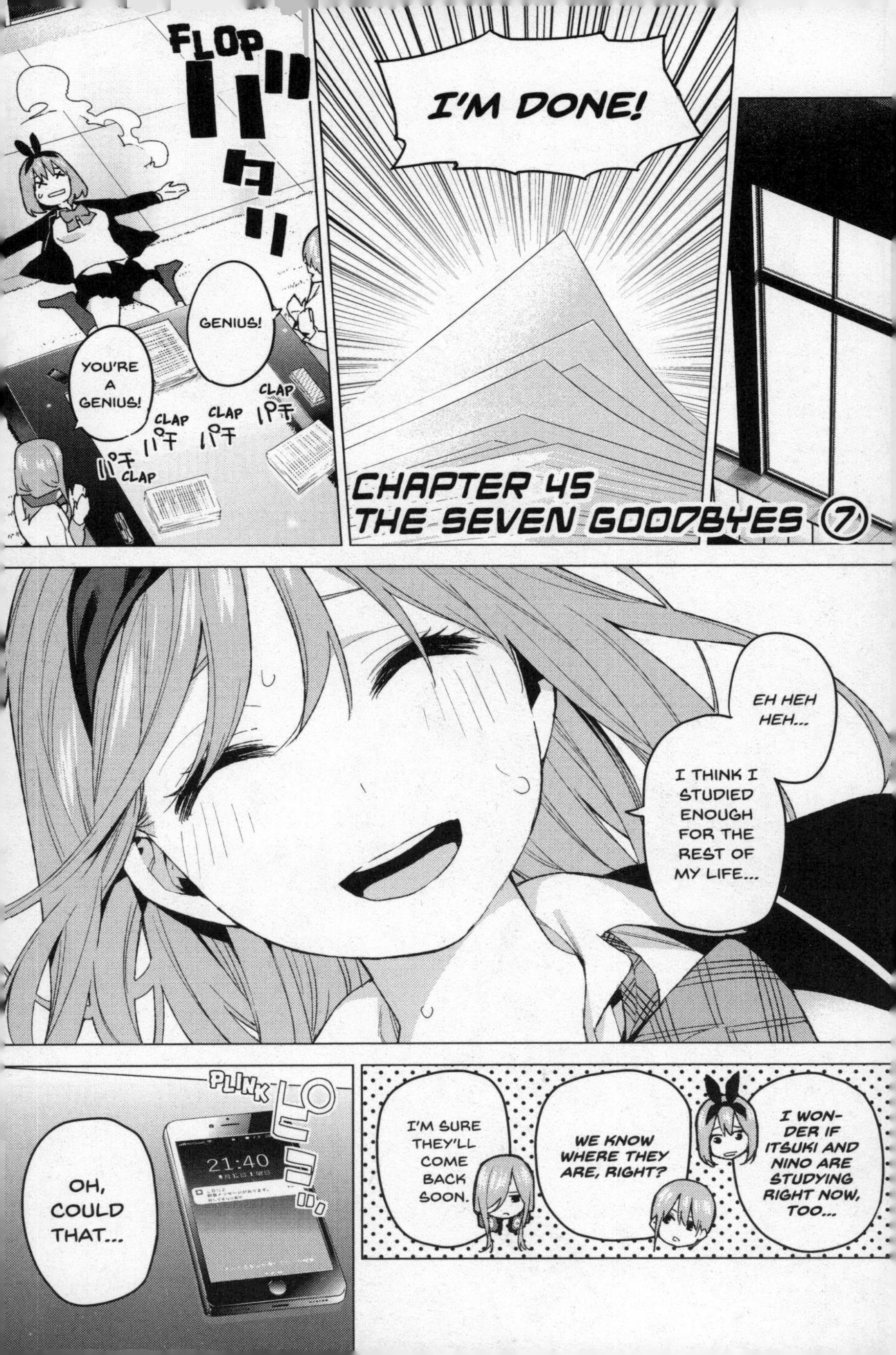
I'M DONE!
CHAPTER 45
THE SEVEN GOODBYES 7
FLOP
GENIUS!
YOU'RE A GENIUS!
CLAP
CLAP
CLAP
CLAP
EH HEH HEH...
I THINK I STUDIED ENOUGH FOR THE REST OF MY LIFE...
I WONDER IF ITSUKI AND NINO ARE STUDYING RIGHT NOW, TOO...
WE KNOW WHERE THEY ARE, RIGHT?
I'M SURE THEY'LL COME BACK SOON.
PLINK
21:40
OH, COULD THAT...

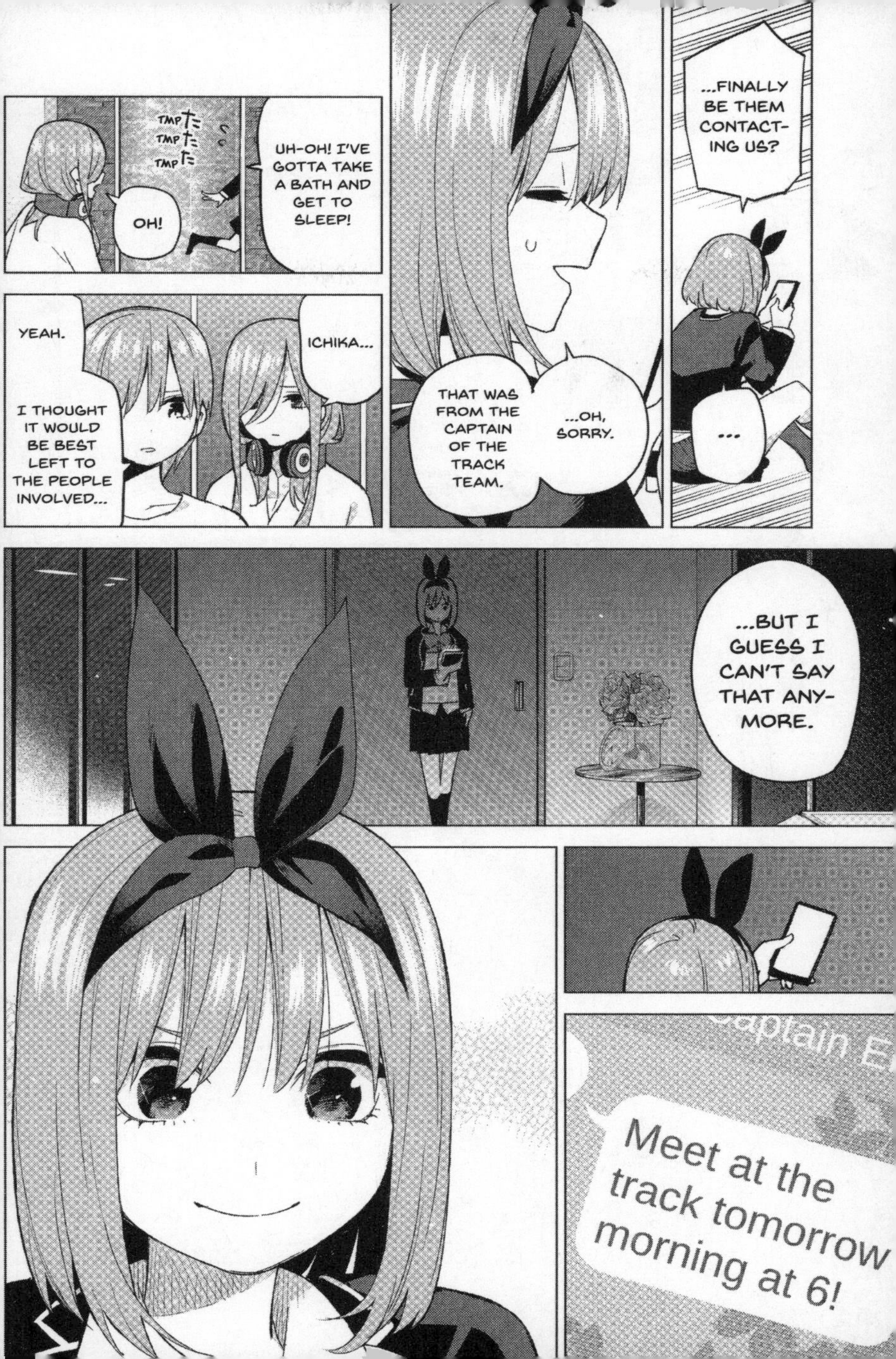
...FINALLY BE THEM CONTACTING US?
...
...OH, SORRY.
THAT WAS FROM THE CAPTAIN OF THE TRACK TEAM.
UH-OH! I'VE GOTTA TAKE A BATH AND GET TO SLEEP!
TMP TMP TMP
OH!
ICHIKA...
YEAH.
I THOUGHT IT WOULD BE BEST LEFT TO THE PEOPLE INVOLVED...
...BUT I GUESS I CAN'T SAY THAT ANYMORE.
Captain
Meet at the track tomorrow morning at 6!

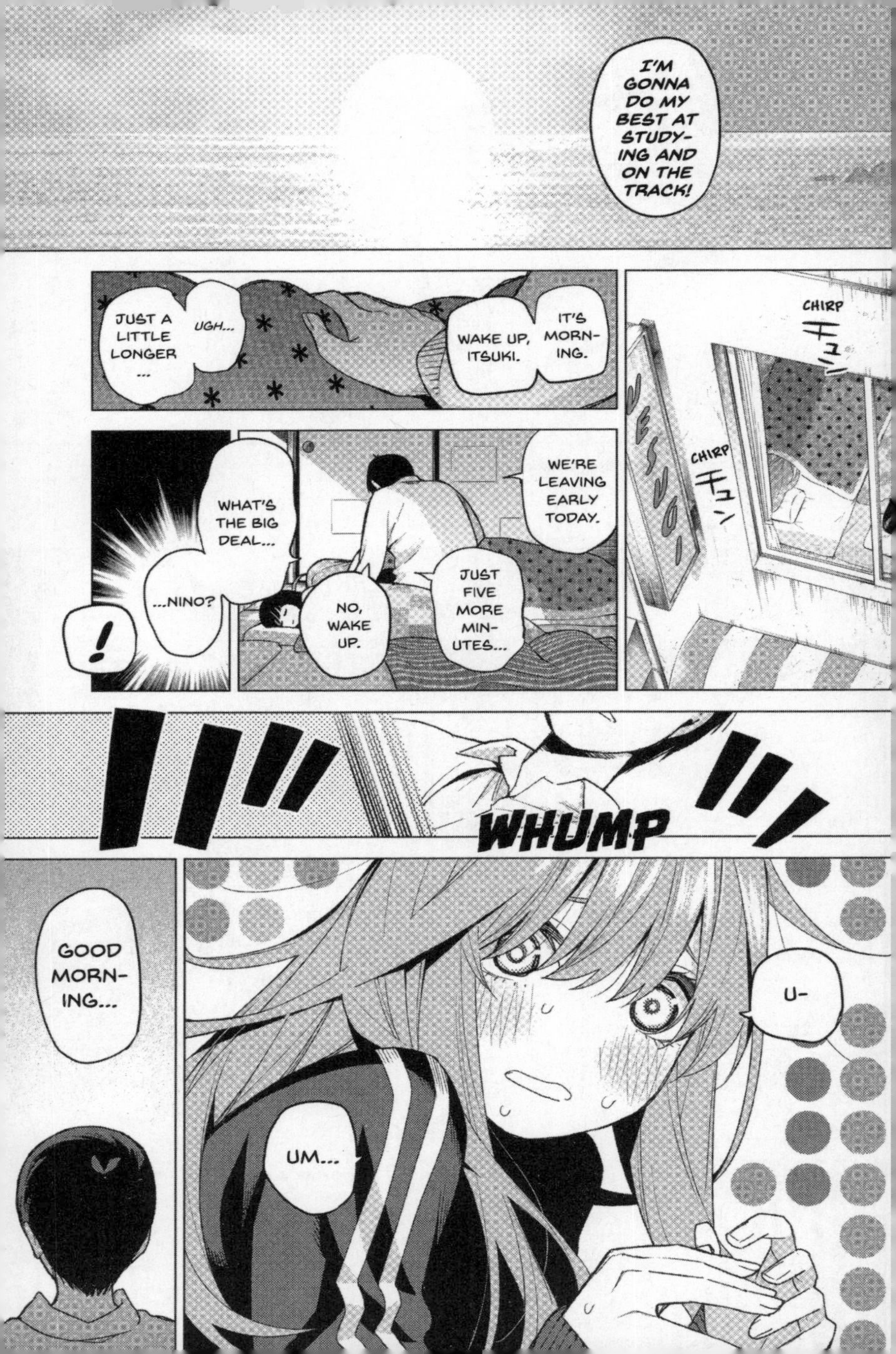

I'M GONNA DO MY BEST AT STUDYING AND ON THE TRACK!
CHIRP
CHIRP
IT'S MORNING.
WAKE UP, ITSUKI.
UGH...
JUST A LITTLE LONGER...
WE'RE LEAVING EARLY TODAY.
JUST FIVE MORE MINUTES...
NO, WAKE UP.
WHAT'S THE BIG DEAL...
...NINO?
!
WHUMP
U-
UM...
GOOD MORNING...

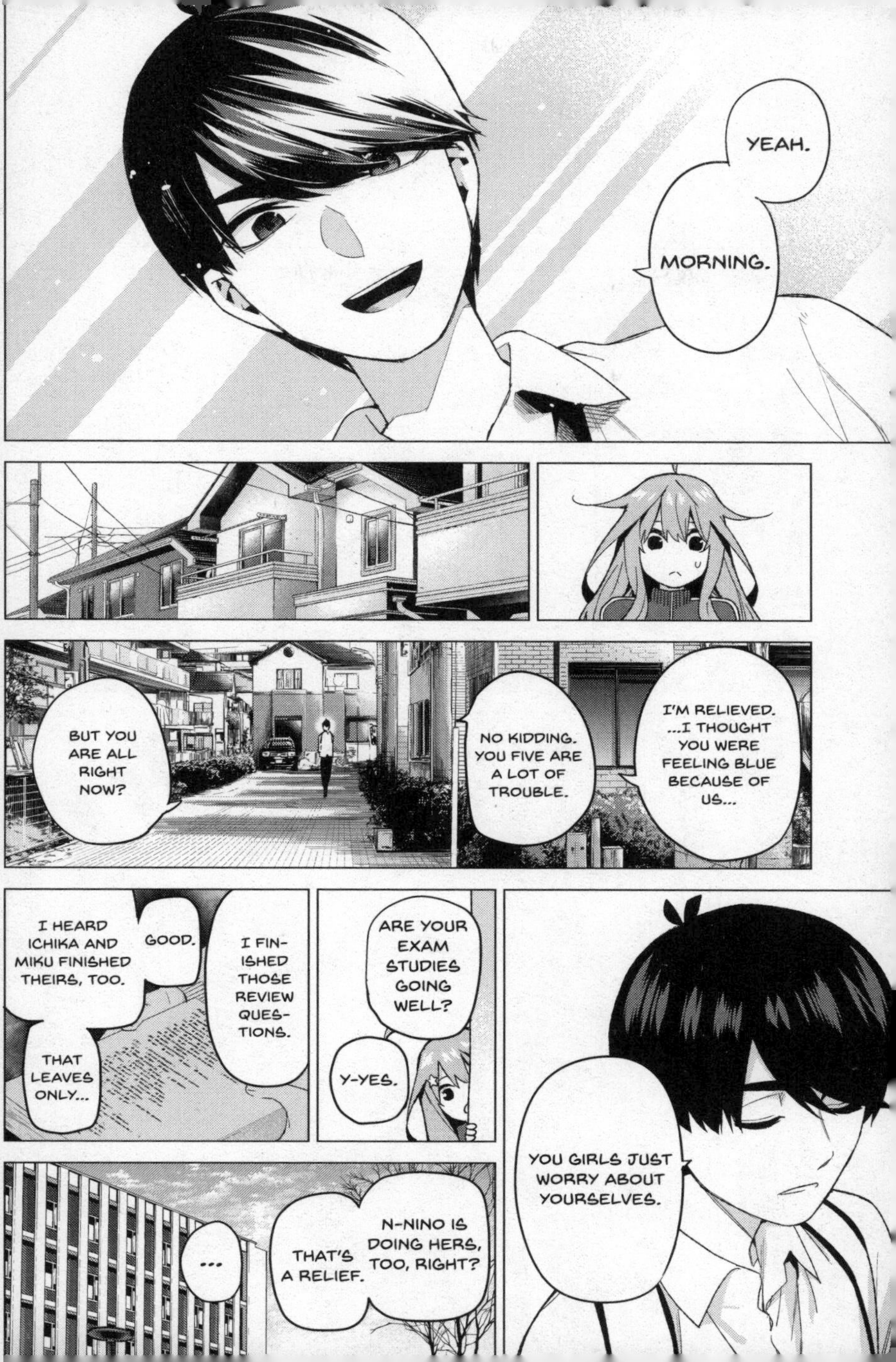

YEAH.
MORNING.
I'M RELIEVED. ...I THOUGHT YOU WERE FEELING BLUE BECAUSE OF US...
NO KIDDING. YOU FIVE ARE A LOT OF TROUBLE.
BUT YOU ARE ALL RIGHT NOW?
YOU GIRLS JUST WORRY ABOUT YOURSELVES.
ARE YOUR EXAM STUDIES GOING WELL?
Y-YES.
I FIN-ISHED THOSE REVIEW QUES-TIONS.
GOOD.
I HEARD ICHIKA AND MIKU FINISHED THEIRS, TOO.
THAT LEAVES ONLY...
N-NINO IS DOING HERS, TOO, RIGHT?
THAT'S A RELIEF.
...

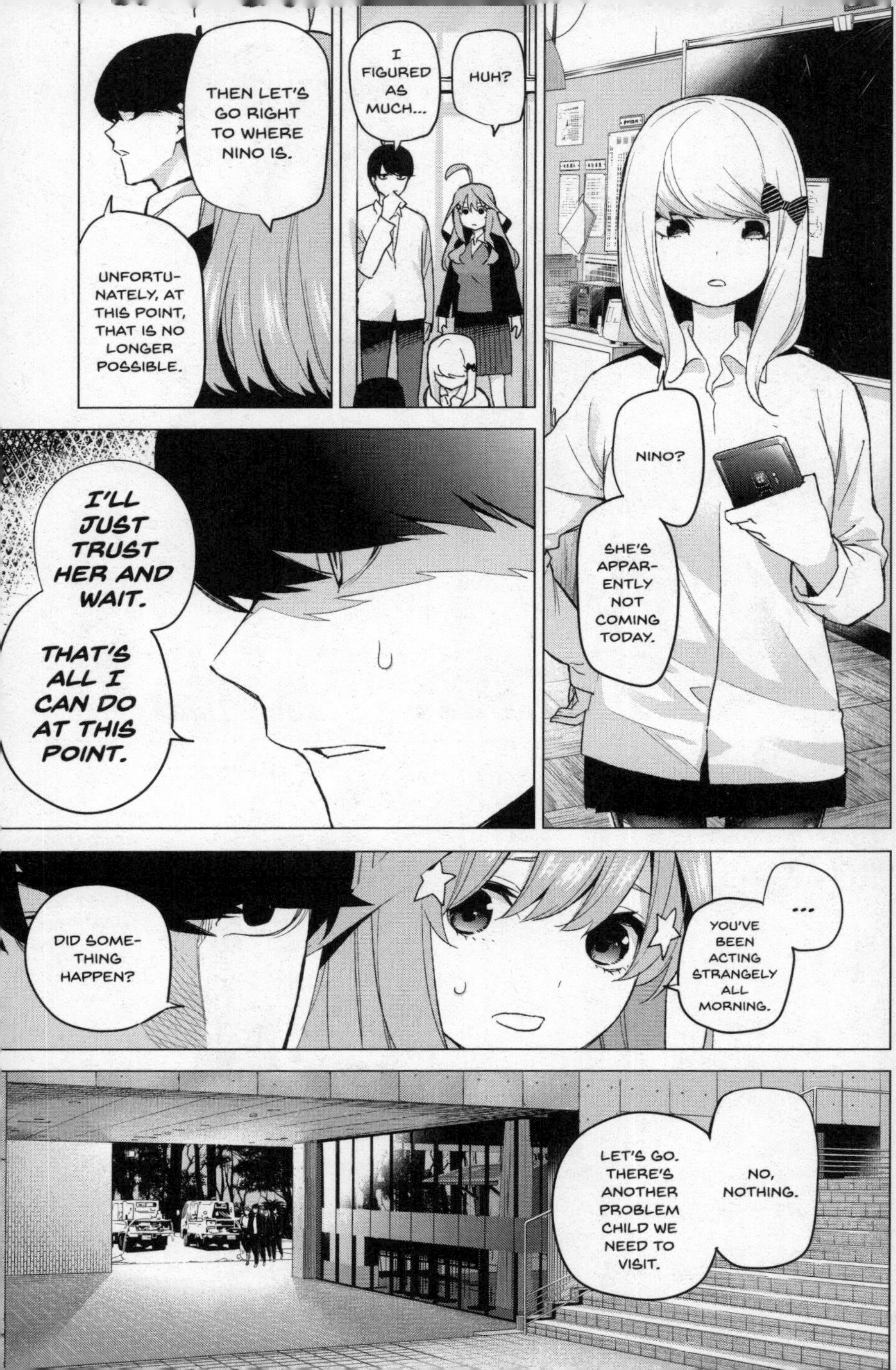
NINO?
SHE'S APPARENTLY NOT COMING TODAY.
HUH?
I FIGURED AS MUCH...
THEN LET'S GO RIGHT TO WHERE NINO IS.
UNFORTUNATELY, AT THIS POINT, THAT IS NO LONGER POSSIBLE.
I'LL JUST TRUST HER AND WAIT.
THAT'S ALL I CAN DO AT THIS POINT.
...
YOU'VE BEEN ACTING STRANGELY ALL MORNING.
DID SOMETHING HAPPEN?
NO, NOTHING.
LET'S GO. THERE'S ANOTHER PROBLEM CHILD WE NEED TO VISIT.

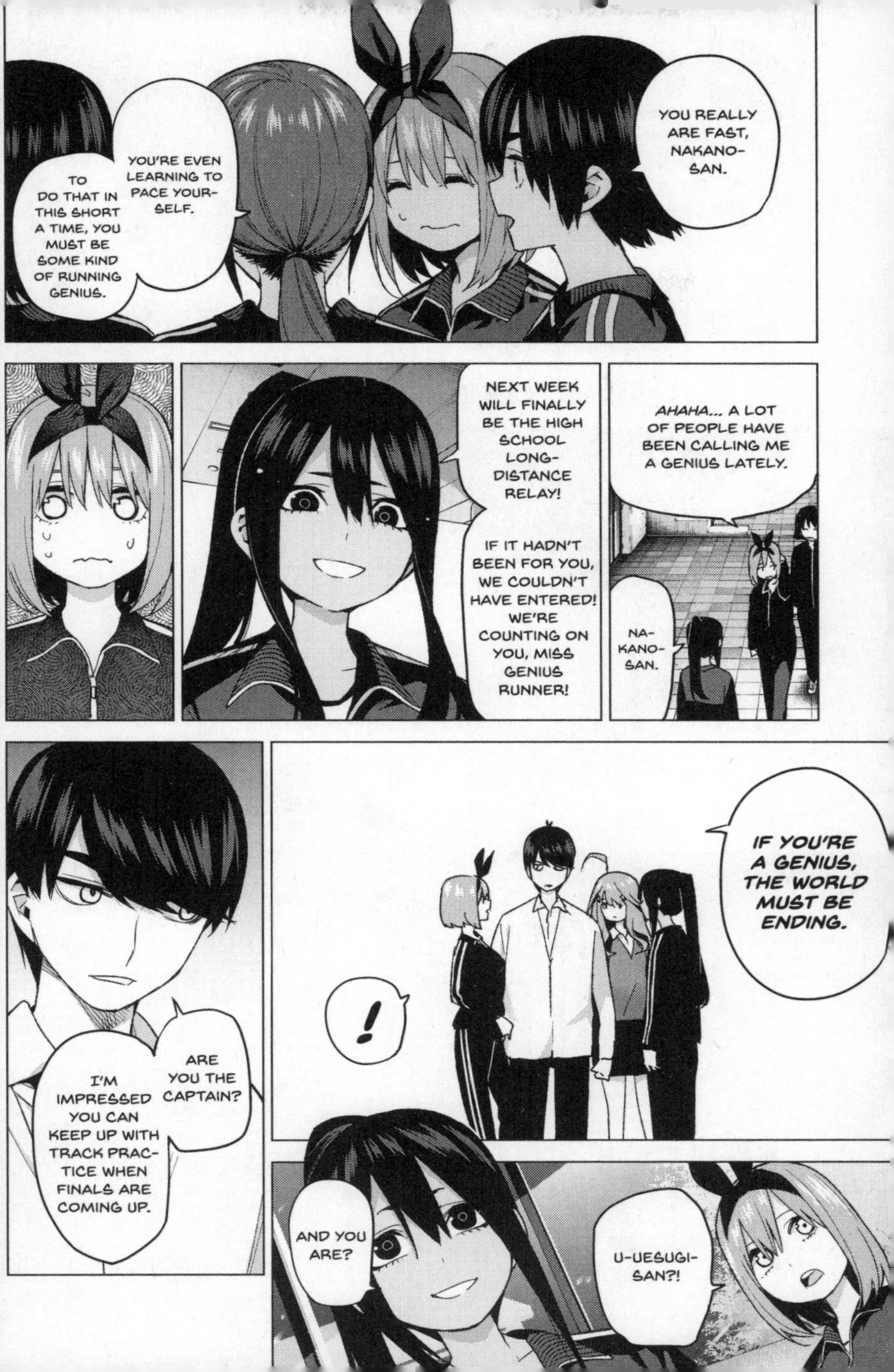
YOU REALLY ARE FAST, NAKANO-SAN.
YOU'RE EVEN LEARNING TO PACE YOUR-SELF.
TO DO THAT IN THIS SHORT A TIME, YOU MUST BE SOME KIND OF RUNNING GENIUS.
AHAHA... A LOT OF PEOPLE HAVE BEEN CALLING ME A GENIUS LATELY.
NA-KANO-SAN.
NEXT WEEK WILL FINALLY BE THE HIGH SCHOOL LONG-DISTANCE RELAY!
IF IT HADN'T BEEN FOR YOU, WE COULDN'T HAVE ENTERED! WE'RE COUNTING ON YOU, MISS GENIUS RUNNER!
IF YOU'RE A GENIUS, THE WORLD MUST BE ENDING.
!
U-UESUGI-SAN?!
AND YOU ARE?
ARE YOU THE CAPTAIN?
I'M IMPRESSED YOU CAN KEEP UP WITH TRACK PRAC-TICE WHEN FINALS ARE COMING UP.

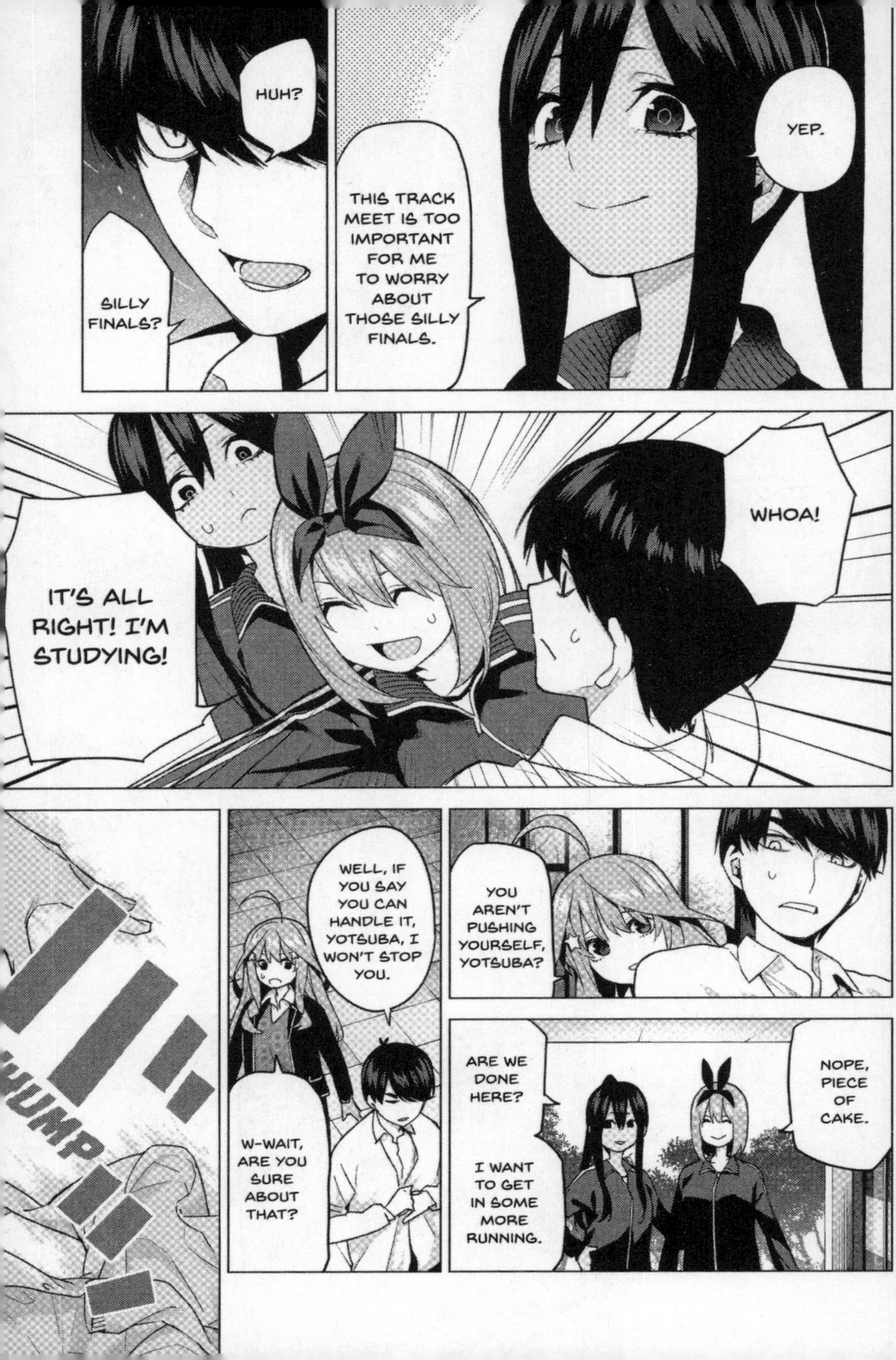
YEP.
THIS TRACK MEET IS TOO IMPORTANT FOR ME TO WORRY ABOUT THOSE SILLY FINALS.
HUH?
SILLY FINALS?
WHOA!
IT'S ALL RIGHT! I'M STUDYING!
YOU AREN'T PUSHING YOURSELF, YOTSUBA?
NOPE, PIECE OF CAKE.
ARE WE DONE HERE?
I WANT TO GET IN SOME MORE RUNNING.
WELL, IF YOU SAY YOU CAN HANDLE IT, YOTSUBA, I WON'T STOP YOU.
W-WAIT, ARE YOU SURE ABOUT THAT?

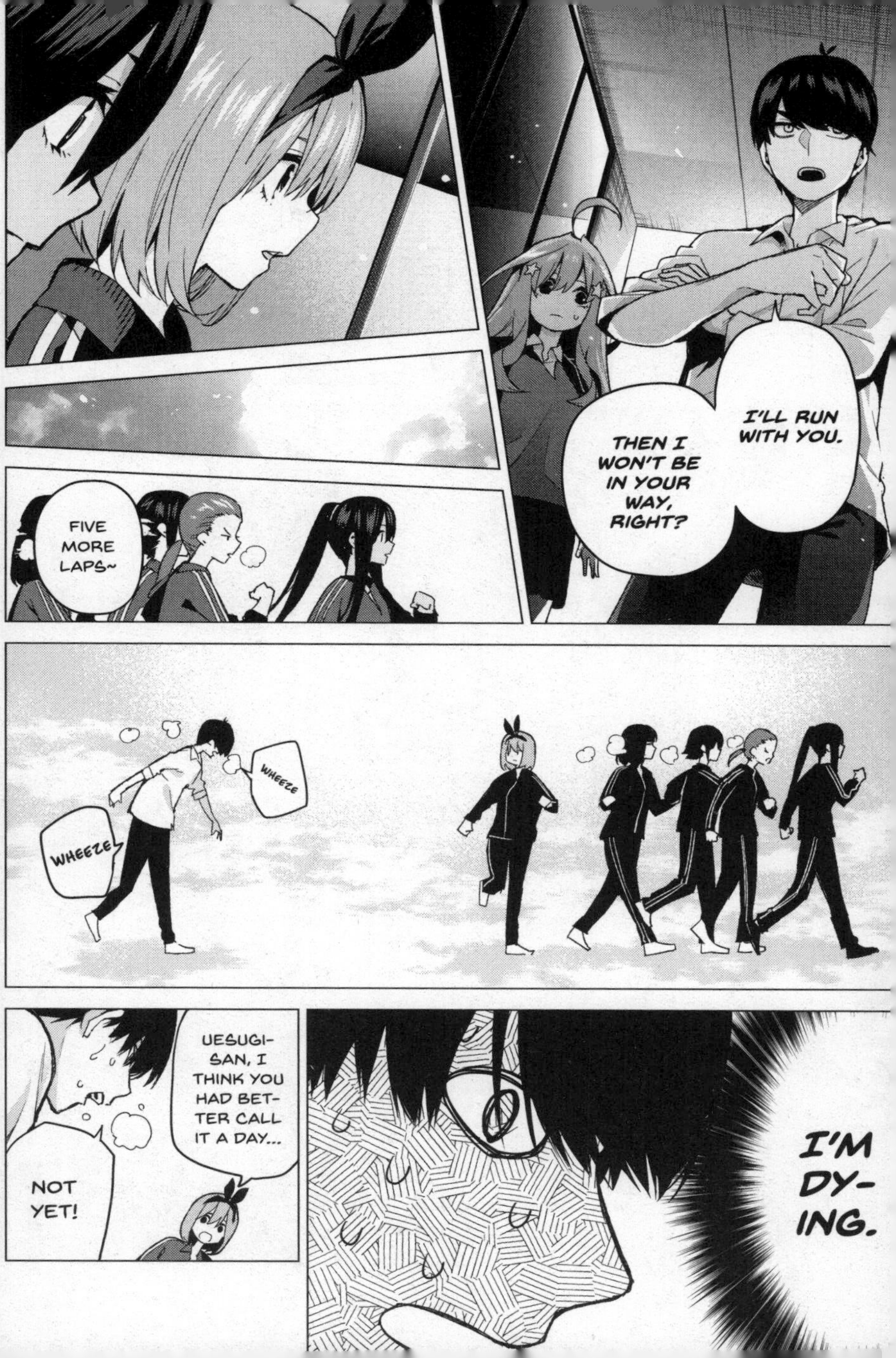
I'LL RUN WITH YOU.
THEN I WON'T BE IN YOUR WAY, RIGHT?
FIVE MORE LAPS~
WHEEZE
WHEEZE
I'M DY-ING.
UESUGI-SAN, I THINK YOU HAD BETTER CALL IT A DAY...
NOT YET!

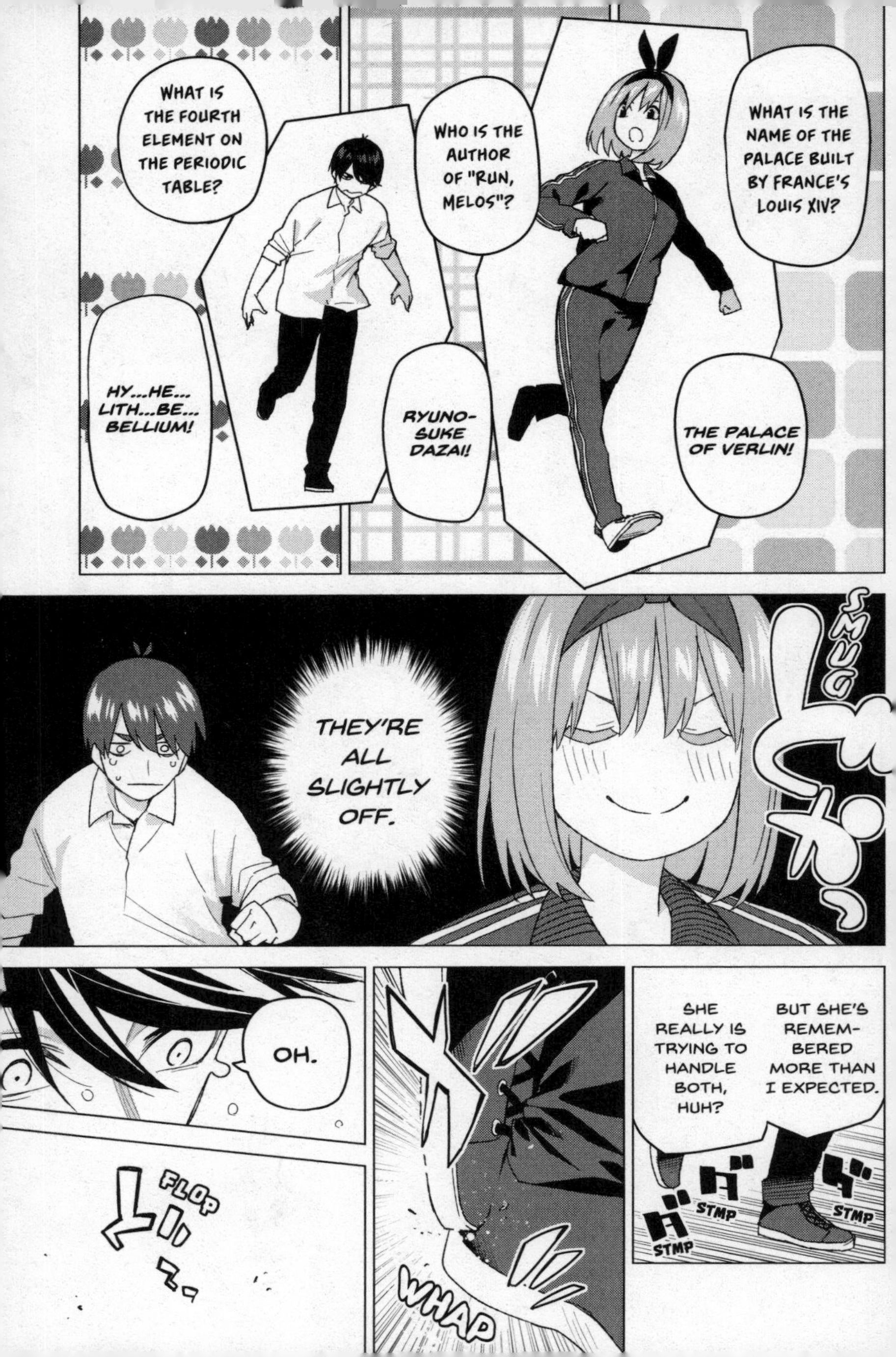
WHAT IS THE NAME OF THE PALACE BUILT BY FRANCE'S LOUIS XIV?
THE PALACE OF VERLIN!
WHO IS THE AUTHOR OF "RUN, MELOS"?
RYUNO-SUKE DAZAI!
WHAT IS THE FOURTH ELEMENT ON THE PERIODIC TABLE?
HY...HE... LITH...BE... BELLIUM!
SMUG
THEY'RE ALL SLIGHTLY OFF.
BUT SHE'S REMEM-BERED MORE THAN I EXPECTED.
SHE REALLY IS TRYING TO HANDLE BOTH, HUH?
STMP
STMP
STMP
WHAP
OH.
FLOP

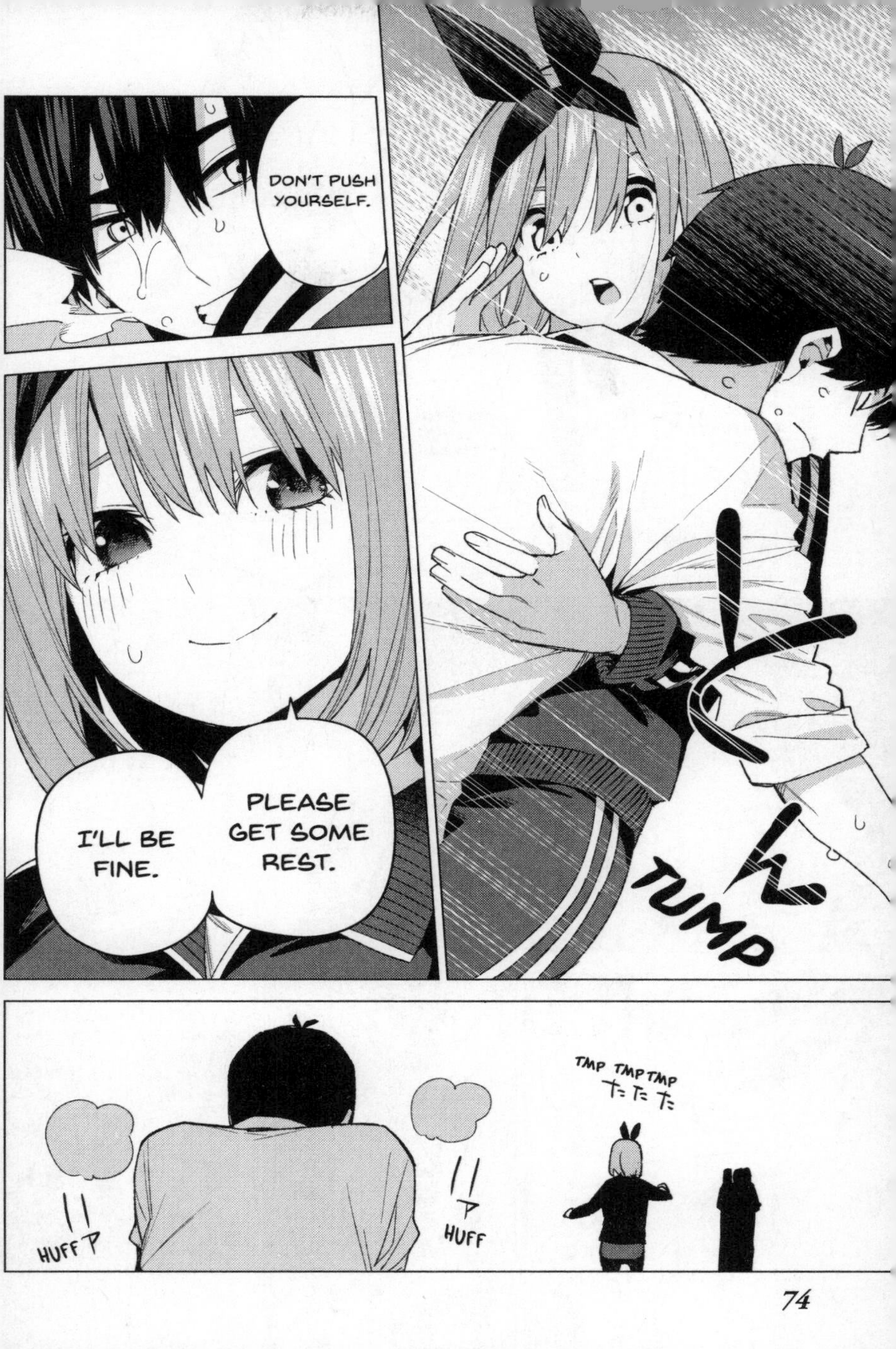
TUMP
DON'T PUSH YOURSELF.
PLEASE GET SOME REST.
I'LL BE FINE.
TMP TMP TMP
HUFF
HUFF

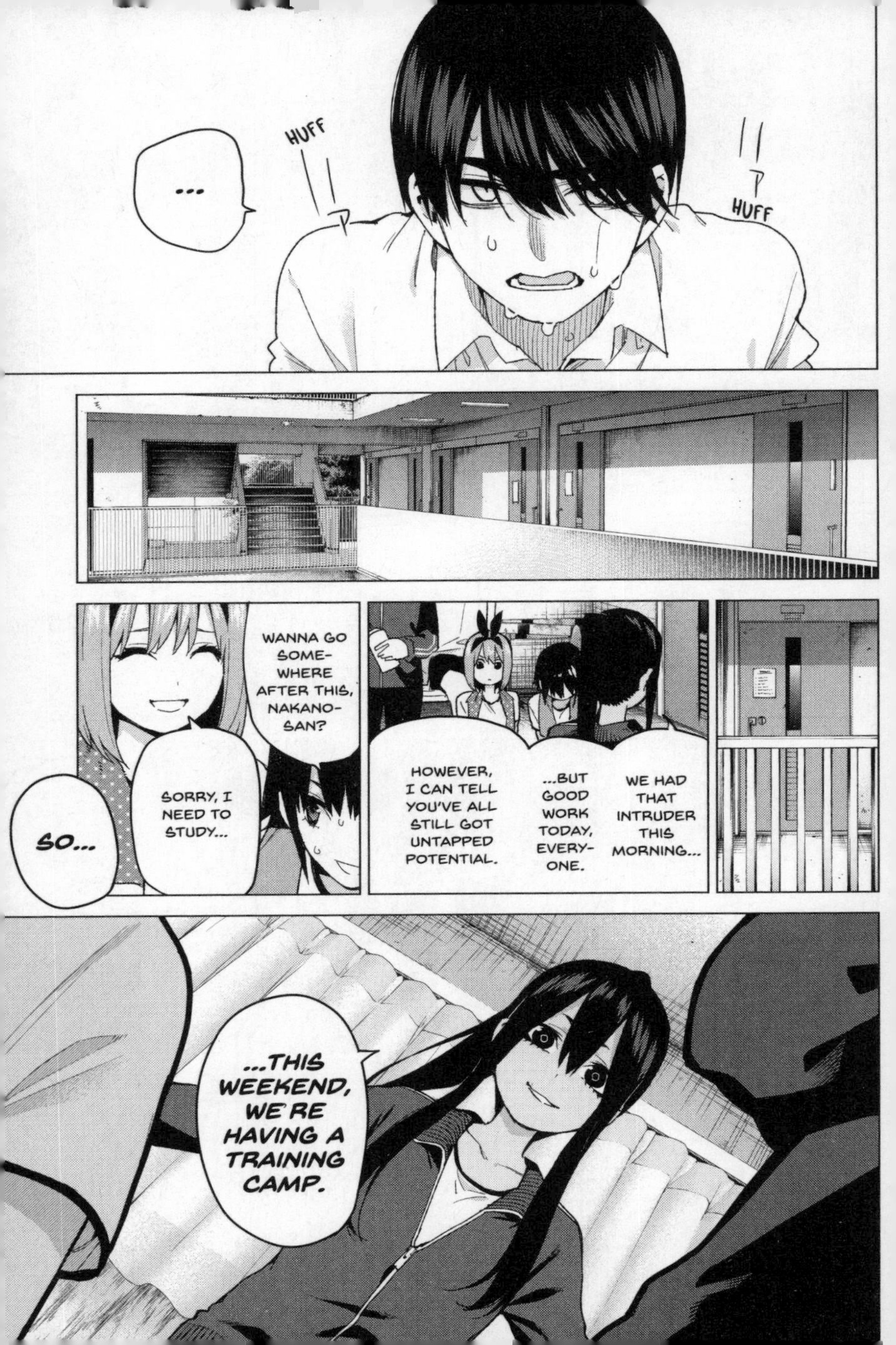
HUFF
HUFF
...
WE HAD THAT INTRUDER THIS MORNING...
...BUT GOOD WORK TODAY, EVERY-ONE.
HOWEVER, I CAN TELL YOU'VE ALL STILL GOT UNTAPPED POTENTIAL.
WANNA GO SOME-WHERE AFTER THIS, NAKANO-SAN?
SORRY, I NEED TO STUDY...
SO...
...THIS WEEKEND, WE'RE HAVING A TRAINING CAMP.

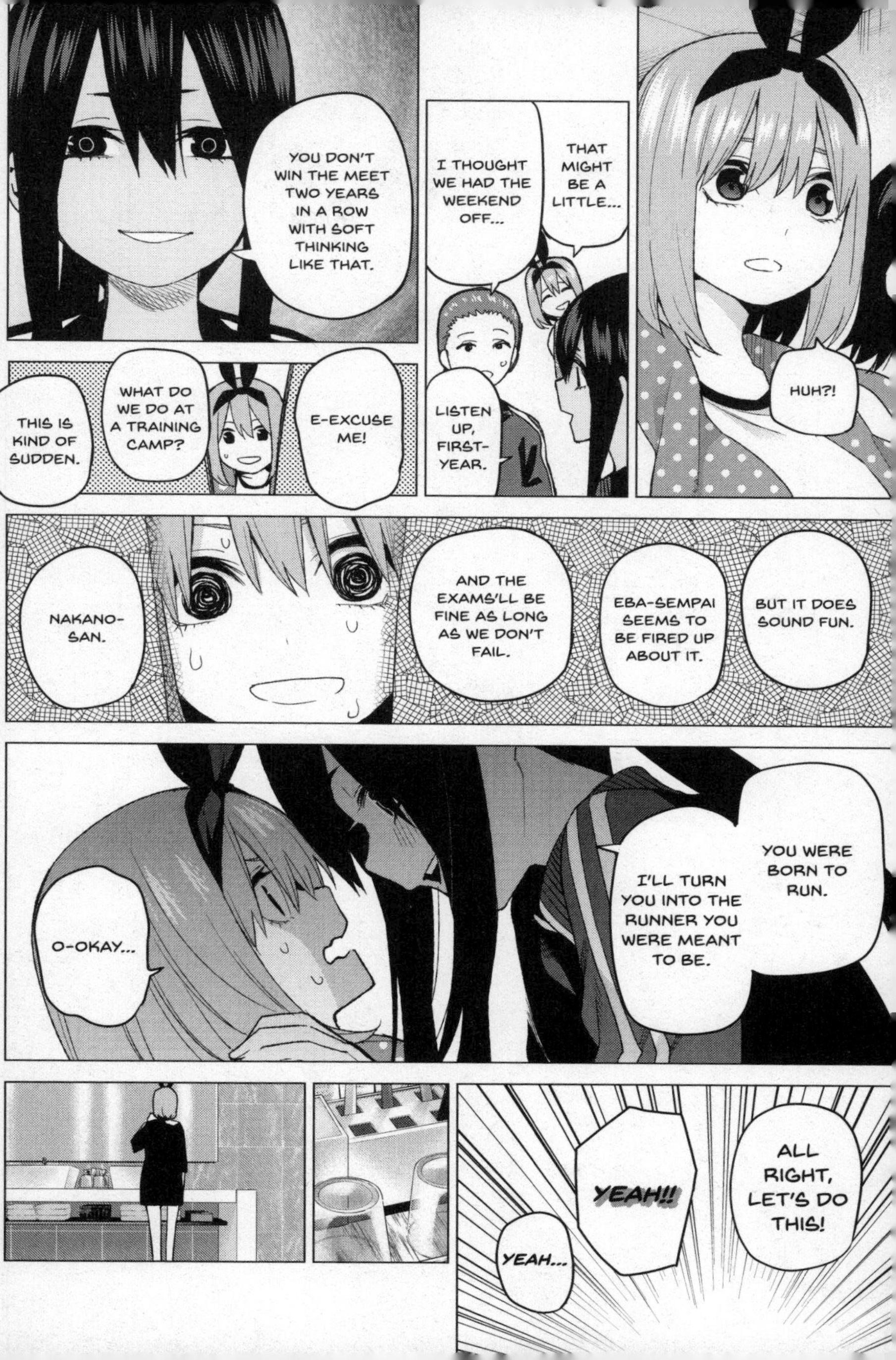
HUH?!
THAT MIGHT BE A LITTLE...
I THOUGHT WE HAD THE WEEKEND OFF...
LISTEN UP, FIRST-YEAR.
YOU DON'T WIN THE MEET TWO YEARS IN A ROW WITH SOFT THINKING LIKE THAT.
E-EXCUSE ME!
WHAT DO WE DO AT A TRAINING CAMP?
THIS IS KIND OF SUDDEN.
BUT IT DOES SOUND FUN.
EBA-SEMPAI SEEMS TO BE FIRED UP ABOUT IT.
AND THE EXAMS'LL BE FINE AS LONG AS WE DON'T FAIL.
NAKANO-SAN.
YOU WERE BORN TO RUN.
I'LL TURN YOU INTO THE RUNNER YOU WERE MEANT TO BE.
O-OKAY...
ALL RIGHT, LET'S DO THIS!
YEAH!!
YEAH...

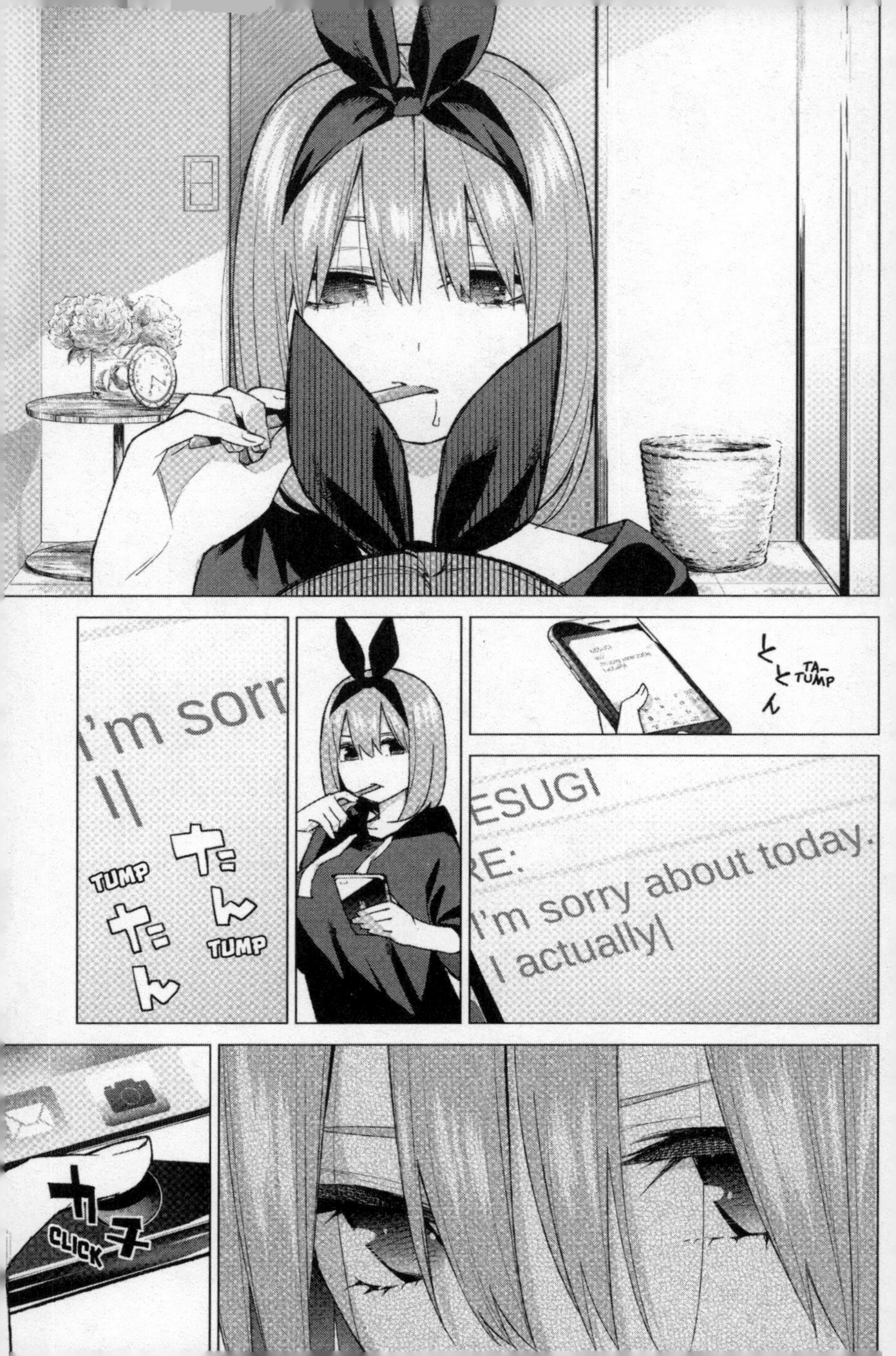

とと
TA-TUMP
ん
ESUGI
RE:
I'm sorry about today.
I actually|
I'm sorr
たん
TUMP
たん
TUMP
カチ
CLICK

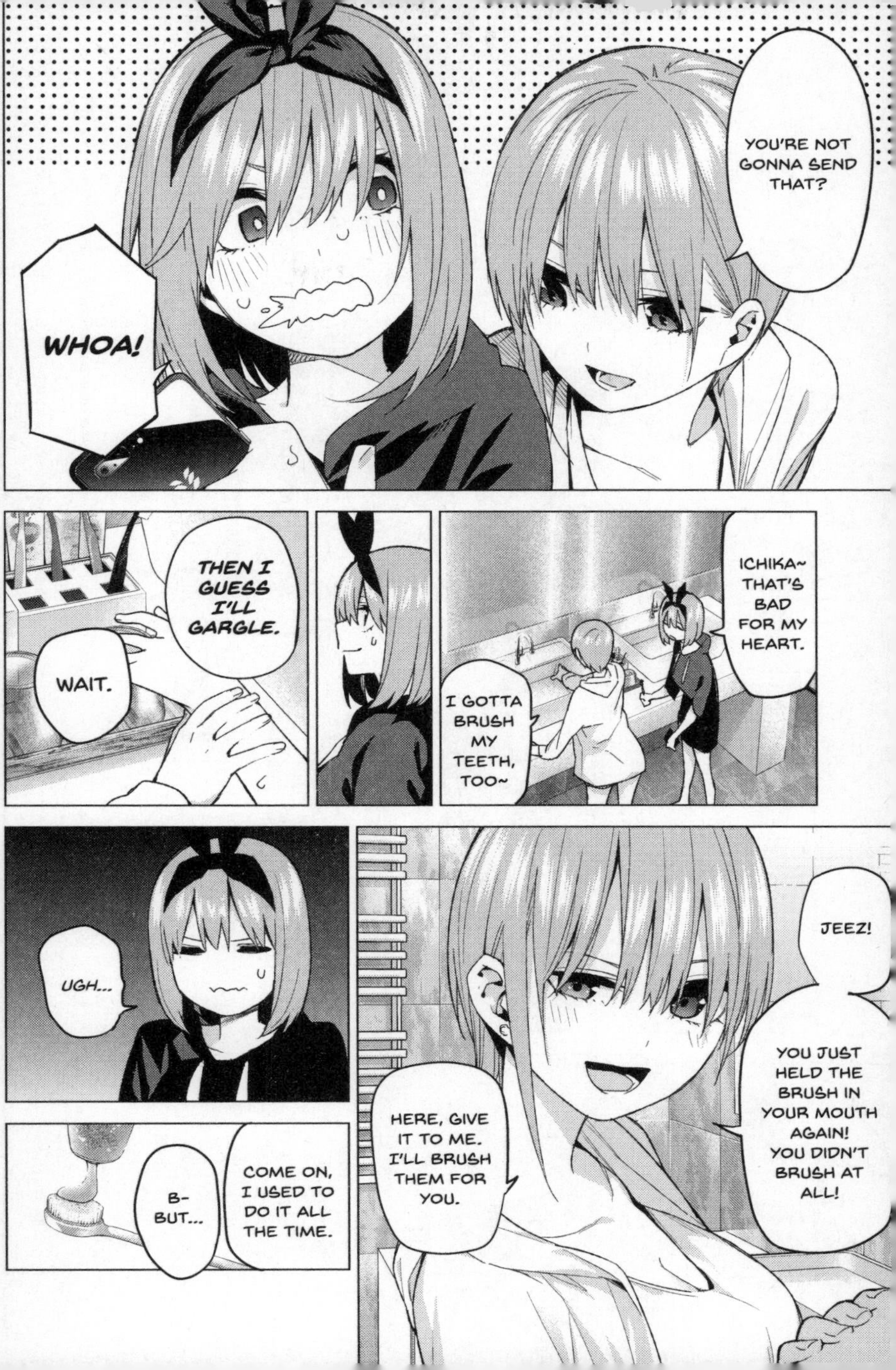
YOU'RE NOT GONNA SEND THAT?
WHOA!
ICHIKA~ THAT'S BAD FOR MY HEART.
I GOTTA BRUSH MY TEETH, TOO~
THEN I GUESS I'LL GARGLE.
WAIT.
JEEZ!
YOU JUST HELD THE BRUSH IN YOUR MOUTH AGAIN! YOU DIDN'T BRUSH AT ALL!
HERE, GIVE IT TO ME. I'LL BRUSH THEM FOR YOU.
UGH...
COME ON, I USED TO DO IT ALL THE TIME.
B-BUT...

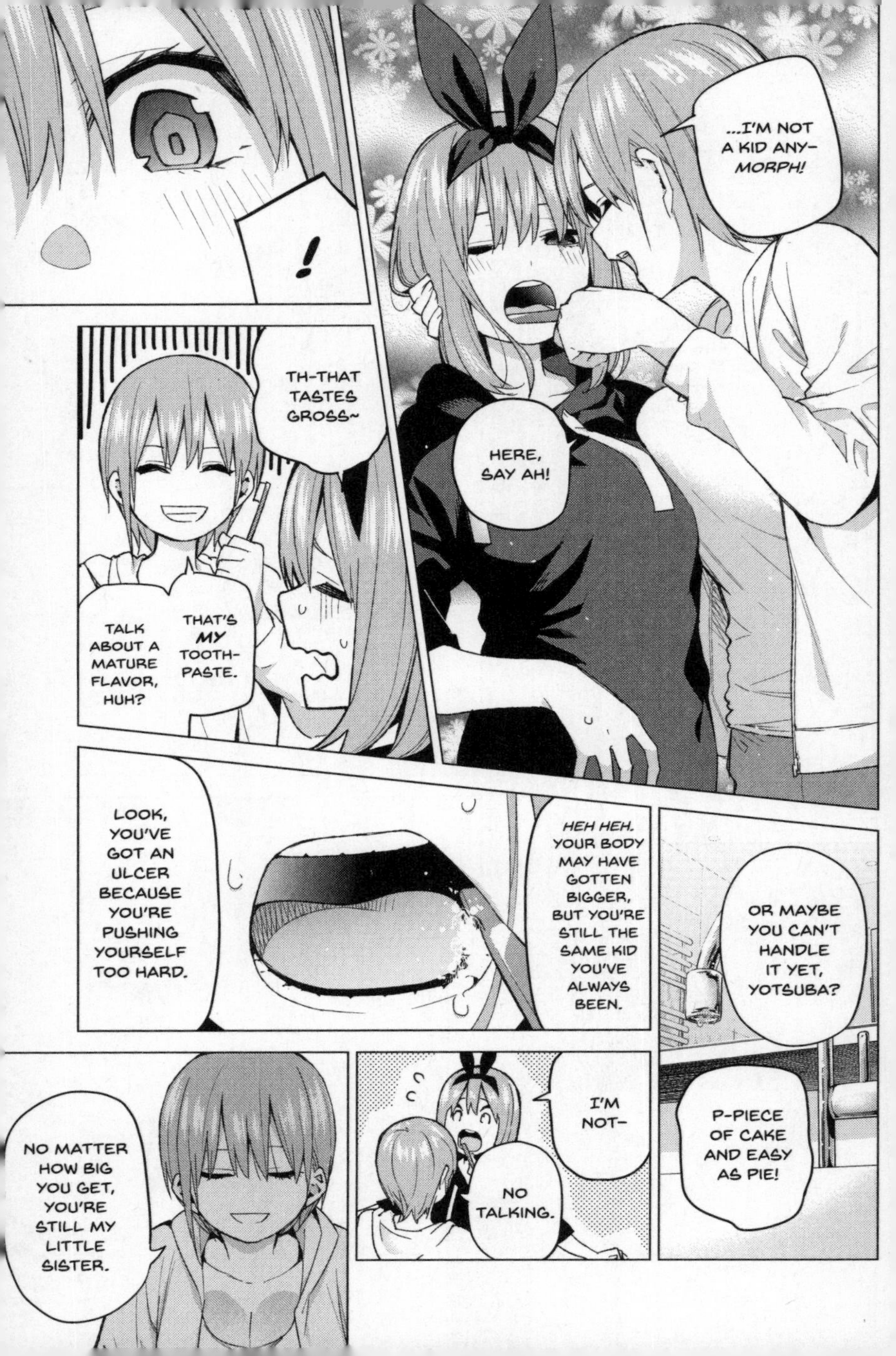
...I'M NOT A KID ANY-MORPH!
HERE, SAY AH!
!
TH-THAT TASTES GROSS~
THAT'S *MY* TOOTH-PASTE.
TALK ABOUT A MATURE FLAVOR, HUH?
OR MAYBE YOU CAN'T HANDLE IT YET, YOTSUBA?
P-PIECE OF CAKE AND EASY AS PIE!
*HEH HEH.* YOUR BODY MAY HAVE GOTTEN BIGGER, BUT YOU'RE STILL THE SAME KID YOU'VE ALWAYS BEEN.
LOOK, YOU'VE GOT AN ULCER BECAUSE YOU'RE PUSHING YOURSELF TOO HARD.
I'M NOT-
NO TALKING.
NO MATTER HOW BIG YOU GET, YOU'RE STILL MY LITTLE SISTER.

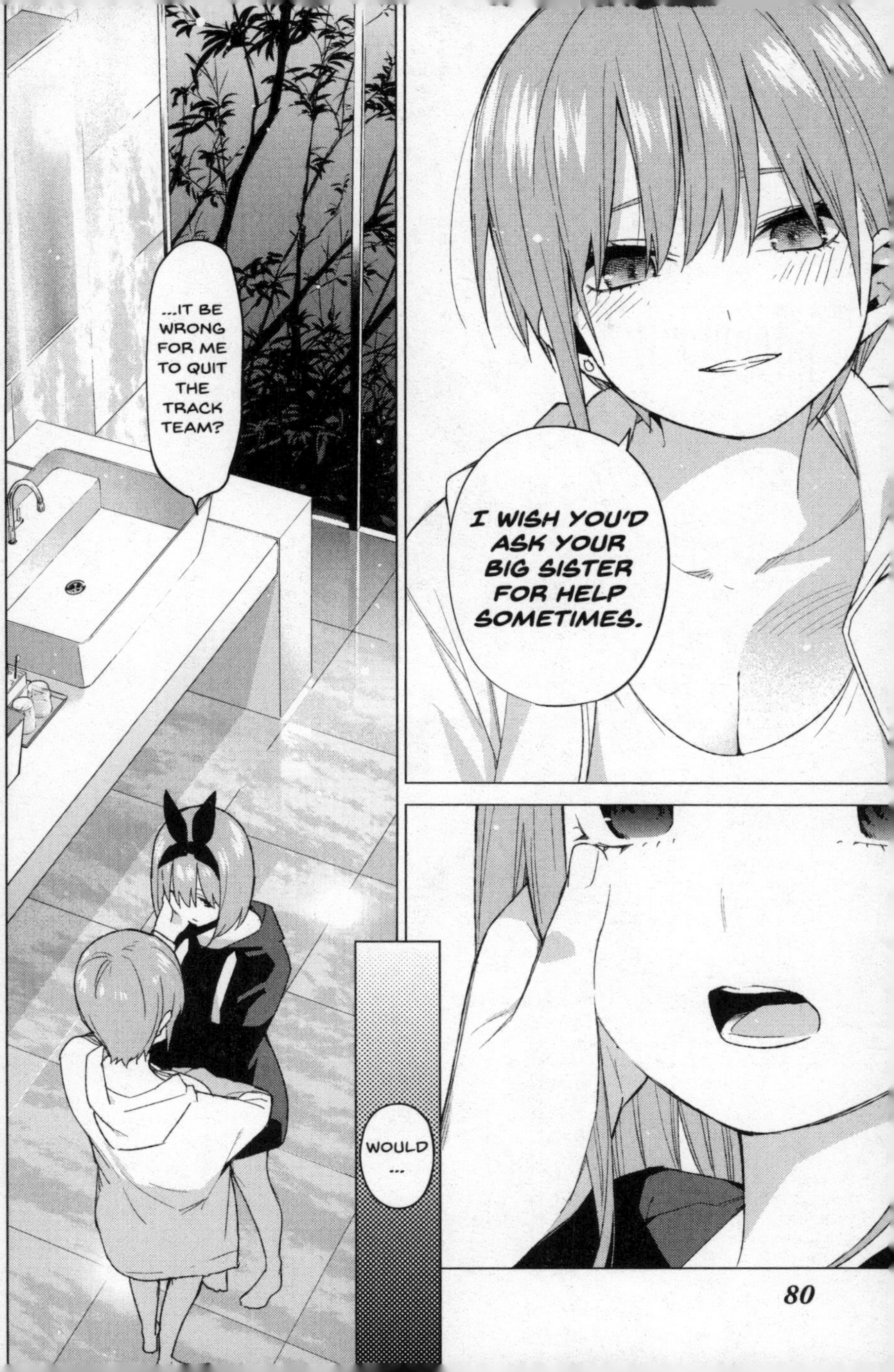
I WISH YOU'D ASK YOUR BIG SISTER FOR HELP SOMETIMES.
WOULD ...
...IT BE WRONG FOR ME TO QUIT THE TRACK TEAM?

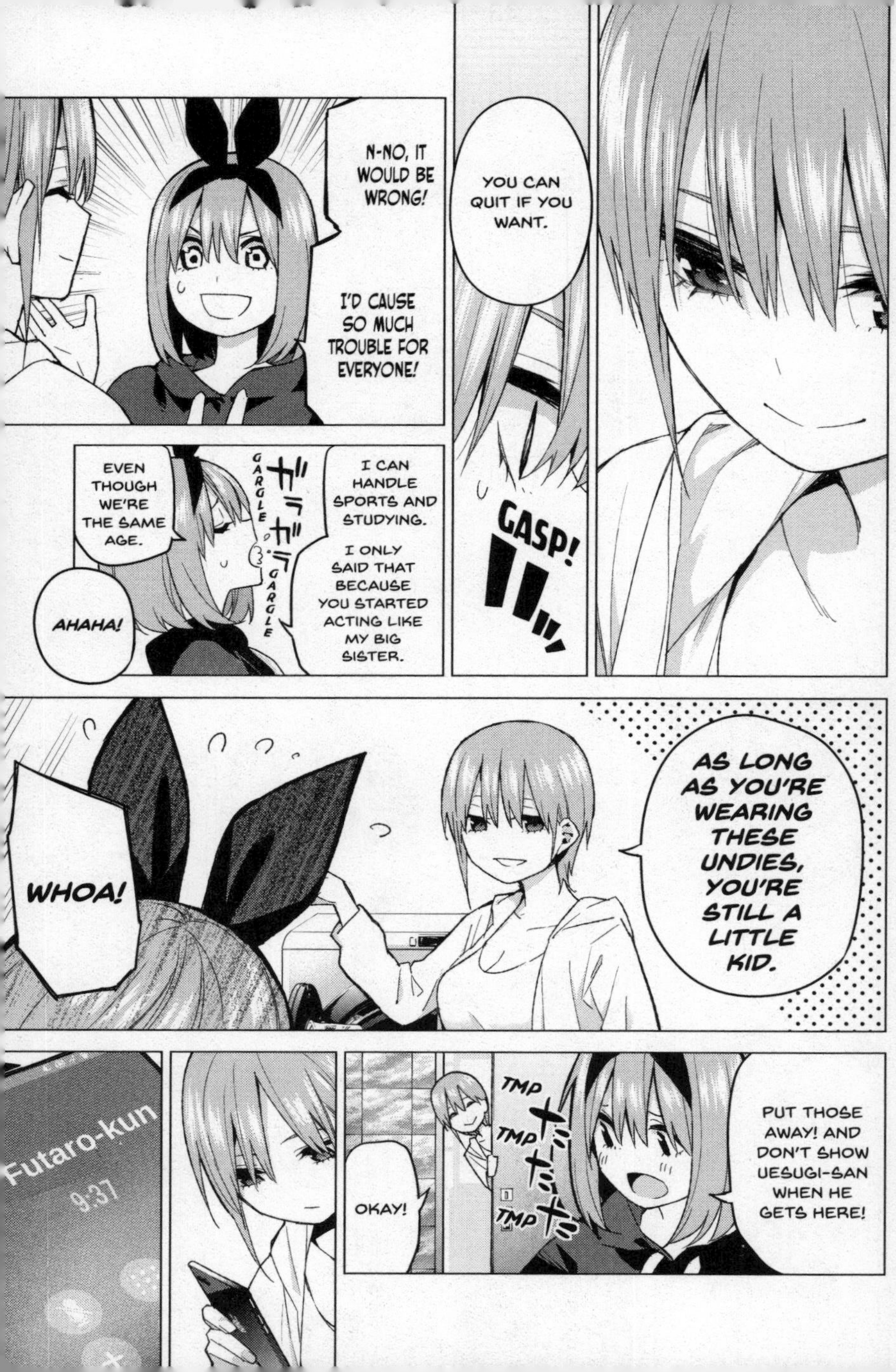
YOU CAN QUIT IF YOU WANT.
GASP!
N-NO, IT WOULD BE WRONG!
I'D CAUSE SO MUCH TROUBLE FOR EVERYONE!
I CAN HANDLE SPORTS AND STUDYING.
I ONLY SAID THAT BECAUSE YOU STARTED ACTING LIKE MY BIG SISTER.
GARGLE
GARGLE
EVEN THOUGH WE'RE THE SAME AGE.
AHAHA!
AS LONG AS YOU'RE WEARING THESE UNDIES, YOU'RE STILL A LITTLE KID.
WHOA!
PUT THOSE AWAY! AND DON'T SHOW UESUGI-SAN WHEN HE GETS HERE!
TMP
TMP
TMP
OKAY!
Futaro-kun
9:37

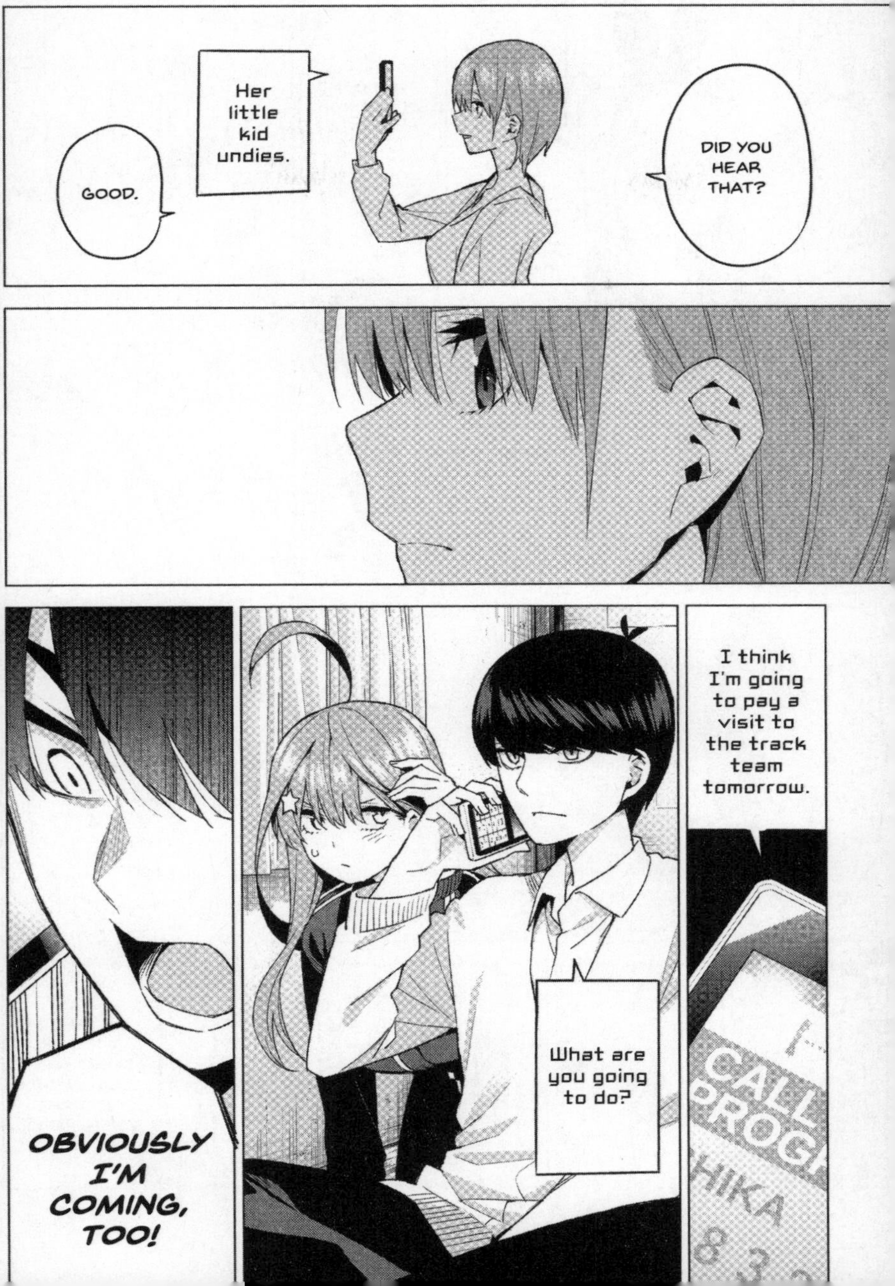
DID YOU HEAR THAT?
Her little kid undies.
GOOD.
I think I'm going to pay a visit to the track team tomorrow.
What are you going to do?
OBVIOUSLY I'M COMING, TOO!

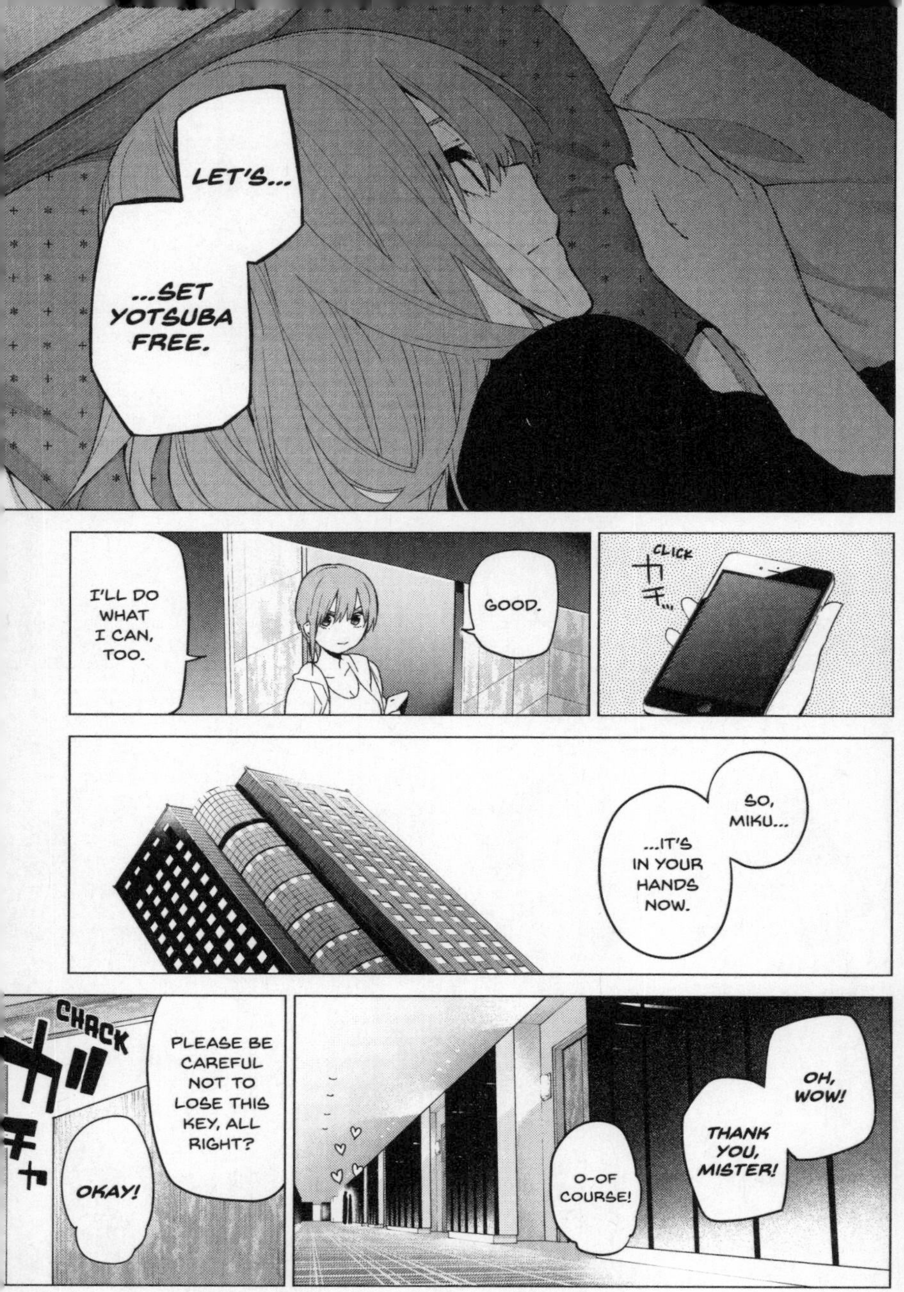
LET'S...
...SET YOTSUBA FREE.
CLICK
カチ...
GOOD.
I'LL DO WHAT I CAN, TOO.
SO, MIKU...
...IT'S IN YOUR HANDS NOW.
OH, WOW!
THANK YOU, MISTER!
O-OF COURSE!
PLEASE BE CAREFUL NOT TO LOSE THIS KEY, ALL RIGHT?
OKAY!
CHACK
ガチャ

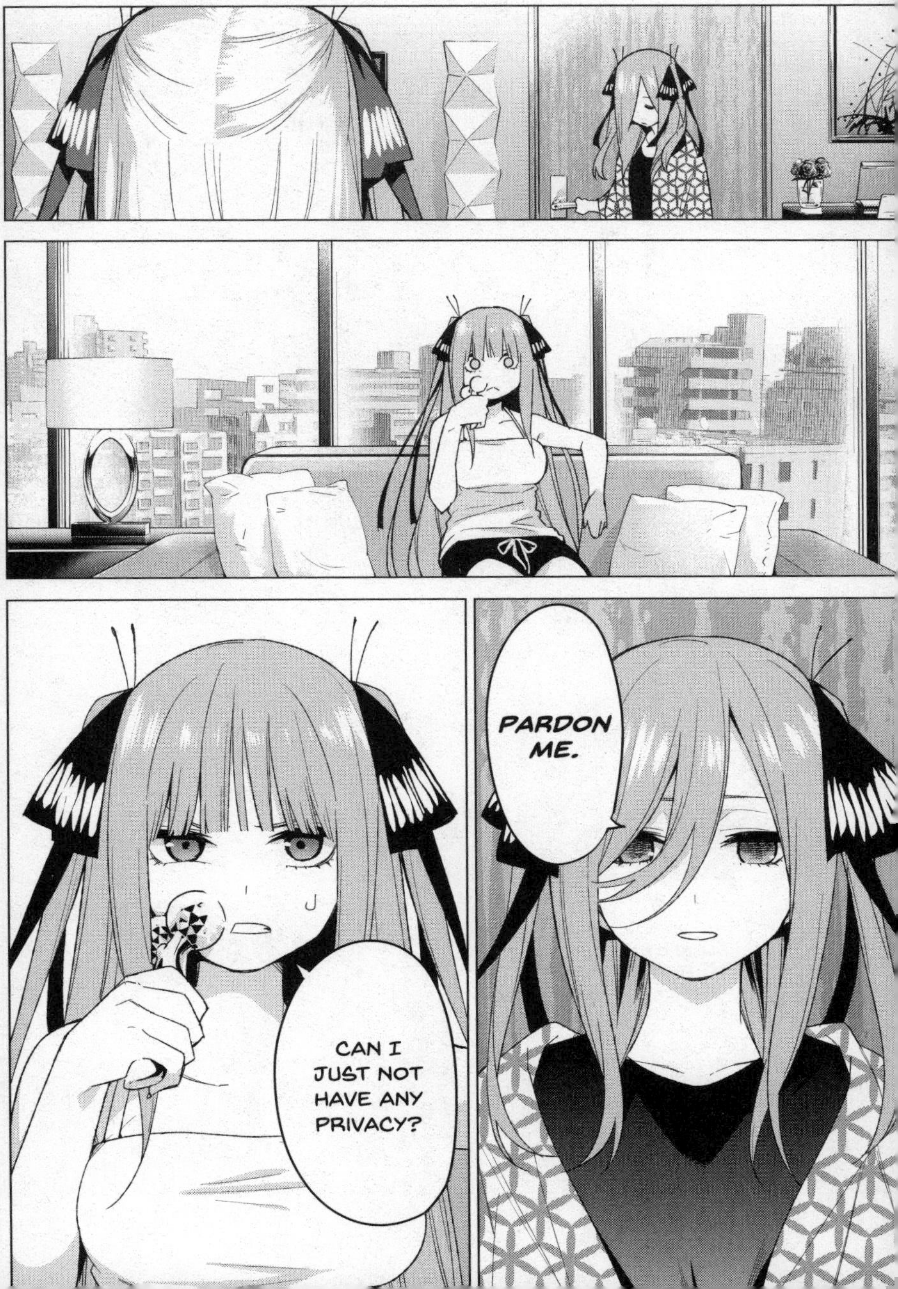
PARDON ME.
CAN I JUST NOT HAVE ANY PRIVACY?

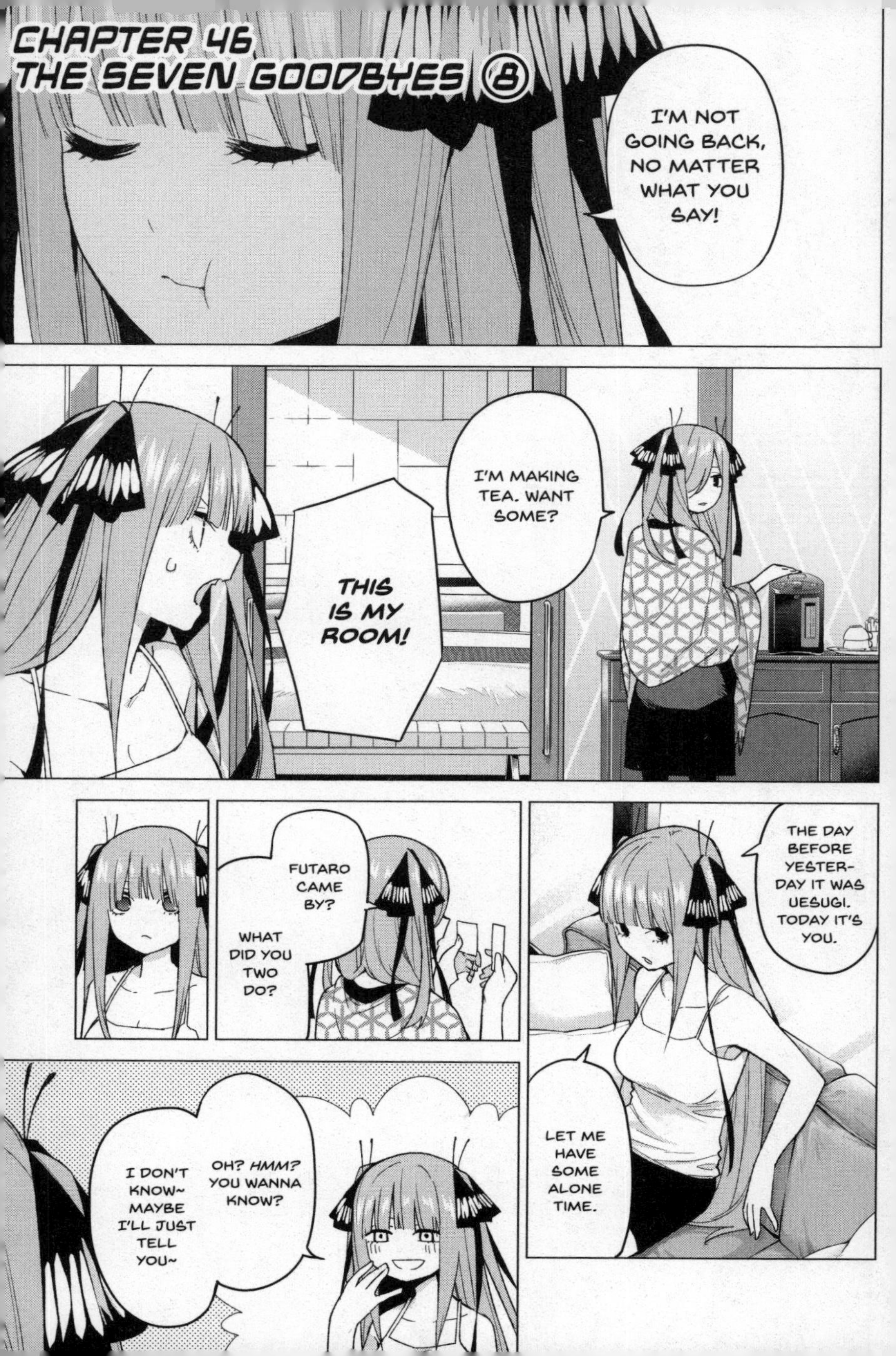
CHAPTER 46
THE SEVEN GOODBYES ⑧
I'M NOT GOING BACK, NO MATTER WHAT YOU SAY!
I'M MAKING TEA. WANT SOME?
THIS IS MY ROOM!
THE DAY BEFORE YESTER-DAY IT WAS UESUGI. TODAY IT'S YOU.
LET ME HAVE SOME ALONE TIME.
FUTARO CAME BY?
WHAT DID YOU TWO DO?
OH? HMM? YOU WANNA KNOW?
I DON'T KNOW~ MAYBE I'LL JUST TELL YOU~

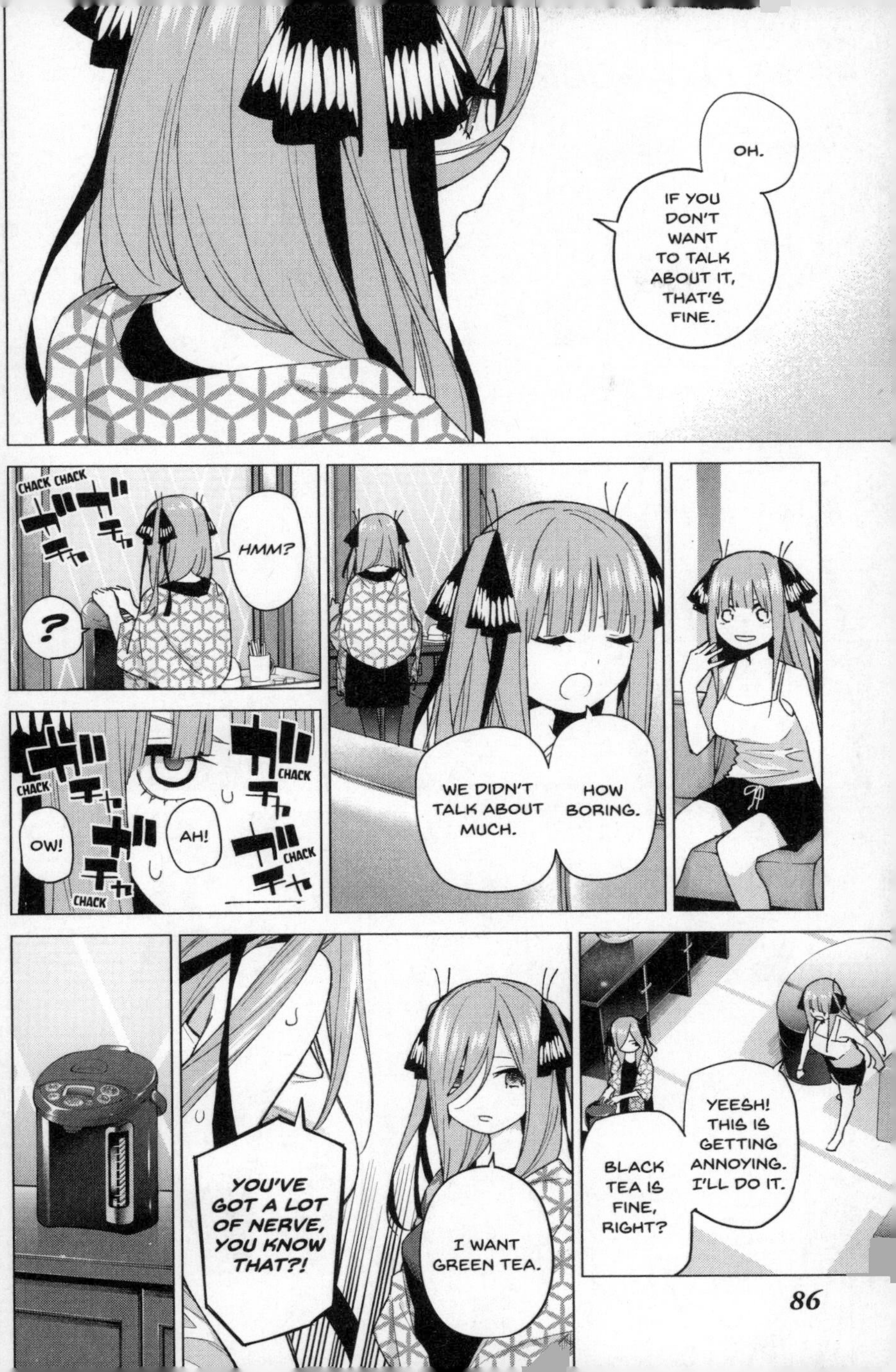
OH.
IF YOU DON'T WANT TO TALK ABOUT IT, THAT'S FINE.
HOW BORING.
WE DIDN'T TALK ABOUT MUCH.
CHACK CHACK
HMM?
?
CHACK
CHACK
AH!
CHACK
OW!
CHACK
YEESH! THIS IS GETTING ANNOYING. I'LL DO IT.
BLACK TEA IS FINE, RIGHT?
I WANT GREEN TEA.
YOU'VE GOT A LOT OF NERVE, YOU KNOW THAT?!

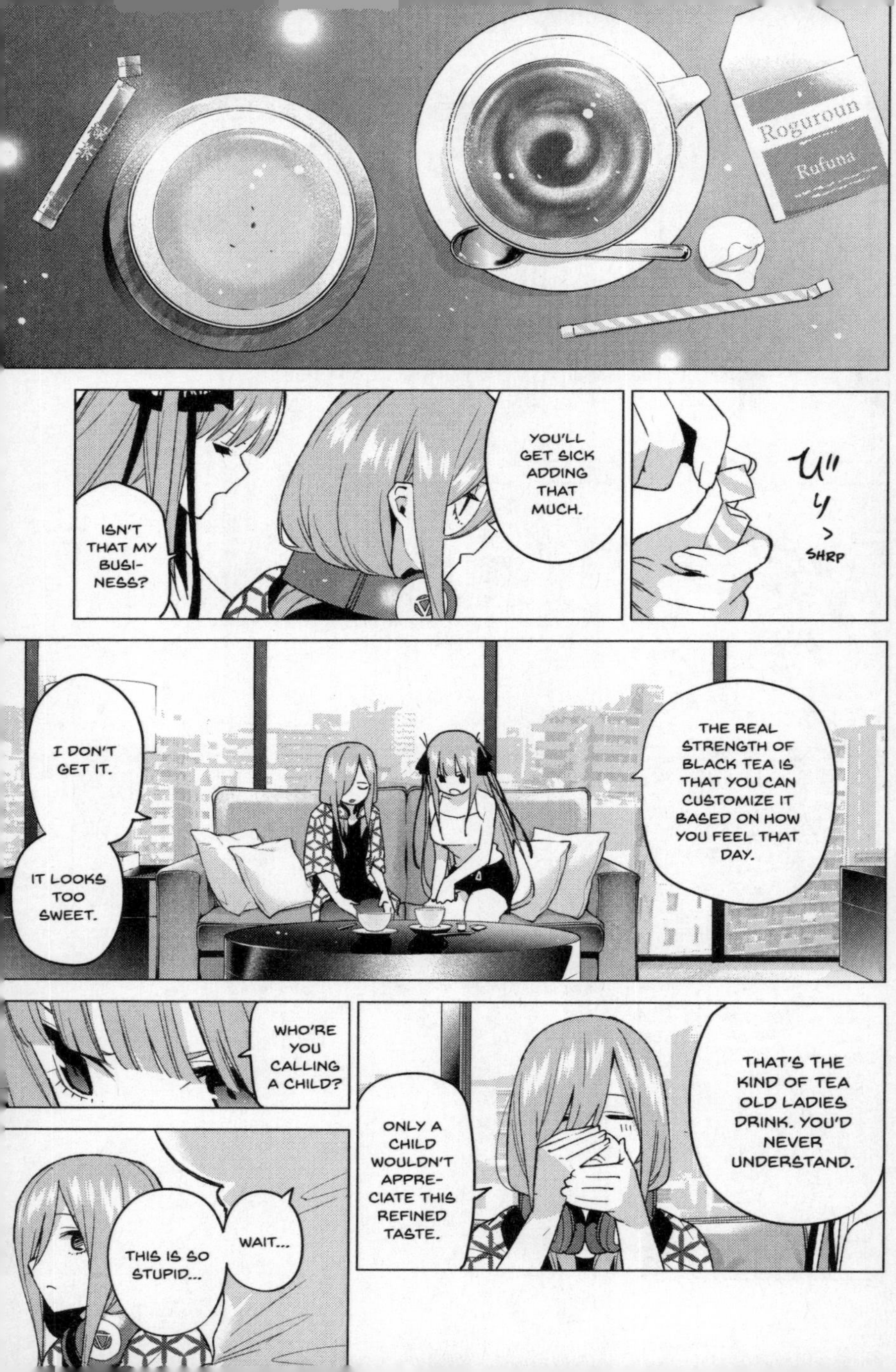

Roguroun
Rufuna
SHRP
YOU'LL GET SICK ADDING THAT MUCH.
ISN'T THAT MY BUSINESS?
THE REAL STRENGTH OF BLACK TEA IS THAT YOU CAN CUSTOMIZE IT BASED ON HOW YOU FEEL THAT DAY.
I DON'T GET IT.
IT LOOKS TOO SWEET.
THAT'S THE KIND OF TEA OLD LADIES DRINK. YOU'D NEVER UNDERSTAND.
ONLY A CHILD WOULDN'T APPRECIATE THIS REFINED TASTE.
WHO'RE YOU CALLING A CHILD?
WAIT...
THIS IS SO STUPID...

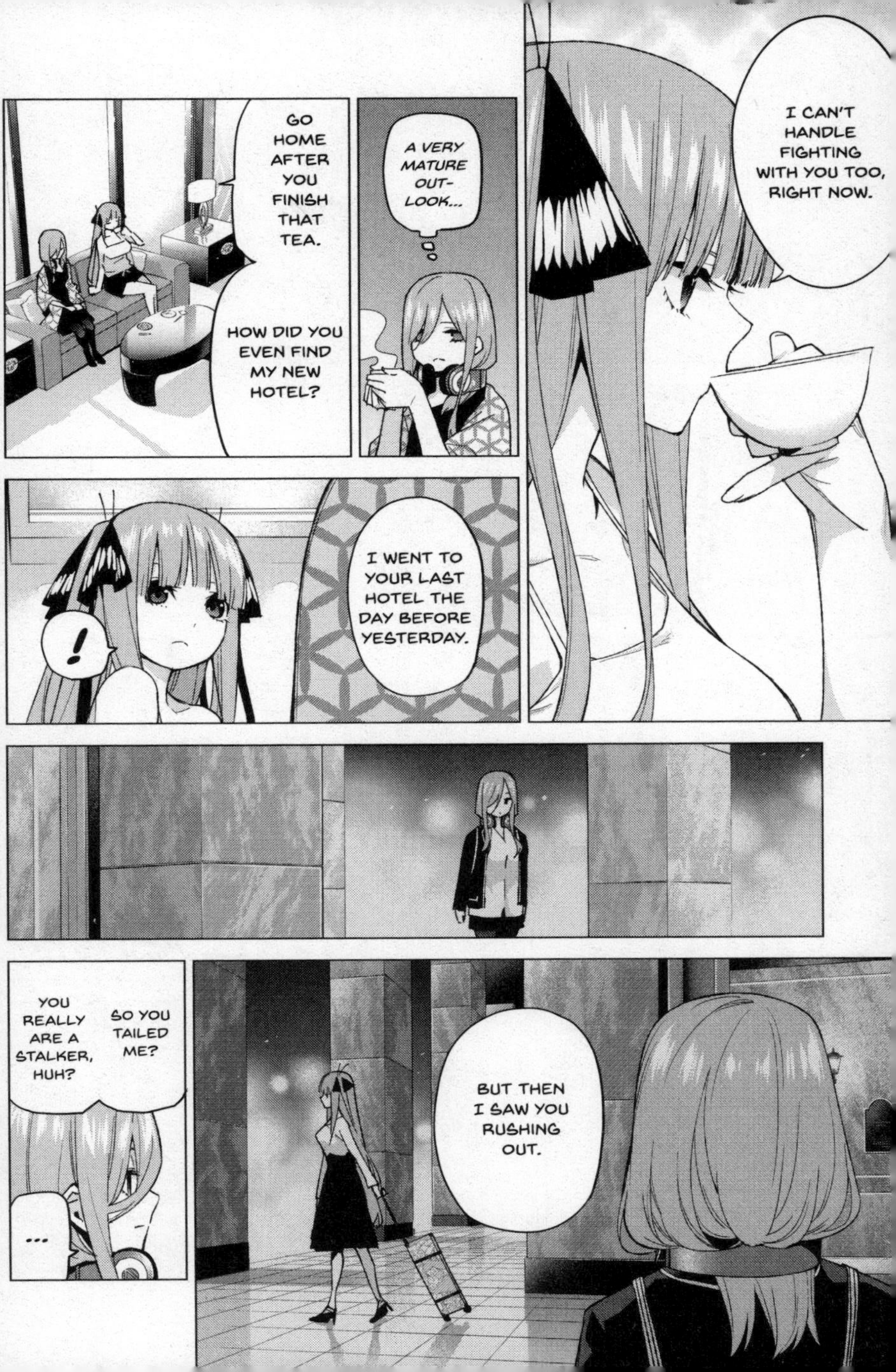
I CAN'T HANDLE FIGHTING WITH YOU TOO, RIGHT NOW.
A VERY MATURE OUT-LOOK...
GO HOME AFTER YOU FINISH THAT TEA.
HOW DID YOU EVEN FIND MY NEW HOTEL?
I WENT TO YOUR LAST HOTEL THE DAY BEFORE YESTERDAY.
!
BUT THEN I SAW YOU RUSHING OUT.
SO YOU TAILED ME?
YOU REALLY ARE A STALKER, HUH?
...

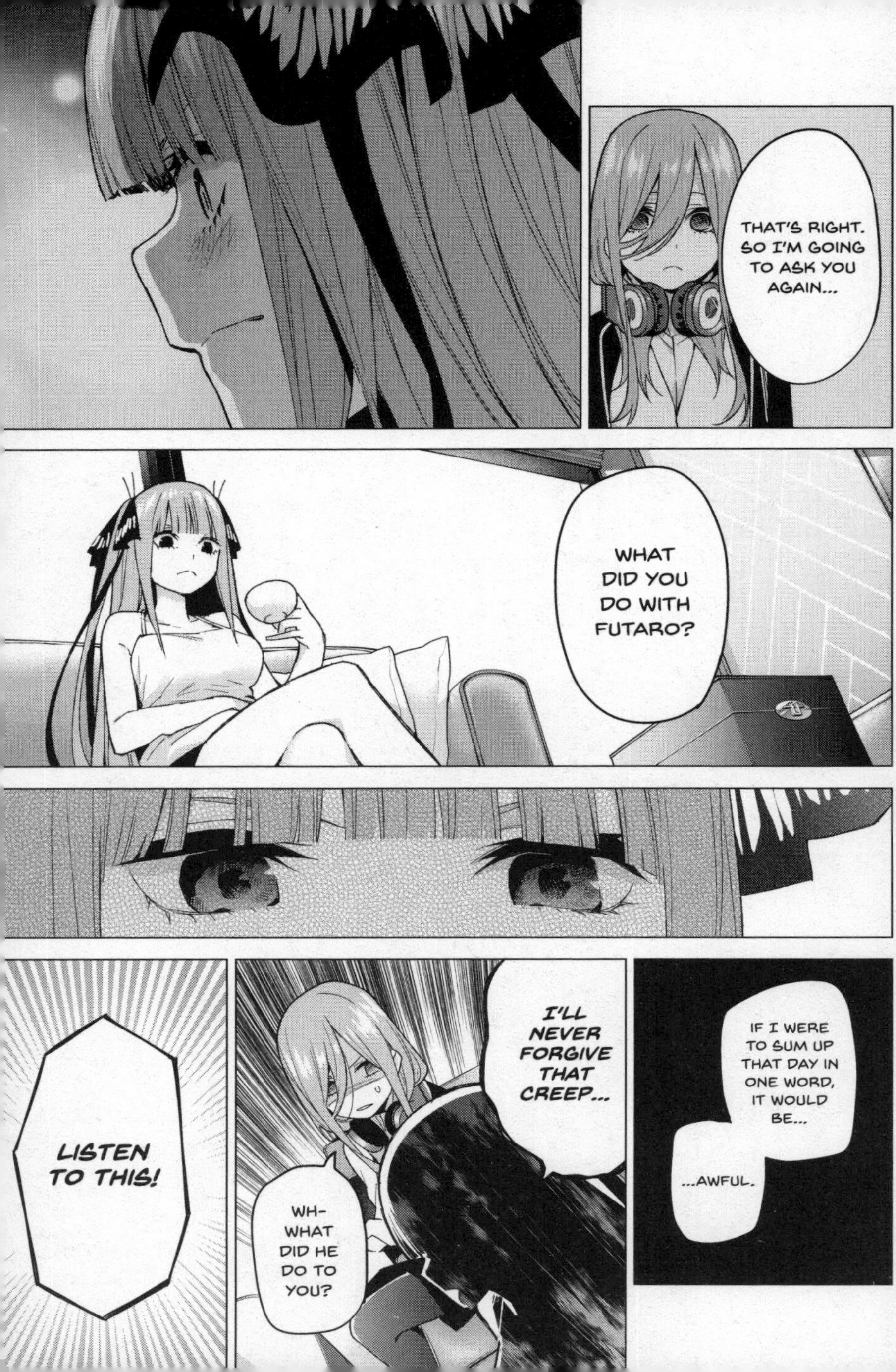
THAT'S RIGHT. SO I'M GOING TO ASK YOU AGAIN...
WHAT DID YOU DO WITH FUTARO?
IF I WERE TO SUM UP THAT DAY IN ONE WORD, IT WOULD BE...
...AWFUL.
I'LL NEVER FORGIVE THAT CREEP...
WH- WHAT DID HE DO TO YOU?
LISTEN TO THIS!

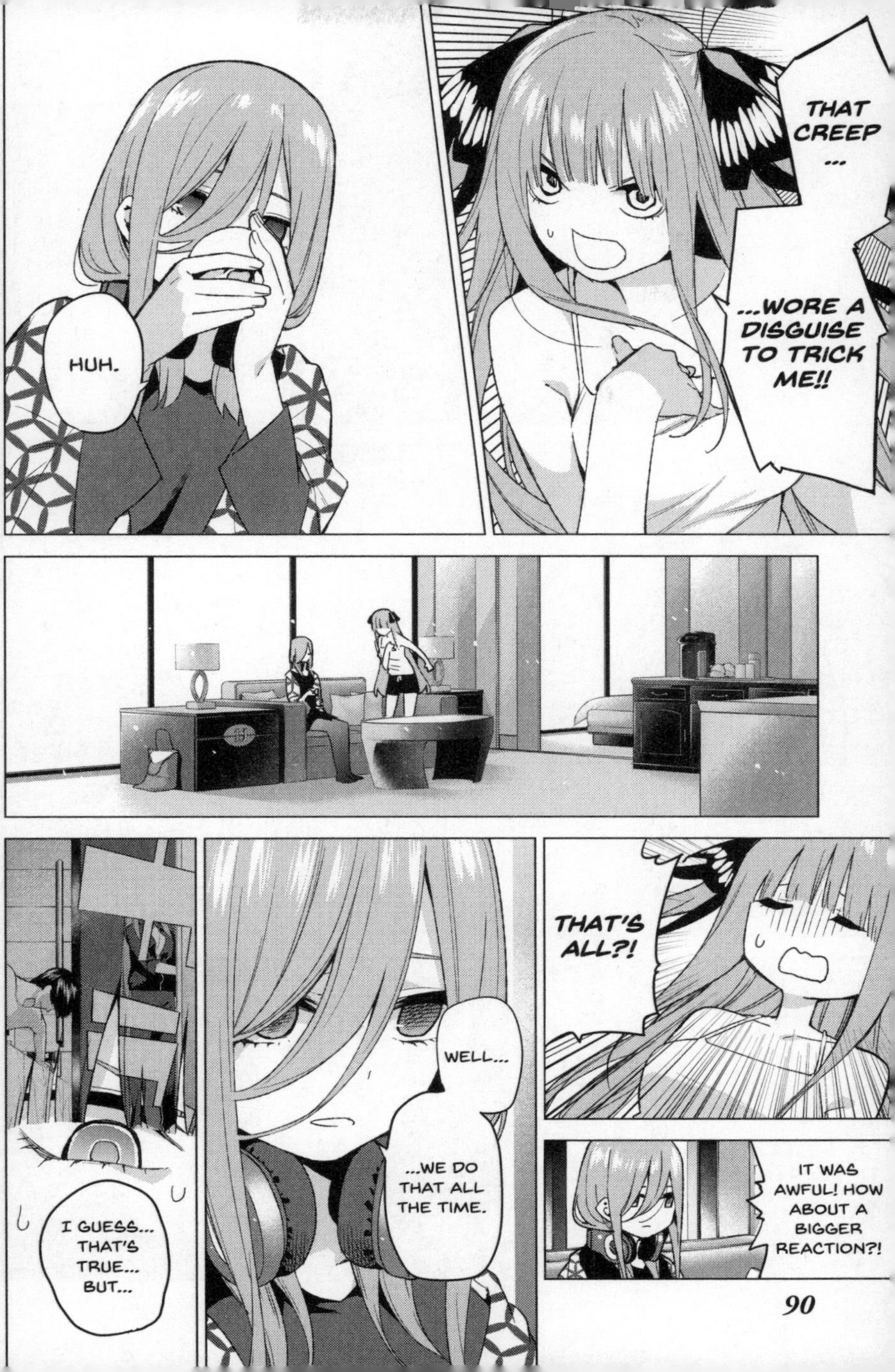
THAT CREEP ...
...WORE A DISGUISE TO TRICK ME!!
HUH.
THAT'S ALL?!
IT WAS AWFUL! HOW ABOUT A BIGGER REACTION?!
WELL...
...WE DO THAT ALL THE TIME.
I GUESS... THAT'S TRUE... BUT...

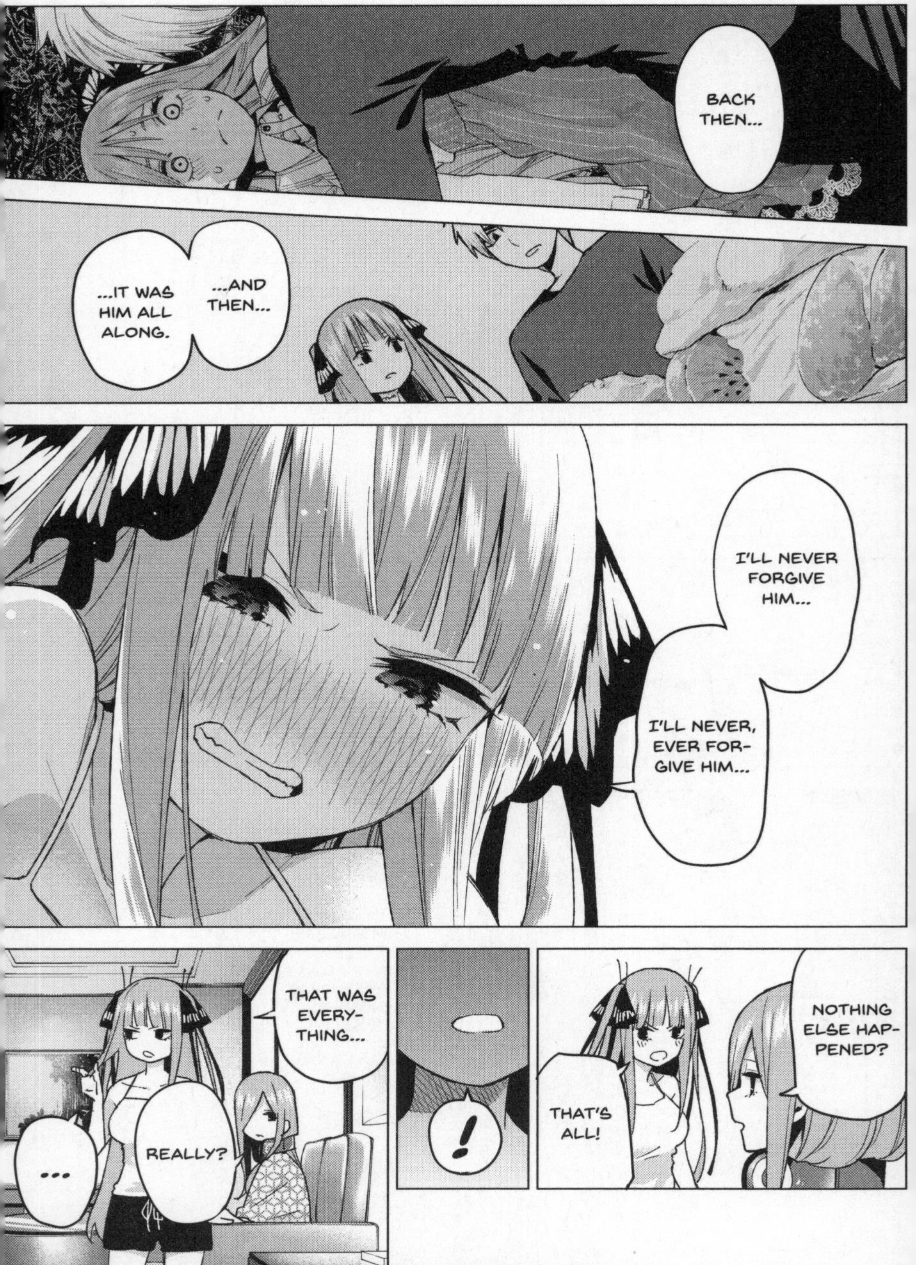
BACK THEN...
...AND THEN...
...IT WAS HIM ALL ALONG.
I'LL NEVER FORGIVE HIM...
I'LL NEVER, EVER FOR-GIVE HIM...
NOTHING ELSE HAP-PENED?
THAT'S ALL!
!
THAT WAS EVERY-THING...
REALLY?
...

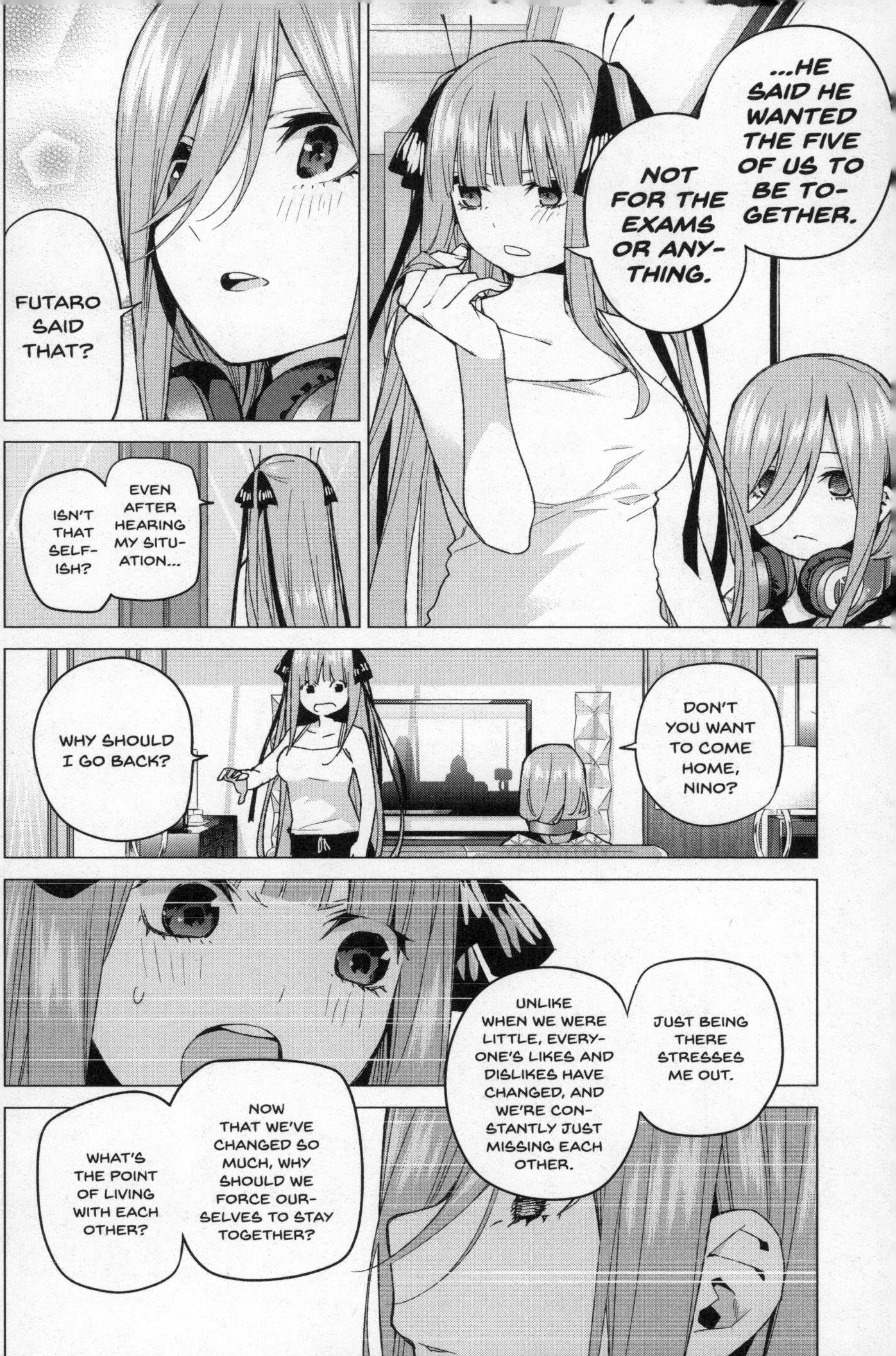
...HE SAID HE WANTED THE FIVE OF US TO BE TO-GETHER.
NOT FOR THE EXAMS OR ANY-THING.
FUTARO SAID THAT?
EVEN AFTER HEARING MY SITU-ATION...
ISN'T THAT SELF-ISH?
DON'T YOU WANT TO COME HOME, NINO?
WHY SHOULD I GO BACK?
JUST BEING THERE STRESSES ME OUT.
UNLIKE WHEN WE WERE LITTLE, EVERY-ONE'S LIKES AND DISLIKES HAVE CHANGED, AND WE'RE CON-STANTLY JUST MISSING EACH OTHER.
NOW THAT WE'VE CHANGED SO MUCH, WHY SHOULD WE FORCE OUR-SELVES TO STAY TOGETHER?
WHAT'S THE POINT OF LIVING WITH EACH OTHER?

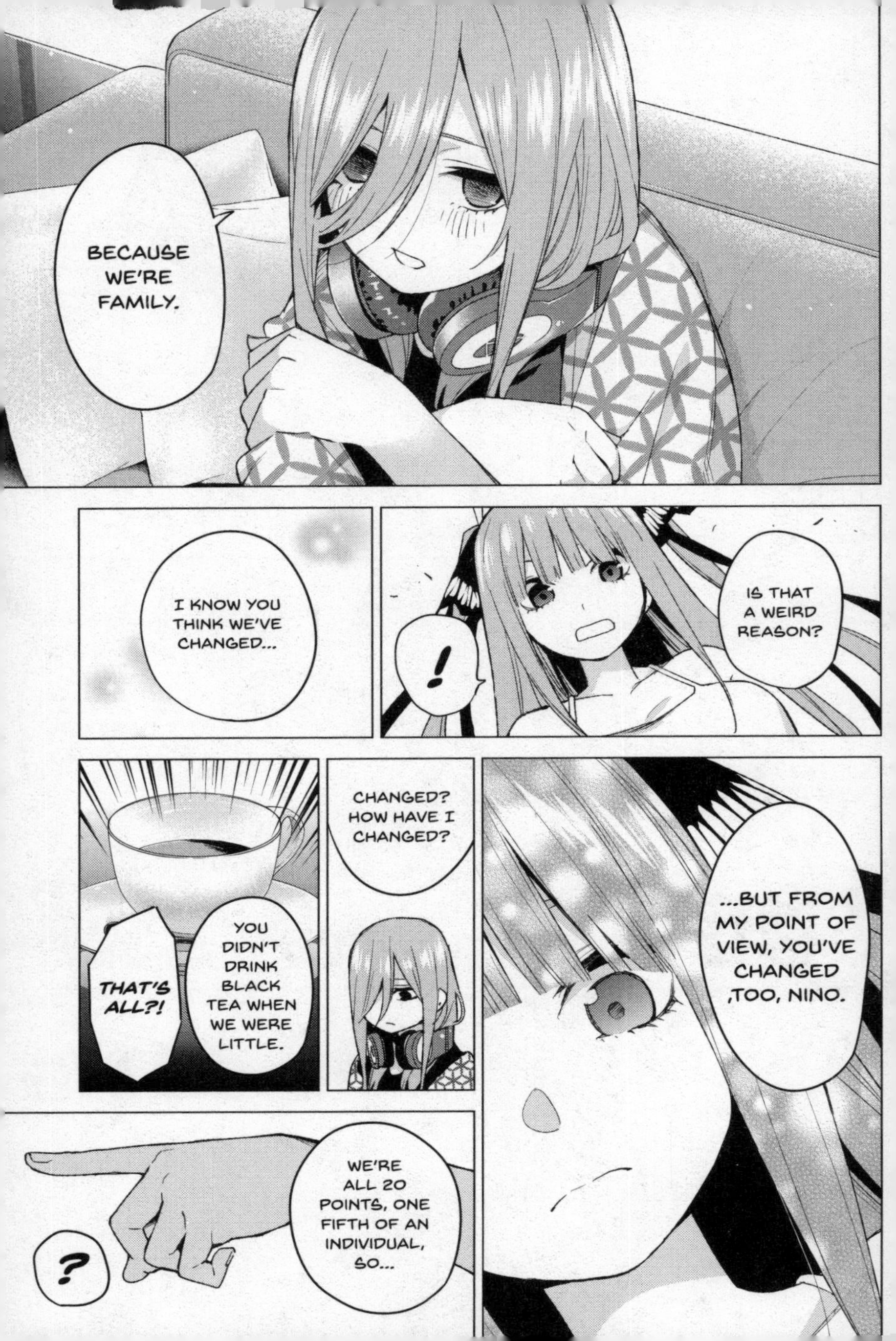
BECAUSE WE'RE FAMILY.
IS THAT A WEIRD REASON?
!
I KNOW YOU THINK WE'VE CHANGED...
...BUT FROM MY POINT OF VIEW, YOU'VE CHANGED ,TOO, NINO.
CHANGED? HOW HAVE I CHANGED?
YOU DIDN'T DRINK BLACK TEA WHEN WE WERE LITTLE.
THAT'S ALL?!
WE'RE ALL 20 POINTS, ONE FIFTH OF AN INDIVIDUAL, SO...
?

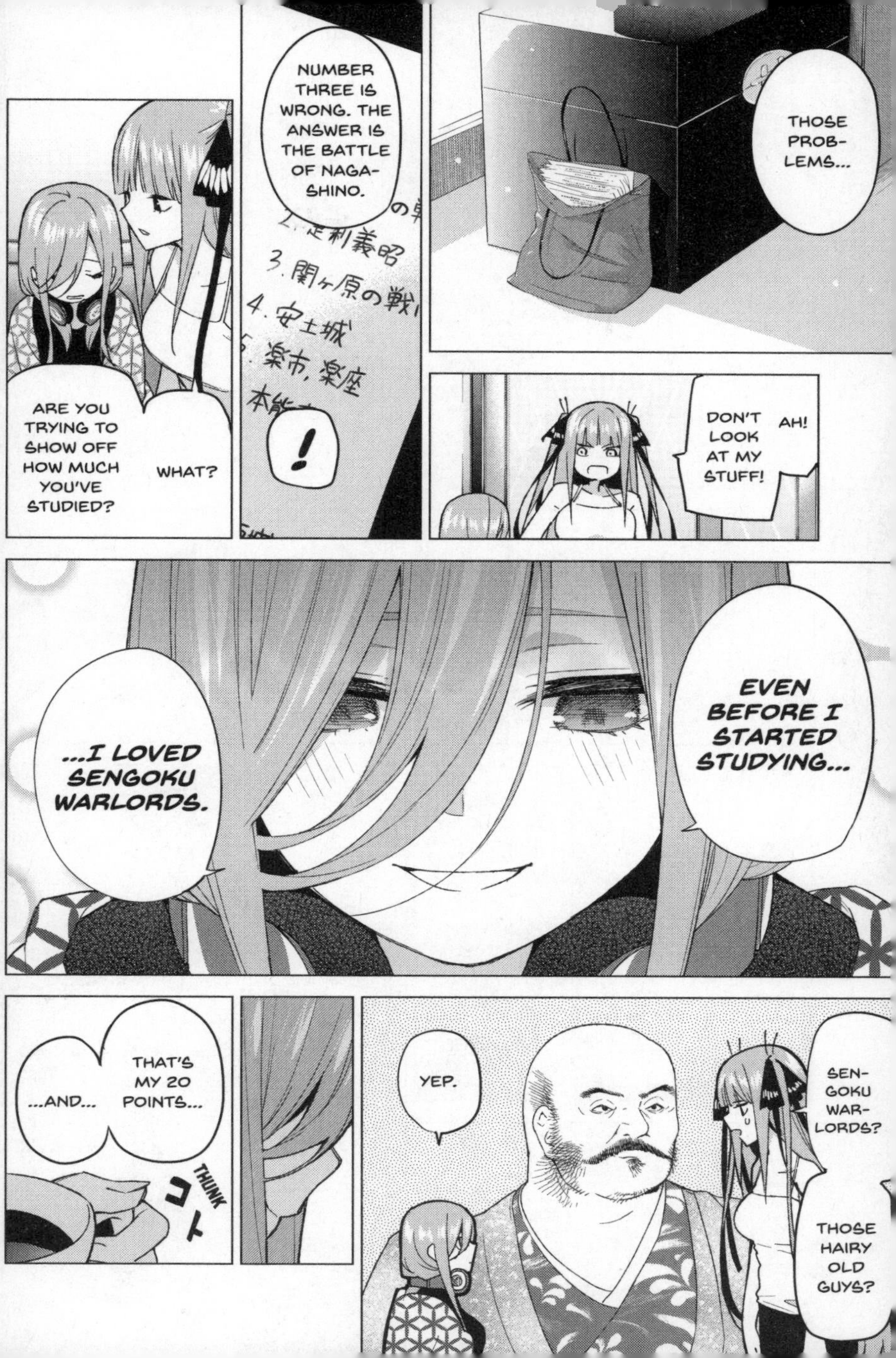
THOSE PROB-LEMS...
AH!
DON'T LOOK AT MY STUFF!
NUMBER THREE IS WRONG. THE ANSWER IS THE BATTLE OF NAGA-SHINO.
3.関ヶ原の戦
4.安土城
5.楽市,楽座
!
WHAT?
ARE YOU TRYING TO SHOW OFF HOW MUCH YOU'VE STUDIED?
EVEN BEFORE I STARTED STUDYING...
...I LOVED SENGOKU WARLORDS.
SEN-GOKU WAR-LORDS?
YEP.
THOSE HAIRY OLD GUYS?
THAT'S MY 20 POINTS...
...AND...
THUNK

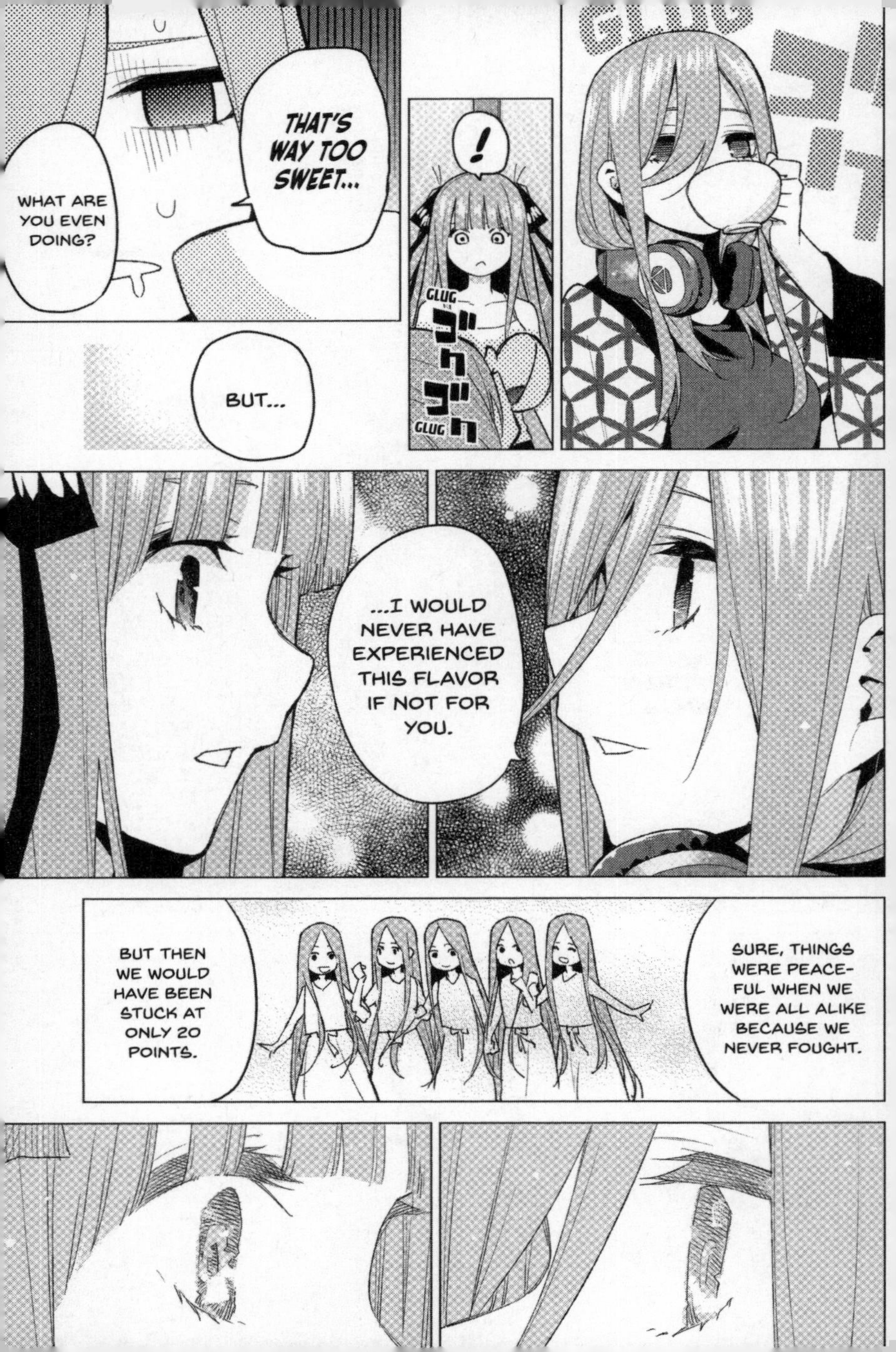
GLUG
!
GLUG
GLUG
THAT'S WAY TOO SWEET...
WHAT ARE YOU EVEN DOING?
BUT...
...I WOULD NEVER HAVE EXPERIENCED THIS FLAVOR IF NOT FOR YOU.
SURE, THINGS WERE PEACE-FUL WHEN WE WERE ALL ALIKE BECAUSE WE NEVER FOUGHT.
BUT THEN WE WOULD HAVE BEEN STUCK AT ONLY 20 POINTS.

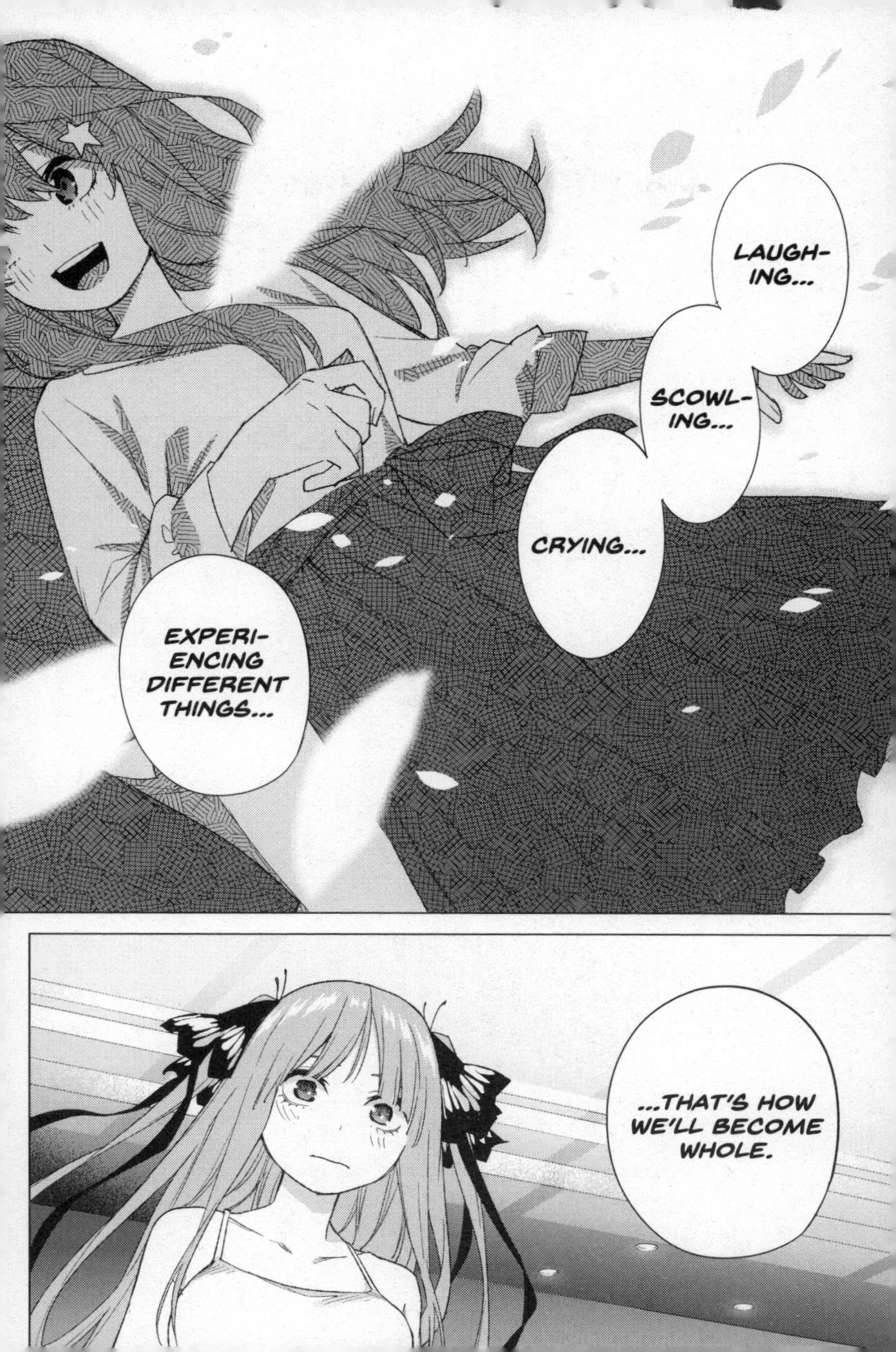
LAUGHING-
ING...
SCOWL-
ING...
CRYING...
EXPERI-
ENCING
DIFFERENT
THINGS...
...THAT'S HOW
WE'LL BECOME
WHOLE.

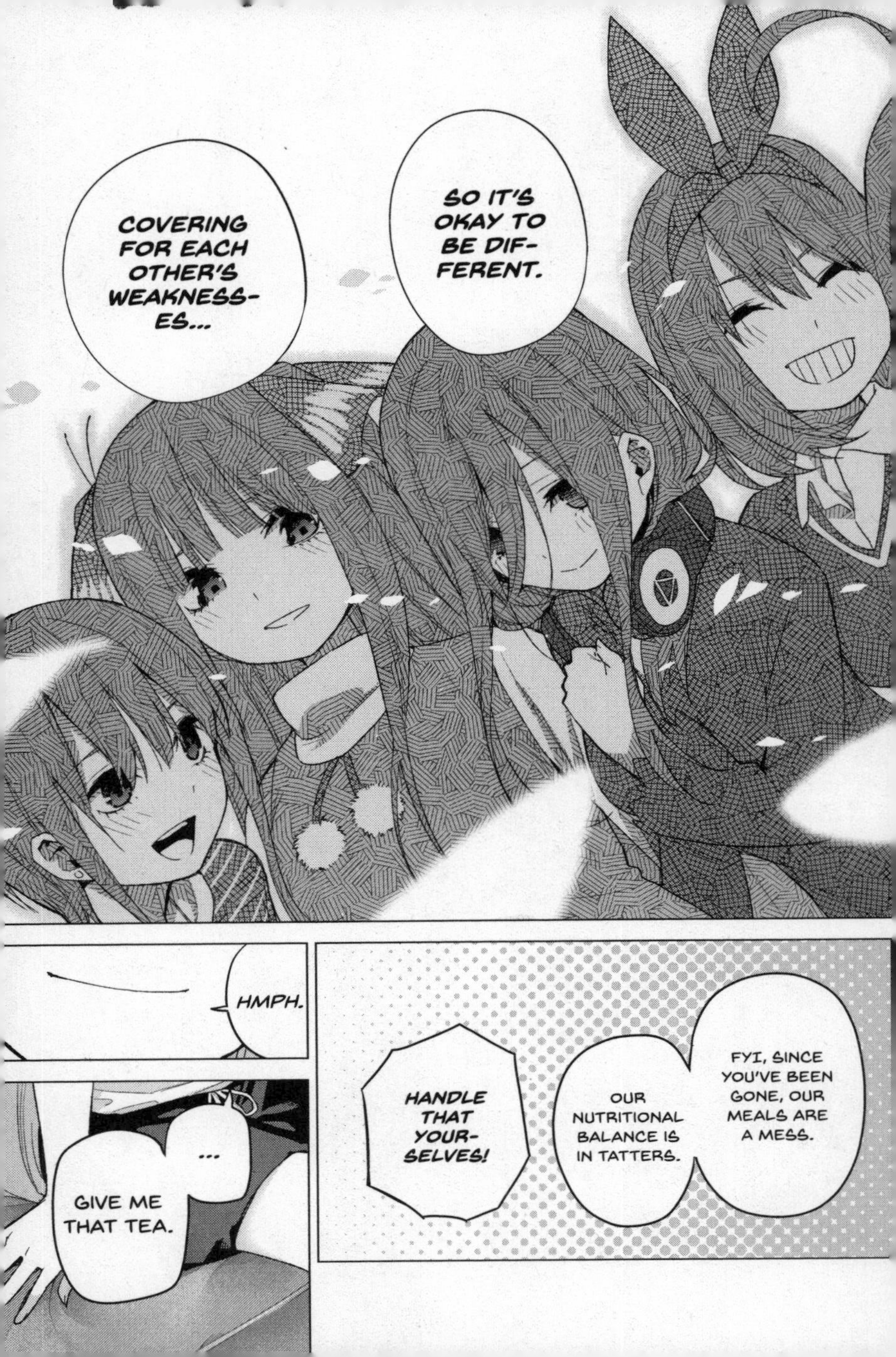
SO IT'S OKAY TO BE DIF-FERENT.
COVERING FOR EACH OTHER'S WEAKNESS-ES...
FYI, SINCE YOU'VE BEEN GONE, OUR MEALS ARE A MESS.
OUR NUTRITIONAL BALANCE IS IN TATTERS.
HANDLE THAT YOUR-SELVES!
HMPH.
...
GIVE ME THAT TEA.

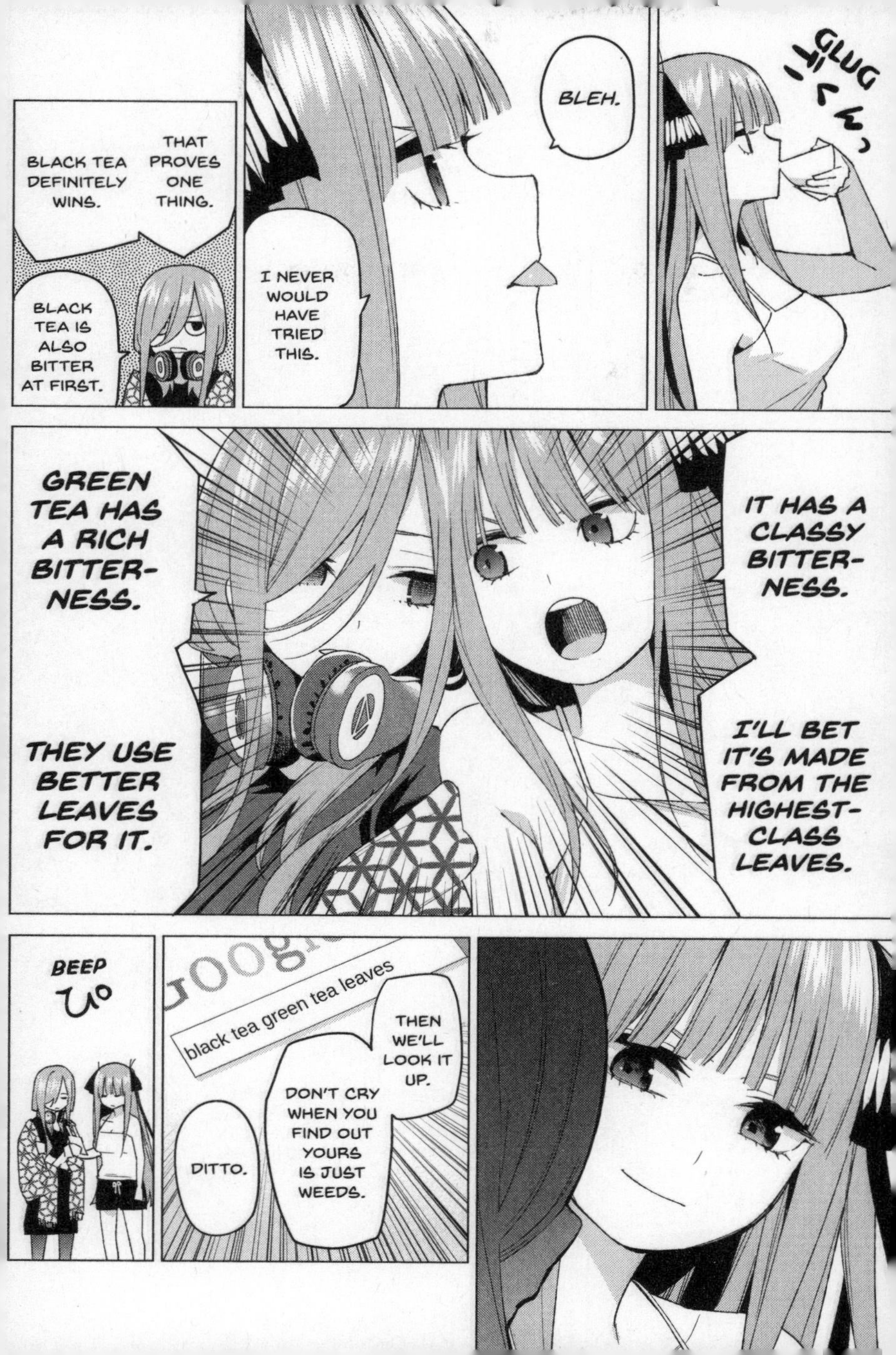
GLUG
BLEH.
I NEVER WOULD HAVE TRIED THIS.
THAT PROVES ONE THING.
BLACK TEA DEFINITELY WINS.
BLACK TEA IS ALSO BITTER AT FIRST.
IT HAS A CLASSY BITTERNESS.
I'LL BET IT'S MADE FROM THE HIGHEST-CLASS LEAVES.
GREEN TEA HAS A RICH BITTERNESS.
THEY USE BETTER LEAVES FOR IT.
black tea green tea leaves
THEN WE'LL LOOK IT UP.
DON'T CRY WHEN YOU FIND OUT YOURS IS JUST WEEDS.
DITTO.
BEEP

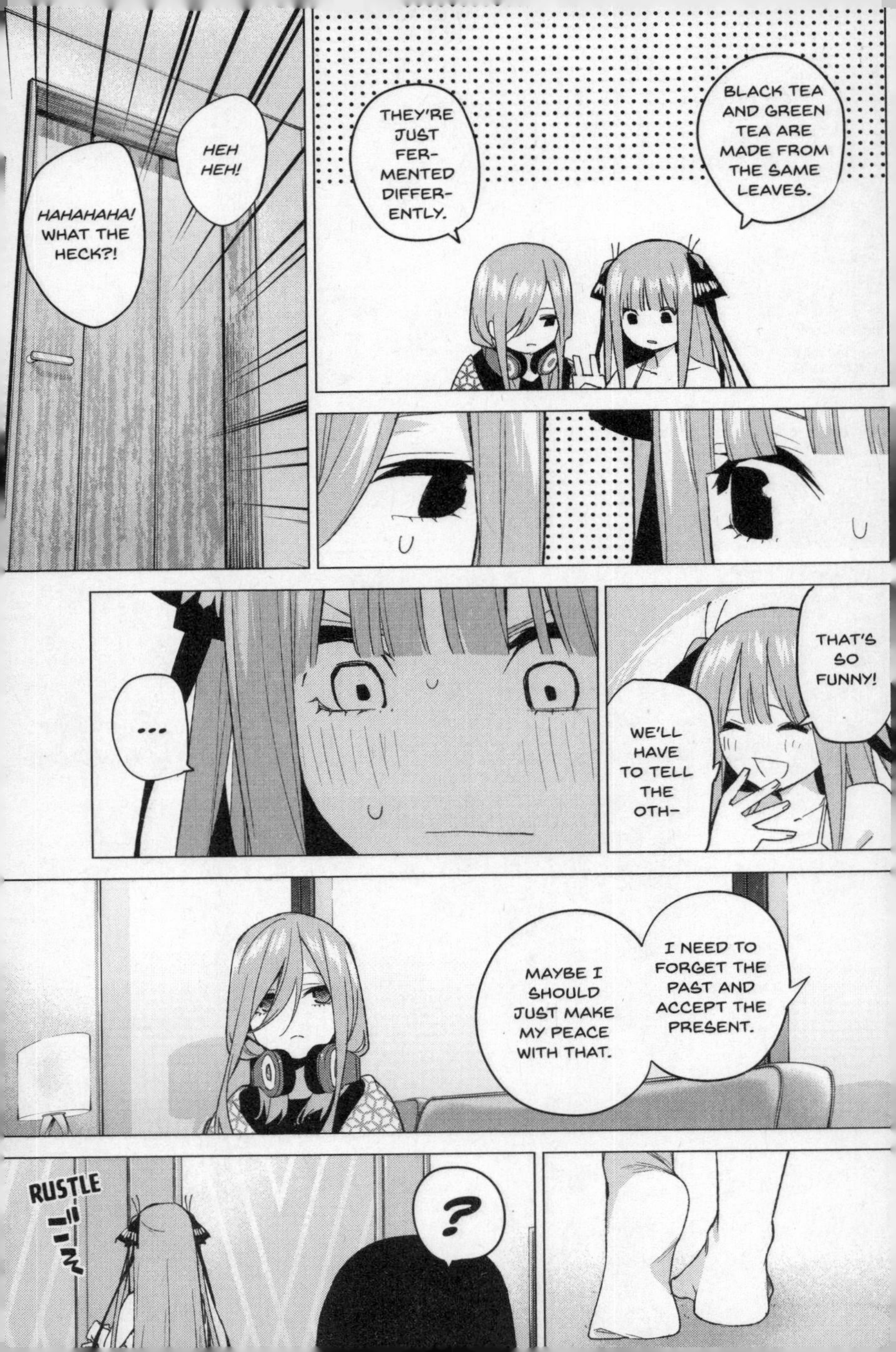

BLACK TEA AND GREEN TEA ARE MADE FROM THE SAME LEAVES.
THEY'RE JUST FER-MENTED DIFFER-ENTLY.
HEH HEH!
HAHAHAHA! WHAT THE HECK?!
THAT'S SO FUNNY!
WE'LL HAVE TO TELL THE OTH-
...
I NEED TO FORGET THE PAST AND ACCEPT THE PRESENT.
MAYBE I SHOULD JUST MAKE MY PEACE WITH THAT.
?
RUSTLE

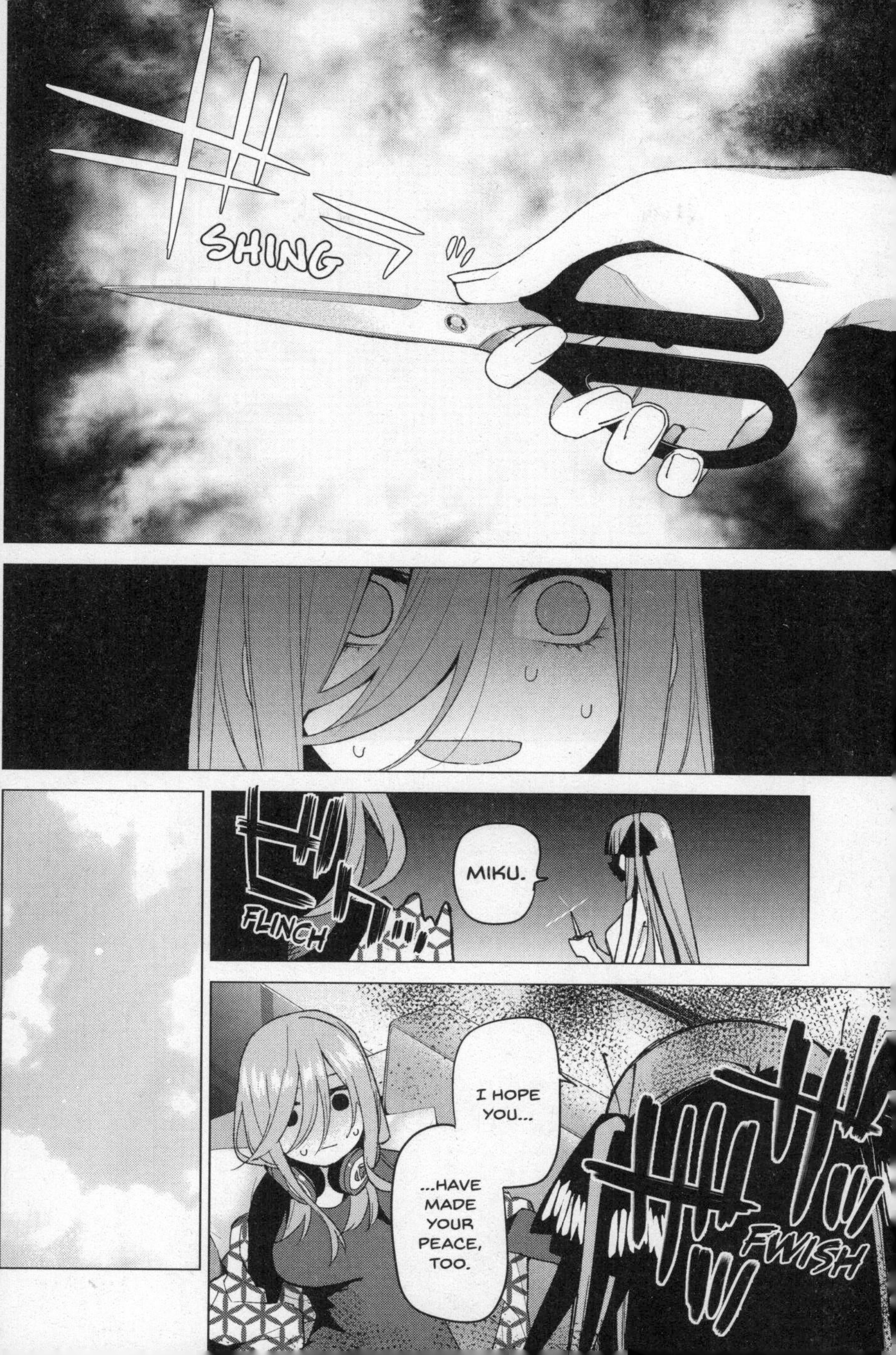
SHING
MIKU.
FLINCH
I HOPE YOU...
...HAVE MADE YOUR PEACE, TOO.
FWISH

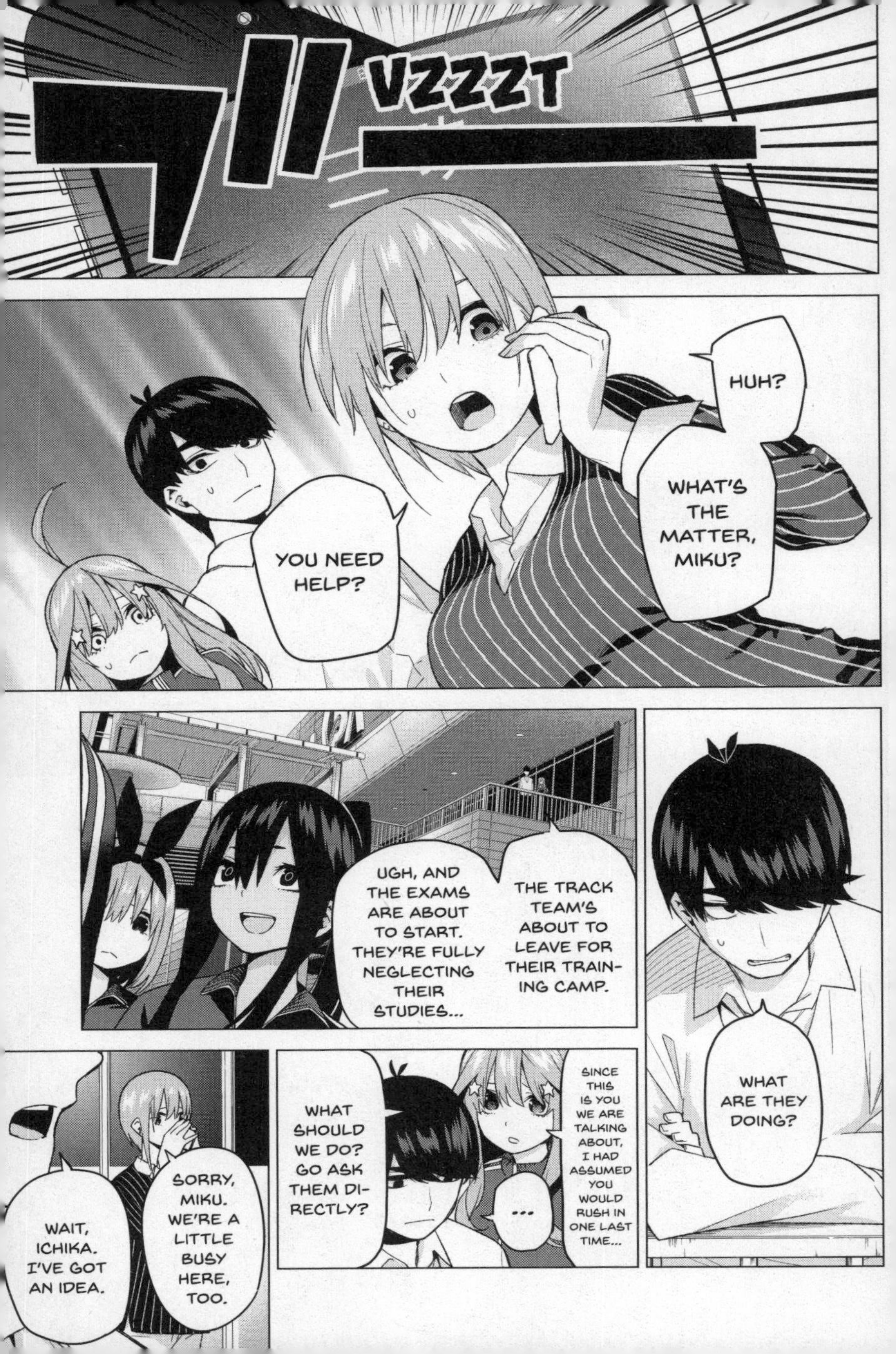
VZZZT
HUH?
WHAT'S THE MATTER, MIKU?
YOU NEED HELP?
WHAT ARE THEY DOING?
THE TRACK TEAM'S ABOUT TO LEAVE FOR THEIR TRAIN-ING CAMP.
UGH, AND THE EXAMS ARE ABOUT TO START. THEY'RE FULLY NEGLECTING THEIR STUDIES...
SINCE THIS IS YOU WE ARE TALKING ABOUT, I HAD ASSUMED YOU WOULD RUSH IN ONE LAST TIME...
WHAT SHOULD WE DO? GO ASK THEM DI-RECTLY?
...
SORRY, MIKU. WE'RE A LITTLE BUSY HERE, TOO.
WAIT, ICHIKA. I'VE GOT AN IDEA.

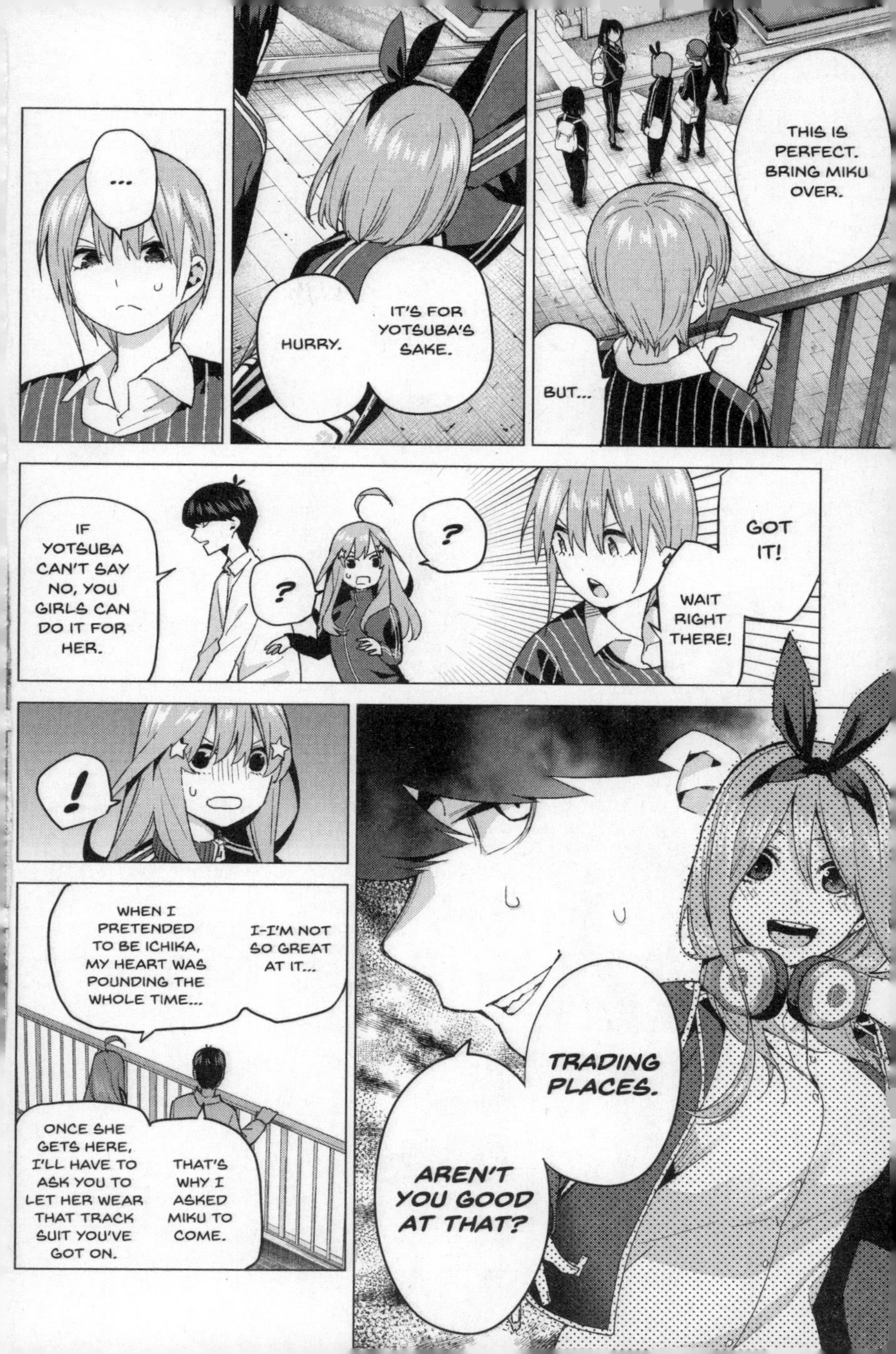
THIS IS PERFECT. BRING MIKU OVER.
BUT...
IT'S FOR YOTSUBA'S SAKE.
HURRY.
...
GOT IT!
WAIT RIGHT THERE!
?
?
IF YOTSUBA CAN'T SAY NO, YOU GIRLS CAN DO IT FOR HER.
TRADING PLACES.
AREN'T YOU GOOD AT THAT?
!
I-I'M NOT SO GREAT AT IT...
WHEN I PRETENDED TO BE ICHIKA, MY HEART WAS POUNDING THE WHOLE TIME...
THAT'S WHY I ASKED MIKU TO COME.
ONCE SHE GETS HERE, I'LL HAVE TO ASK YOU TO LET HER WEAR THAT TRACK SUIT YOU'VE GOT ON.

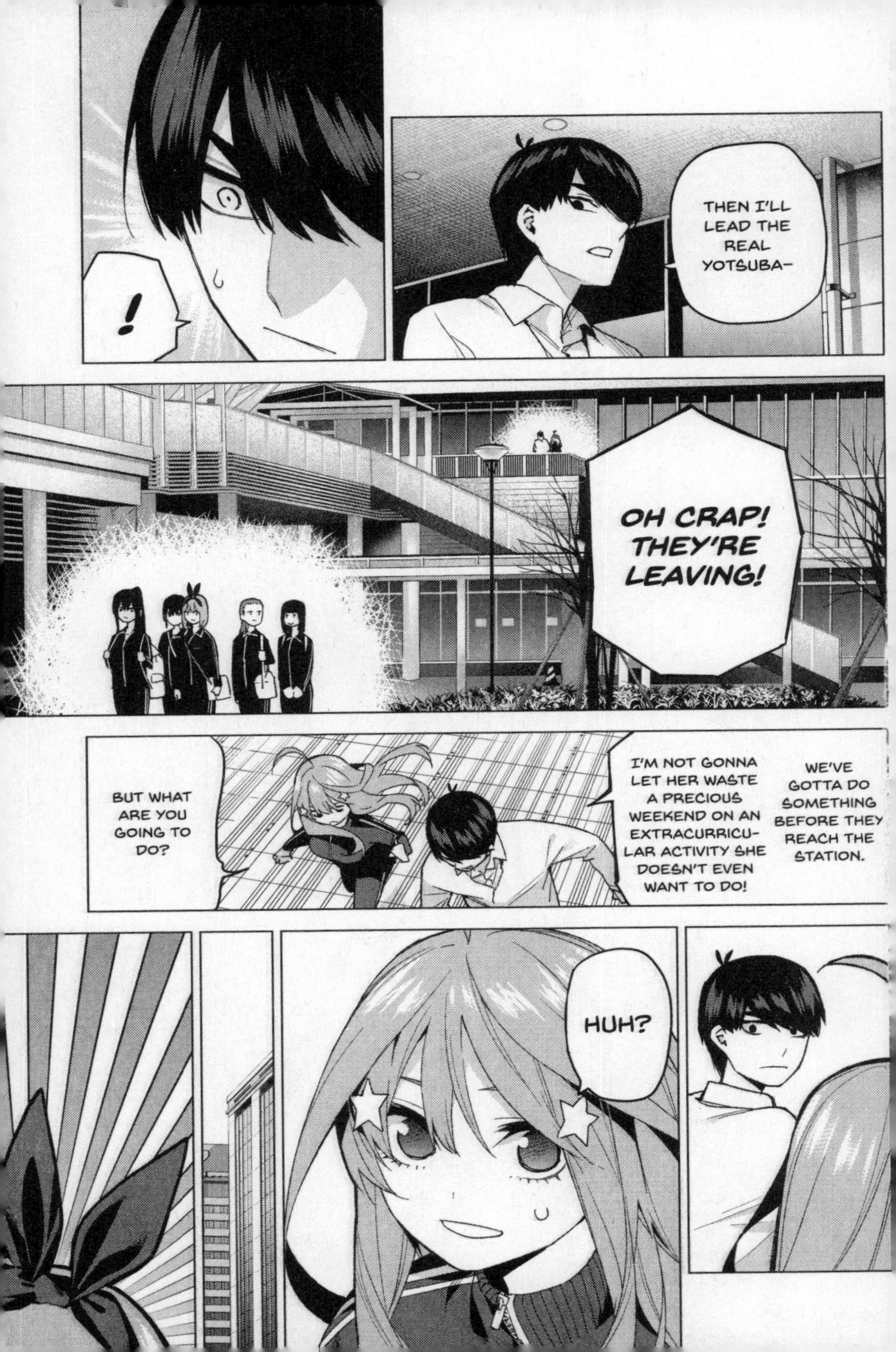
THEN I'LL LEAD THE REAL YOTSUBA-
!
OH CRAP! THEY'RE LEAVING!
WE'VE GOTTA DO SOMETHING BEFORE THEY REACH THE STATION.
I'M NOT GONNA LET HER WASTE A PRECIOUS WEEKEND ON AN EXTRACURRICU-LAR ACTIVITY SHE DOESN'T EVEN WANT TO DO!
BUT WHAT ARE YOU GOING TO DO?
HUH?

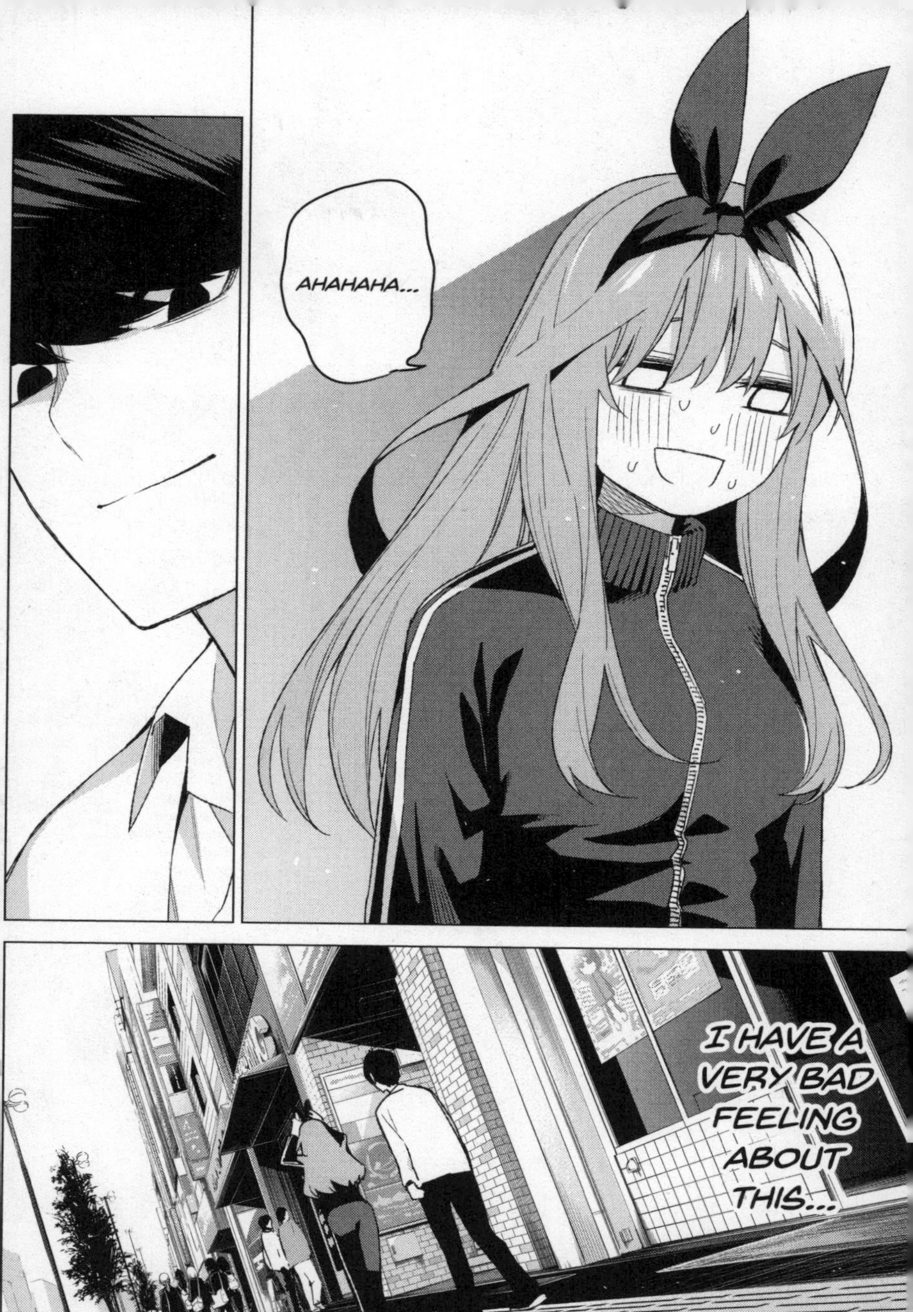
AHAHAHA...
I HAVE A VERY BAD FEELING ABOUT THIS...

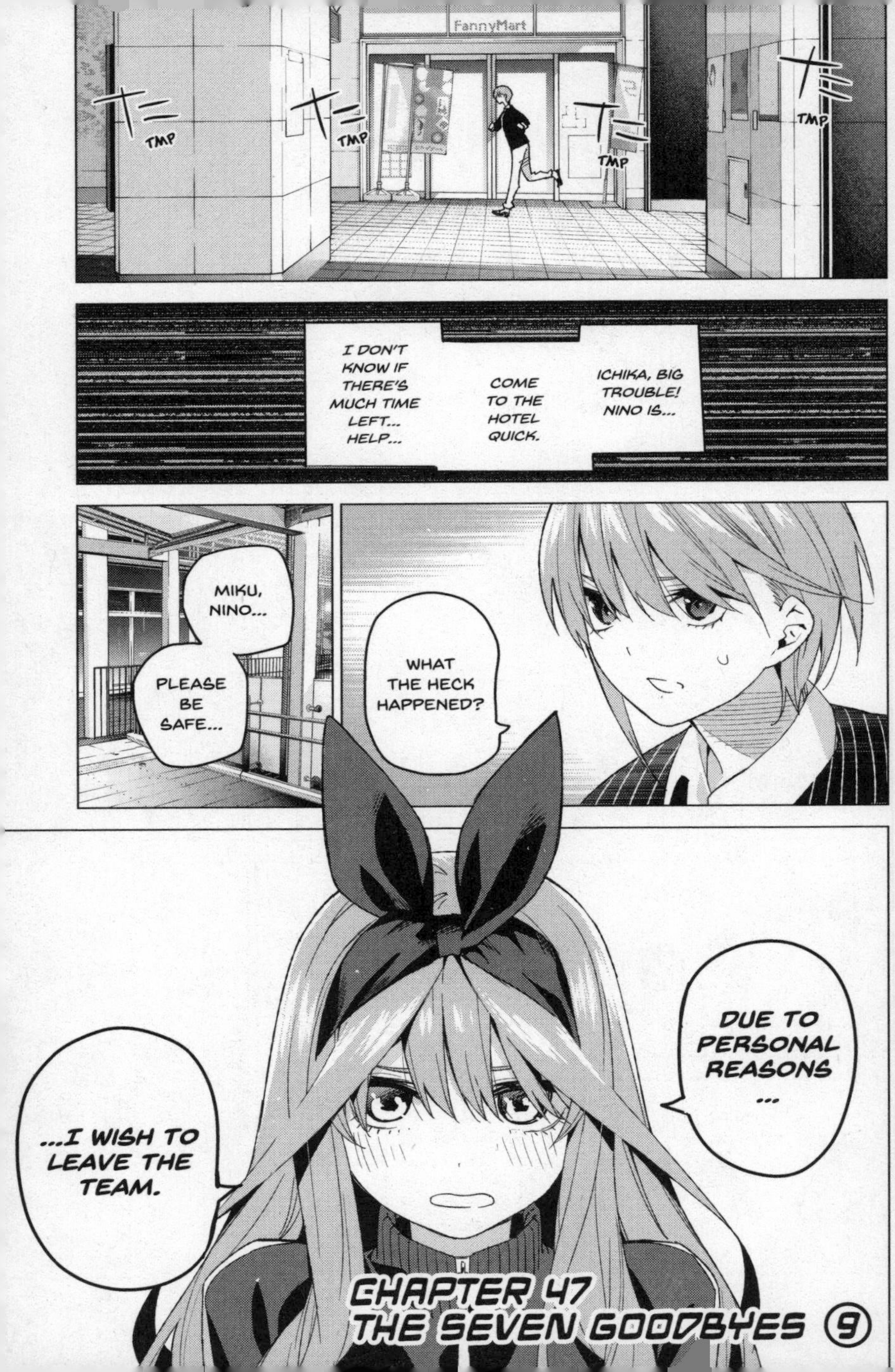
TMP
TMP
TMP
TMP
ICHIKA, BIG TROUBLE! NINO IS...
COME TO THE HOTEL QUICK.
I DON'T KNOW IF THERE'S MUCH TIME LEFT... HELP...
WHAT THE HECK HAPPENED?
MIKU, NINO...
PLEASE BE SAFE...
DUE TO PERSONAL REASONS ...
...I WISH TO LEAVE THE TEAM.
CHAPTER 47
THE SEVEN GOODBYES ⑨

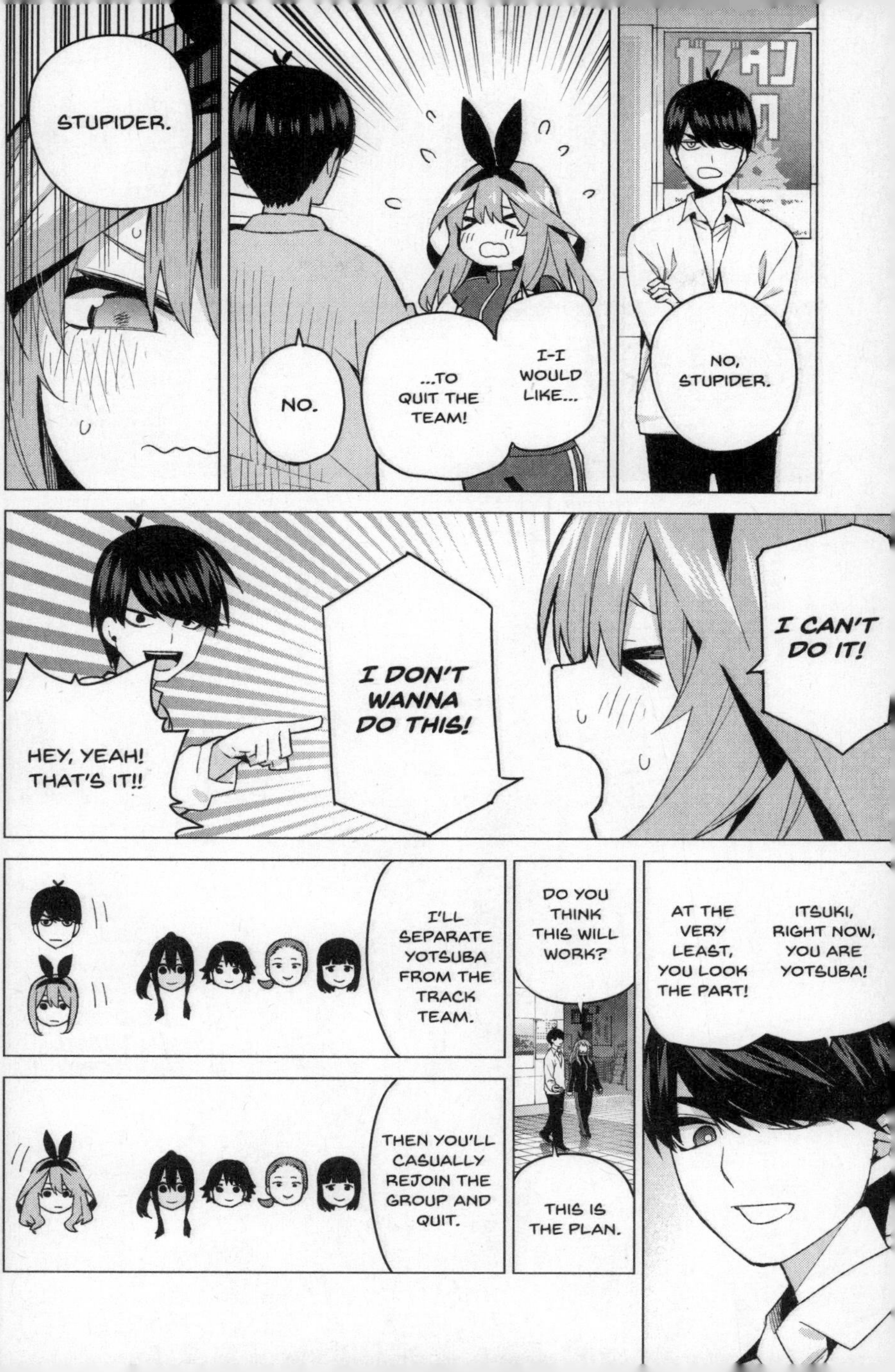
NO, STUPIDER.
I-I WOULD LIKE...
...TO QUIT THE TEAM!
NO.
STUPIDER.
I CAN'T DO IT!
I DON'T WANNA DO THIS!
HEY, YEAH! THAT'S IT!!
ITSUKI, RIGHT NOW, YOU ARE YOTSUBA!
AT THE VERY LEAST, YOU LOOK THE PART!
DO YOU THINK THIS WILL WORK?
THIS IS THE PLAN.
I'LL SEPARATE YOTSUBA FROM THE TRACK TEAM.
THEN YOU'LL CASUALLY REJOIN THE GROUP AND QUIT.

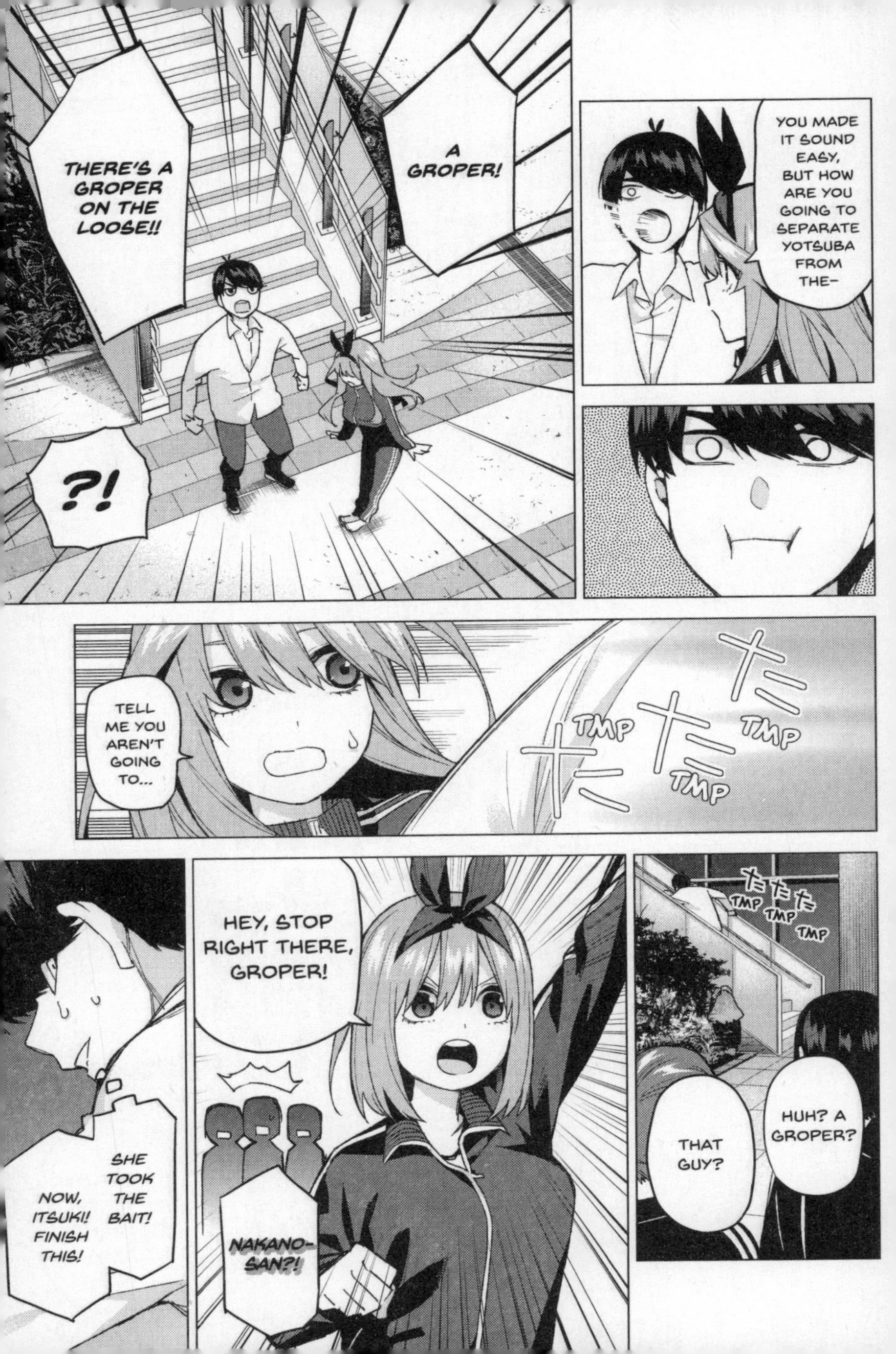
YOU MADE IT SOUND EASY, BUT HOW ARE YOU GOING TO SEPARATE YOTSUBA FROM THE-
A GROPER!
THERE'S A GROPER ON THE LOOSE!!
?!
TMP TMP TMP
TELL ME YOU AREN'T GOING TO...
たたた
TMP TMP TMP
HUH? A GROPER?
THAT GUY?
HEY, STOP RIGHT THERE, GROPER!
NAKANO-SAN?!
SHE TOOK THE BAIT!
NOW, ITSUKI! FINISH THIS!

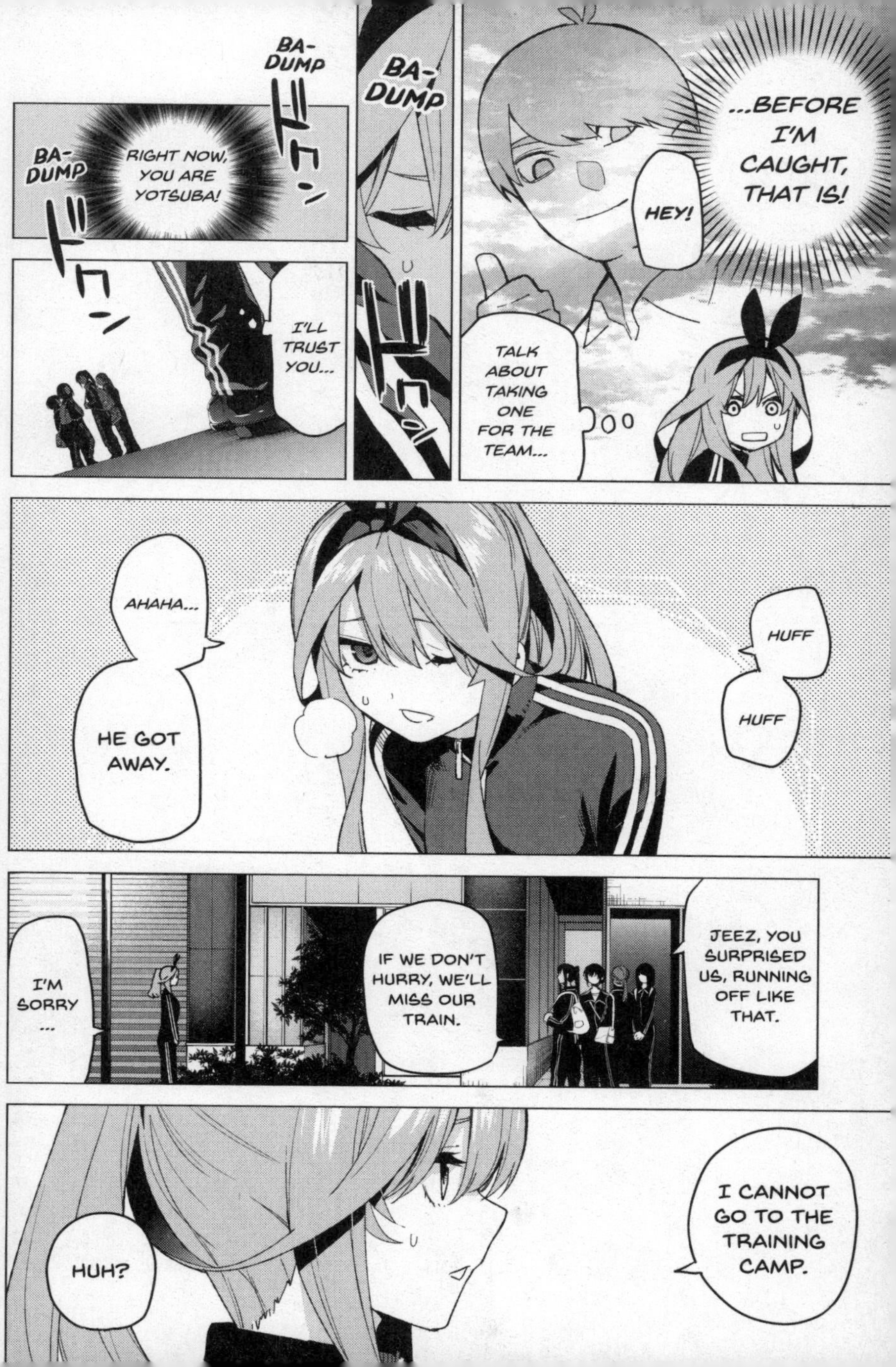
...BEFORE I'M CAUGHT, THAT IS!
HEY!
TALK ABOUT TAKING ONE FOR THE TEAM...
BA-DUMP
BA-DUMP
BA-DUMP
RIGHT NOW, YOU ARE YOTSUBA!
I'LL TRUST YOU...
HUFF
HUFF
AHAHA...
HE GOT AWAY.
JEEZ, YOU SURPRISED US, RUNNING OFF LIKE THAT.
IF WE DON'T HURRY, WE'LL MISS OUR TRAIN.
I'M SORRY ...
I CANNOT GO TO THE TRAINING CAMP.
HUH?

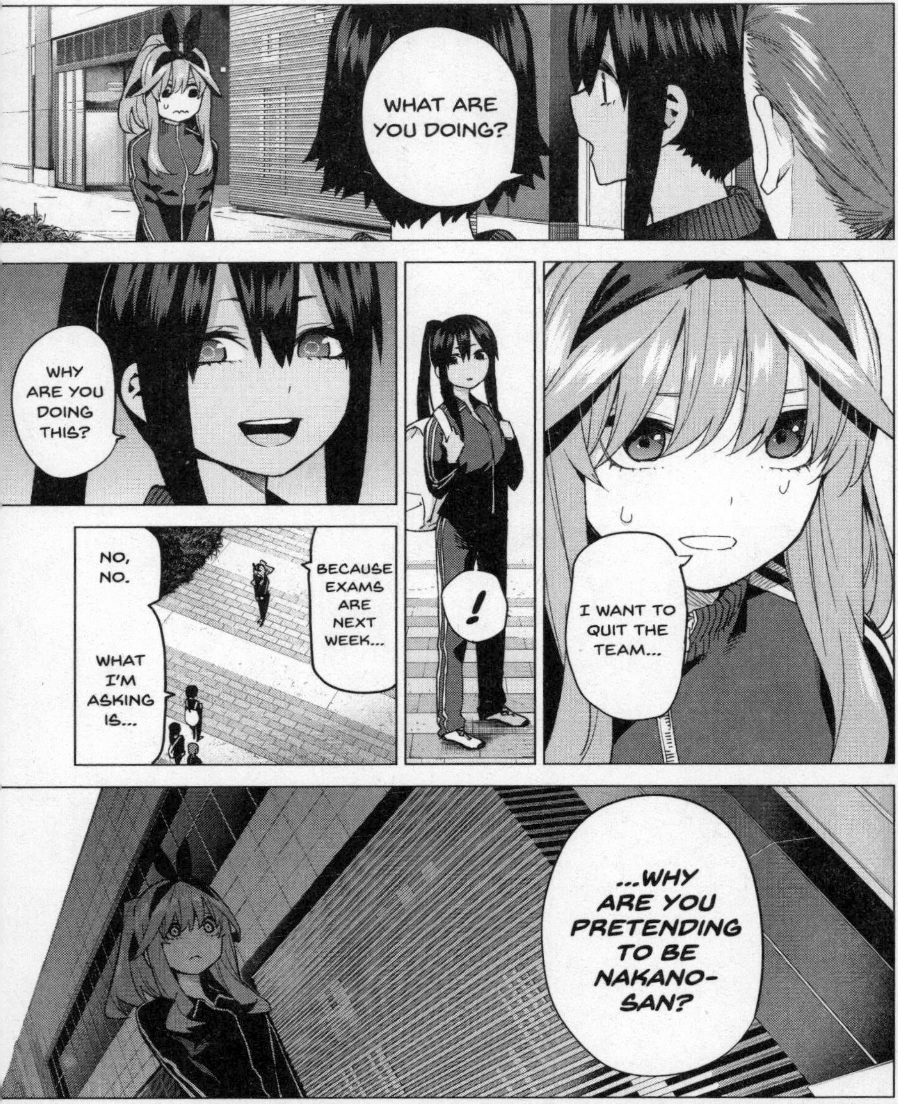
WHAT ARE YOU DOING?
I WANT TO QUIT THE TEAM...
!
WHY ARE YOU DOING THIS?
BECAUSE EXAMS ARE NEXT WEEK...
NO, NO.
WHAT I'M ASKING IS...
...WHY ARE YOU PRETENDING TO BE NAKANO-SAN?

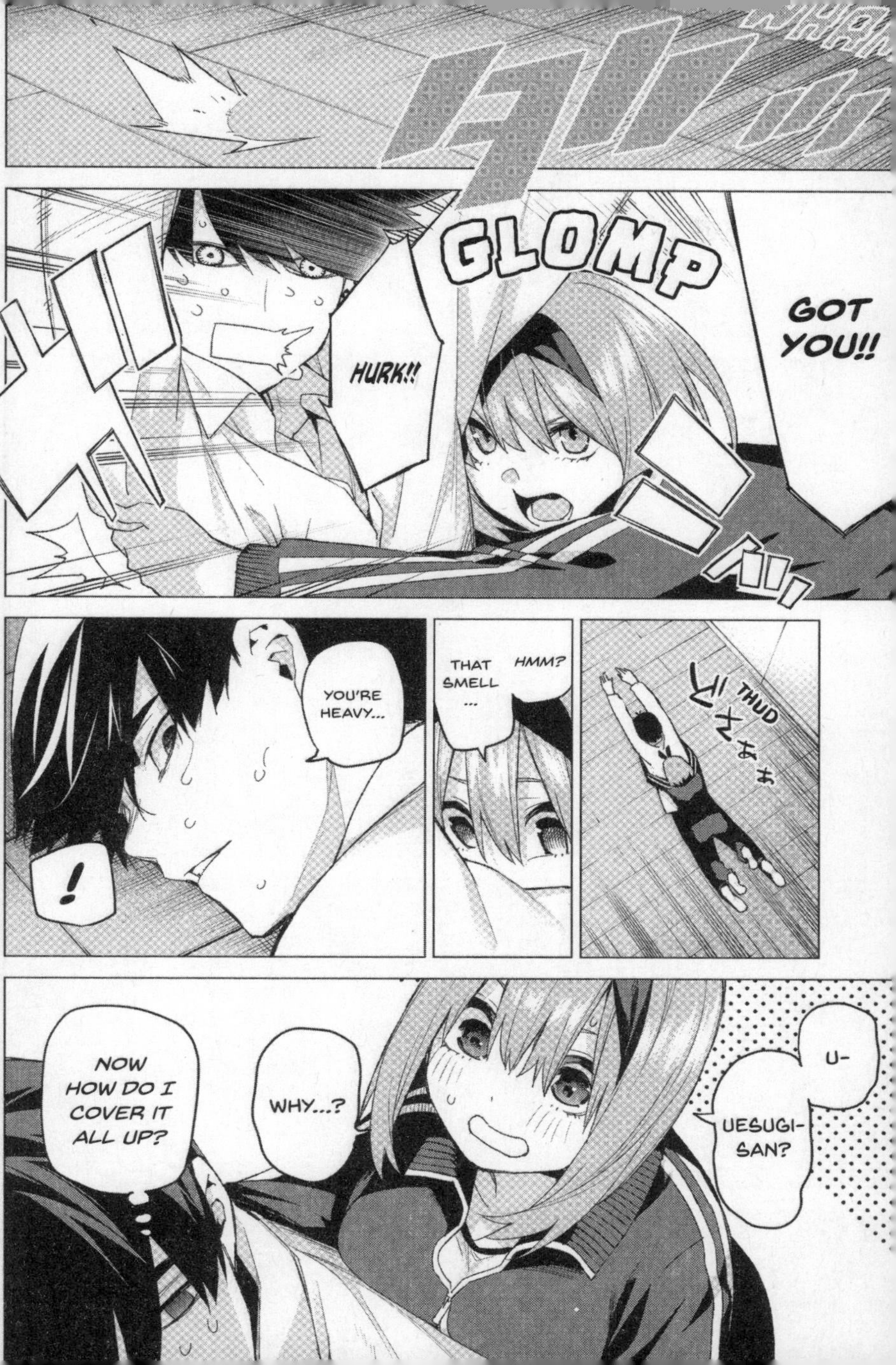
GLOMP
GOT YOU!!
HURK!!
THUD
HMM?
THAT SMELL ...
YOU'RE HEAVY...
!
U-
UESUGI-SAN?
WHY...?
NOW HOW DO I COVER IT ALL UP?

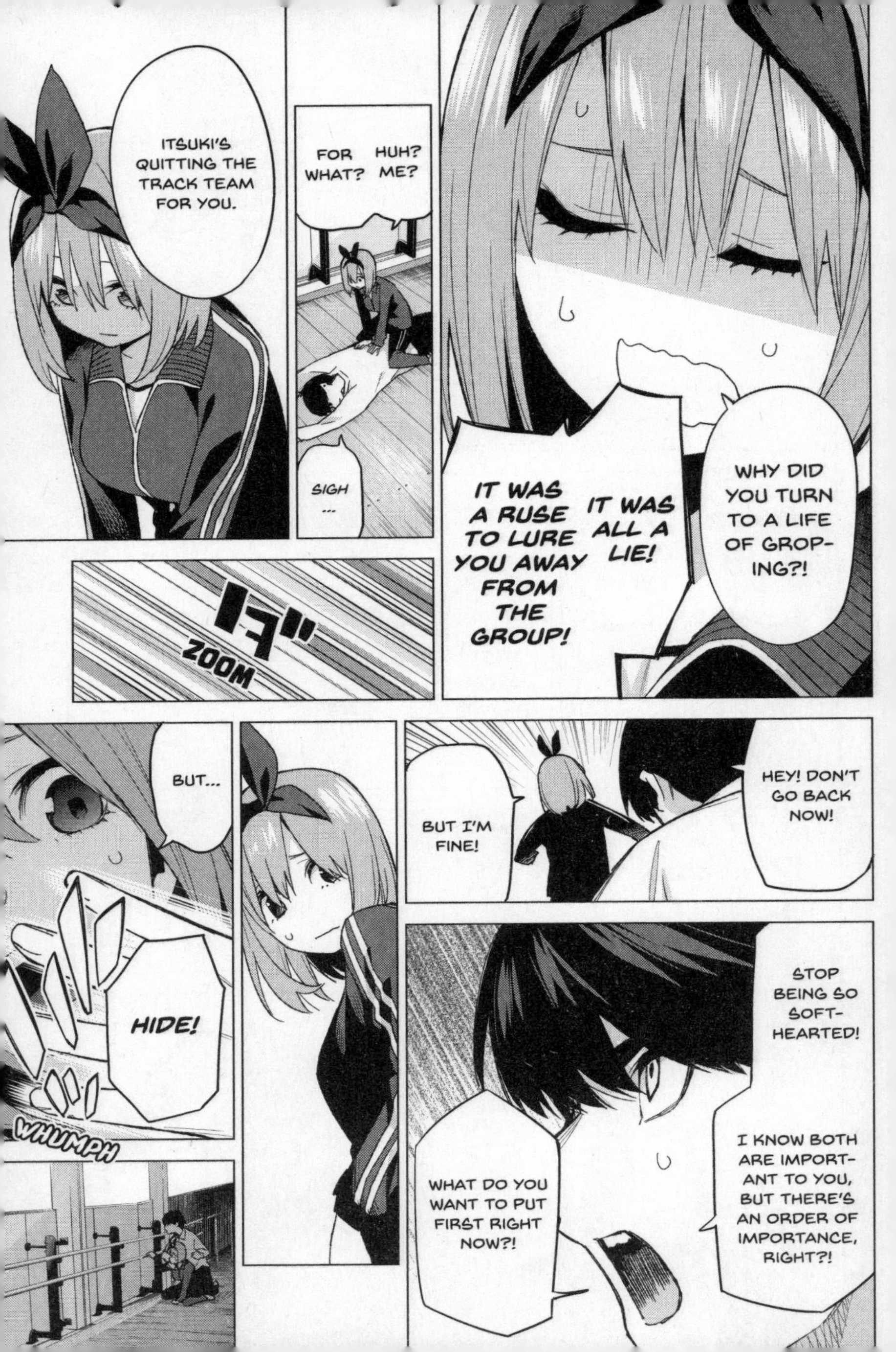
WHY DID YOU TURN TO A LIFE OF GROP-ING?!
IT WAS ALL A LIE!
IT WAS A RUSE TO LURE YOU AWAY FROM THE GROUP!
HUH? ME?
FOR WHAT?
SIGH ...
ITSUKI'S QUITTING THE TRACK TEAM FOR YOU.
ZOOM
HEY! DON'T GO BACK NOW!
BUT I'M FINE!
STOP BEING SO SOFT-HEARTED!
I KNOW BOTH ARE IMPORT-ANT TO YOU, BUT THERE'S AN ORDER OF IMPORTANCE, RIGHT?!
WHAT DO YOU WANT TO PUT FIRST RIGHT NOW?!
BUT...
HIDE!
WHUMPH

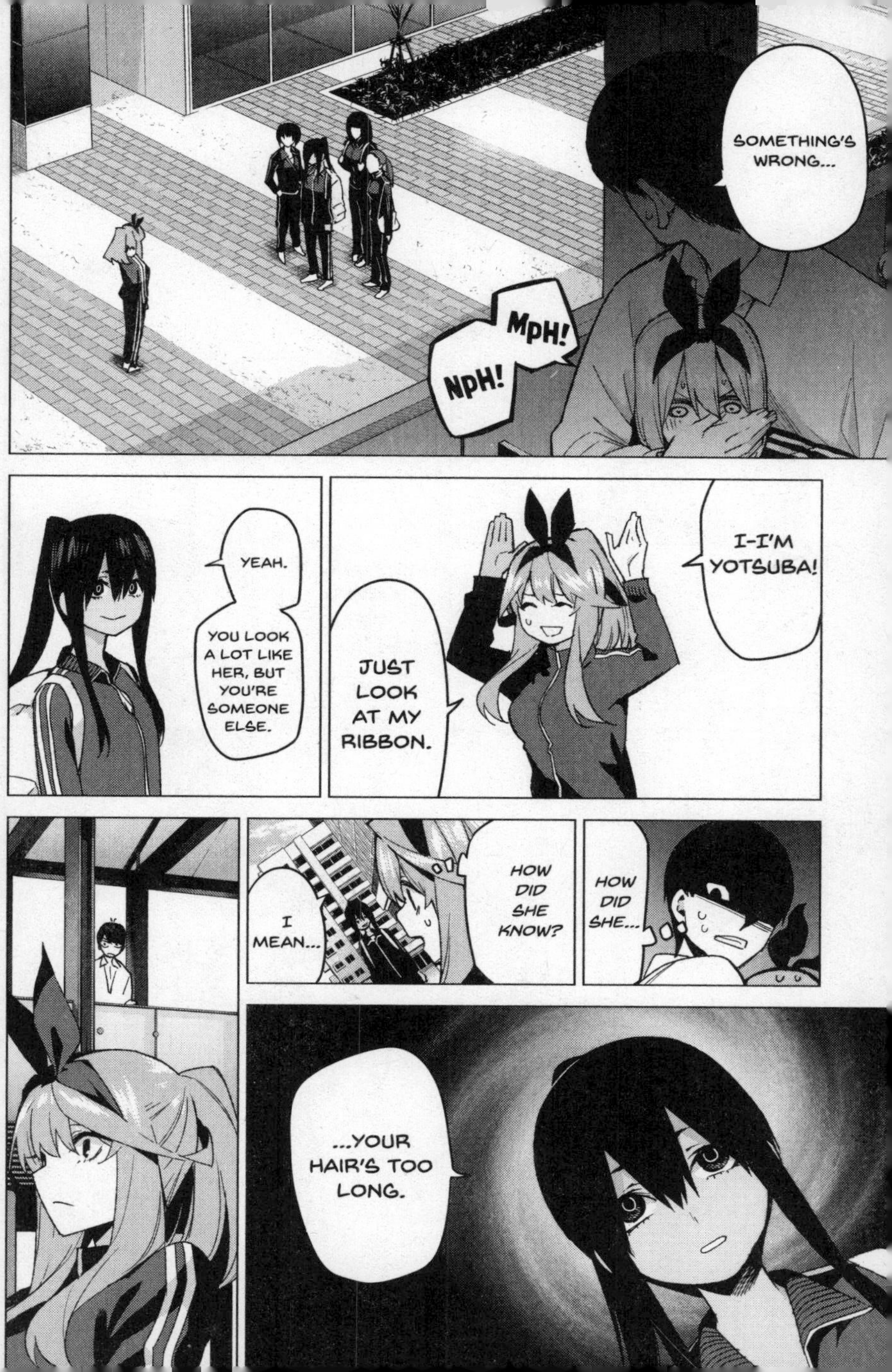
SOMETHING'S WRONG...
MPH!
NPH!
I-I'M YOTSUBA!
JUST LOOK AT MY RIBBON.
YEAH.
YOU LOOK A LOT LIKE HER, BUT YOU'RE SOMEONE ELSE.
HOW DID SHE...
HOW DID SHE KNOW?
I MEAN...
...YOUR HAIR'S TOO LONG.

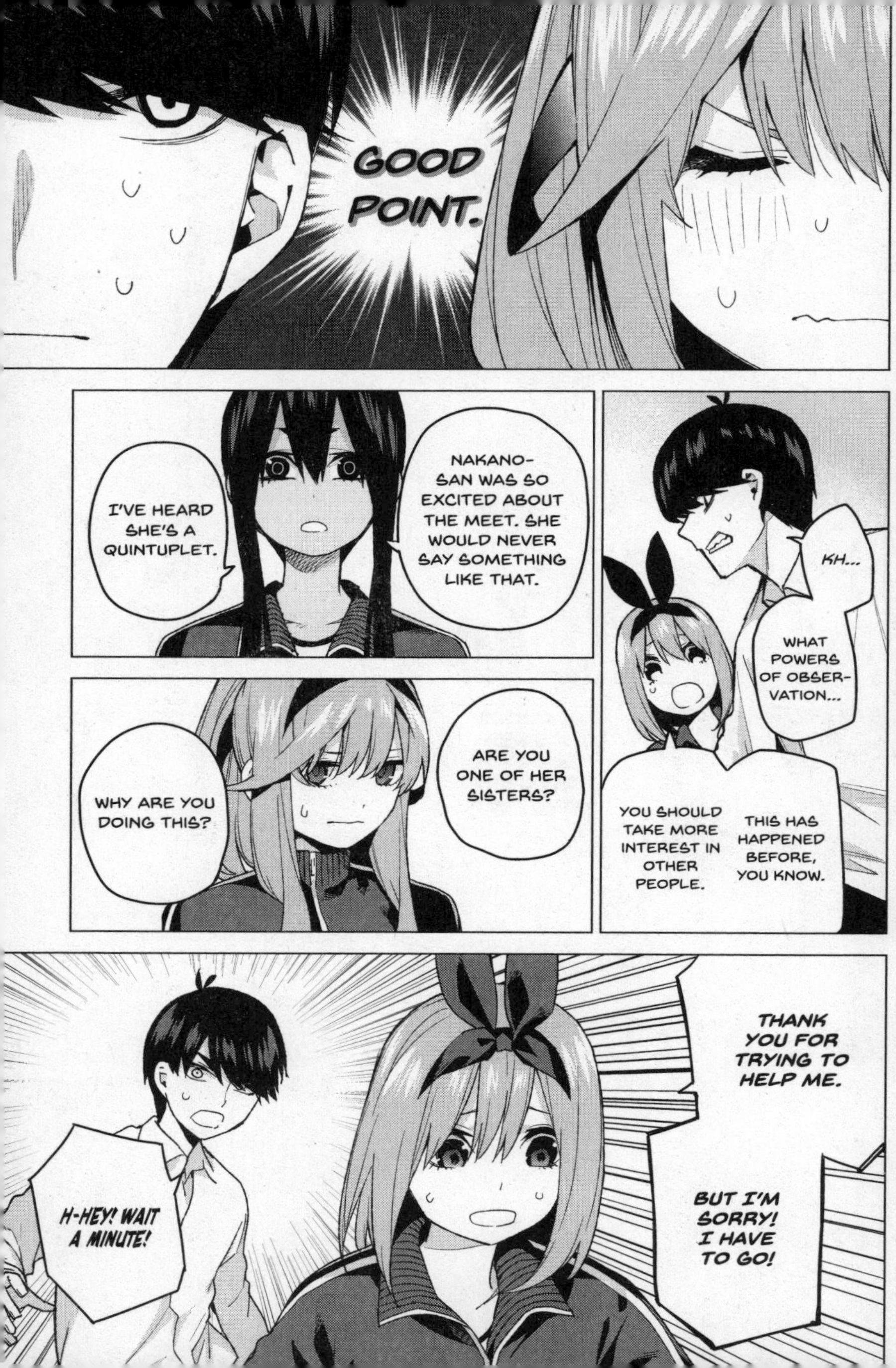
GOOD POINT.
KH...
WHAT POWERS OF OBSERVATION...
THIS HAS HAPPENED BEFORE, YOU KNOW.
YOU SHOULD TAKE MORE INTEREST IN OTHER PEOPLE.
NAKANO-SAN WAS SO EXCITED ABOUT THE MEET. SHE WOULD NEVER SAY SOMETHING LIKE THAT.
I'VE HEARD SHE'S A QUINTUPLET.
ARE YOU ONE OF HER SISTERS?
WHY ARE YOU DOING THIS?
THANK YOU FOR TRYING TO HELP ME.
BUT I'M SORRY! I HAVE TO GO!
H-HEY! WAIT A MINUTE!

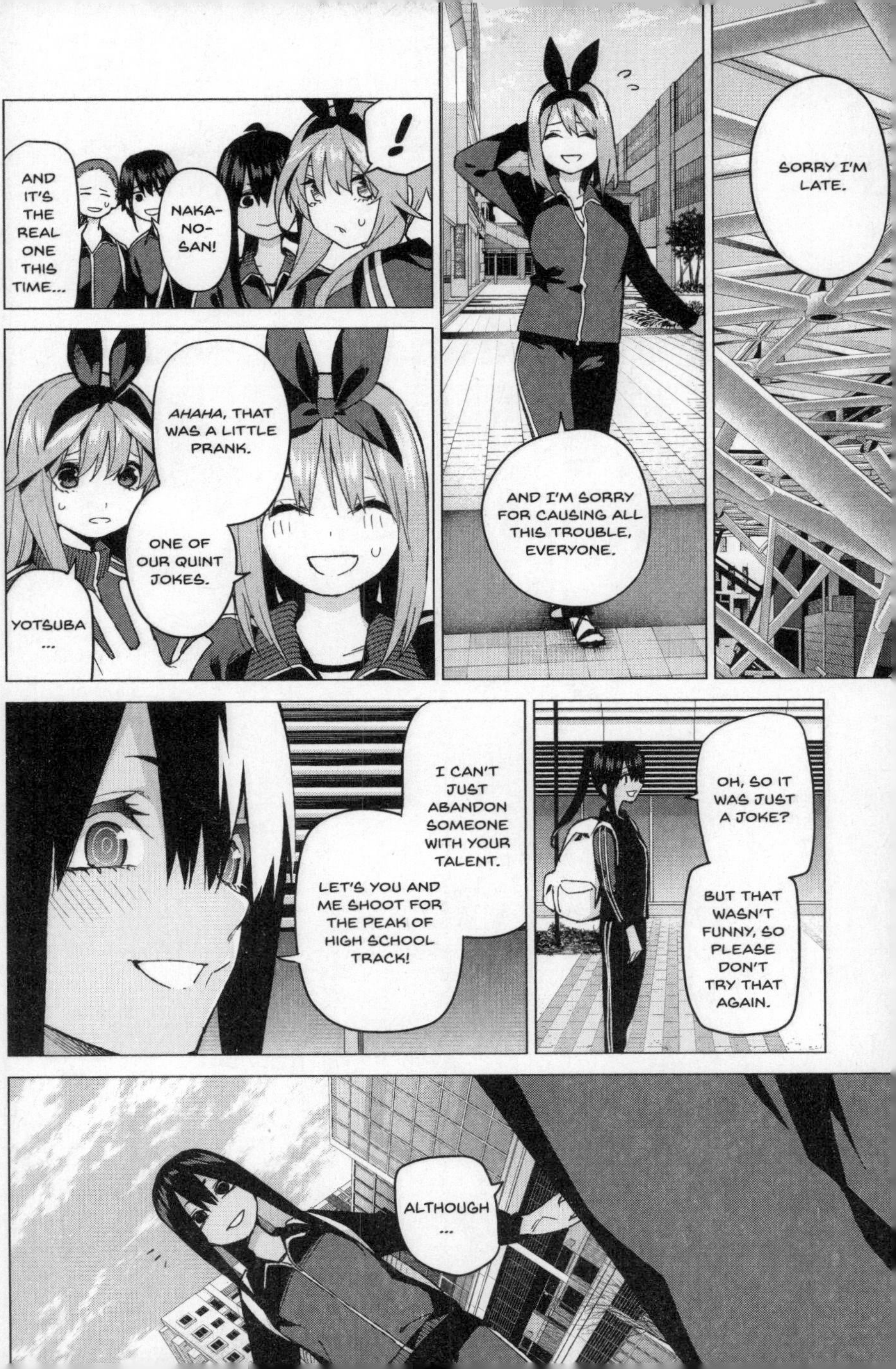
SORRY I'M LATE.
AND I'M SORRY FOR CAUSING ALL THIS TROUBLE, EVERYONE.
!
NAKA-NO-SAN!
AND IT'S THE REAL ONE THIS TIME...
*AHAHA*, THAT WAS A LITTLE PRANK.
ONE OF OUR QUINT JOKES.
YOTSUBA...
OH, SO IT WAS JUST A JOKE?
BUT THAT WASN'T FUNNY, SO PLEASE DON'T TRY THAT AGAIN.
I CAN'T JUST ABANDON SOMEONE WITH YOUR TALENT.
LET'S YOU AND ME SHOOT FOR THE PEAK OF HIGH SCHOOL TRACK!
ALTHOUGH...

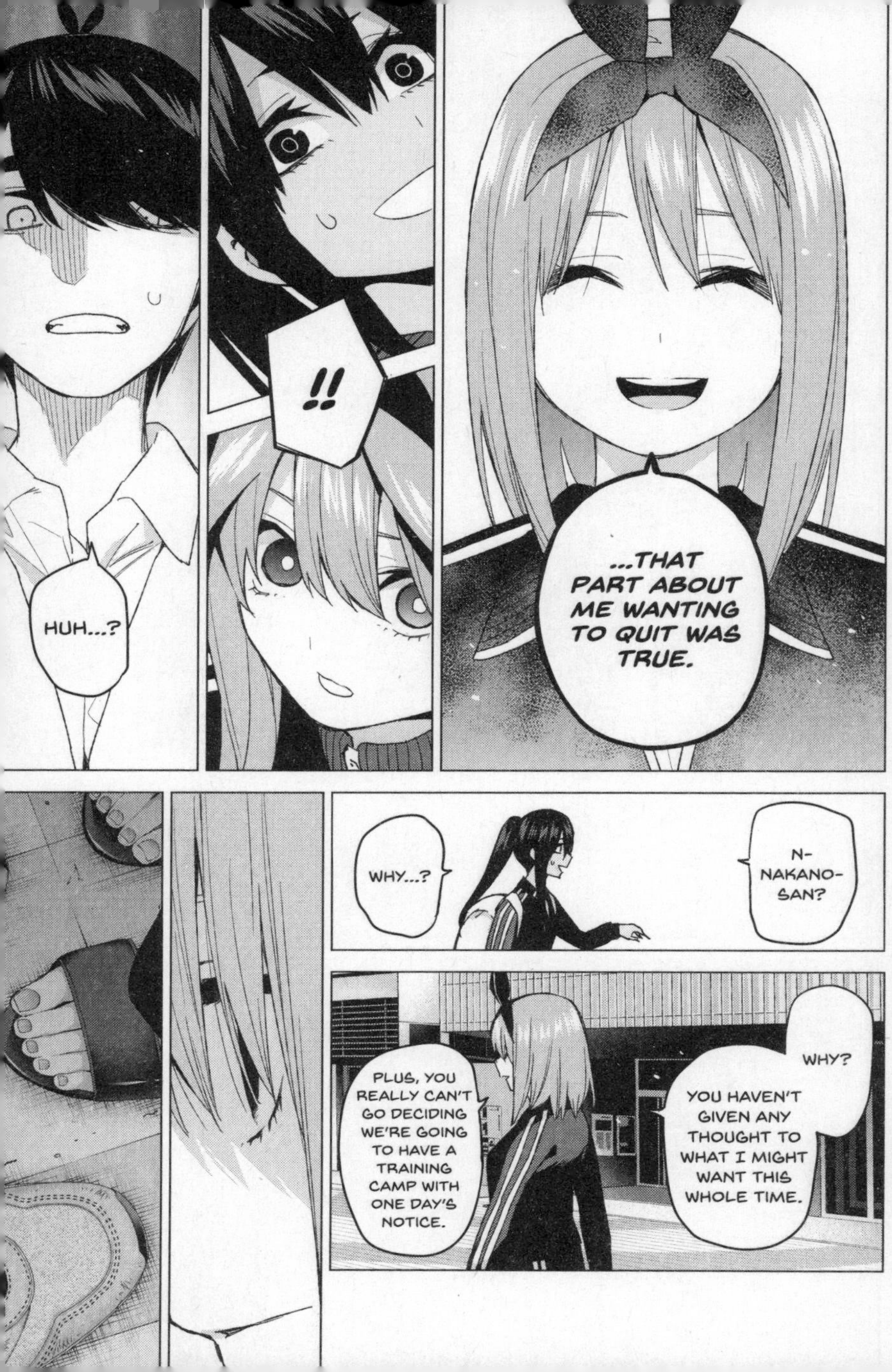
...THAT PART ABOUT ME WANTING TO QUIT WAS TRUE.
!!
HUH...?
N-NAKANO-SAN?
WHY...?
WHY? YOU HAVEN'T GIVEN ANY THOUGHT TO WHAT I MIGHT WANT THIS WHOLE TIME.
PLUS, YOU REALLY CAN'T GO DECIDING WE'RE GOING TO HAVE A TRAINING CAMP WITH ONE DAY'S NOTICE.

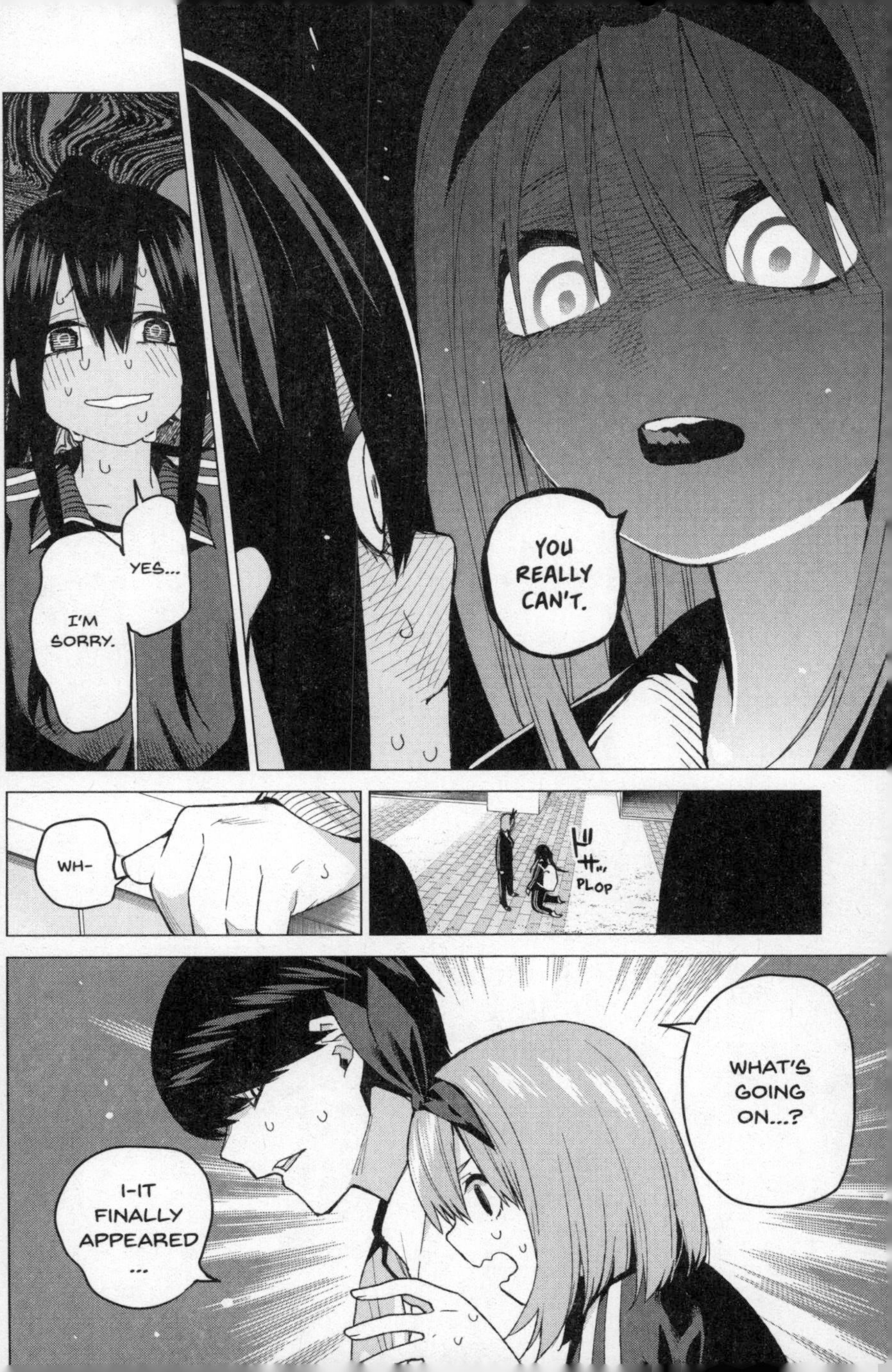
YOU REALLY CAN'T.
YES...
I'M SORRY.
PLOP
WH-
WHAT'S GOING ON...?
I-IT FINALLY APPEARED ...

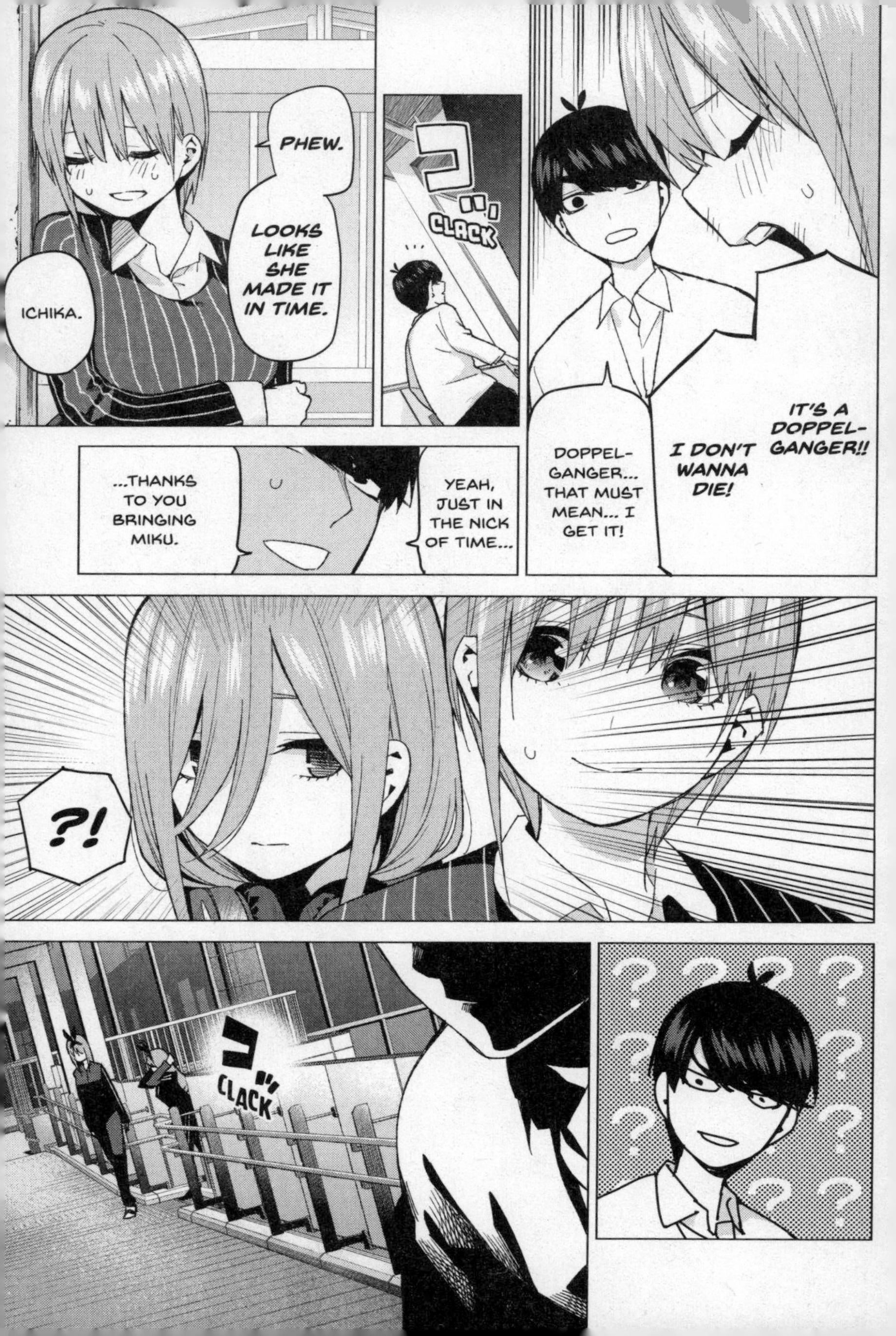

IT'S A DOPPEL-GANGER!!
I DON'T WANNA DIE!
DOPPEL-GANGER... THAT MUST MEAN... I GET IT!
CLACK
PHEW.
LOOKS LIKE SHE MADE IT IN TIME.
ICHIKA.
YEAH, JUST IN THE NICK OF TIME...
...THANKS TO YOU BRINGING MIKU.
?!
CLACK

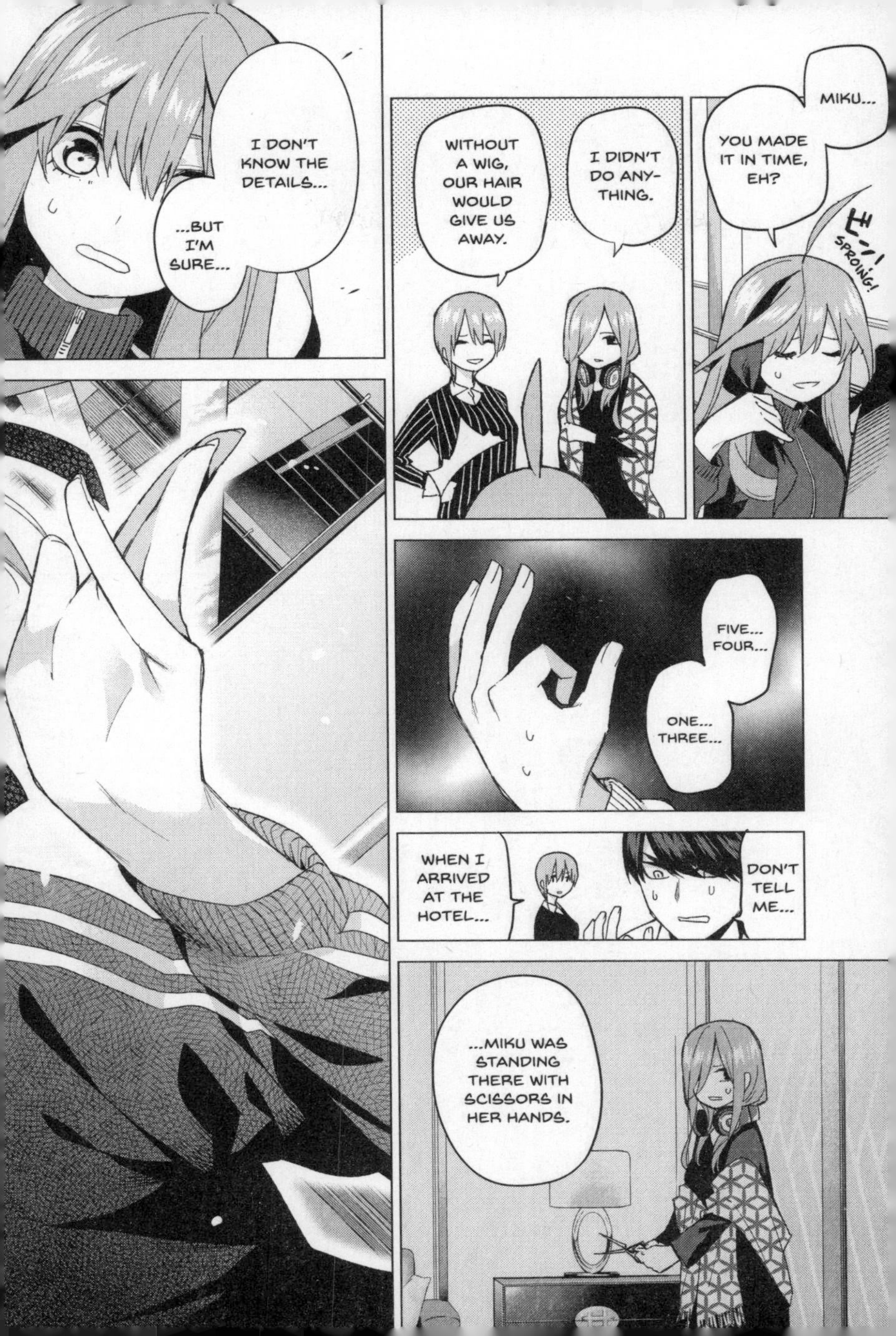

MIKU...
YOU MADE IT IN TIME, EH?
SPROING!
I DIDN'T DO ANY-THING.
WITHOUT A WIG, OUR HAIR WOULD GIVE US AWAY.
I DON'T KNOW THE DETAILS...
...BUT I'M SURE...
FIVE... FOUR...
ONE... THREE...
DON'T TELL ME...
WHEN I ARRIVED AT THE HOTEL...
...MIKU WAS STANDING THERE WITH SCISSORS IN HER HANDS.

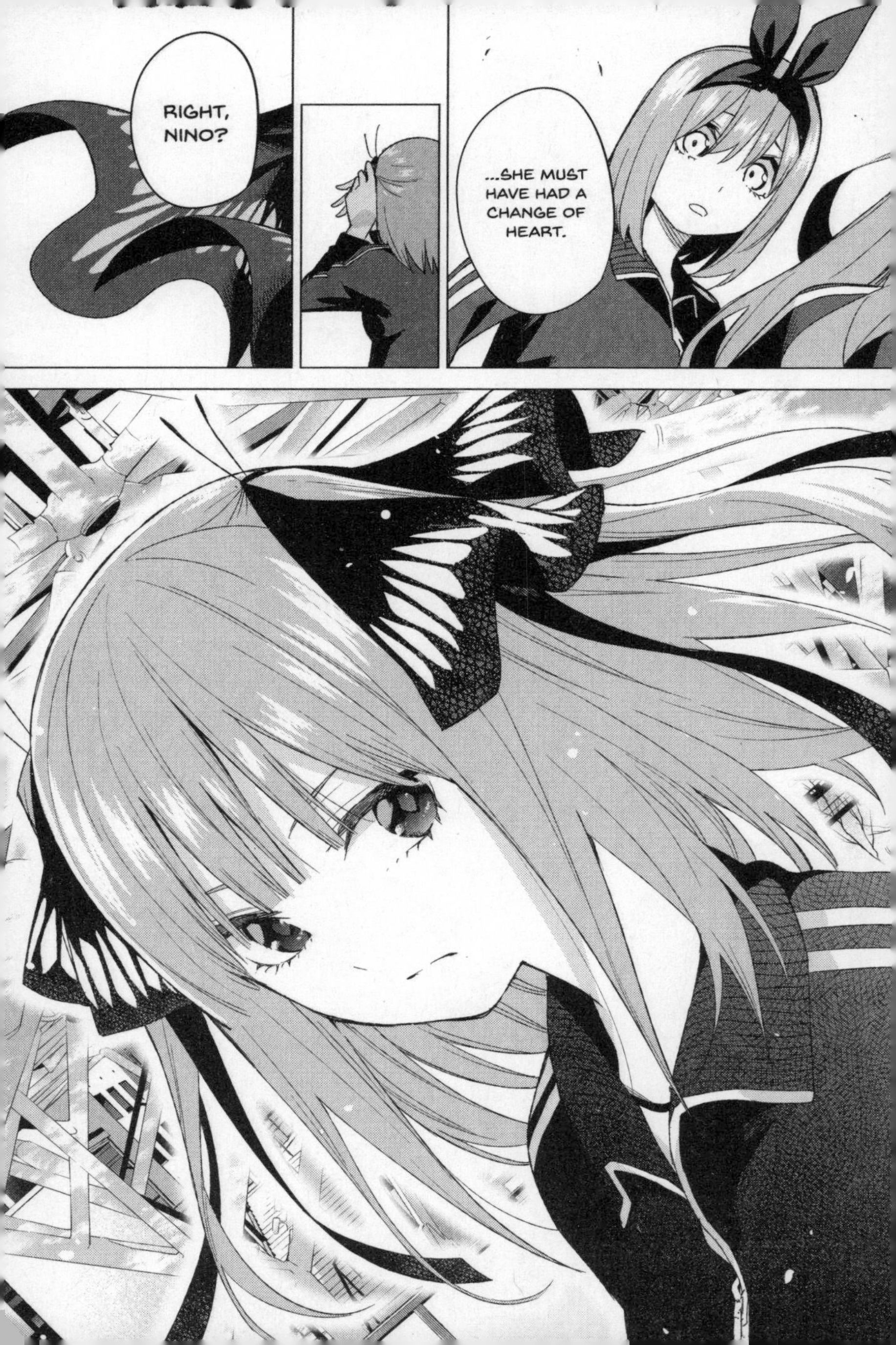
...SHE MUST HAVE HAD A CHANGE OF HEART.
RIGHT, NINO?

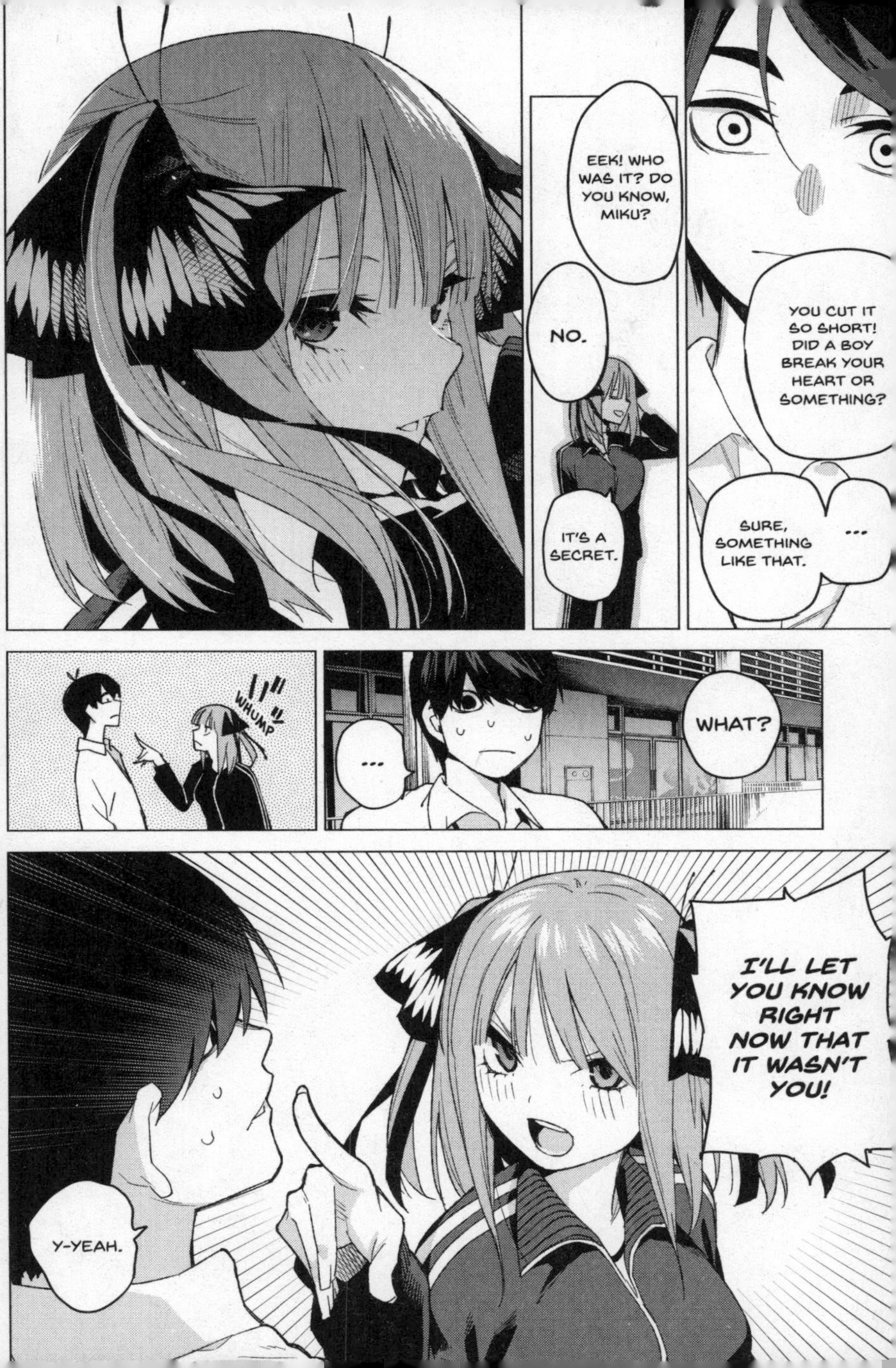
YOU CUT IT SO SHORT! DID A BOY BREAK YOUR HEART OR SOMETHING?
...
SURE, SOMETHING LIKE THAT.
EEK! WHO WAS IT? DO YOU KNOW, MIKU?
NO.
IT'S A SECRET.
WHAT?
...
WHUMP
I'LL LET YOU KNOW RIGHT NOW THAT IT WASN'T YOU!
Y-YEAH.

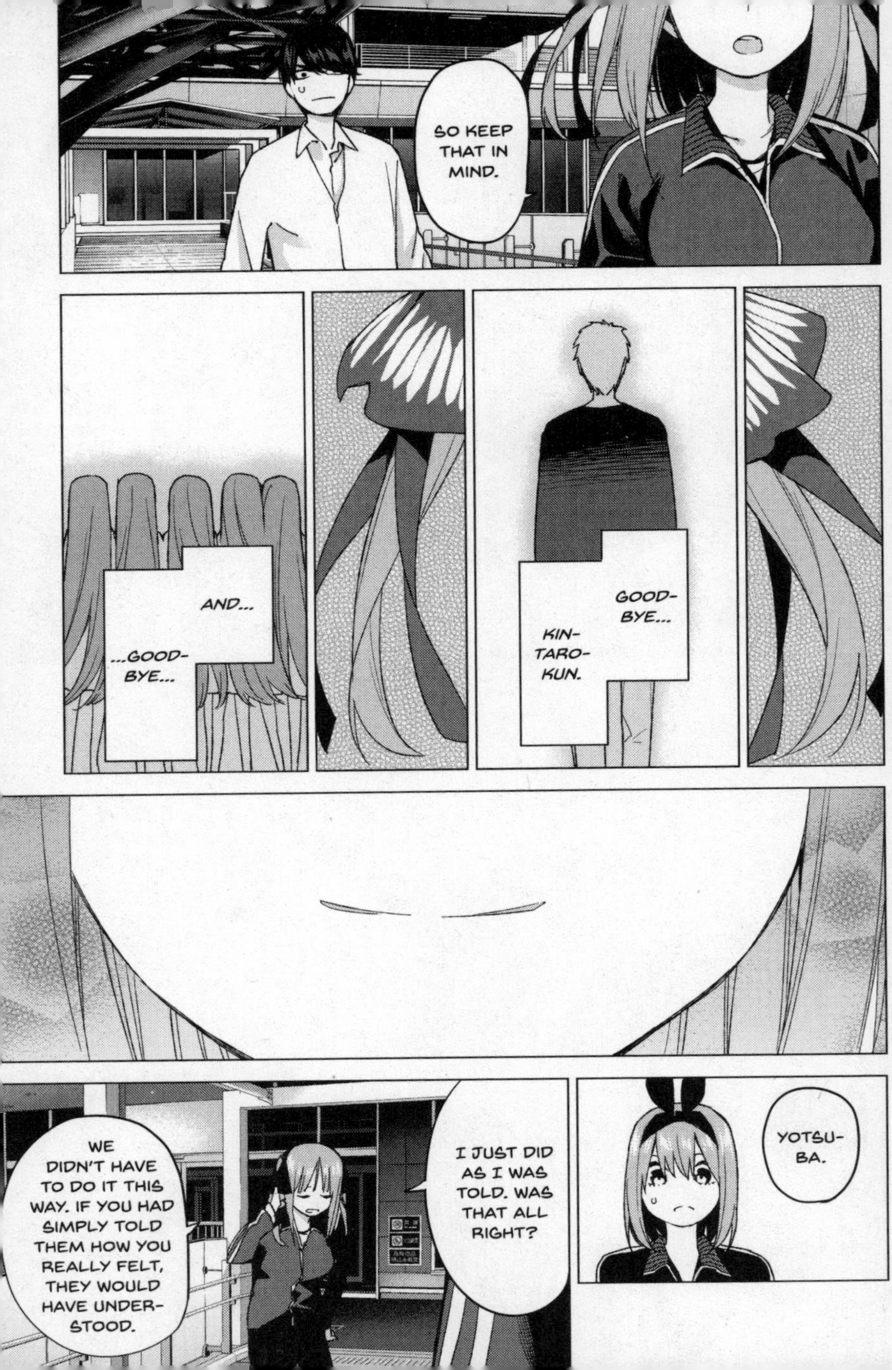
SO KEEP THAT IN MIND.
GOOD-BYE...
KIN-TARO-KUN.
AND...
...GOOD-BYE...
YOTSU-BA.
I JUST DID AS I WAS TOLD. WAS THAT ALL RIGHT?
WE DIDN'T HAVE TO DO IT THIS WAY. IF YOU HAD SIMPLY TOLD THEM HOW YOU REALLY FELT, THEY WOULD HAVE UNDER-STOOD.

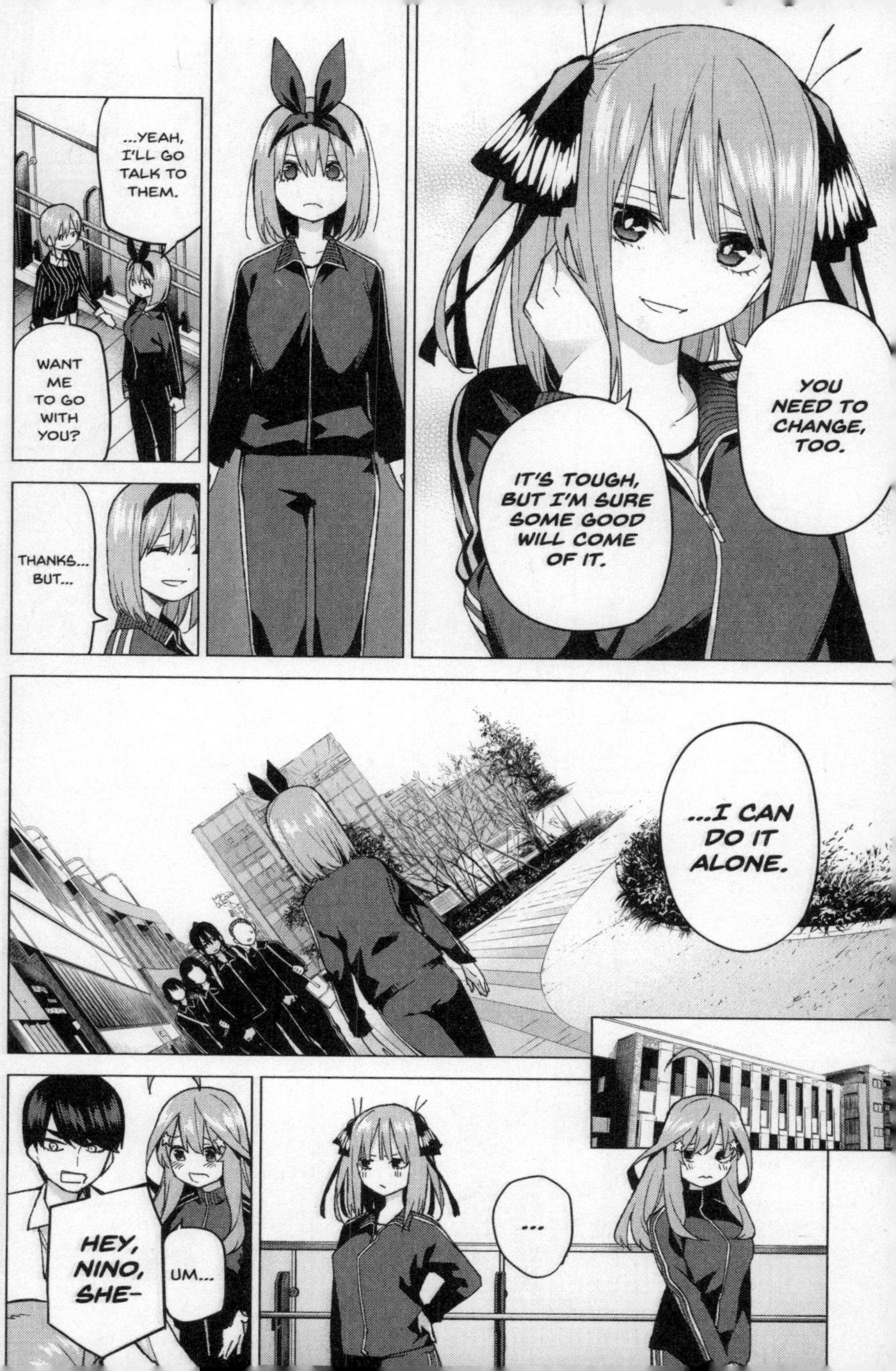
YOU NEED TO CHANGE, TOO.
IT'S TOUGH, BUT I'M SURE SOME GOOD WILL COME OF IT.
...YEAH, I'LL GO TALK TO THEM.
WANT ME TO GO WITH YOU?
THANKS... BUT...
...I CAN DO IT ALONE.
...
UM...
HEY, NINO, SHE-

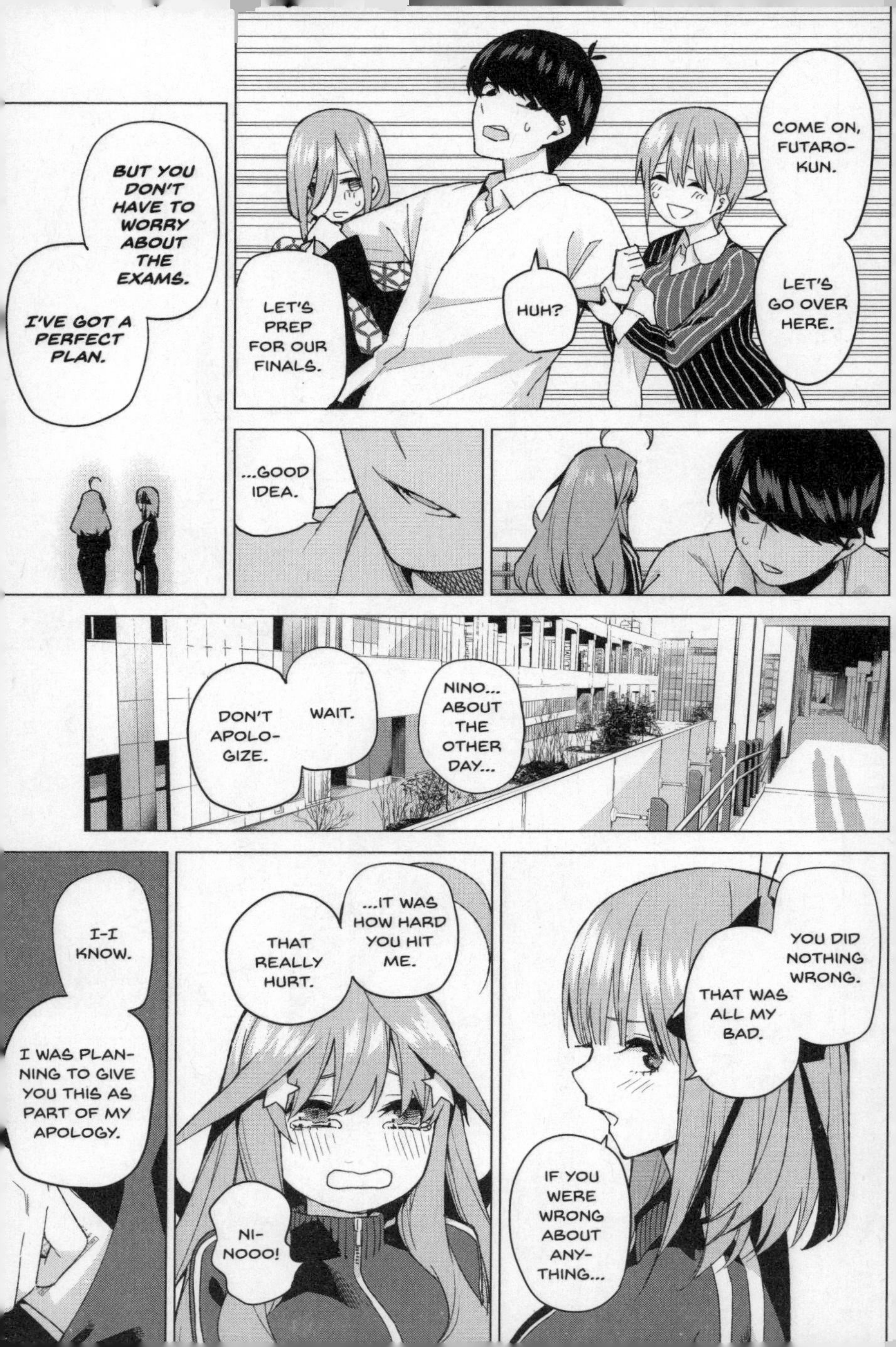
COME ON, FUTARO-KUN.
LET'S GO OVER HERE.
HUH?
LET'S PREP FOR OUR FINALS.
...GOOD IDEA.
BUT YOU DON'T HAVE TO WORRY ABOUT THE EXAMS.
I'VE GOT A PERFECT PLAN.
NINO... ABOUT THE OTHER DAY...
WAIT.
DON'T APOLO-GIZE.
YOU DID NOTHING WRONG.
THAT WAS ALL MY BAD.
IF YOU WERE WRONG ABOUT ANY-THING...
...IT WAS HOW HARD YOU HIT ME.
THAT REALLY HURT.
NI-NOOO!
I-I KNOW.
I WAS PLAN-NING TO GIVE YOU THIS AS PART OF MY APOLOGY.

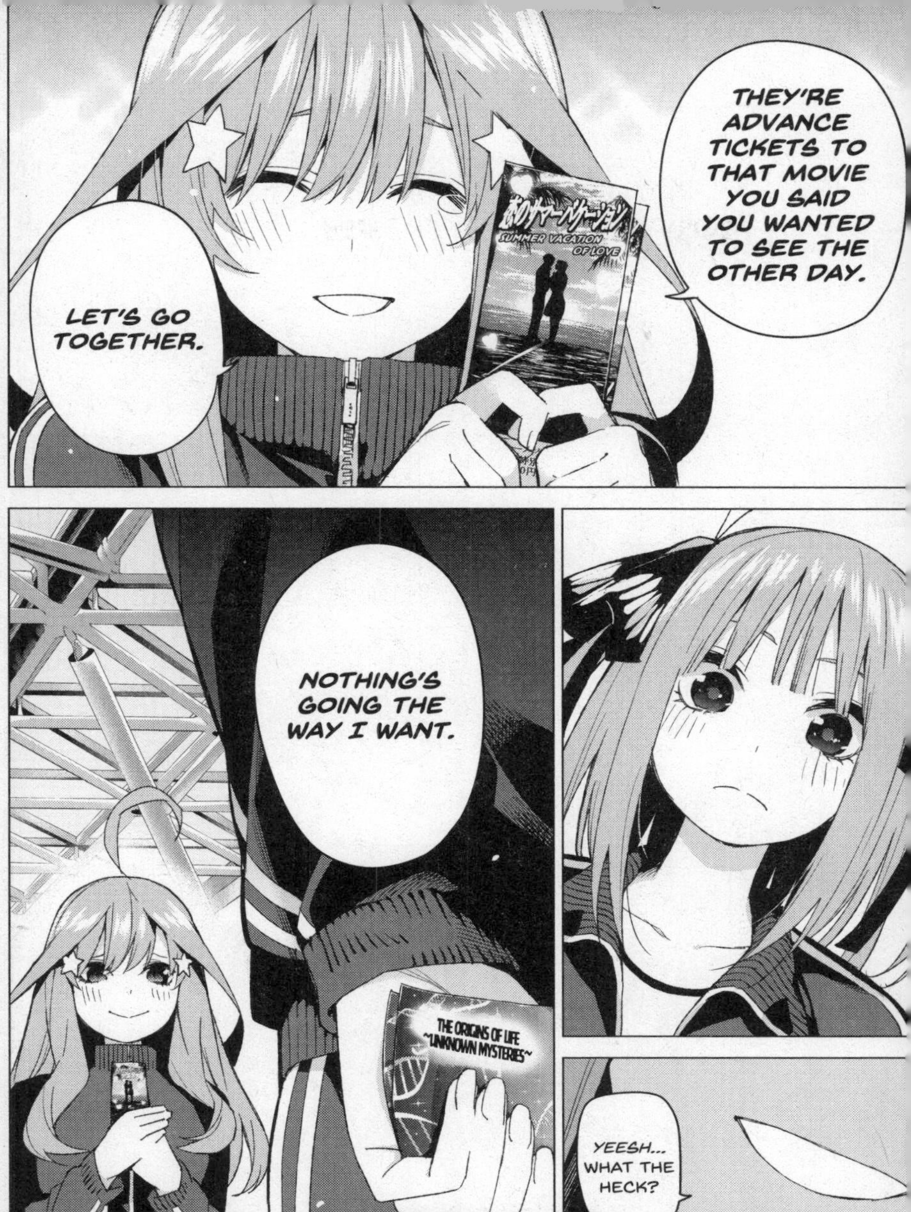
THEY'RE ADVANCE TICKETS TO THAT MOVIE YOU SAID YOU WANTED TO SEE THE OTHER DAY.
SUMMER VACATION OF LOVE
LET'S GO TOGETHER.
YEESH... WHAT THE HECK?
NOTHING'S GOING THE WAY I WANT.
THE ORIGINS OF LIFE ~UNKNOWN MYSTERIES~

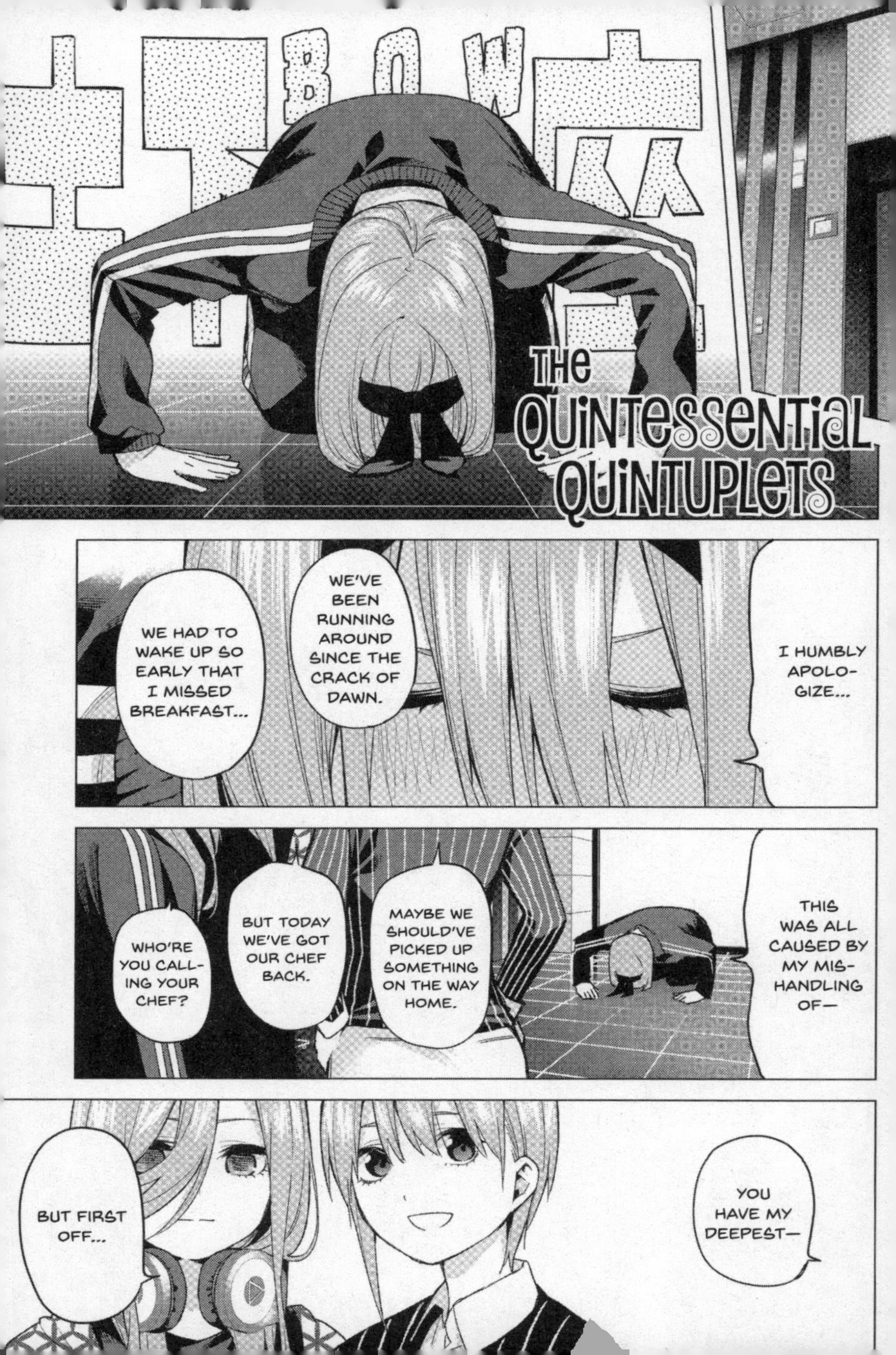
BOW
THE QUINTESSENTIAL QUINTUPLETS
I HUMBLY APOLO-GIZE...
WE'VE BEEN RUNNING AROUND SINCE THE CRACK OF DAWN.
WE HAD TO WAKE UP SO EARLY THAT I MISSED BREAKFAST...
THIS WAS ALL CAUSED BY MY MIS-HANDLING OF—
MAYBE WE SHOULD'VE PICKED UP SOMETHING ON THE WAY HOME.
BUT TODAY WE'VE GOT OUR CHEF BACK.
WHO'RE YOU CALL-ING YOUR CHEF?
YOU HAVE MY DEEPEST—
BUT FIRST OFF...

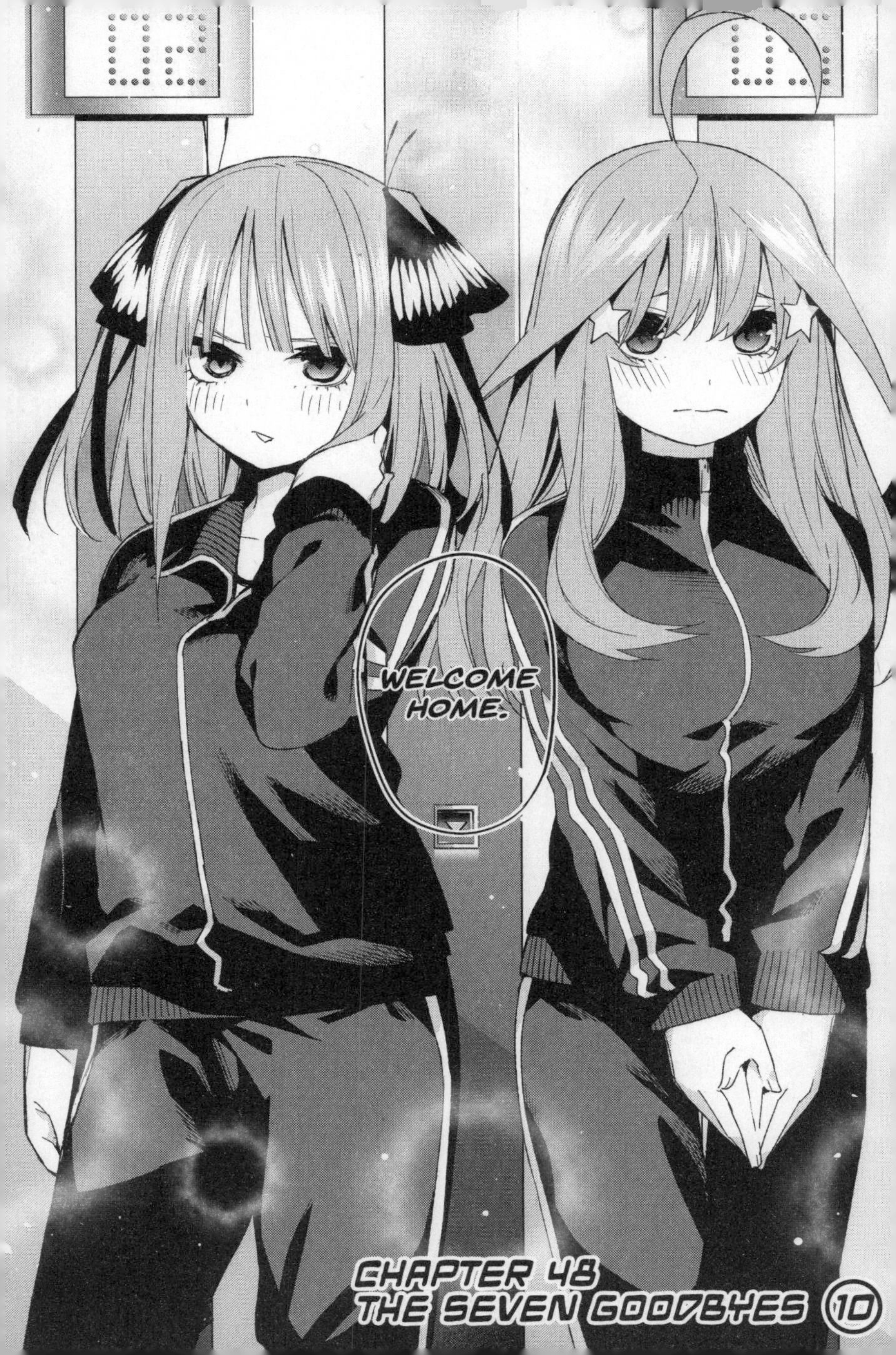
WELCOME HOME.
CHAPTER 48
THE SEVEN GOODBYES 10

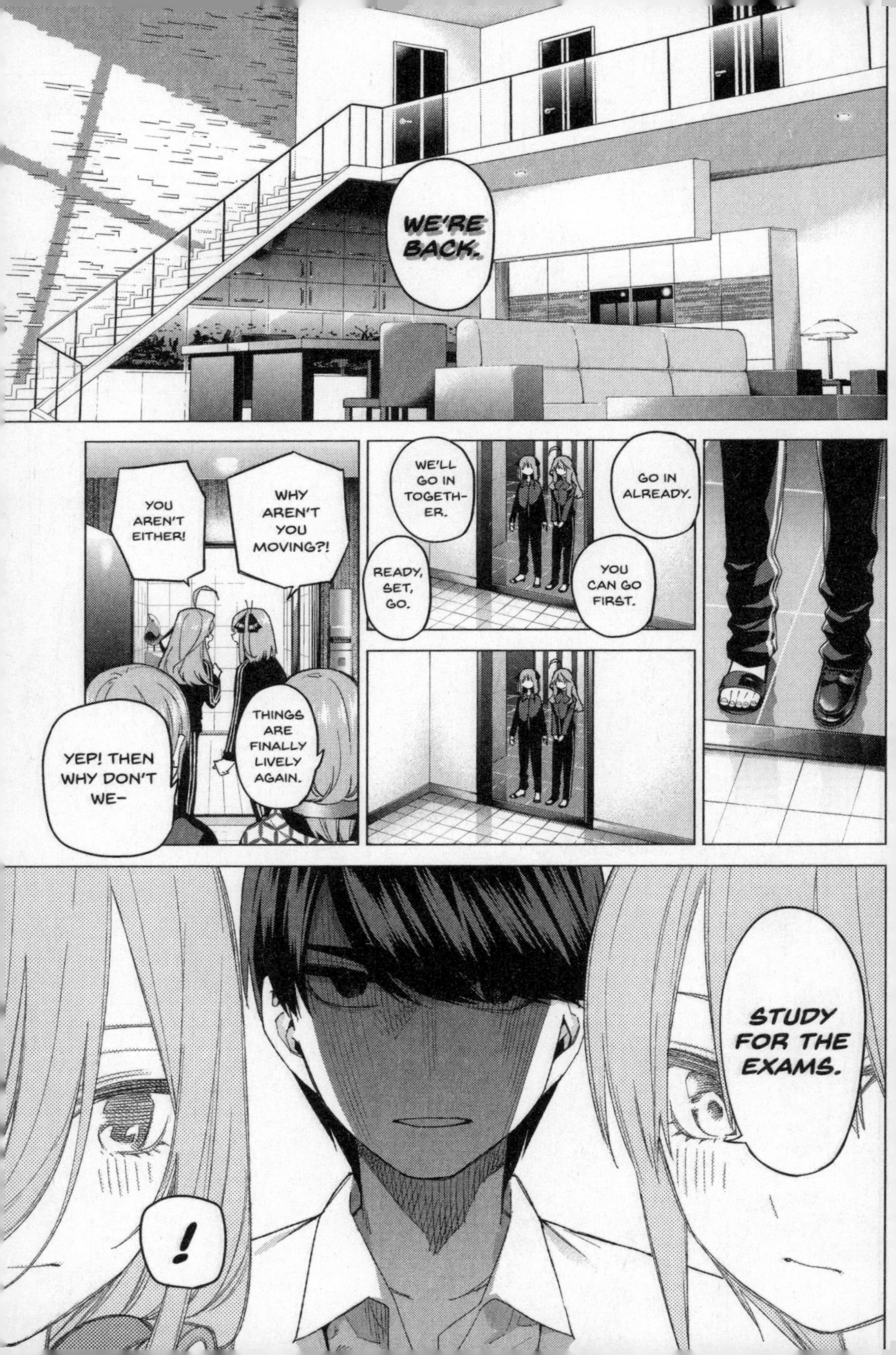
WE'RE BACK.
GO IN ALREADY.
WE'LL GO IN TOGETH-ER.
YOU CAN GO FIRST.
READY, SET, GO.
WHY AREN'T YOU MOVING?!
YOU AREN'T EITHER!
THINGS ARE FINALLY LIVELY AGAIN.
YEP! THEN WHY DON'T WE-
STUDY FOR THE EXAMS.
!

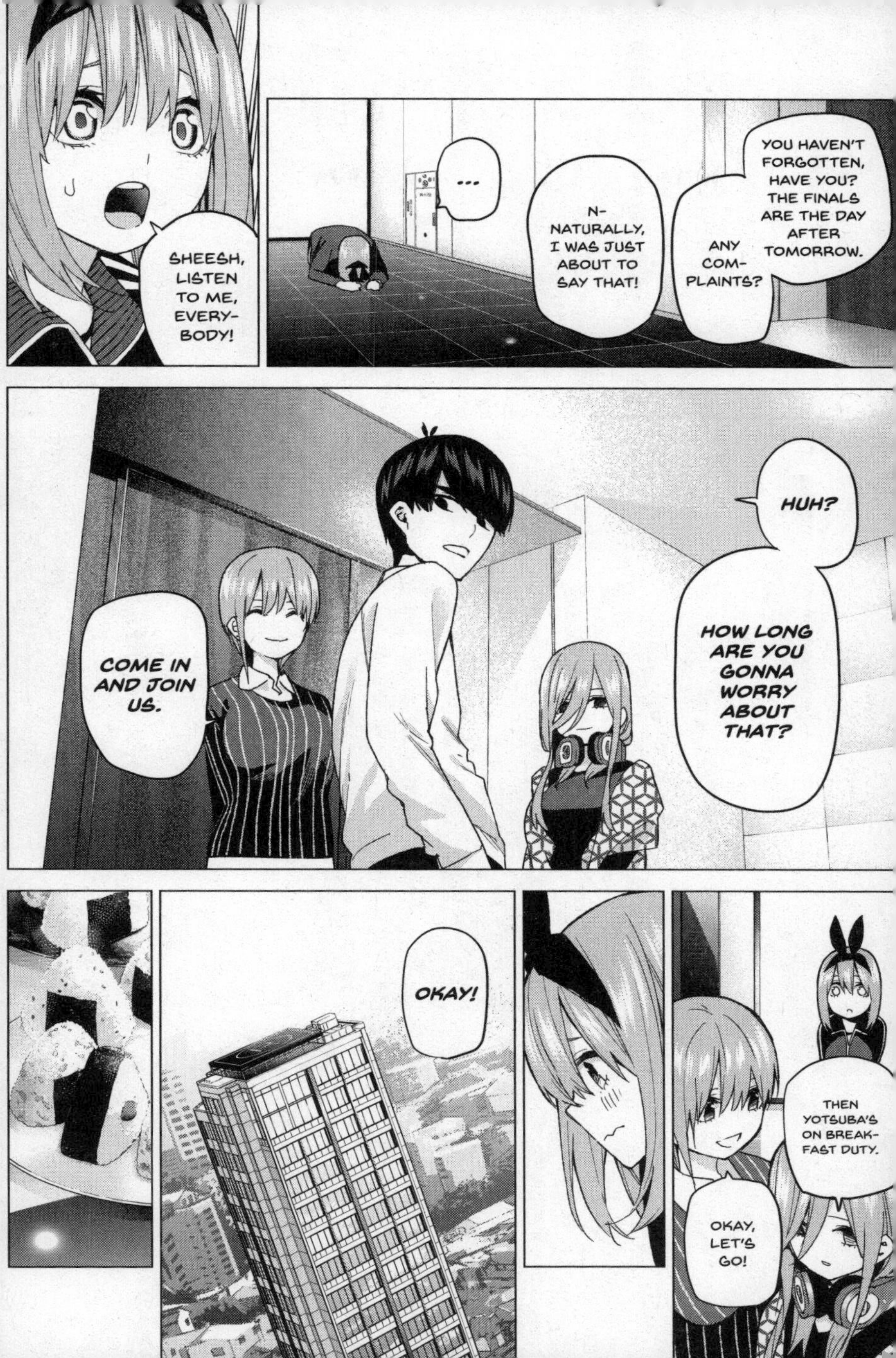
YOU HAVEN'T FORGOTTEN, HAVE YOU? THE FINALS ARE THE DAY AFTER TOMORROW.
ANY COM-PLAINTS?
N- NATURALLY, I WAS JUST ABOUT TO SAY THAT!
...
SHEESH, LISTEN TO ME, EVERY-BODY!
HUH?
HOW LONG ARE YOU GONNA WORRY ABOUT THAT?
COME IN AND JOIN US.
THEN YOTSUBA'S ON BREAK-FAST DUTY.
OKAY, LET'S GO!
OKAY!

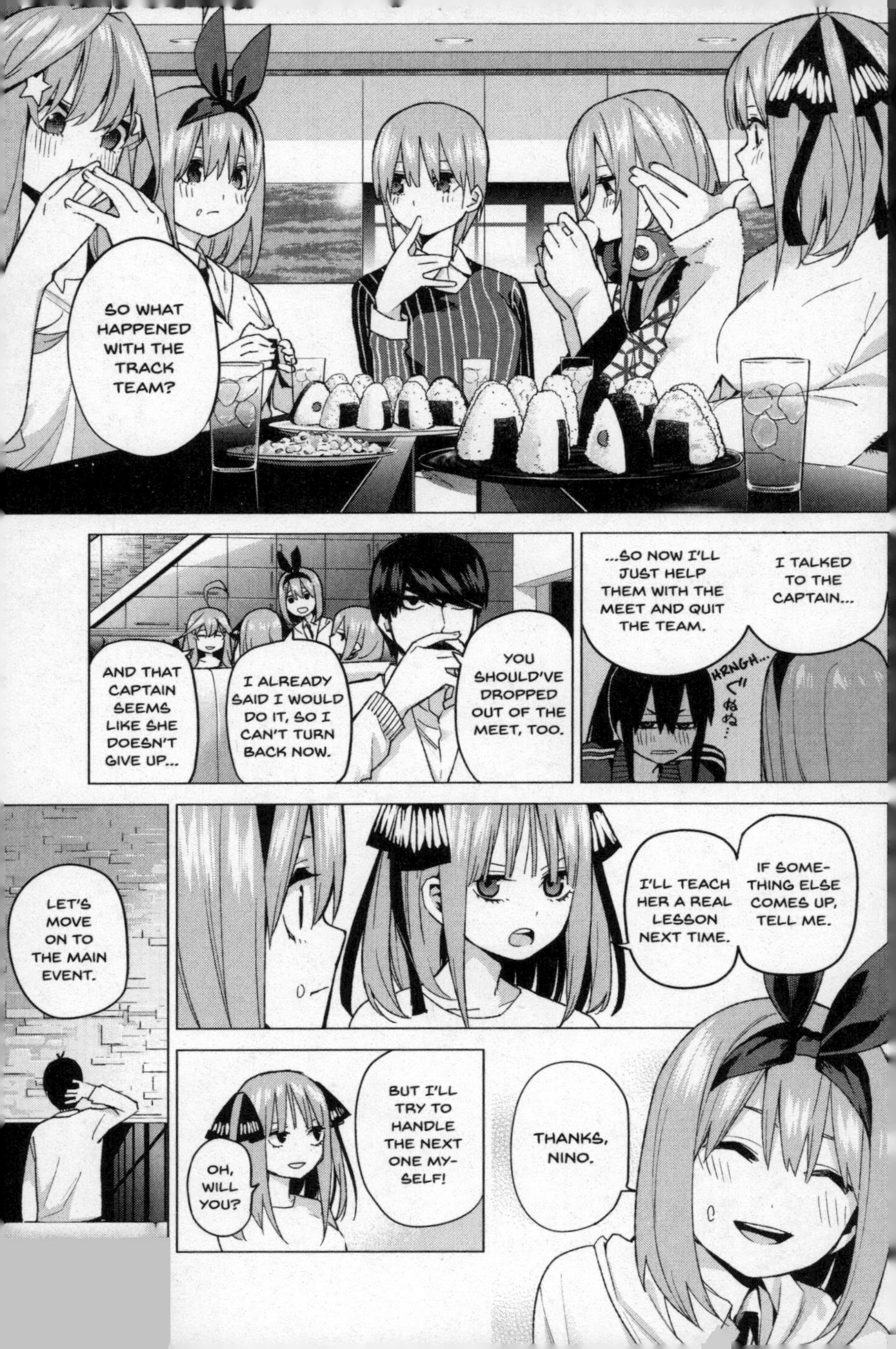
SO WHAT HAPPENED WITH THE TRACK TEAM?
I TALKED TO THE CAPTAIN...
...SO NOW I'LL JUST HELP THEM WITH THE MEET AND QUIT THE TEAM.
HRNGH...
ぐぬぬ...
YOU SHOULD'VE DROPPED OUT OF THE MEET, TOO.
I ALREADY SAID I WOULD DO IT, SO I CAN'T TURN BACK NOW.
AND THAT CAPTAIN SEEMS LIKE SHE DOESN'T GIVE UP...
IF SOME-THING ELSE COMES UP, TELL ME.
I'LL TEACH HER A REAL LESSON NEXT TIME.
THANKS, NINO.
BUT I'LL TRY TO HANDLE THE NEXT ONE MY-SELF!
OH, WILL YOU?
LET'S MOVE ON TO THE MAIN EVENT.

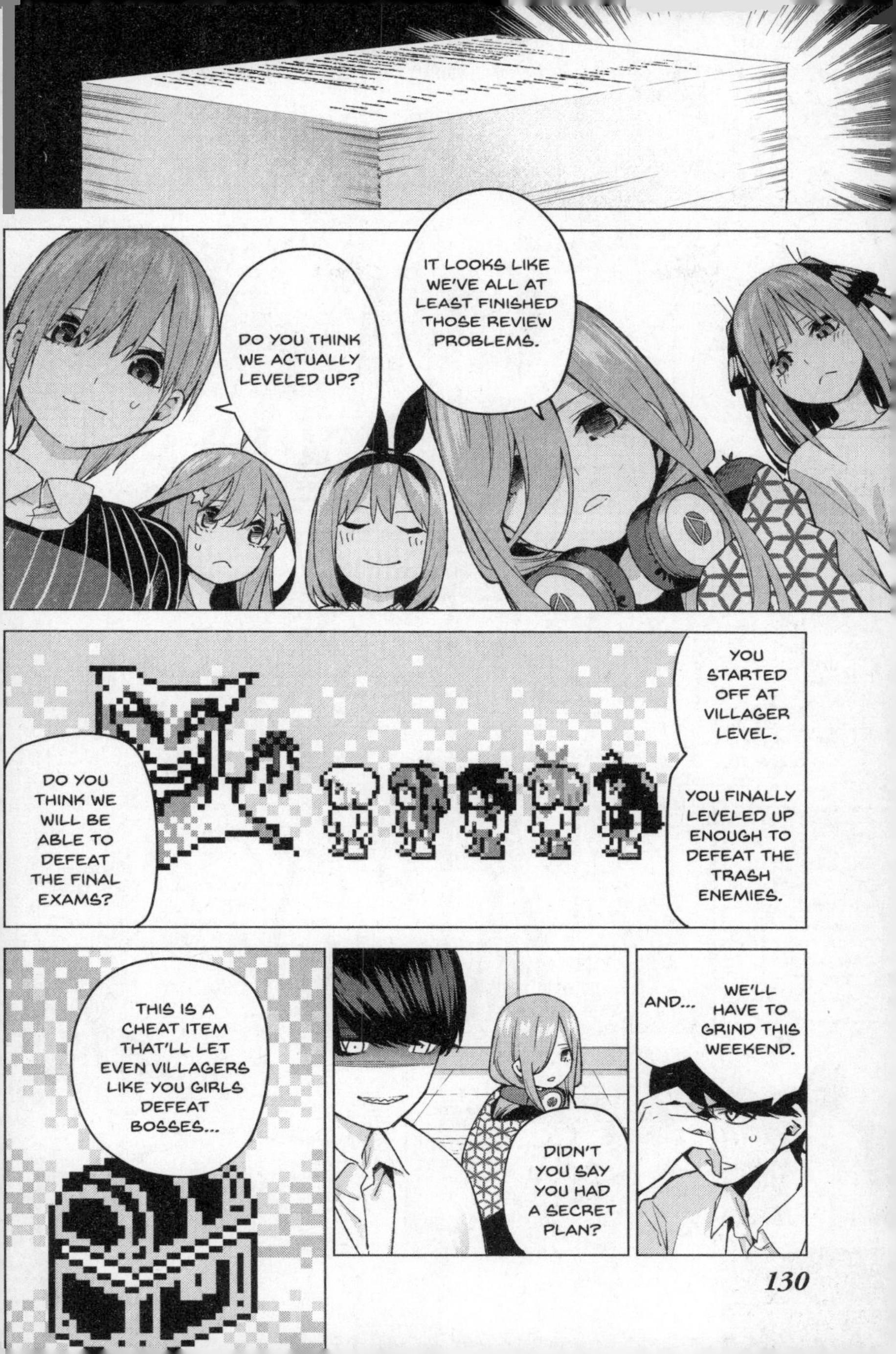
IT LOOKS LIKE WE'VE ALL AT LEAST FINISHED THOSE REVIEW PROBLEMS.
DO YOU THINK WE ACTUALLY LEVELED UP?
YOU STARTED OFF AT VILLAGER LEVEL.
YOU FINALLY LEVELED UP ENOUGH TO DEFEAT THE TRASH ENEMIES.
DO YOU THINK WE WILL BE ABLE TO DEFEAT THE FINAL EXAMS?
WE'LL HAVE TO GRIND THIS WEEKEND.
AND...
DIDN'T YOU SAY YOU HAD A SECRET PLAN?
THIS IS A CHEAT ITEM THAT'LL LET EVEN VILLAGERS LIKE YOU GIRLS DEFEAT BOSSES...

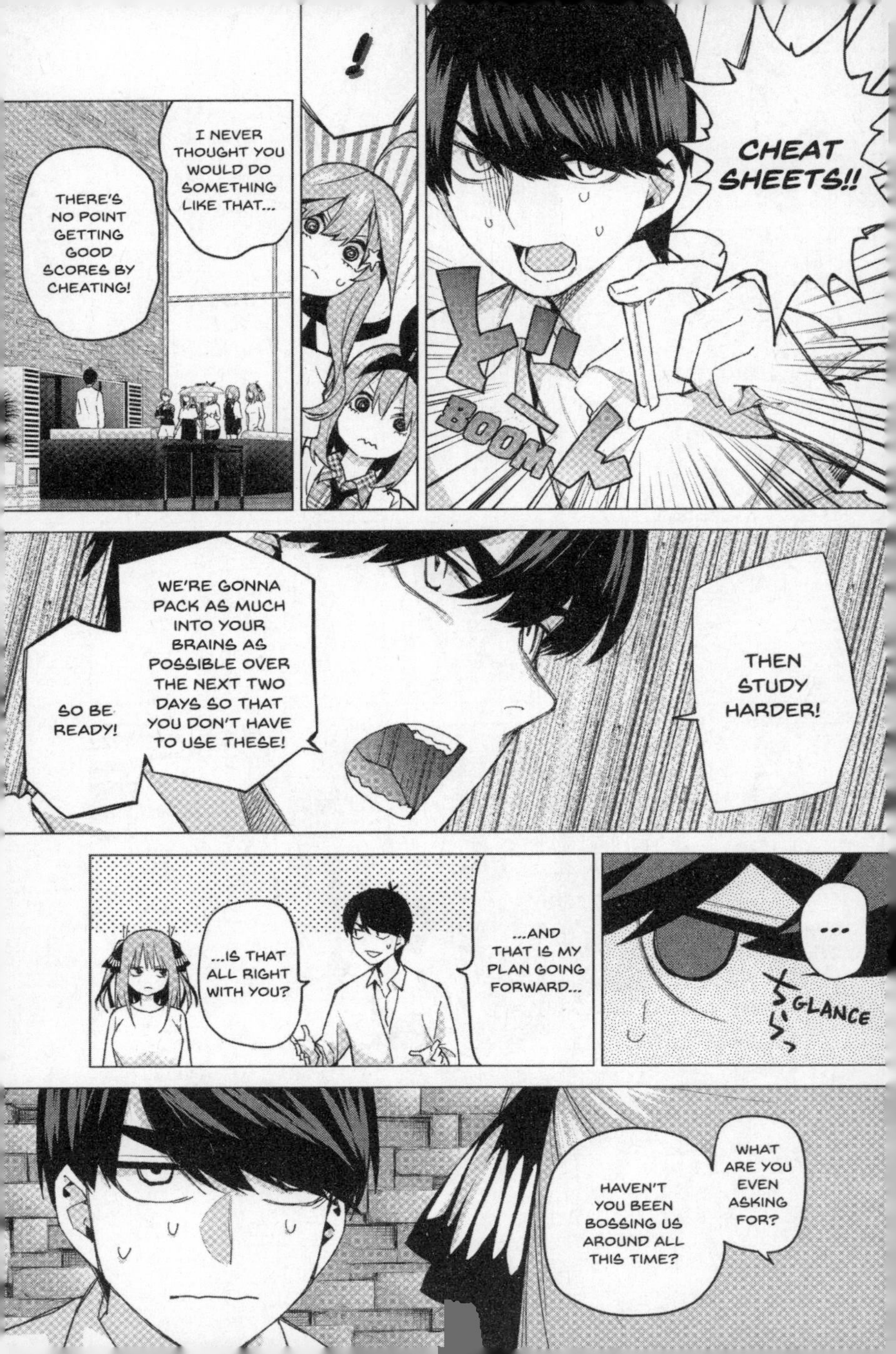
CHEAT SHEETS!!
BOOM
!
I NEVER THOUGHT YOU WOULD DO SOMETHING LIKE THAT...
THERE'S NO POINT GETTING GOOD SCORES BY CHEATING!
THEN STUDY HARDER!
WE'RE GONNA PACK AS MUCH INTO YOUR BRAINS AS POSSIBLE OVER THE NEXT TWO DAYS SO THAT YOU DON'T HAVE TO USE THESE!
SO BE READY!
...
GLANCE
...AND THAT IS MY PLAN GOING FORWARD...
...IS THAT ALL RIGHT WITH YOU?
WHAT ARE YOU EVEN ASKING FOR?
HAVEN'T YOU BEEN BOSSING US AROUND ALL THIS TIME?

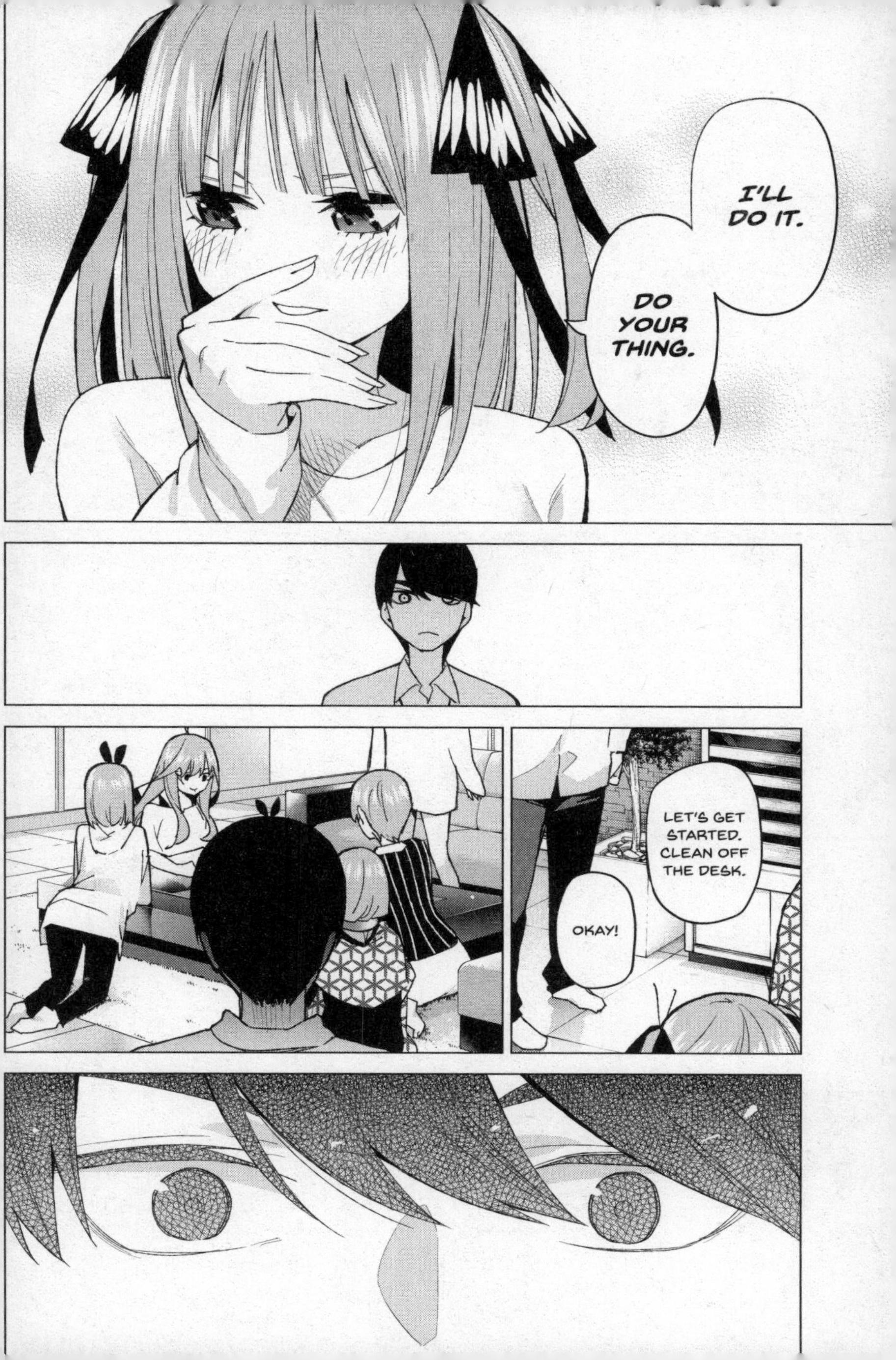
I'LL DO IT.
DO YOUR THING.
LET'S GET STARTED. CLEAN OFF THE DESK.
OKAY!

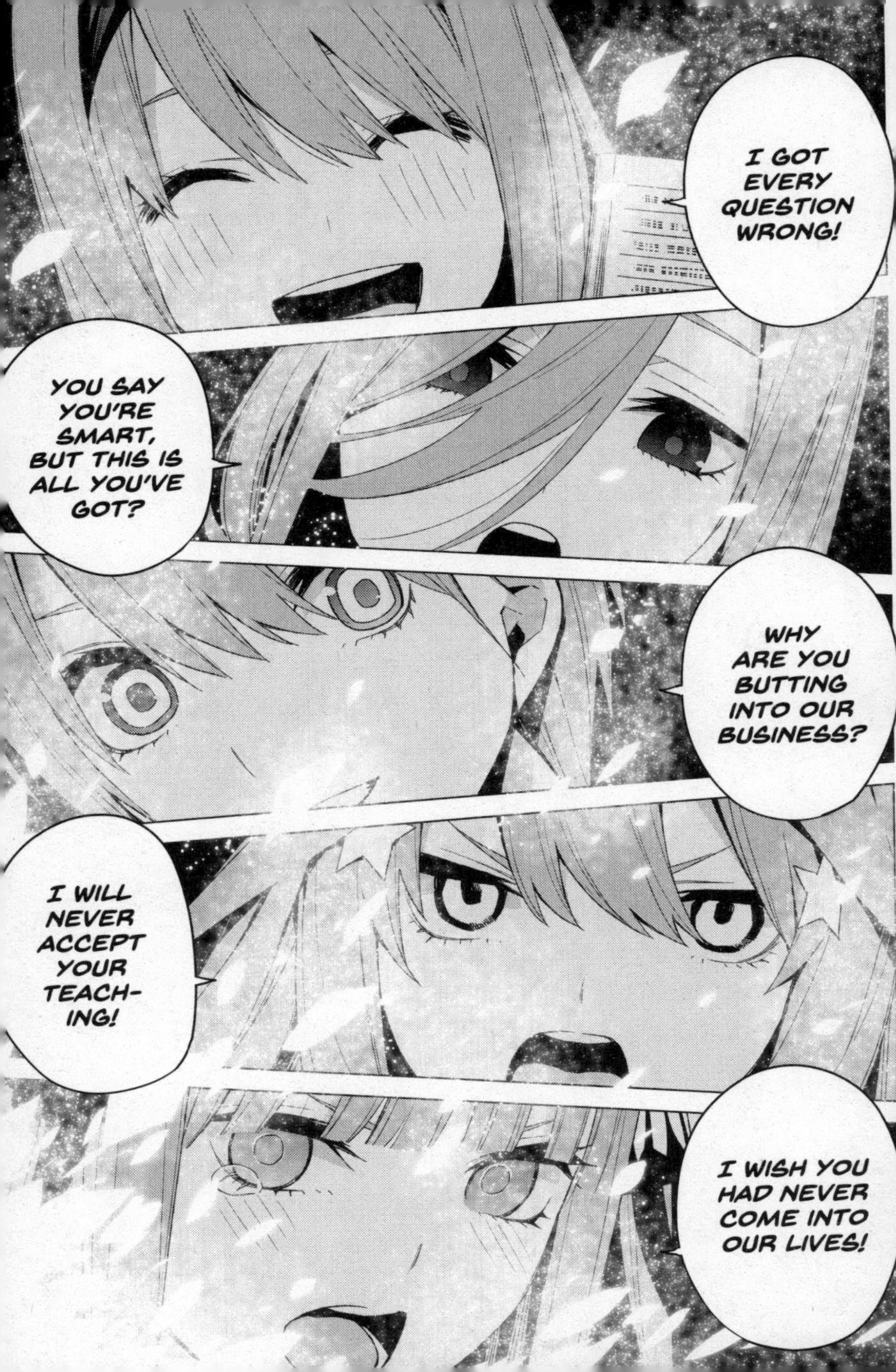
I GOT EVERY QUESTION WRONG!
YOU SAY YOU'RE SMART, BUT THIS IS ALL YOU'VE GOT?
WHY ARE YOU BUTTING INTO OUR BUSINESS?
I WILL NEVER ACCEPT YOUR TEACH-ING!
I WISH YOU HAD NEVER COME INTO OUR LIVES!

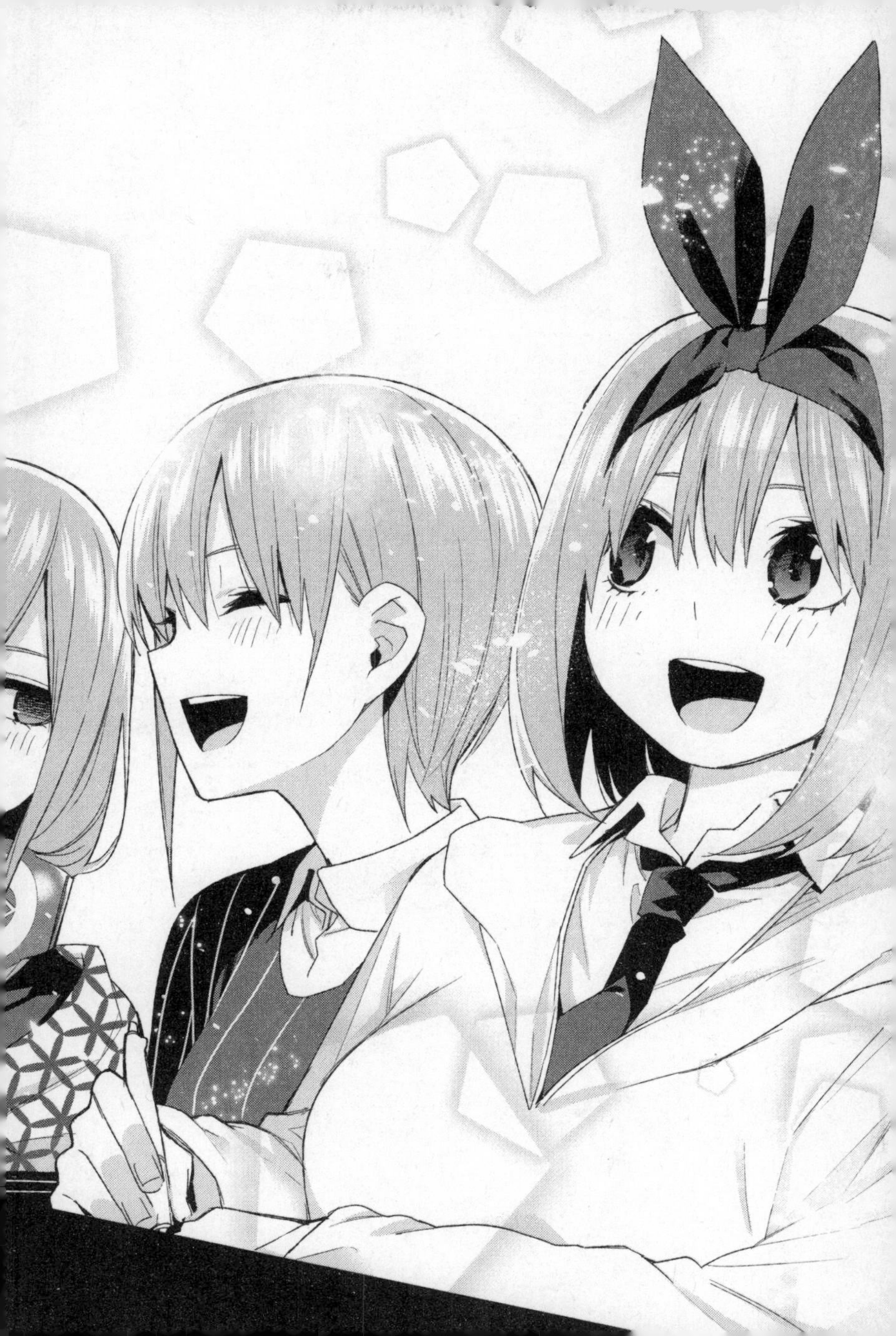

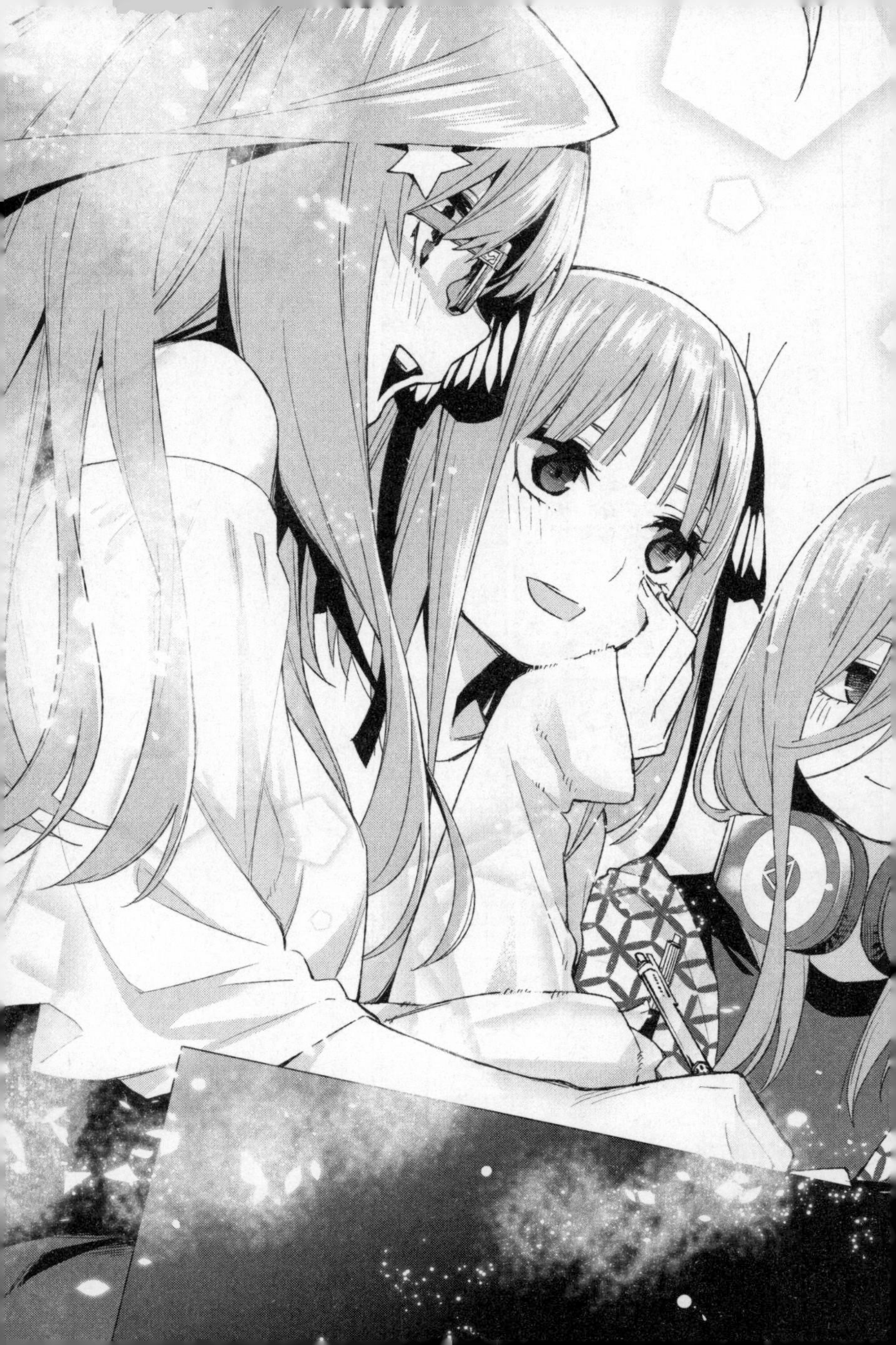

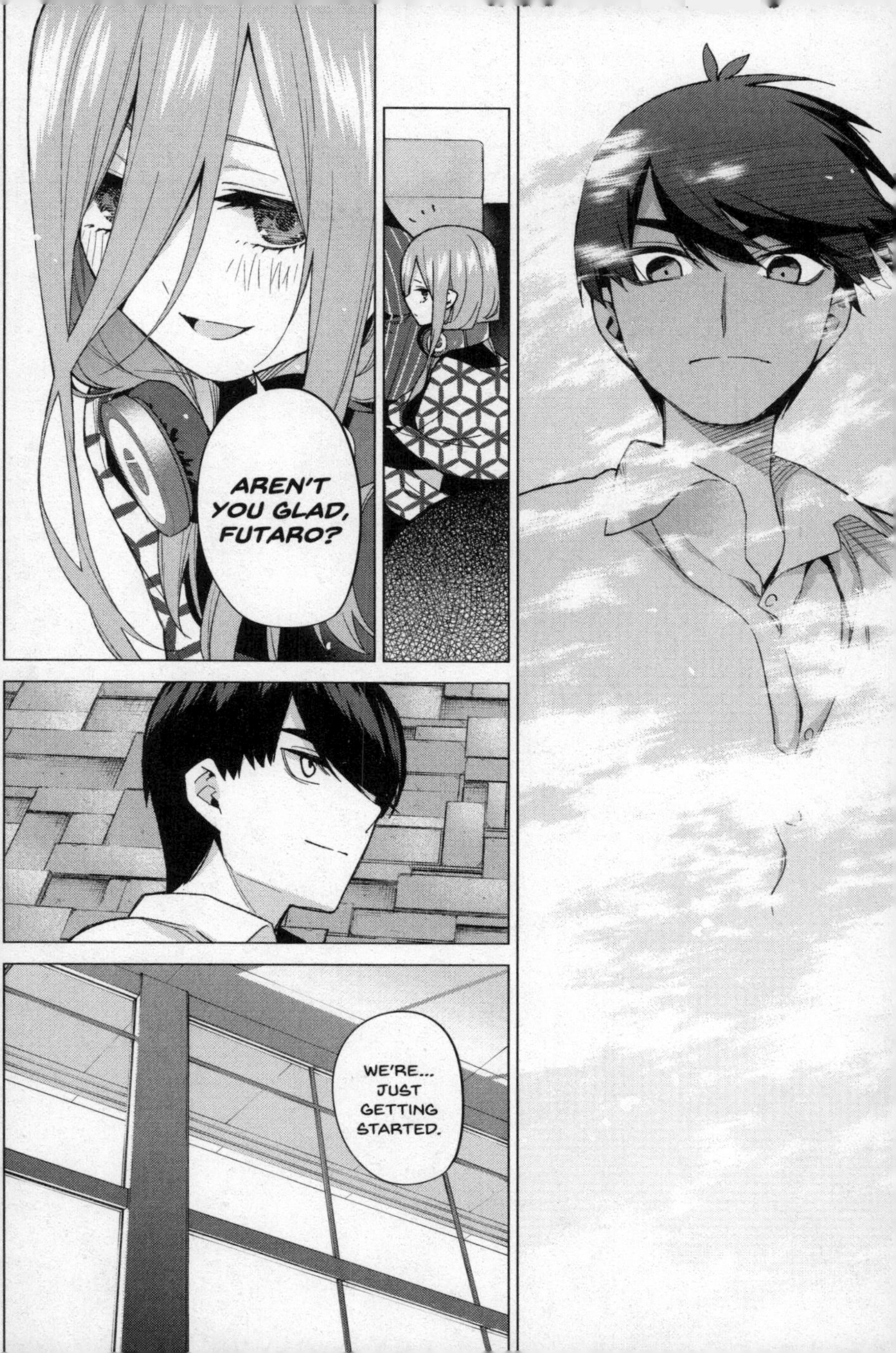
AREN'T YOU GLAD, FUTARO?
WE'RE... JUST GETTING STARTED.

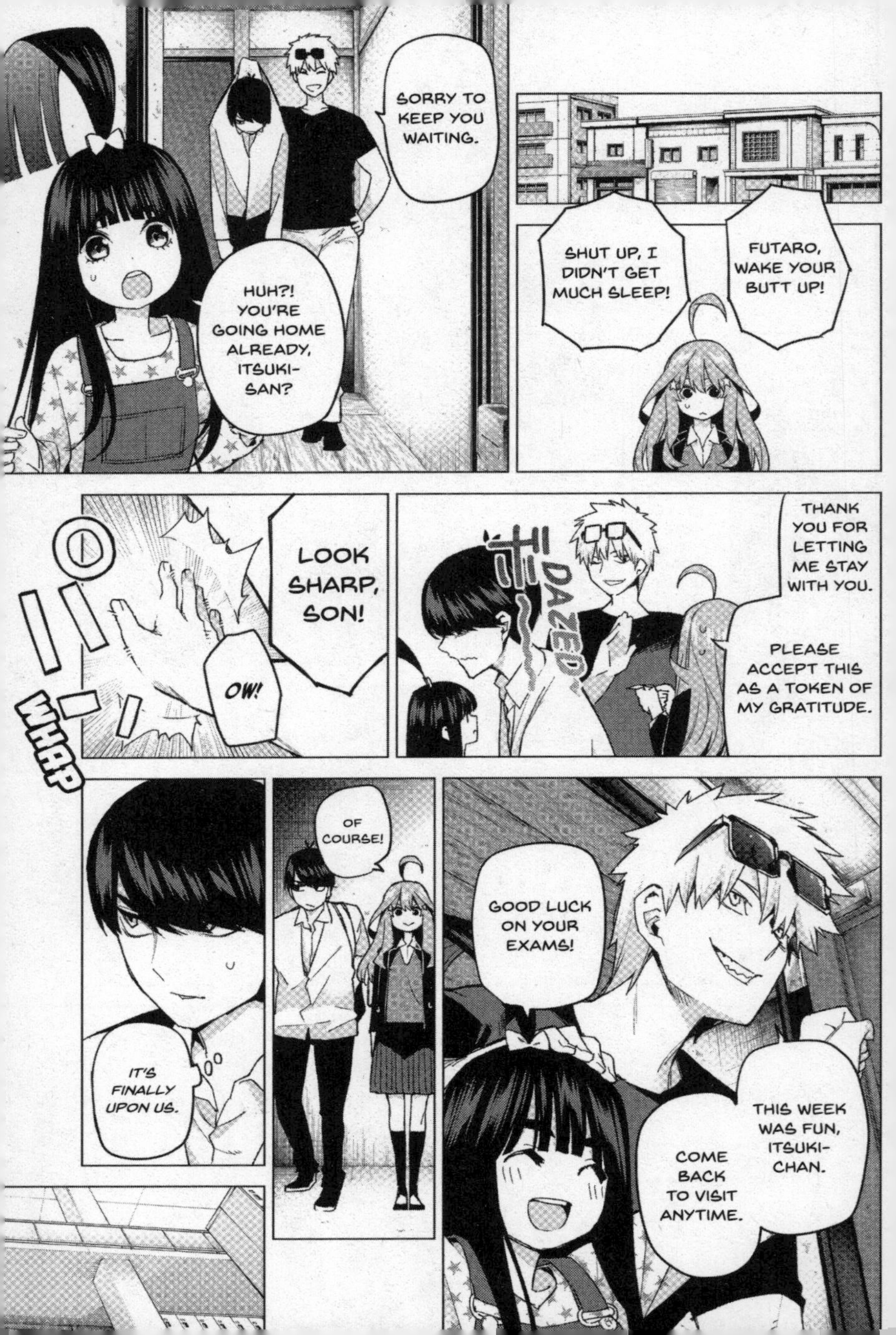
FUTARO, WAKE YOUR BUTT UP!
SHUT UP, I DIDN'T GET MUCH SLEEP!
SORRY TO KEEP YOU WAITING.
HUH?! YOU'RE GOING HOME ALREADY, ITSUKI-SAN?
THANK YOU FOR LETTING ME STAY WITH YOU.
PLEASE ACCEPT THIS AS A TOKEN OF MY GRATITUDE.
DAZED
LOOK SHARP, SON!
OW!
WHAP
GOOD LUCK ON YOUR EXAMS!
THIS WEEK WAS FUN, ITSUKI-CHAN.
COME BACK TO VISIT ANYTIME.
OF COURSE!
IT'S FINALLY UPON US.

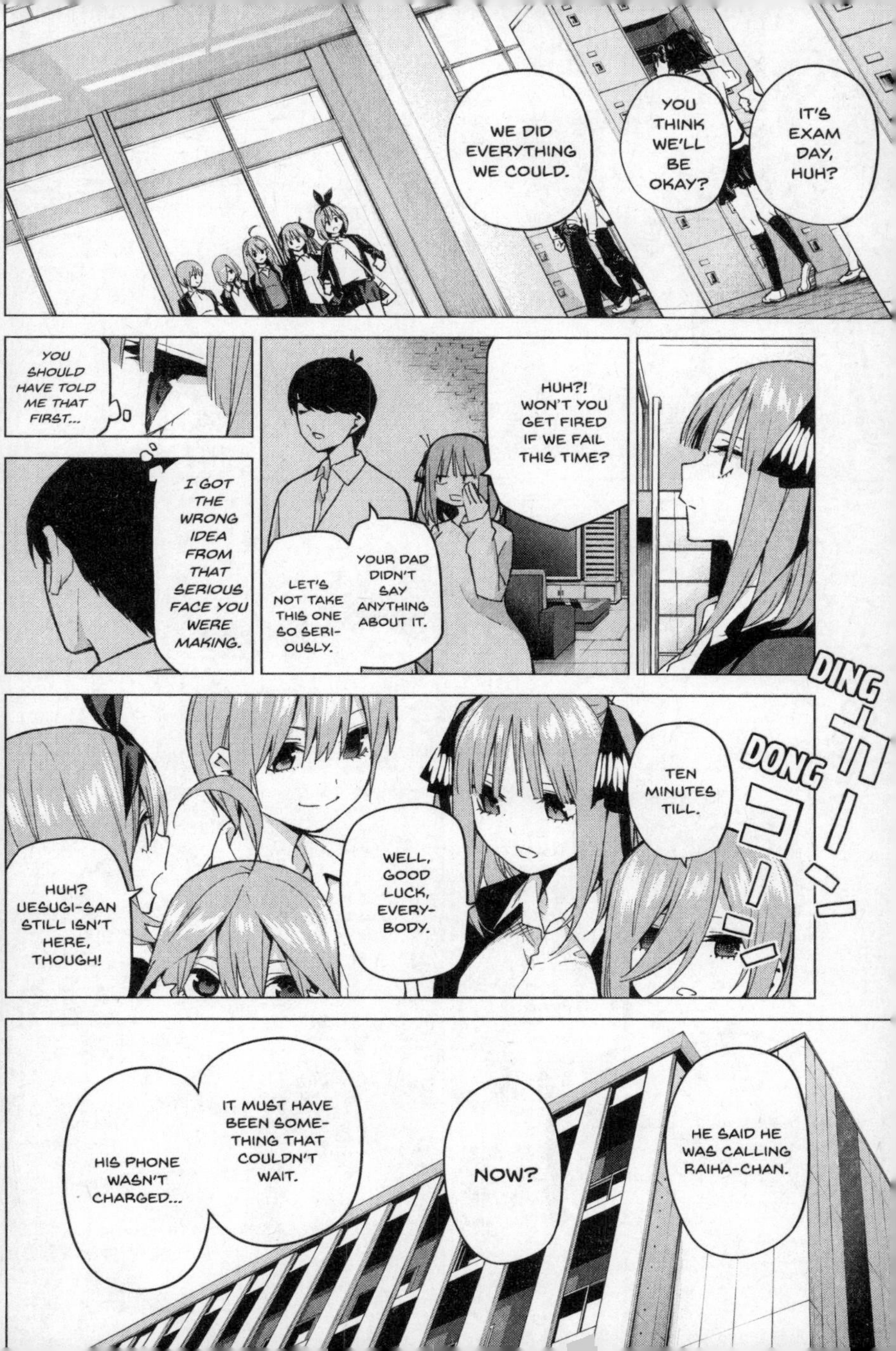
IT'S EXAM DAY, HUH?
YOU THINK WE'LL BE OKAY?
WE DID EVERYTHING WE COULD.
HUH?! WON'T YOU GET FIRED IF WE FAIL THIS TIME?
YOUR DAD DIDN'T SAY ANYTHING ABOUT IT.
LET'S NOT TAKE THIS ONE SO SERIOUSLY.
YOU SHOULD HAVE TOLD ME THAT FIRST...
I GOT THE WRONG IDEA FROM THAT SERIOUS FACE YOU WERE MAKING.
DING
DONG
TEN MINUTES TILL.
WELL, GOOD LUCK, EVERYBODY.
HUH? UESUGI-SAN STILL ISN'T HERE, THOUGH!
HE SAID HE WAS CALLING RAIHA-CHAN.
NOW?
IT MUST HAVE BEEN SOMETHING THAT COULDN'T WAIT.
HIS PHONE WASN'T CHARGED...

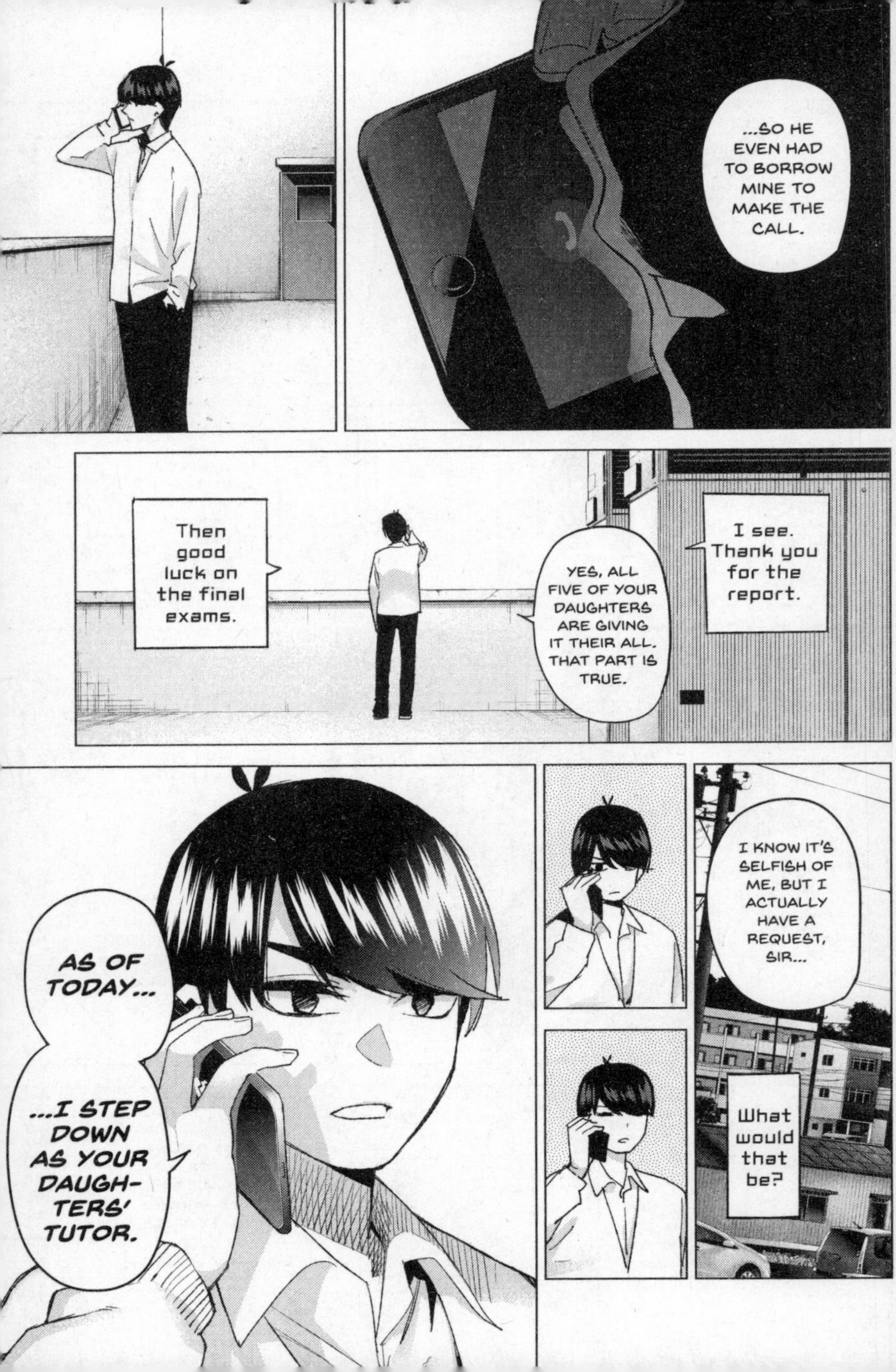
...SO HE EVEN HAD TO BORROW MINE TO MAKE THE CALL.
I see. Thank you for the report.
YES, ALL FIVE OF YOUR DAUGHTERS ARE GIVING IT THEIR ALL. THAT PART IS TRUE.
Then good luck on the final exams.
I KNOW IT'S SELFISH OF ME, BUT I ACTUALLY HAVE A REQUEST, SIR...
What would that be?
AS OF TODAY...
...I STEP DOWN AS YOUR DAUGHTERS' TUTOR.

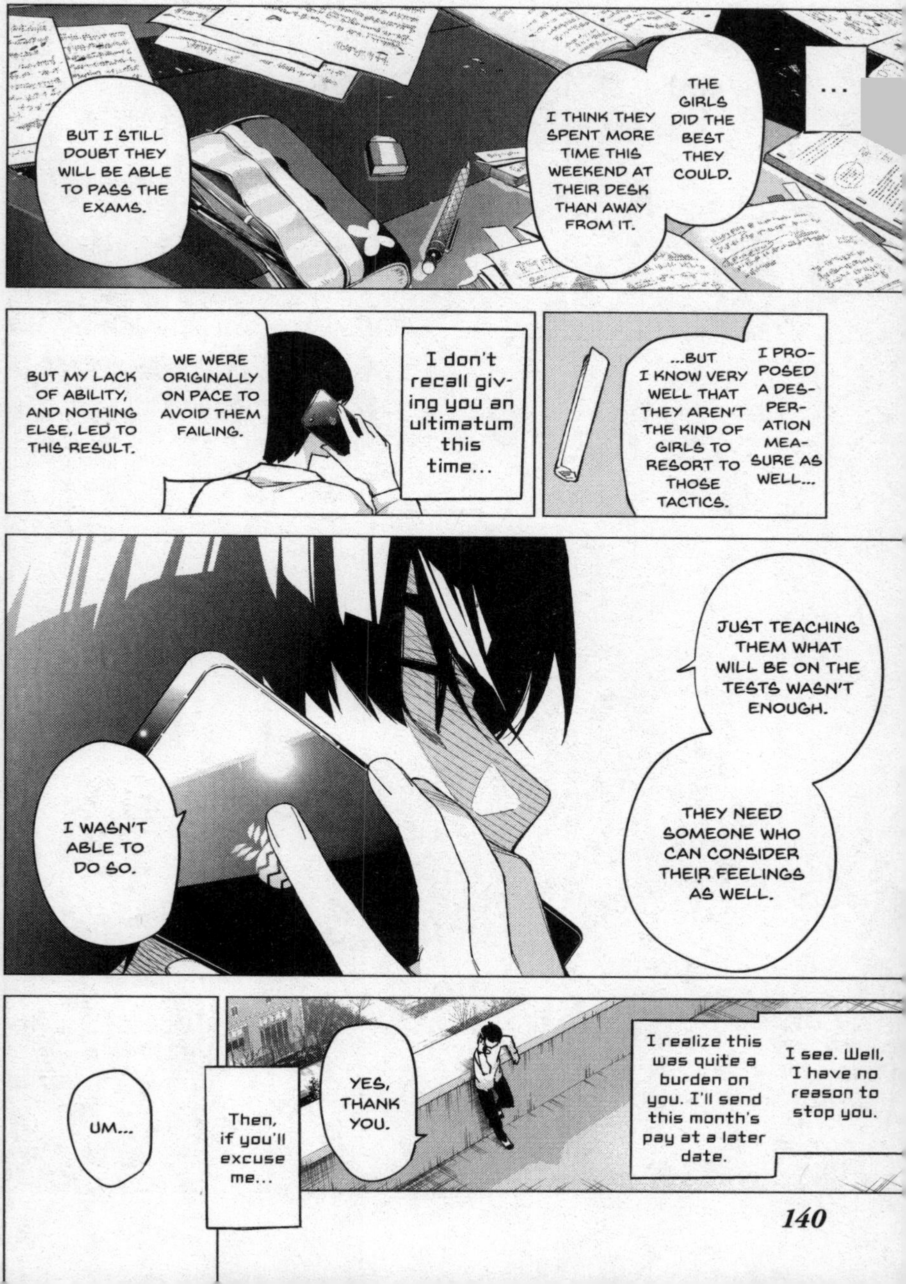
...
THE GIRLS DID THE BEST THEY COULD.
I THINK THEY SPENT MORE TIME THIS WEEKEND AT THEIR DESK THAN AWAY FROM IT.
BUT I STILL DOUBT THEY WILL BE ABLE TO PASS THE EXAMS.
I PROPOSED A DESPERATION MEASURE AS WELL...
...BUT I KNOW VERY WELL THAT THEY AREN'T THE KIND OF GIRLS TO RESORT TO THOSE TACTICS.
I don't recall giving you an ultimatum this time...
WE WERE ORIGINALLY ON PACE TO AVOID THEM FAILING.
BUT MY LACK OF ABILITY, AND NOTHING ELSE, LED TO THIS RESULT.
JUST TEACHING THEM WHAT WILL BE ON THE TESTS WASN'T ENOUGH.
THEY NEED SOMEONE WHO CAN CONSIDER THEIR FEELINGS AS WELL.
I WASN'T ABLE TO DO SO.
I see. Well, I have no reason to stop you.
I realize this was quite a burden on you. I'll send this month's pay at a later date.
YES, THANK YOU.
Then, if you'll excuse me...
UM...

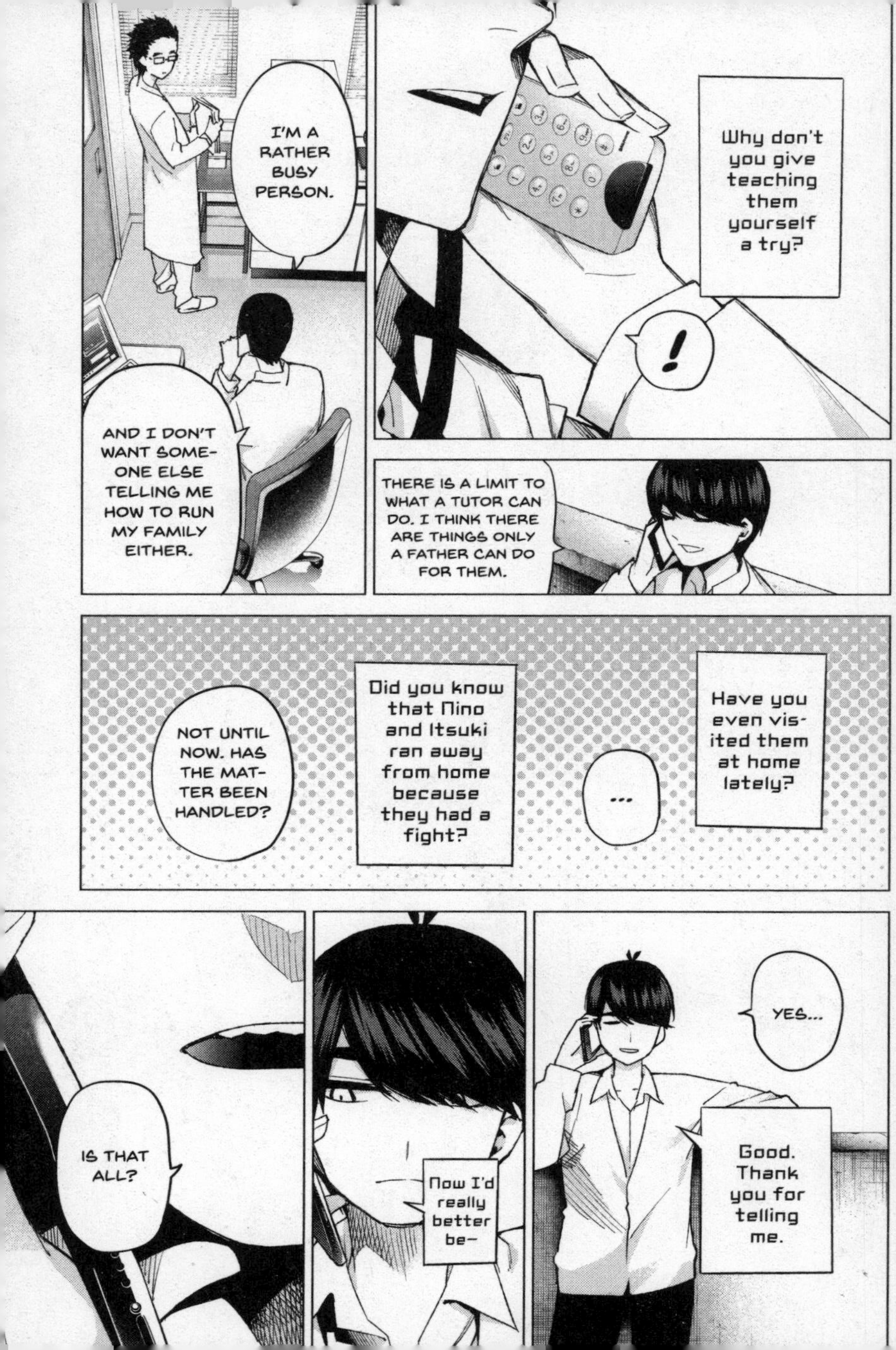
Why don't you give teaching them yourself a try?
!
THERE IS A LIMIT TO WHAT A TUTOR CAN DO. I THINK THERE ARE THINGS ONLY A FATHER CAN DO FOR THEM.
I'M A RATHER BUSY PERSON.
AND I DON'T WANT SOME-ONE ELSE TELLING ME HOW TO RUN MY FAMILY EITHER.
Have you even vis-ited them at home lately?
...
Did you know that Nino and Itsuki ran away from home because they had a fight?
NOT UNTIL NOW. HAS THE MAT-TER BEEN HANDLED?
YES...
Good. Thank you for telling me.
Now I'd really better be—
IS THAT ALL?

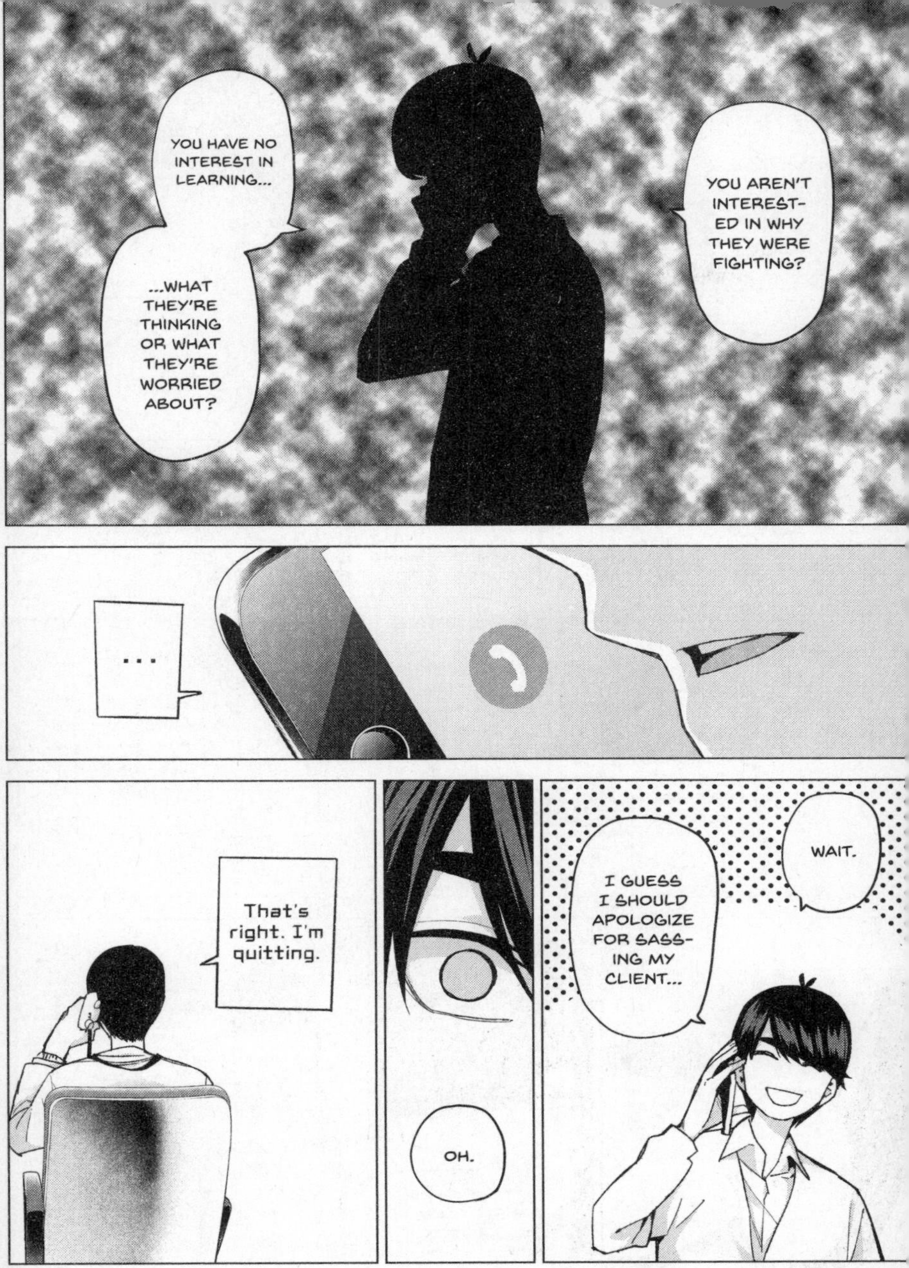
YOU AREN'T INTEREST-ED IN WHY THEY WERE FIGHTING?
YOU HAVE NO INTEREST IN LEARNING...
...WHAT THEY'RE THINKING OR WHAT THEY'RE WORRIED ABOUT?
...
WAIT.
I GUESS I SHOULD APOLOGIZE FOR SASS-ING MY CLIENT...
OH.
That's right. I'm quitting.

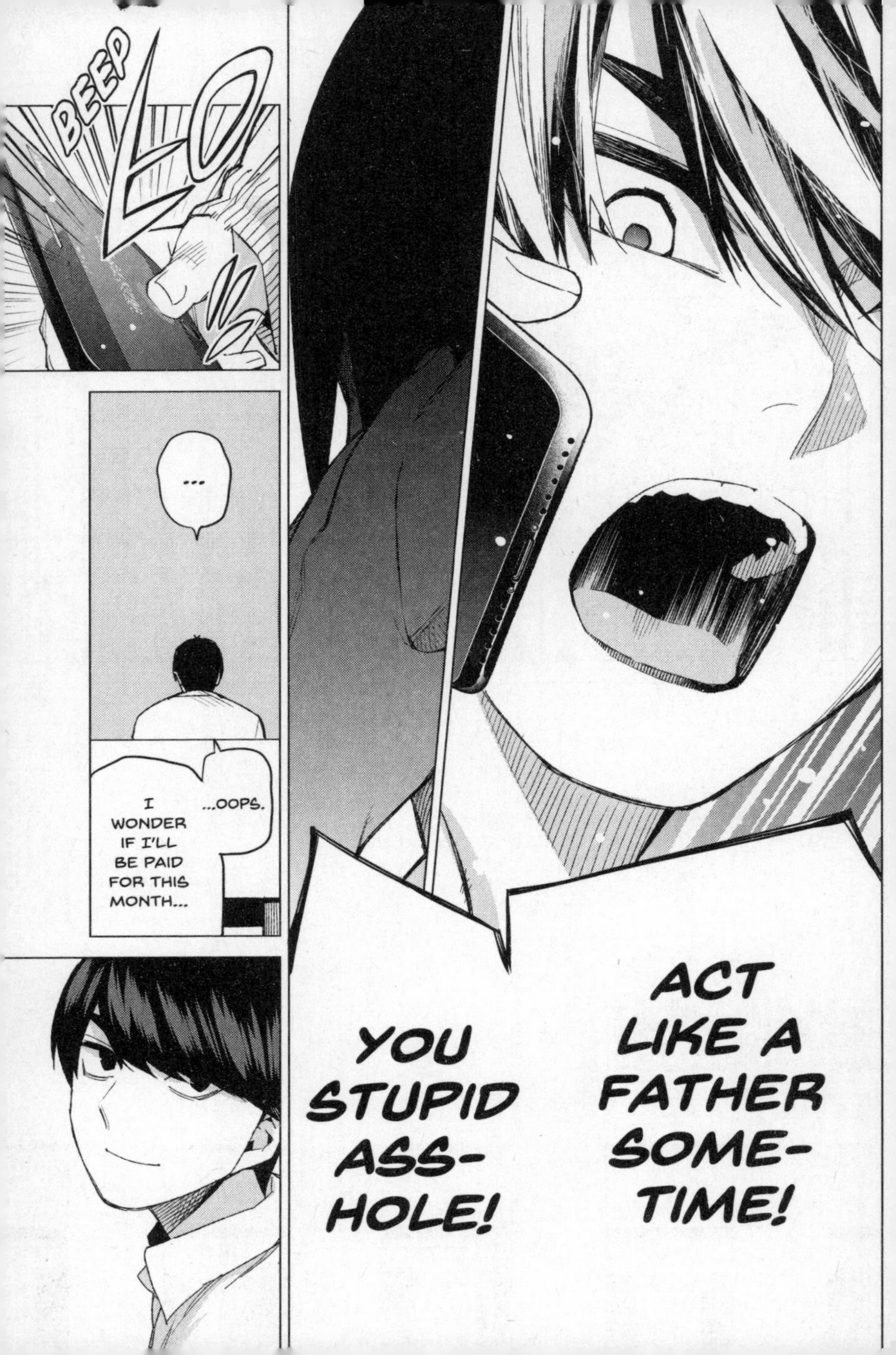
YOU STUPID ASS-HOLE!
ACT LIKE A FATHER SOME-TIME!
BEEP
...
...OOPS.
I WONDER IF I'LL BE PAID FOR THIS MONTH...

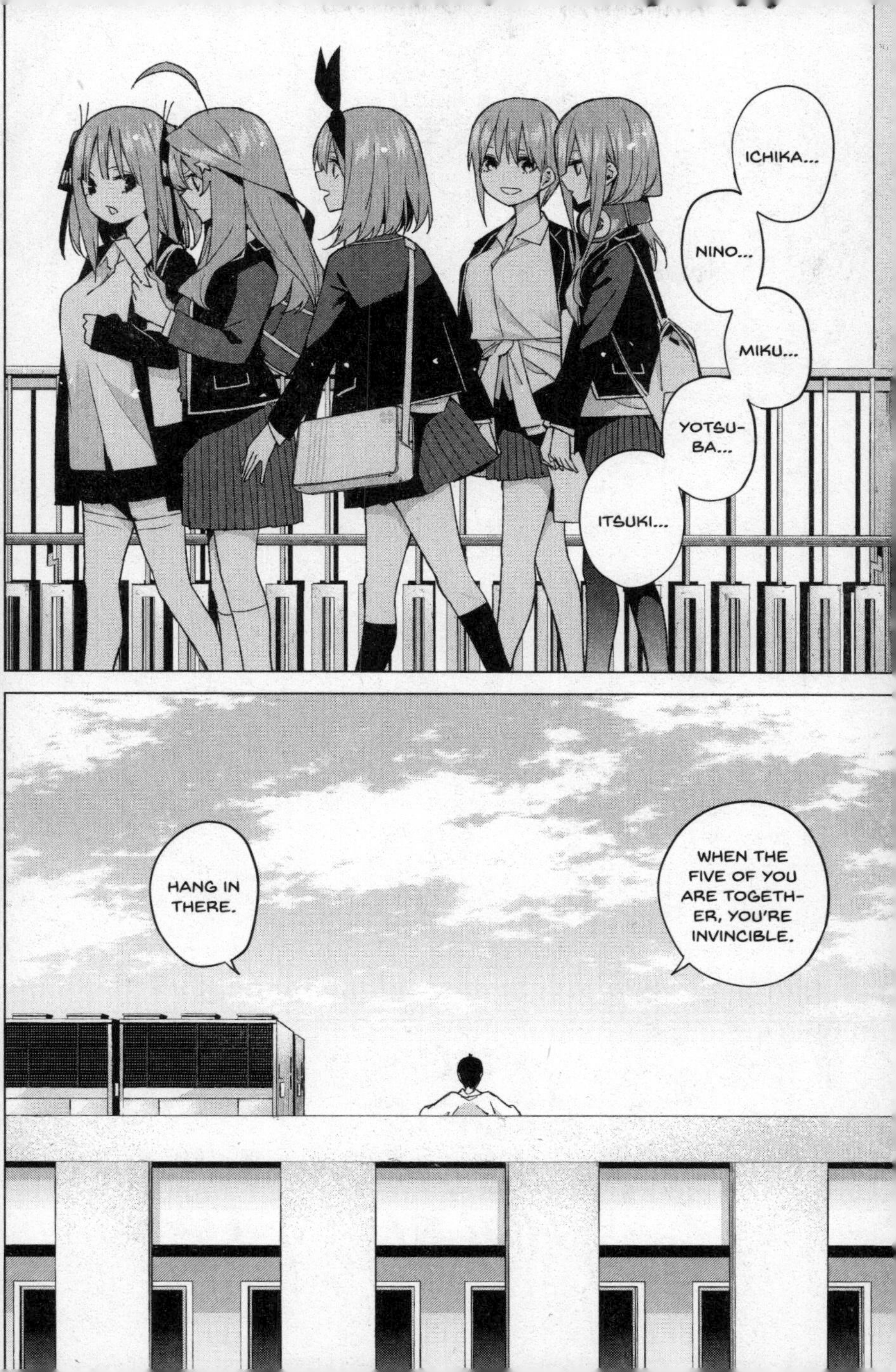
ICHIKA...
NINO...
MIKU...
YOTSUBA...
ITSUKI...
WHEN THE FIVE OF YOU ARE TOGETHER, YOU'RE INVINCIBLE.
HANG IN THERE.

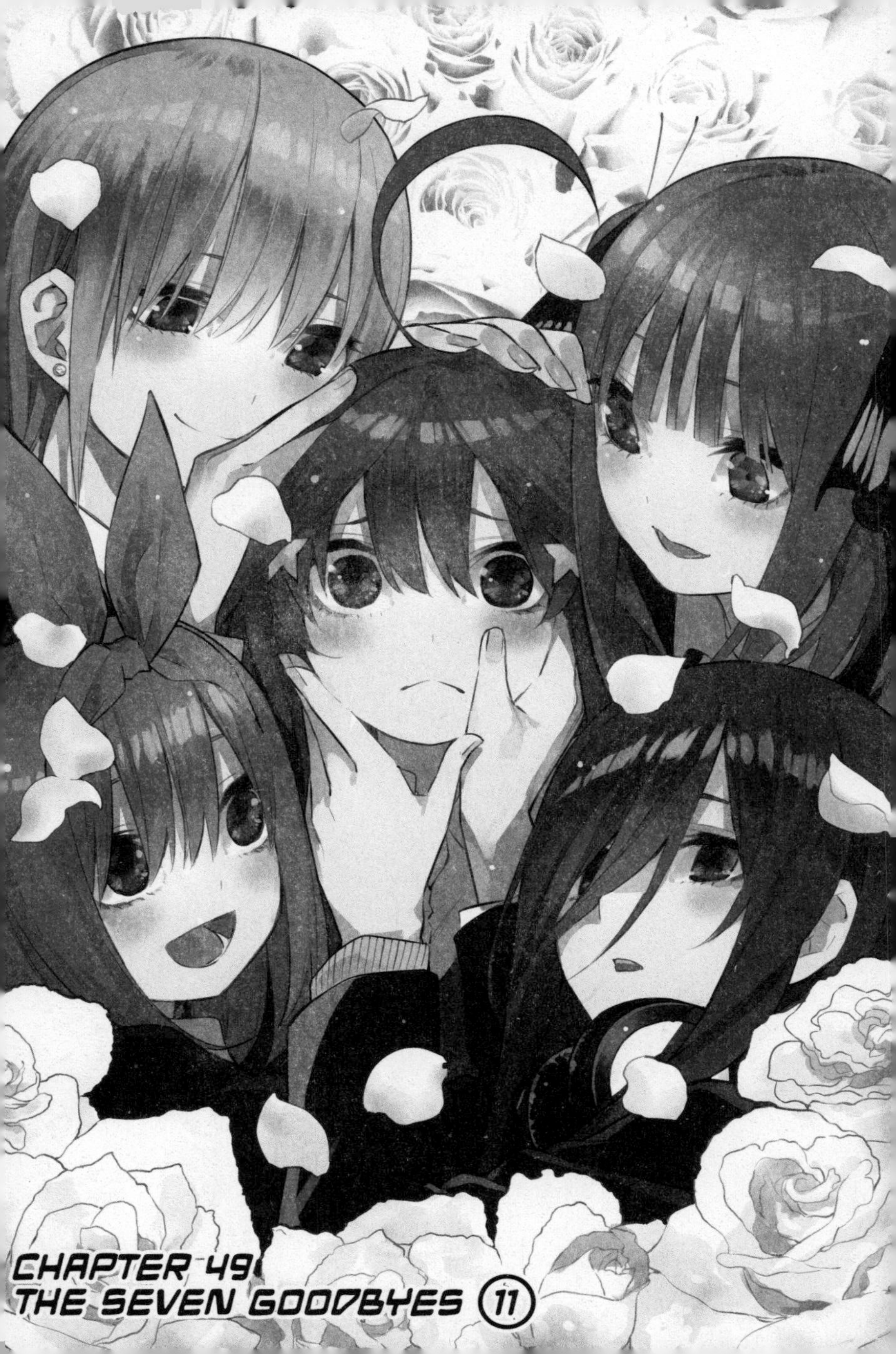
CHAPTER 49:
THE SEVEN GOODBYES ⑪

THE QUINTESSENTIAL QUINTUPLETS

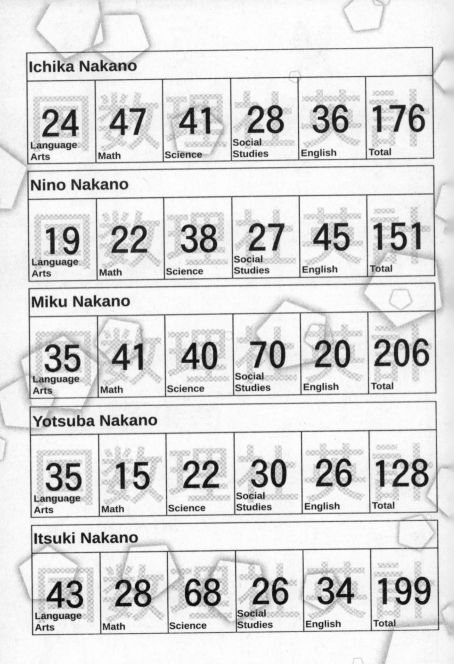

## Ichika Nakano

| 24 | 47 | 41 | 28 | 36 | 176 |
|---|---|---|---|---|---|
| Language Arts | Math | Science | Social Studies | English | Total |

## Nino Nakano

| 19 | 22 | 38 | 27 | 45 | 151 |
|---|---|---|---|---|---|
| Language Arts | Math | Science | Social Studies | English | Total |

## Miku Nakano

| 35 | 41 | 40 | 70 | 20 | 206 |
|---|---|---|---|---|---|
| Language Arts | Math | Science | Social Studies | English | Total |

## Yotsuba Nakano

| 35 | 15 | 22 | 30 | 26 | 128 |
|---|---|---|---|---|---|
| Language Arts | Math | Science | Social Studies | English | Total |

## Itsuki Nakano

| 43 | 28 | 68 | 26 | 34 | 199 |
|---|---|---|---|---|---|
| Language Arts | Math | Science | Social Studies | English | Total |

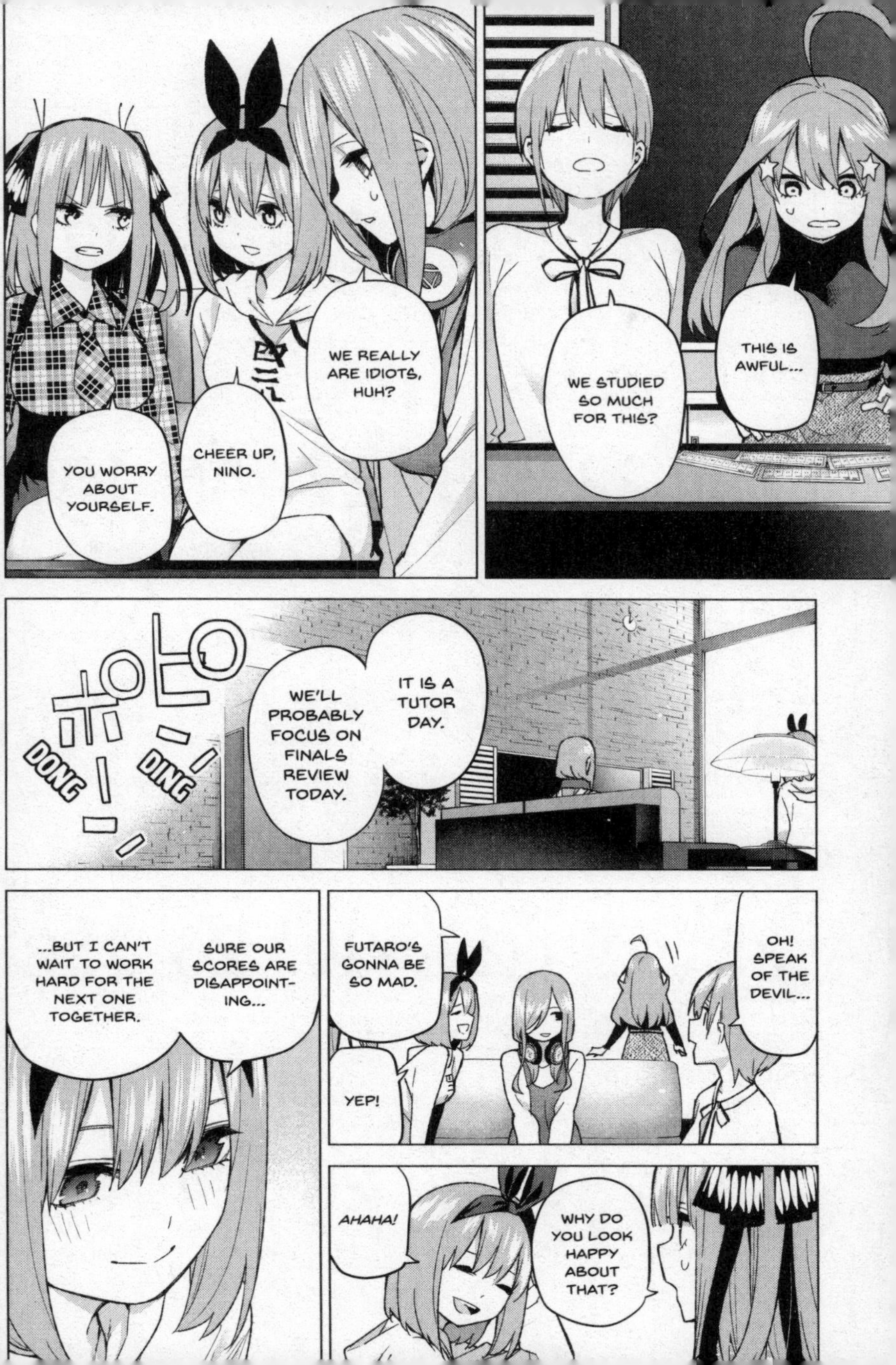
THIS IS AWFUL...
WE STUDIED SO MUCH FOR THIS?
WE REALLY ARE IDIOTS, HUH?
CHEER UP, NINO.
YOU WORRY ABOUT YOURSELF.
DING
DONG
IT IS A TUTOR DAY.
WE'LL PROBABLY FOCUS ON FINALS REVIEW TODAY.
OH! SPEAK OF THE DEVIL...
FUTARO'S GONNA BE SO MAD.
YEP!
WHY DO YOU LOOK HAPPY ABOUT THAT?
AHAHA!
SURE OUR SCORES ARE DISAPPOINTING...
...BUT I CAN'T WAIT TO WORK HARD FOR THE NEXT ONE TOGETHER.

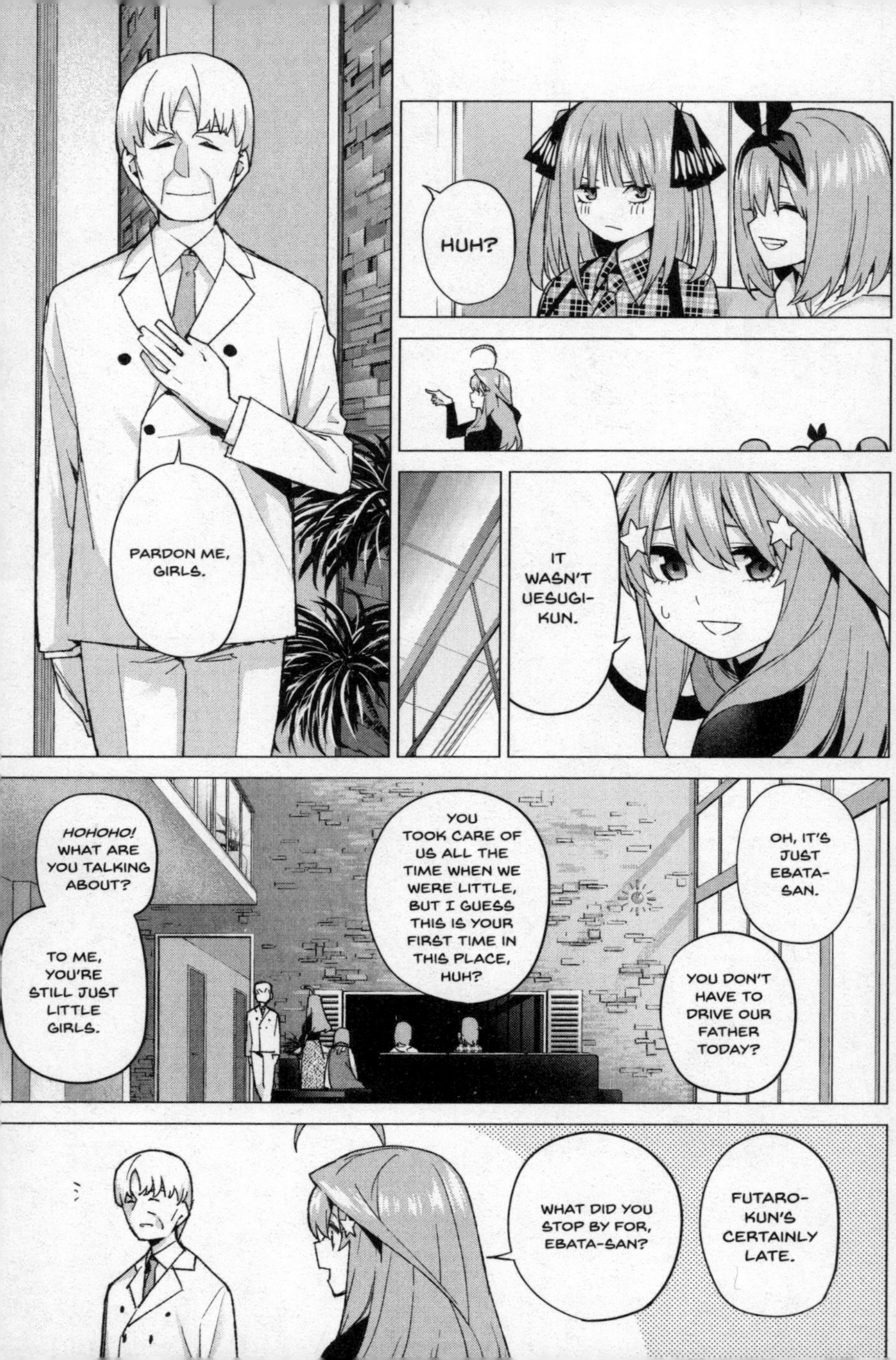
HUH?
IT WASN'T UESUGI-KUN.
PARDON ME, GIRLS.
OH, IT'S JUST EBATA-SAN.
YOU DON'T HAVE TO DRIVE OUR FATHER TODAY?
YOU TOOK CARE OF US ALL THE TIME WHEN WE WERE LITTLE, BUT I GUESS THIS IS YOUR FIRST TIME IN THIS PLACE, HUH?
*HOHOHO!* WHAT ARE YOU TALKING ABOUT?
TO ME, YOU'RE STILL JUST LITTLE GIRLS.
FUTARO-KUN'S CERTAINLY LATE.
WHAT DID YOU STOP BY FOR, EBATA-SAN?

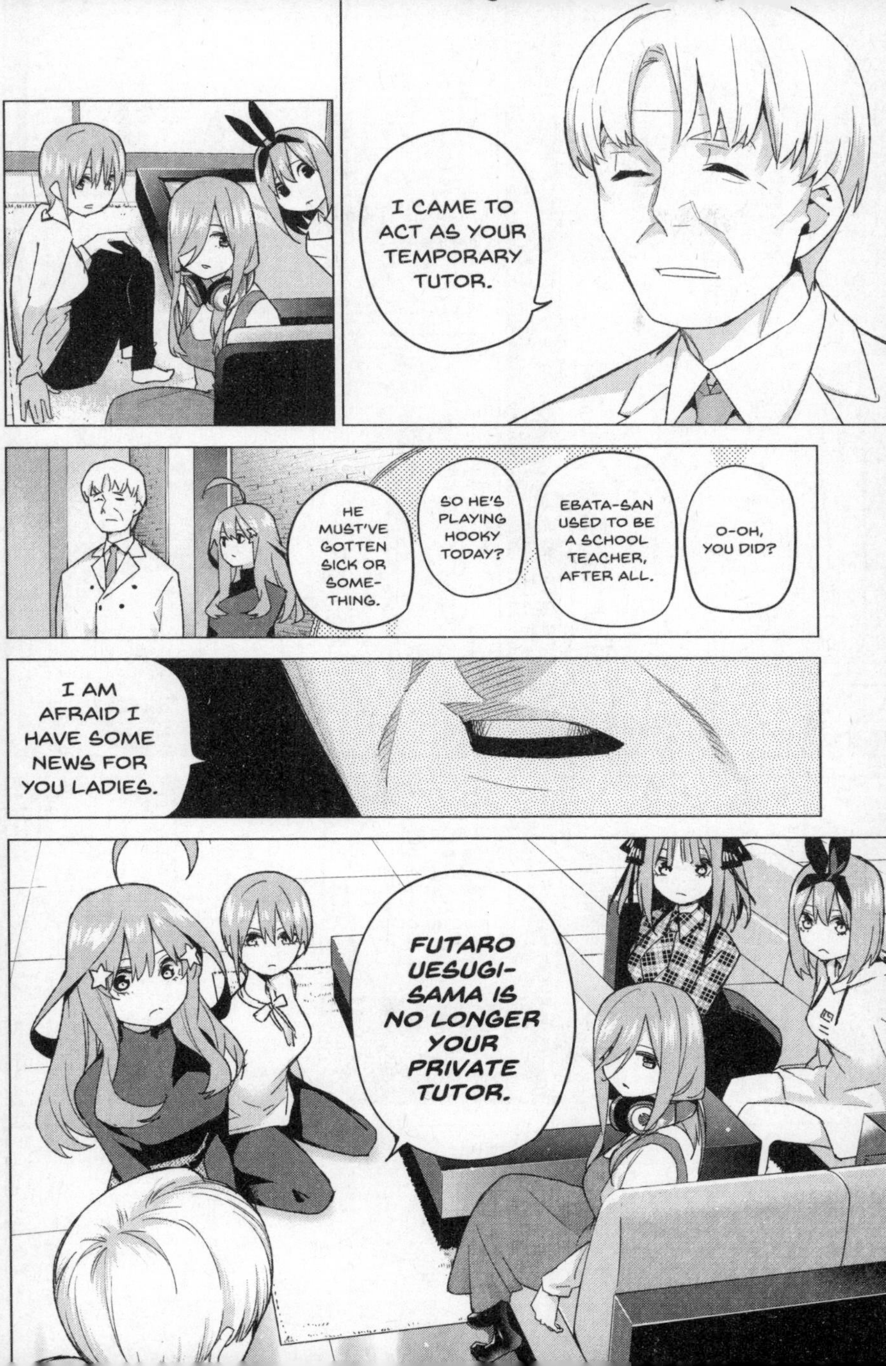
I CAME TO ACT AS YOUR TEMPORARY TUTOR.
O-OH, YOU DID?
EBATA-SAN USED TO BE A SCHOOL TEACHER, AFTER ALL.
SO HE'S PLAYING HOOKY TODAY?
HE MUST'VE GOTTEN SICK OR SOME-THING.
I AM AFRAID I HAVE SOME NEWS FOR YOU LADIES.
FUTARO UESUGI-SAMA IS NO LONGER YOUR PRIVATE TUTOR.

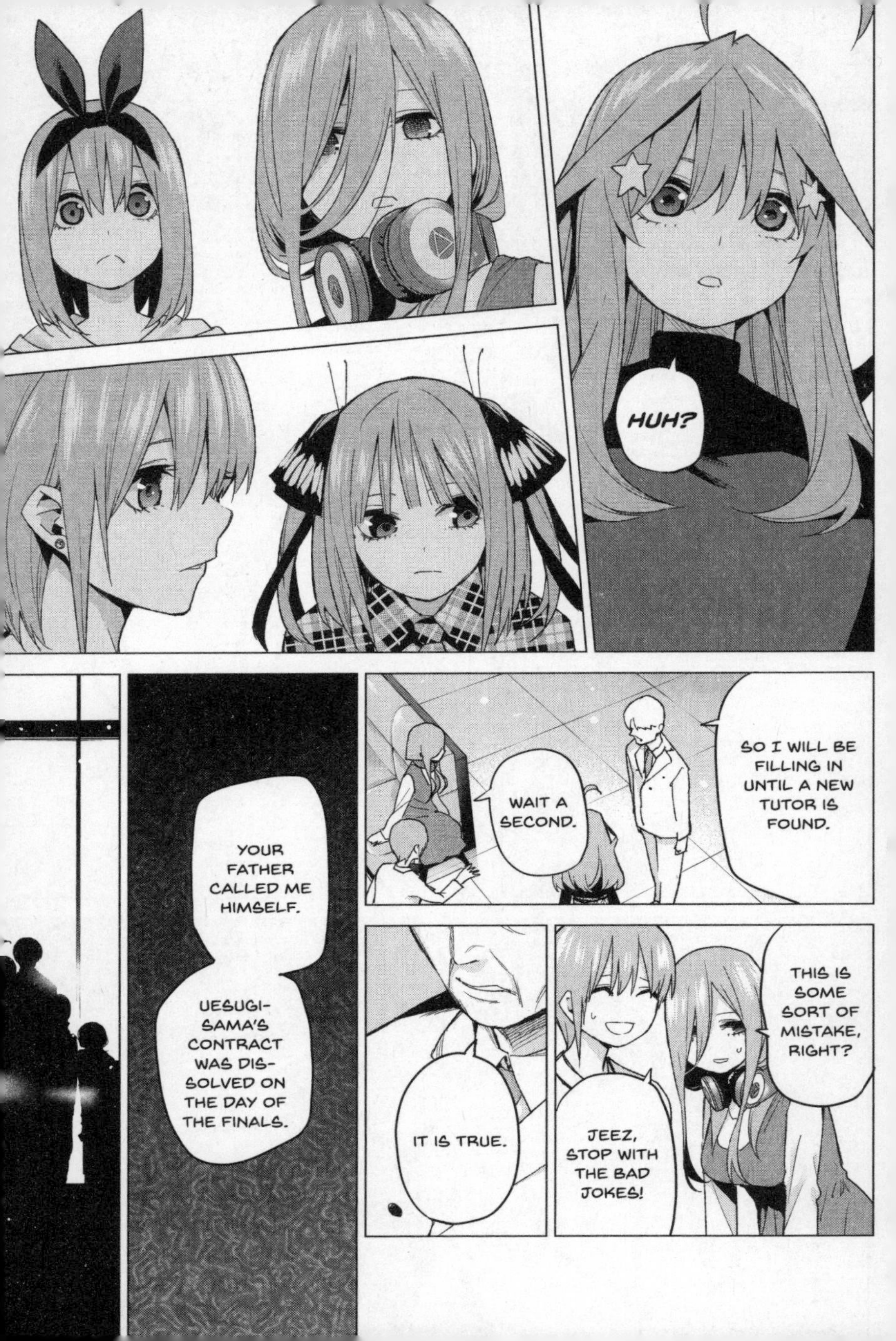
HUH?
SO I WILL BE FILLING IN UNTIL A NEW TUTOR IS FOUND.
WAIT A SECOND.
THIS IS SOME SORT OF MISTAKE, RIGHT?
JEEZ, STOP WITH THE BAD JOKES!
IT IS TRUE.
YOUR FATHER CALLED ME HIMSELF.
UESUGI-SAMA'S CONTRACT WAS DIS-SOLVED ON THE DAY OF THE FINALS.

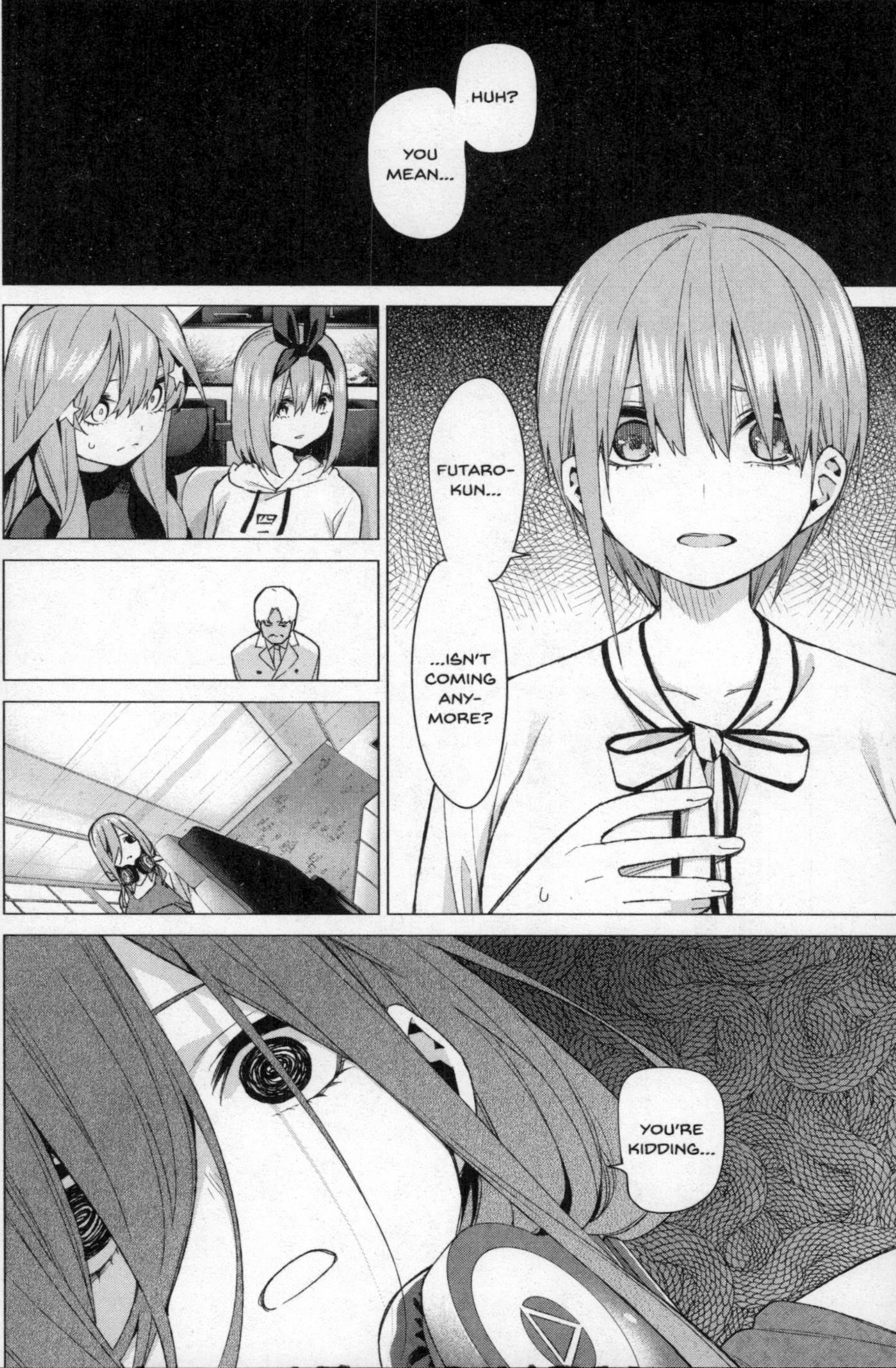
HUH?
YOU MEAN...
FUTARO-KUN...
...ISN'T COMING ANY-MORE?
YOU'RE KIDDING...

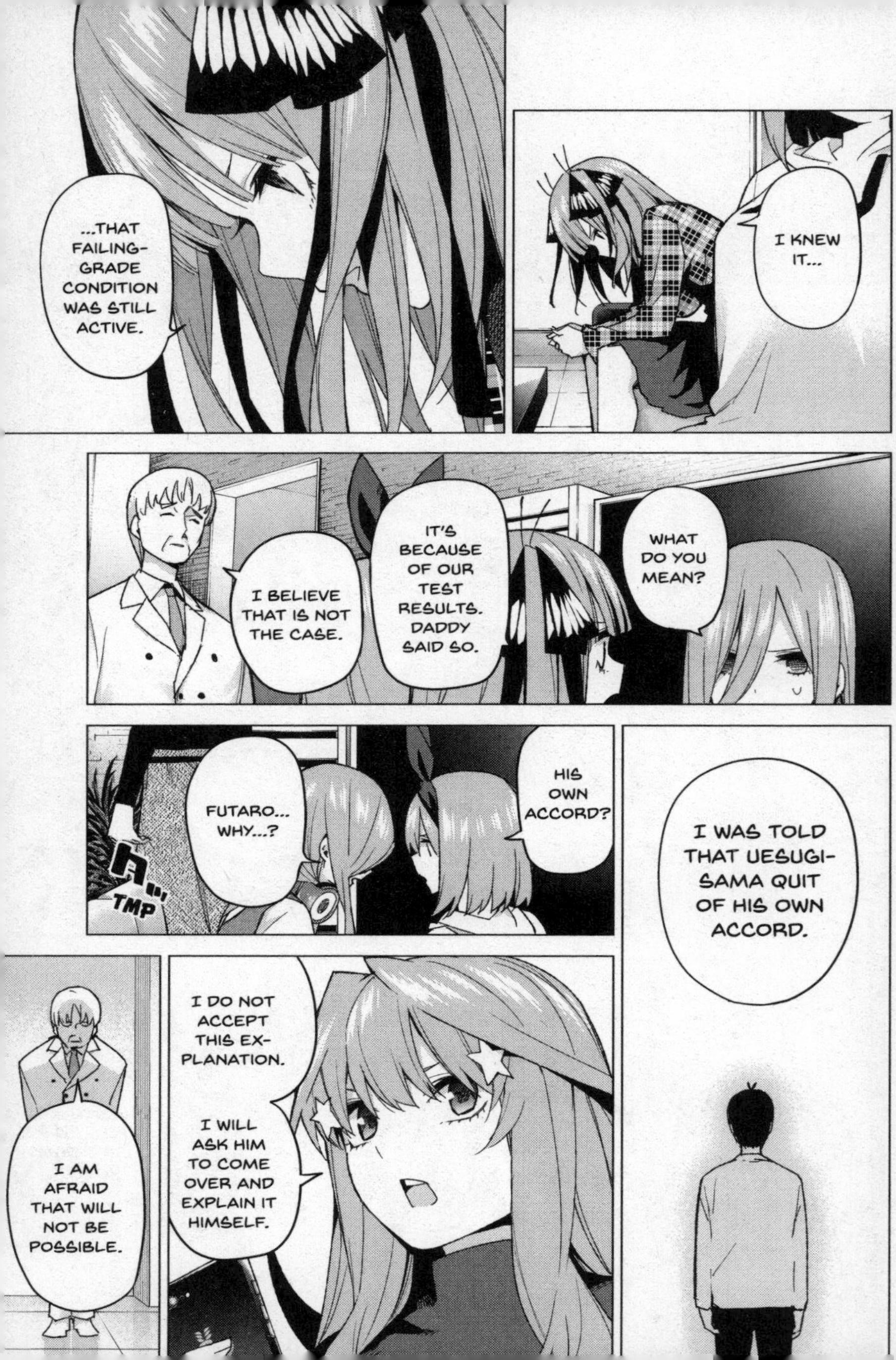
I KNEW IT...
...THAT FAILING-GRADE CONDITION WAS STILL ACTIVE.
WHAT DO YOU MEAN?
IT'S BECAUSE OF OUR TEST RESULTS. DADDY SAID SO.
I BELIEVE THAT IS NOT THE CASE.
I WAS TOLD THAT UESUGI-SAMA QUIT OF HIS OWN ACCORD.
HIS OWN ACCORD?
FUTARO... WHY...?
TMP
I DO NOT ACCEPT THIS EX-PLANATION.
I WILL ASK HIM TO COME OVER AND EXPLAIN IT HIMSELF.
I AM AFRAID THAT WILL NOT BE POSSIBLE.

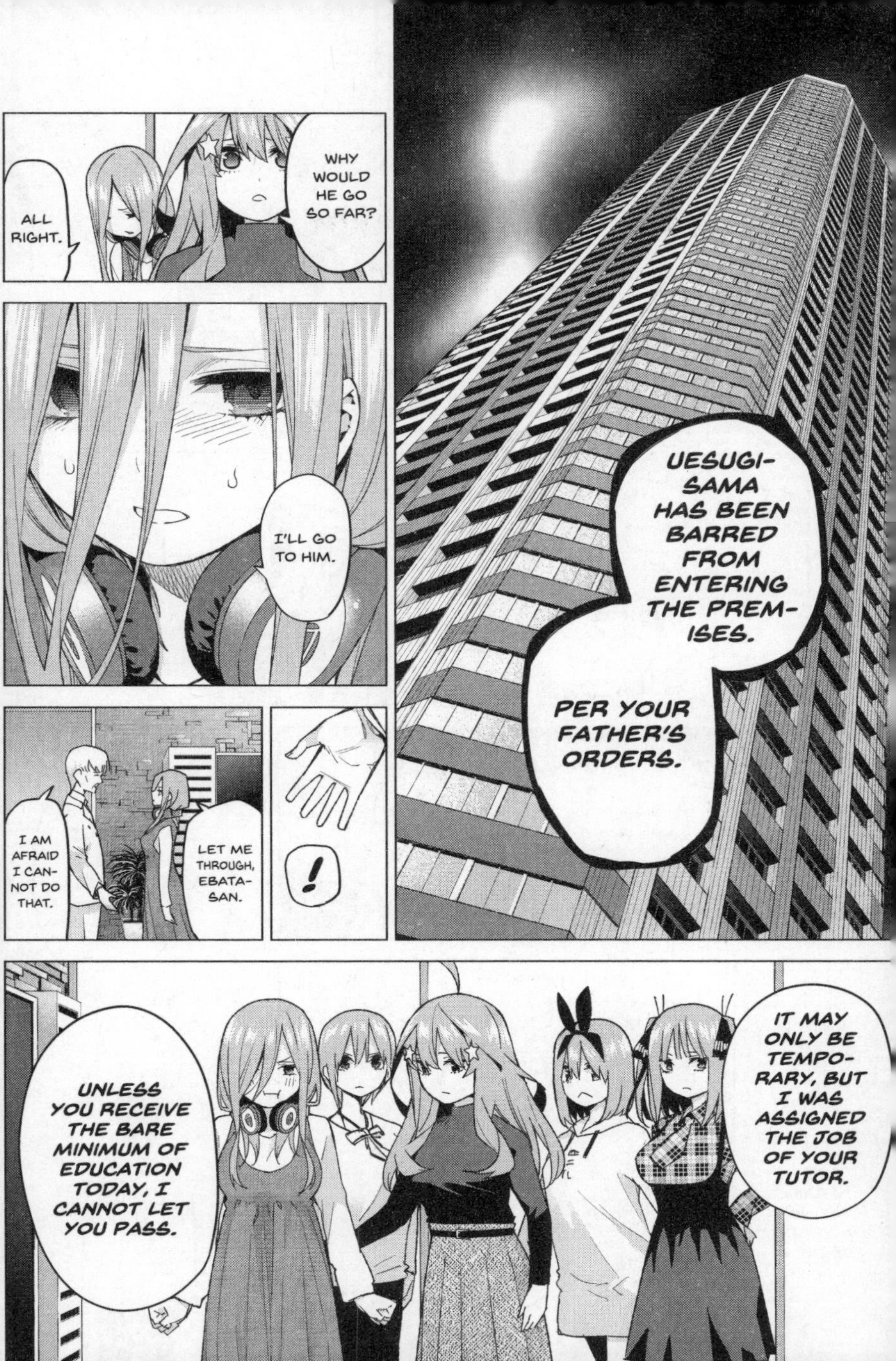
UESUGI-SAMA HAS BEEN BARRED FROM ENTERING THE PREM-ISES.
PER YOUR FATHER'S ORDERS.
WHY WOULD HE GO SO FAR?
ALL RIGHT.
I'LL GO TO HIM.
!
LET ME THROUGH, EBATA-SAN.
I AM AFRAID I CAN-NOT DO THAT.
IT MAY ONLY BE TEMPO-RARY, BUT I WAS ASSIGNED THE JOB OF YOUR TUTOR.
UNLESS YOU RECEIVE THE BARE MINIMUM OF EDUCATION TODAY, I CANNOT LET YOU PASS.

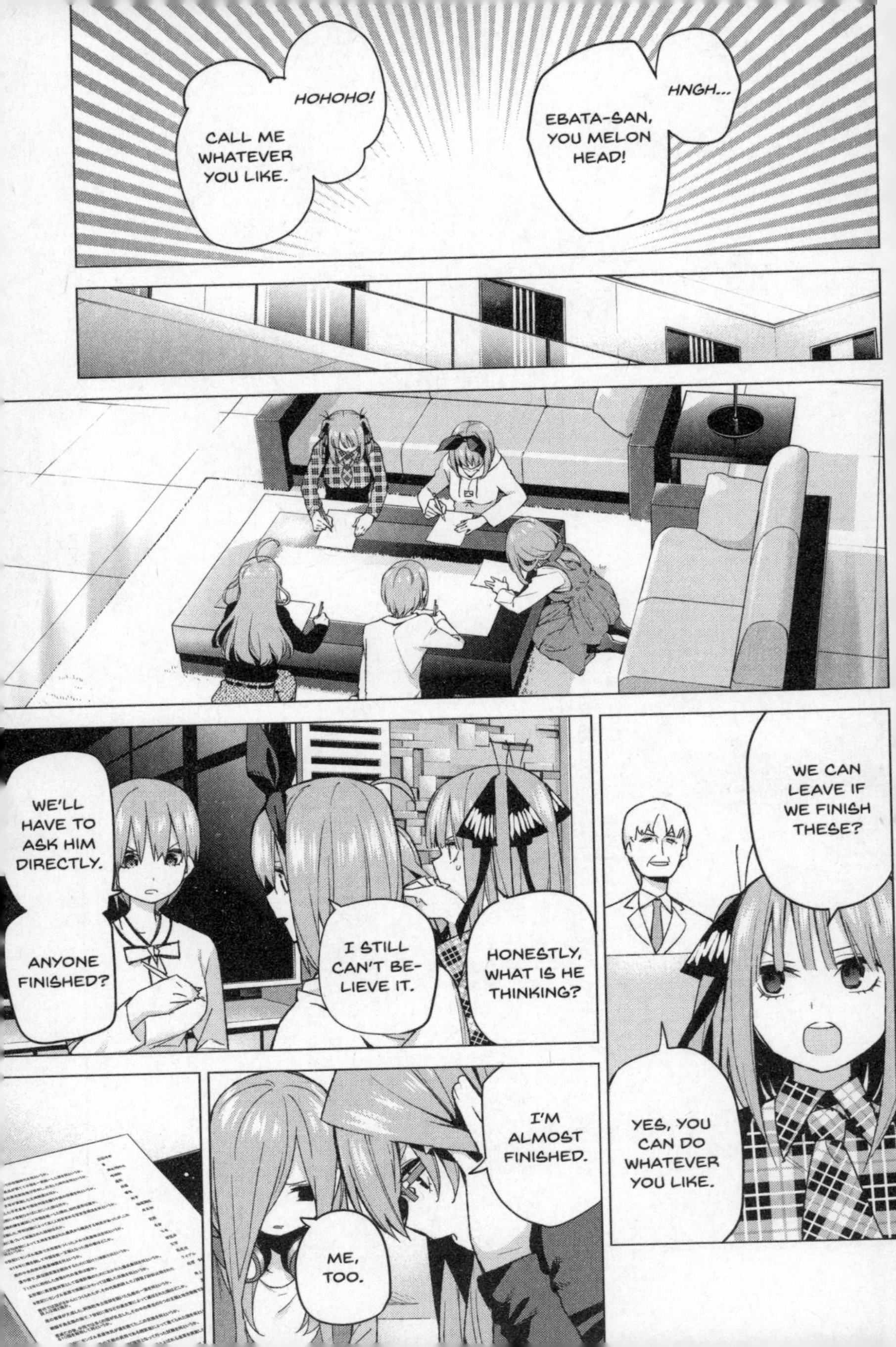
HNGH...
EBATA-SAN, YOU MELON HEAD!
HOHOHO!
CALL ME WHATEVER YOU LIKE.
WE CAN LEAVE IF WE FINISH THESE?
YES, YOU CAN DO WHATEVER YOU LIKE.
HONESTLY, WHAT IS HE THINKING?
I STILL CAN'T BE-LIEVE IT.
WE'LL HAVE TO ASK HIM DIRECTLY.
ANYONE FINISHED?
I'M ALMOST FINISHED.
ME, TOO.

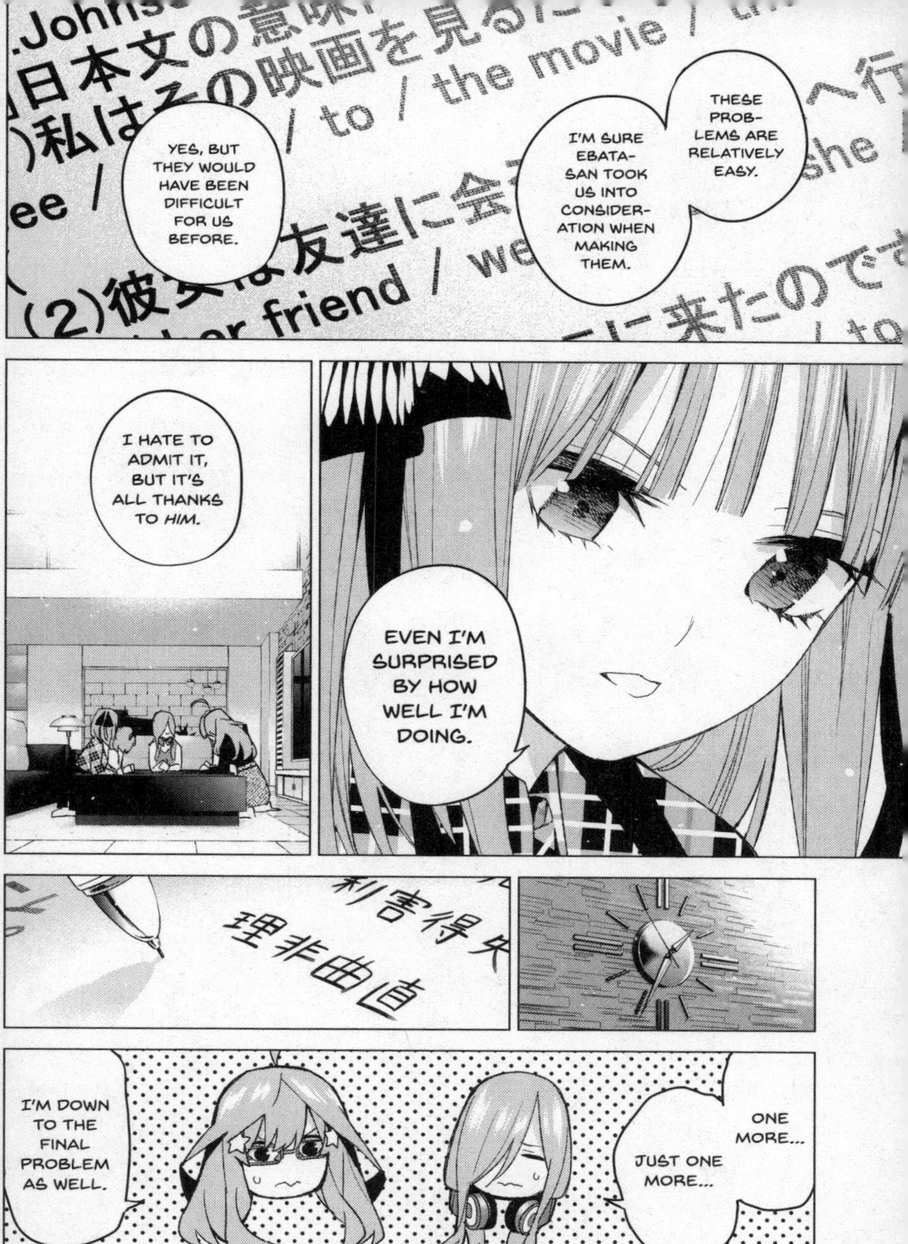
THESE PROB-LEMS ARE RELATIVELY EASY.
I'M SURE EBATA-SAN TOOK US INTO CONSIDER-ATION WHEN MAKING THEM.
YES, BUT THEY WOULD HAVE BEEN DIFFICULT FOR US BEFORE.
EVEN I'M SURPRISED BY HOW WELL I'M DOING.
I HATE TO ADMIT IT, BUT IT'S ALL THANKS TO *HIM*.
ONE MORE... JUST ONE MORE...
I'M DOWN TO THE FINAL PROBLEM AS WELL.

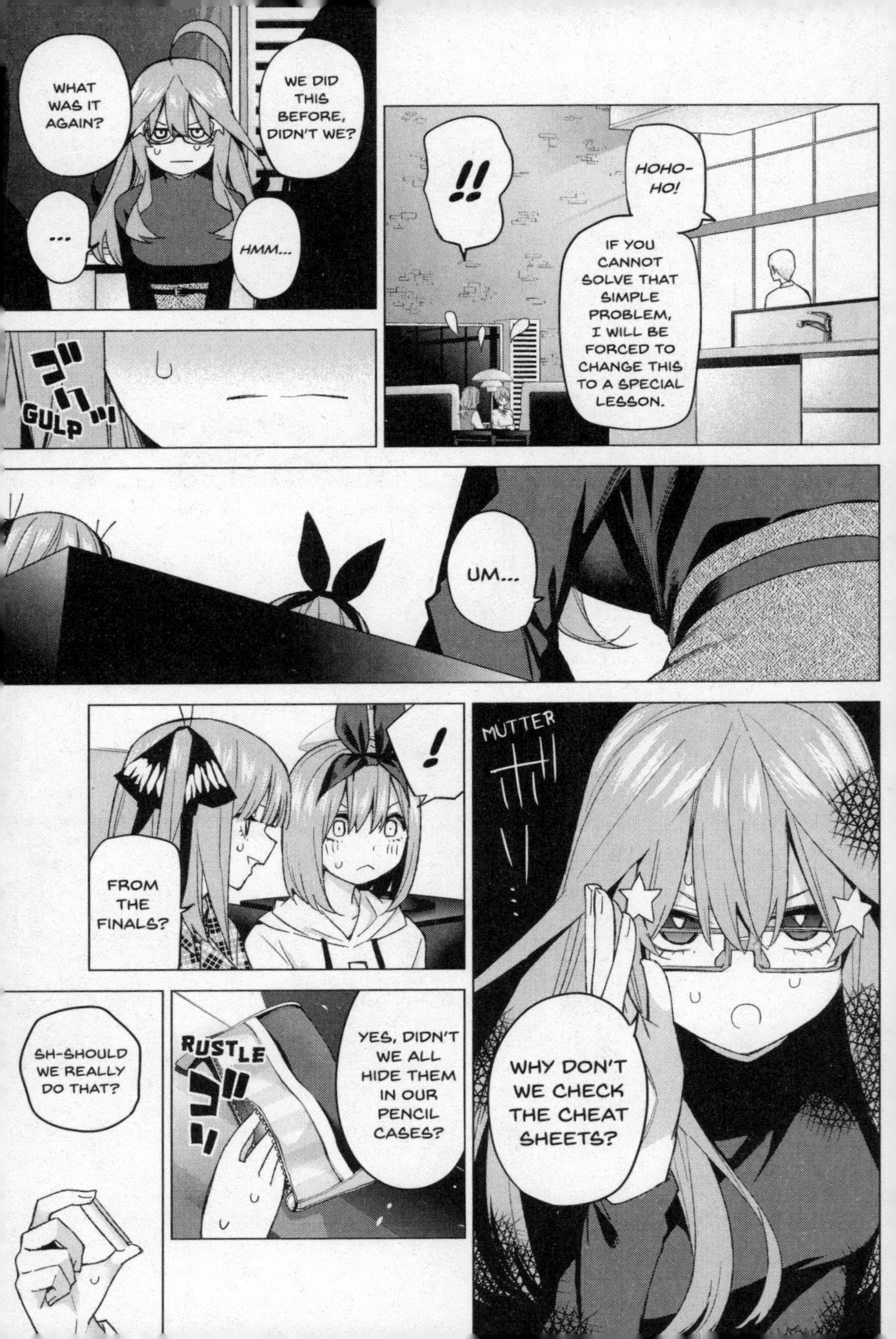

HOHO-HO!
IF YOU CANNOT SOLVE THAT SIMPLE PROBLEM, I WILL BE FORCED TO CHANGE THIS TO A SPECIAL LESSON.
!!
WE DID THIS BEFORE, DIDN'T WE?
WHAT WAS IT AGAIN?
HMM...
...
GULP
UM...
MUTTER
WHY DON'T WE CHECK THE CHEAT SHEETS?
!
FROM THE FINALS?
YES, DIDN'T WE ALL HIDE THEM IN OUR PENCIL CASES?
RUSTLE
SH-SHOULD WE REALLY DO THAT?

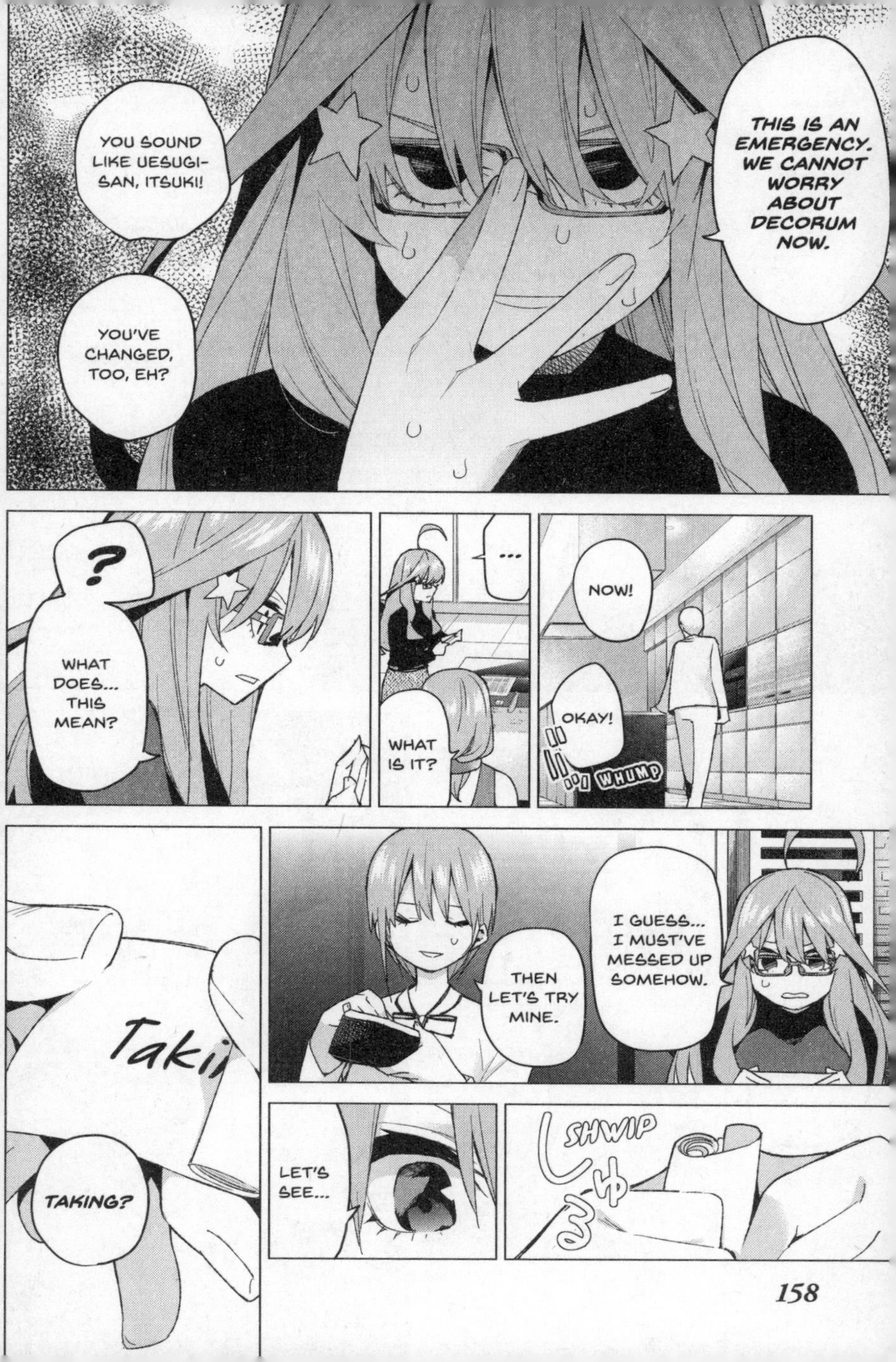

THIS IS AN EMERGENCY. WE CANNOT WORRY ABOUT DECORUM NOW.
YOU SOUND LIKE UESUGI-SAN, ITSUKI!
YOU'VE CHANGED, TOO, EH?
NOW!
OKAY!
WHUMP
...
WHAT IS IT?
?
WHAT DOES... THIS MEAN?
I GUESS... I MUST'VE MESSED UP SOMEHOW.
THEN LET'S TRY MINE.
SHWIP
LET'S SEE...
Taki
TAKING?

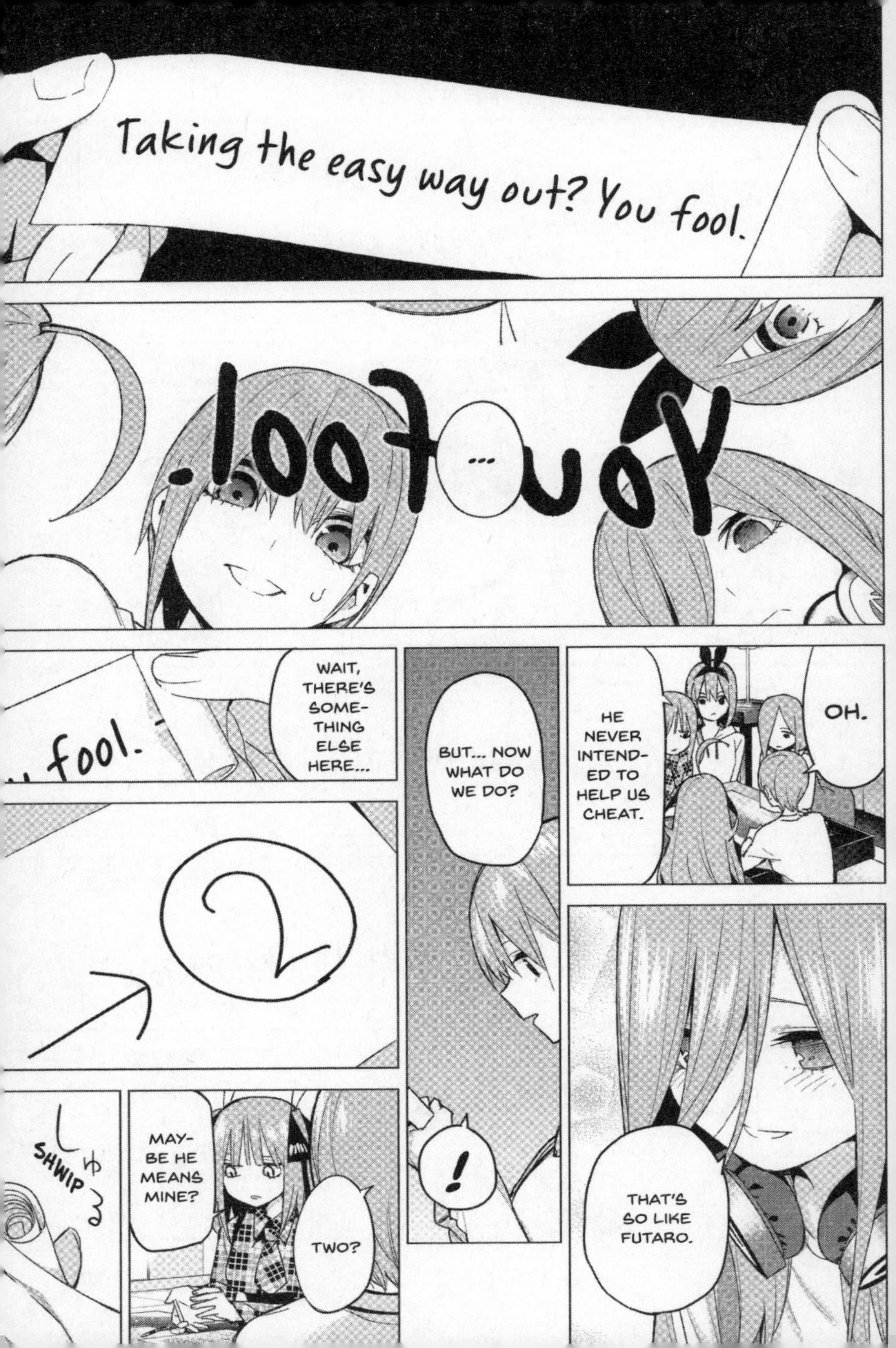
Taking the easy way out? You fool.
You fool.
...
OH.
HE NEVER INTEND-ED TO HELP US CHEAT.
THAT'S SO LIKE FUTARO.
BUT... NOW WHAT DO WE DO?
!
WAIT, THERE'S SOME-THING ELSE HERE...
... fool.
2
TWO?
MAY-BE HE MEANS MINE?
SHWIP
しゅる

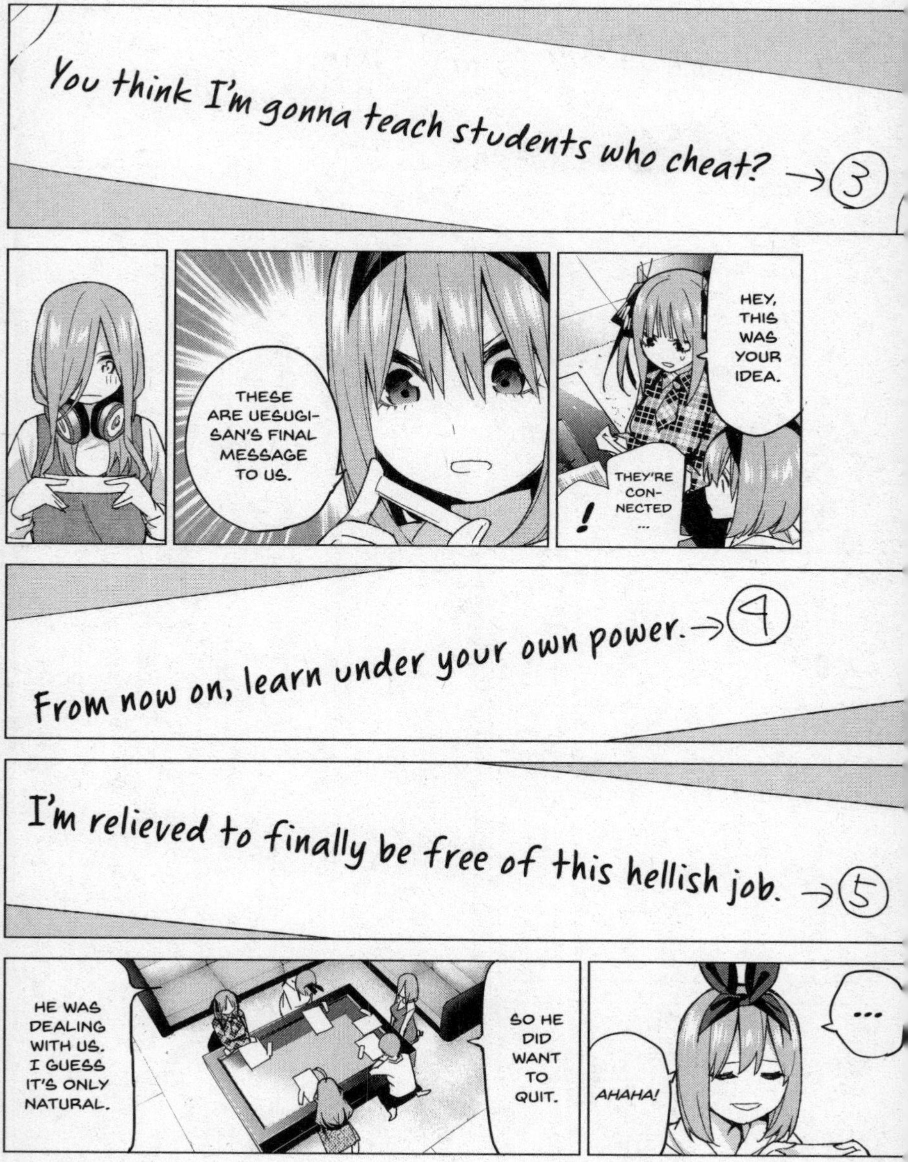
You think I'm gonna teach students who cheat? →③
HEY, THIS WAS YOUR IDEA.
THEY'RE CON- NECTED ...
!
THESE ARE UESUGI-SAN'S FINAL MESSAGE TO US.
From now on, learn under your own power. →④
I'm relieved to finally be free of this hellish job. →⑤
...
AHAHA!
SO HE DID WANT TO QUIT.
HE WAS DEALING WITH US. I GUESS IT'S ONLY NATURAL.

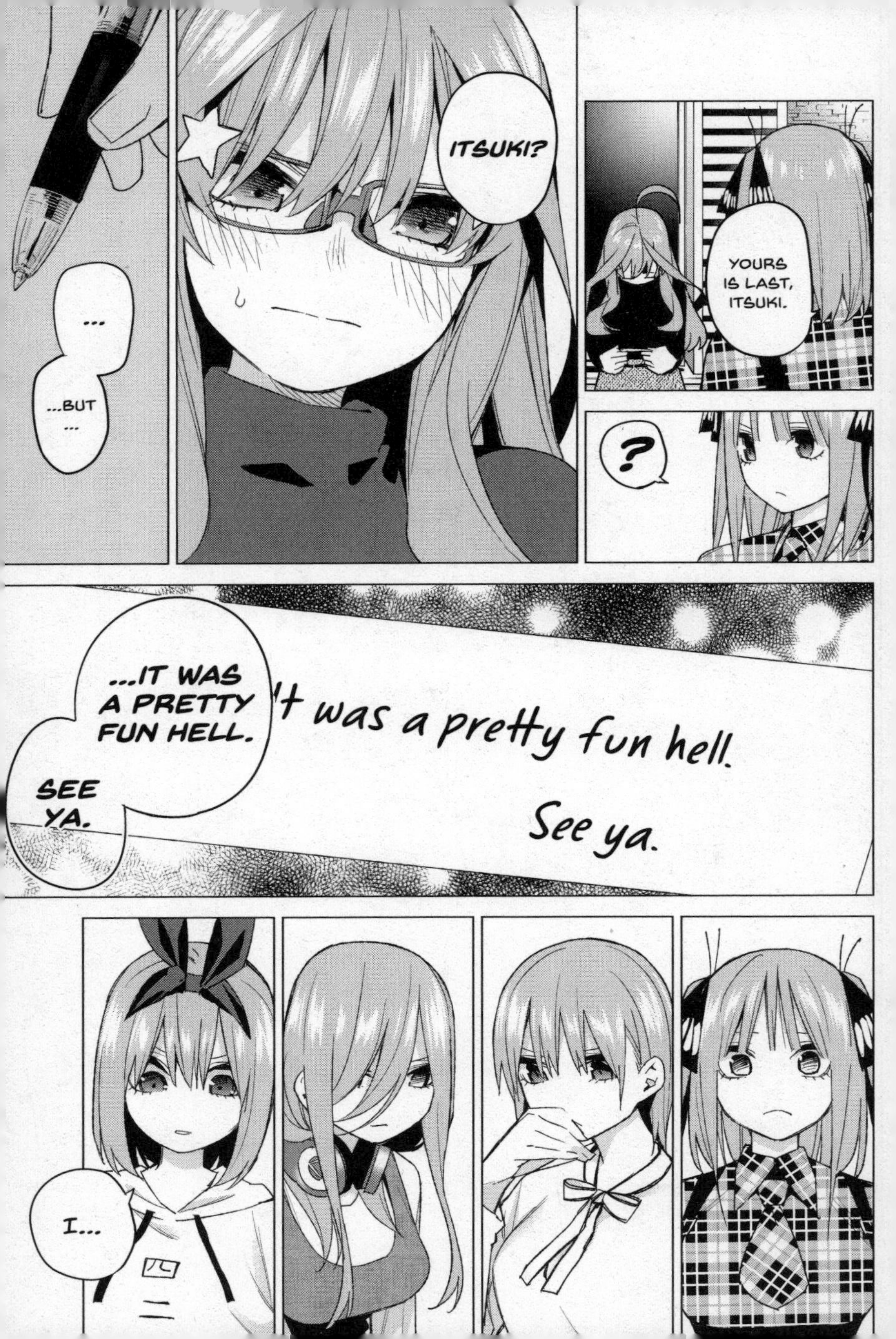
YOURS IS LAST, ITSUKI.
?
ITSUKI?
...
...BUT ...
...IT WAS A PRETTY FUN HELL.
SEE YA.
t was a pretty fun hell.
See ya.
I...

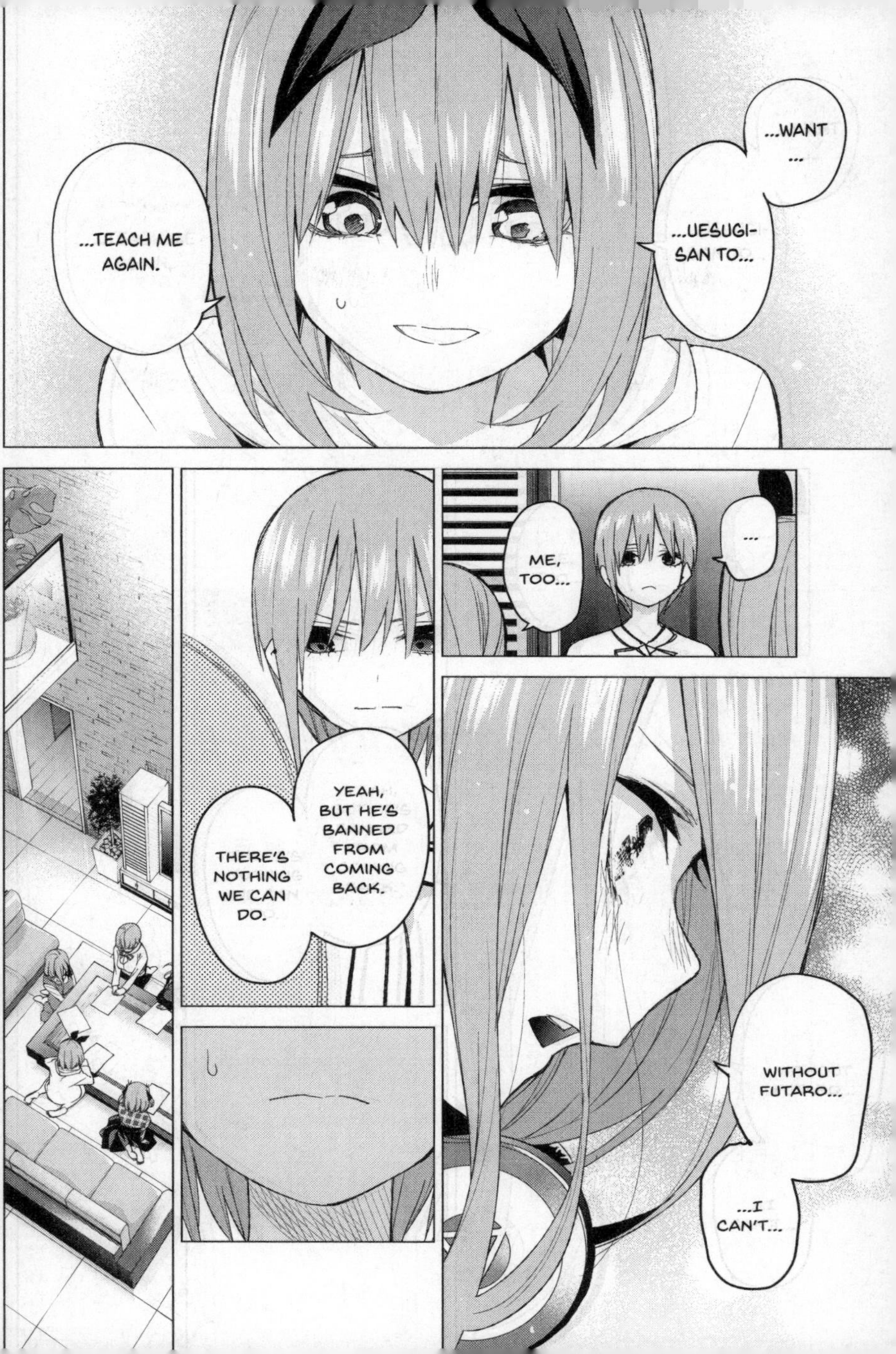
...WANT ...
...UESUGI-SAN TO...
...TEACH ME AGAIN.
...
ME, TOO...
WITHOUT FUTARO...
...I CAN'T...
YEAH, BUT HE'S BANNED FROM COMING BACK.
THERE'S NOTHING WE CAN DO.

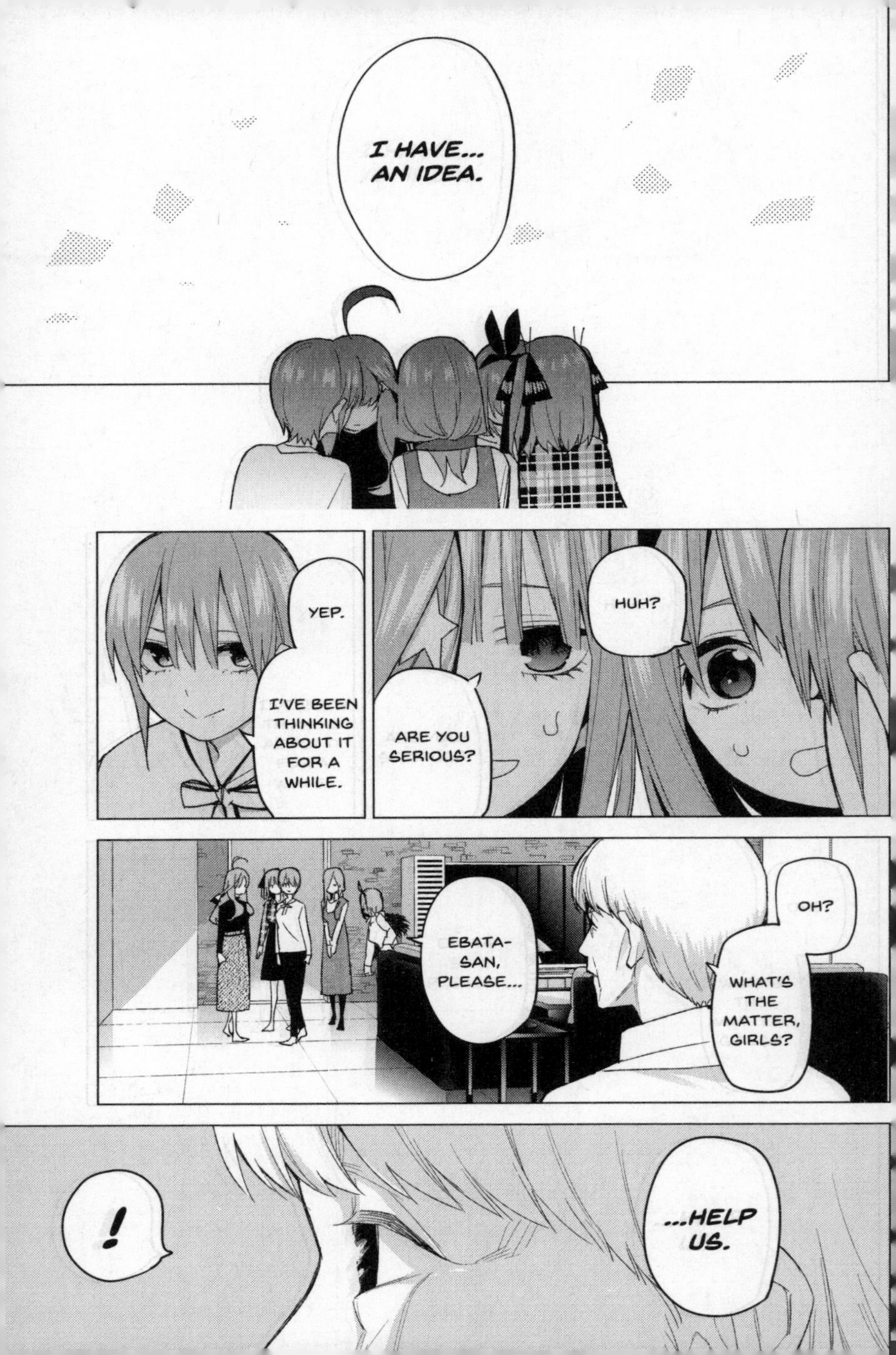
I HAVE... AN IDEA.
HUH?
ARE YOU SERIOUS?
YEP.
I'VE BEEN THINKING ABOUT IT FOR A WHILE.
OH?
WHAT'S THE MATTER, GIRLS?
EBATA-SAN, PLEASE...
...HELP US.
!

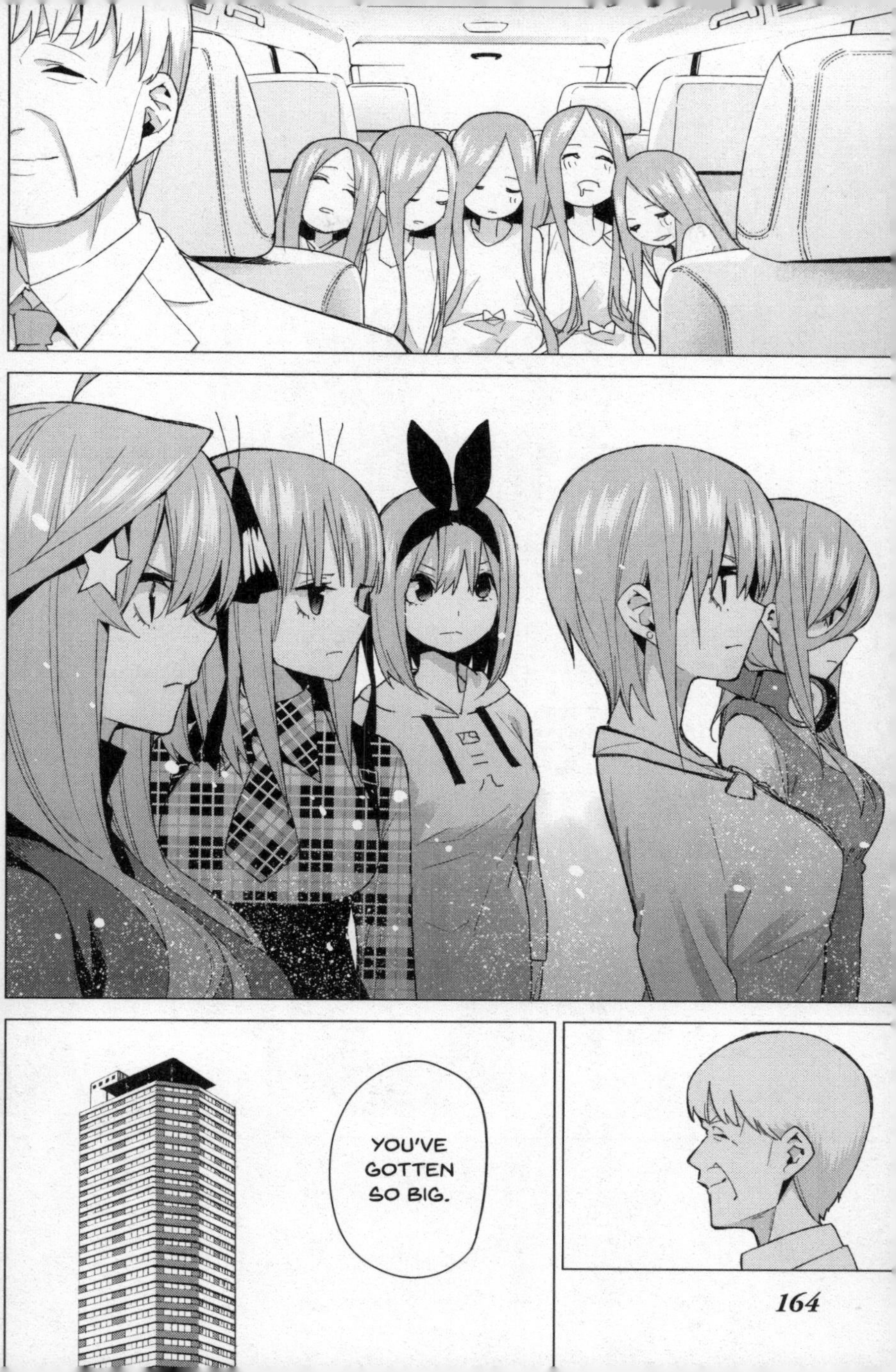
YOU'VE
GOTTEN
SO BIG.

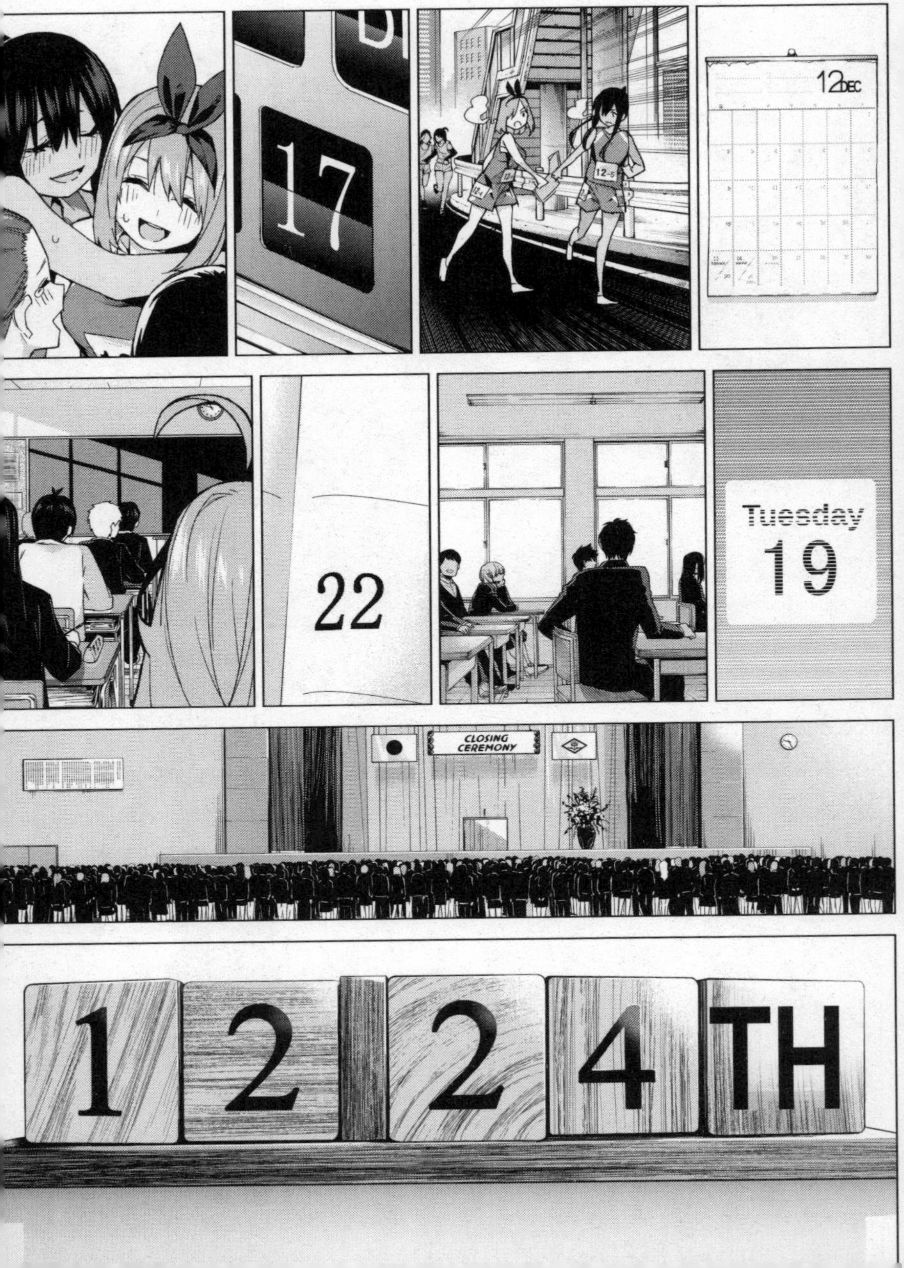
12 DEC
12-5
17
Tuesday
19
22
CLOSING CEREMONY
1 2 2 4 TH

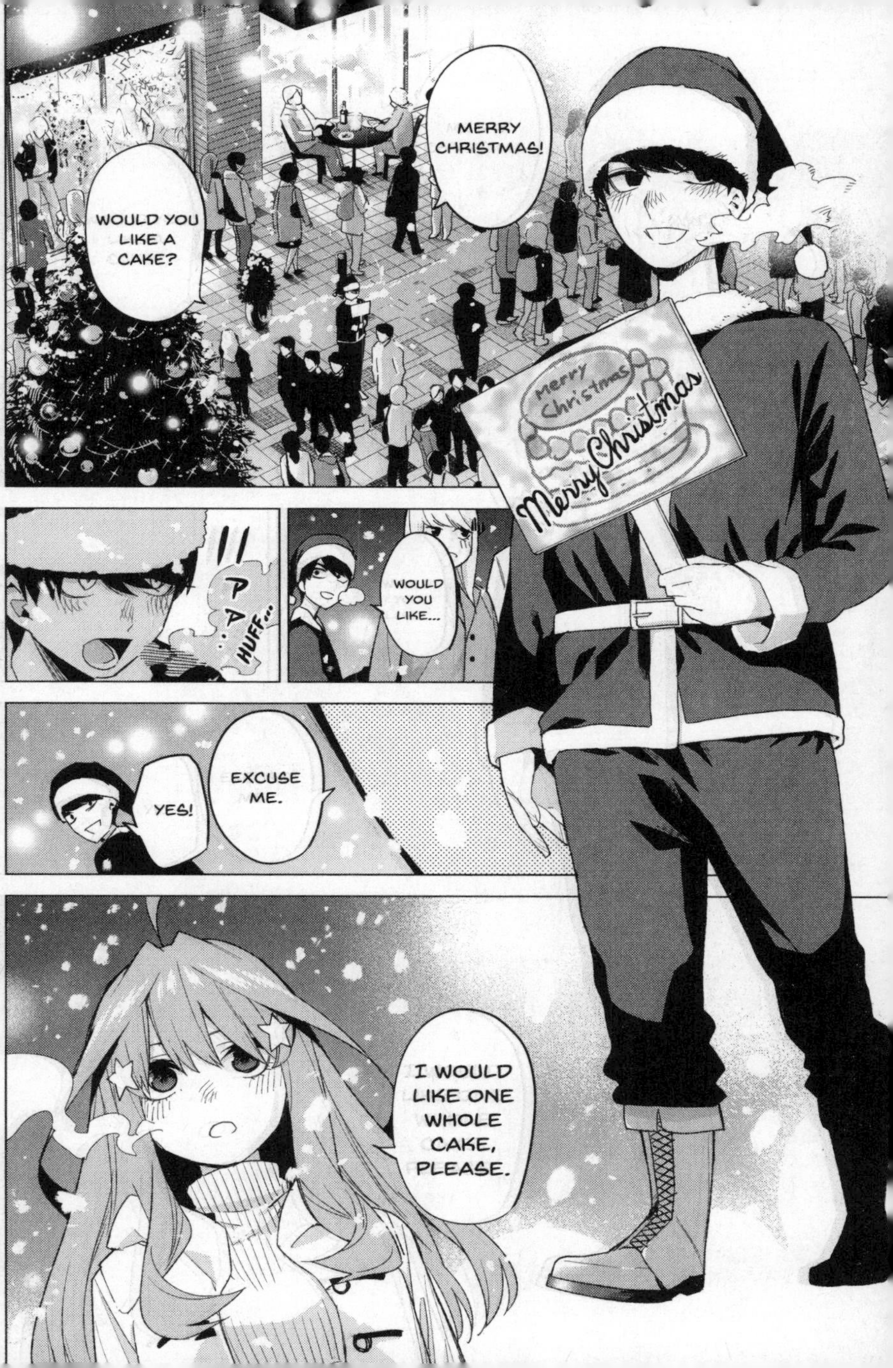
MERRY CHRISTMAS!
WOULD YOU LIKE A CAKE?
Merry Christmas
Merry Christmas
WOULD YOU LIKE...
PA..
HUFF...
EXCUSE ME.
YES!
I WOULD LIKE ONE WHOLE CAKE, PLEASE.

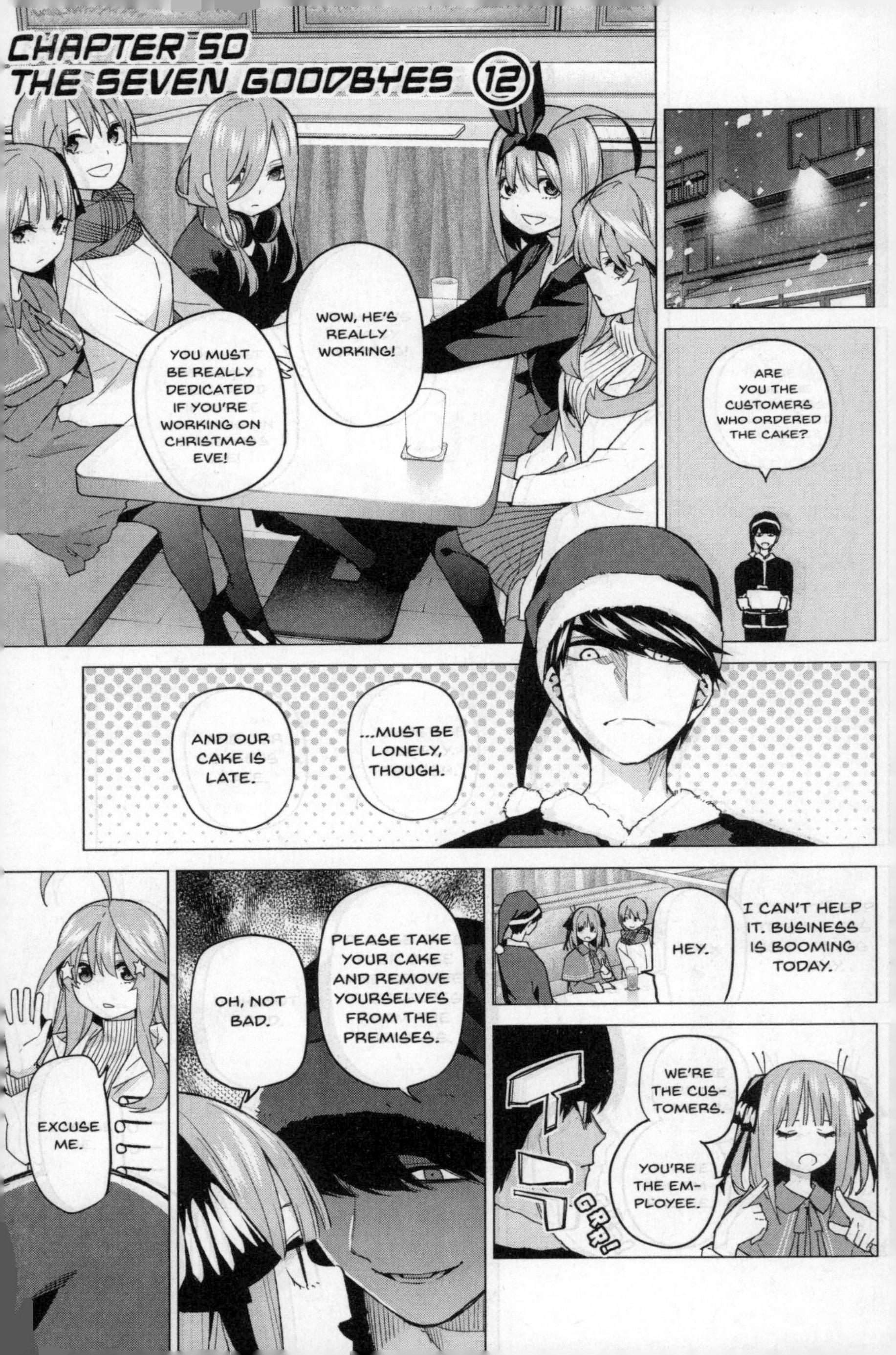
ARE YOU THE CUSTOMERS WHO ORDERED THE CAKE?
CHAPTER 50
THE SEVEN GOODBYES ⑫
WOW, HE'S REALLY WORKING!
YOU MUST BE REALLY DEDICATED IF YOU'RE WORKING ON CHRISTMAS EVE!
...MUST BE LONELY, THOUGH.
AND OUR CAKE IS LATE.
I CAN'T HELP IT. BUSINESS IS BOOMING TODAY.
HEY.
WE'RE THE CUS-TOMERS.
YOU'RE THE EM-PLOYEE.
GRR!
PLEASE TAKE YOUR CAKE AND REMOVE YOURSELVES FROM THE PREMISES.
OH, NOT BAD.
EXCUSE ME.

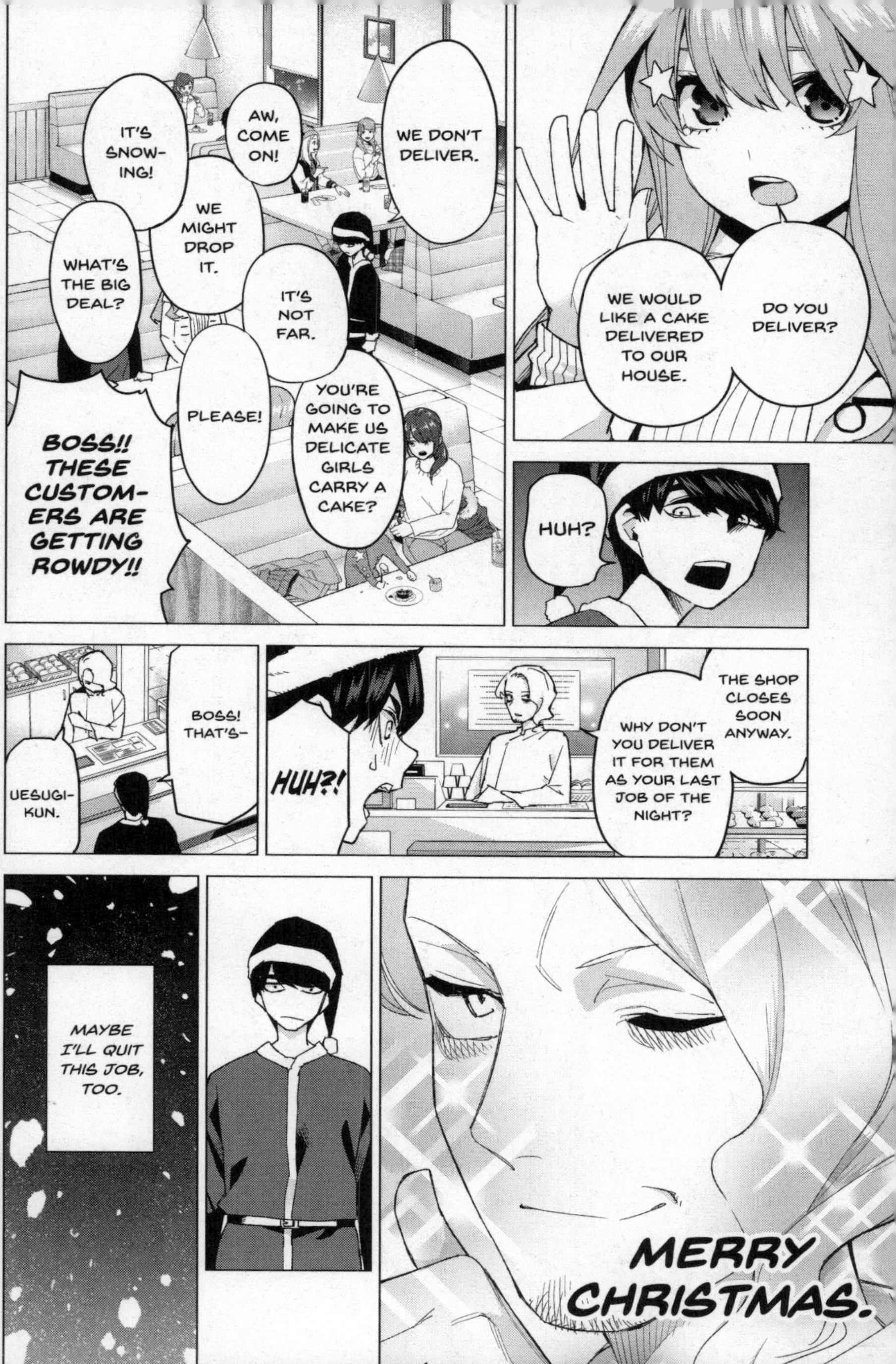
DO YOU DELIVER?
WE WOULD LIKE A CAKE DELIVERED TO OUR HOUSE.
HUH?
WE DON'T DELIVER.
AW, COME ON!
IT'S SNOWING!
WE MIGHT DROP IT.
WHAT'S THE BIG DEAL?
IT'S NOT FAR.
PLEASE!
YOU'RE GOING TO MAKE US DELICATE GIRLS CARRY A CAKE?
BOSS!! THESE CUSTOMERS ARE GETTING ROWDY!!
THE SHOP CLOSES SOON ANYWAY.
WHY DON'T YOU DELIVER IT FOR THEM AS YOUR LAST JOB OF THE NIGHT?
HUH?!
BOSS! THAT'S-
UESUGI-KUN.
MERRY CHRISTMAS.
MAYBE I'LL QUIT THIS JOB, TOO.

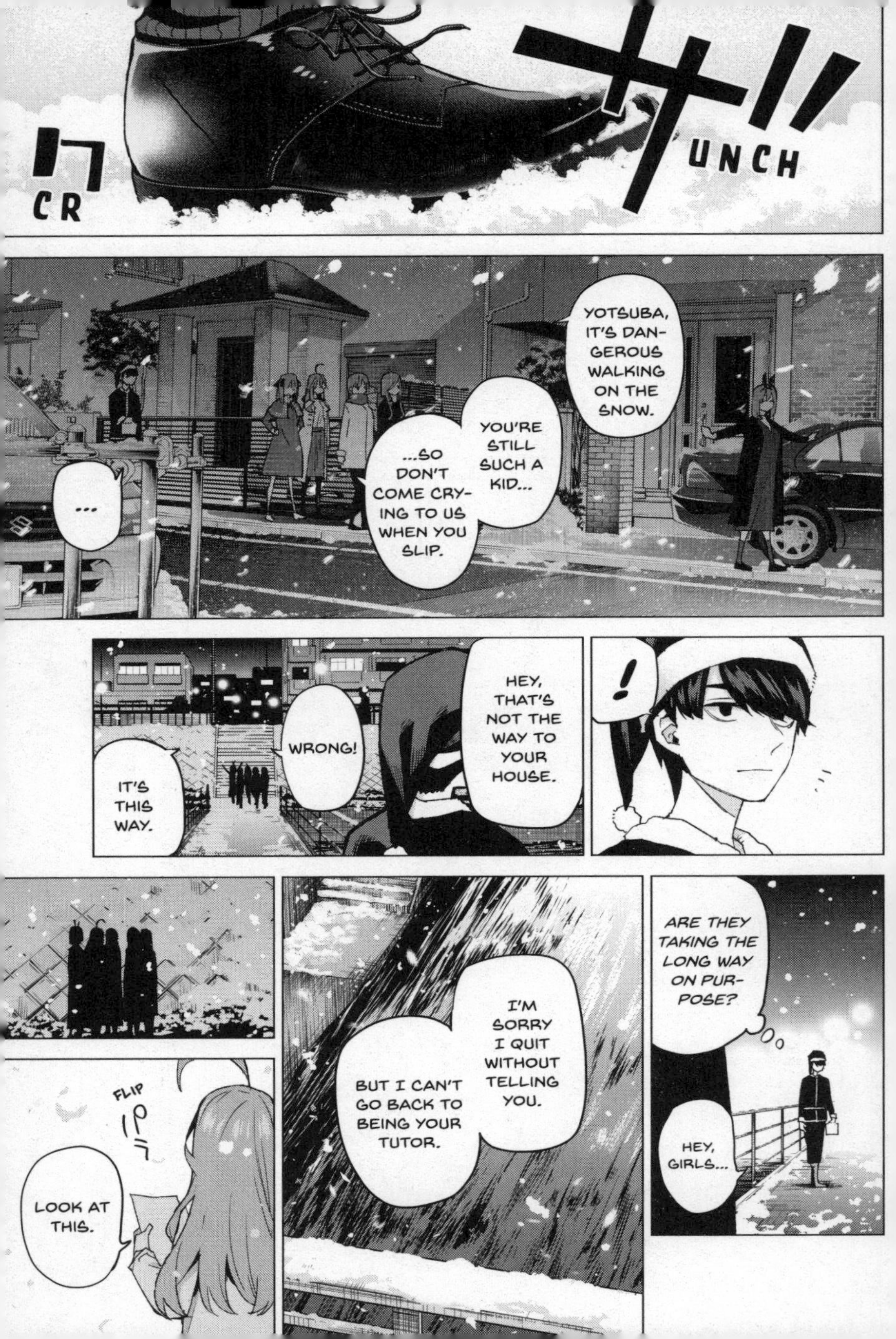

CR UNCH
YOTSUBA, IT'S DANGEROUS WALKING ON THE SNOW.
YOU'RE STILL SUCH A KID...
...SO DON'T COME CRYING TO US WHEN YOU SLIP.
...
!
HEY, THAT'S NOT THE WAY TO YOUR HOUSE.
WRONG!
IT'S THIS WAY.
ARE THEY TAKING THE LONG WAY ON PURPOSE?
HEY, GIRLS...
I'M SORRY I QUIT WITHOUT TELLING YOU.
BUT I CAN'T GO BACK TO BEING YOUR TUTOR.
FLIP
LOOK AT THIS.

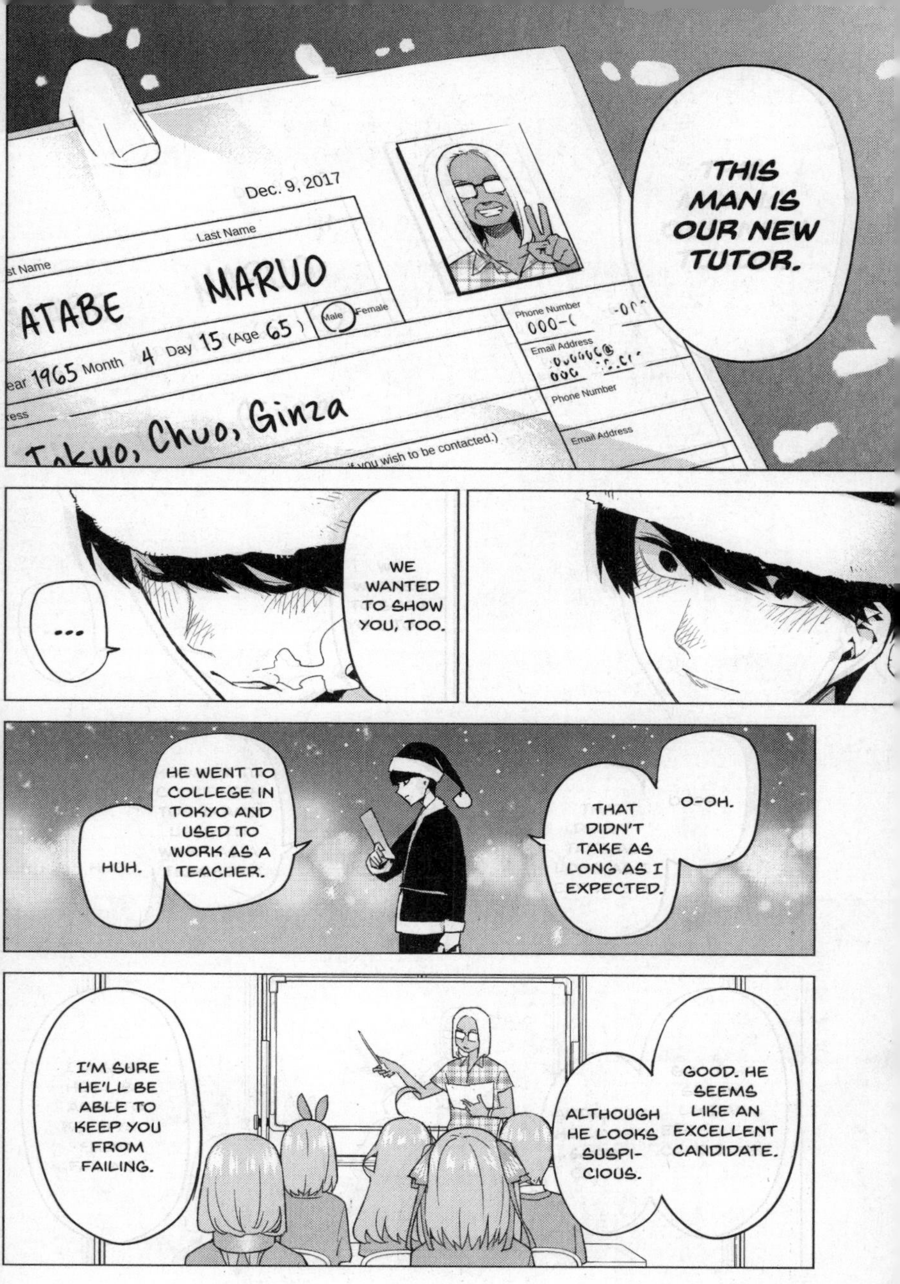

Dec. 9, 2017
Last Name
st Name
ATABE
MARUO
Male Female
ear 1965 Month 4 Day 15 (Age 65)
Phone Number
Email Address
Phone Number
Email Address
ress
Tokyo, Chuo, Ginza
if you wish to be contacted.)
THIS MAN IS OUR NEW TUTOR.
WE WANTED TO SHOW YOU, TOO.
...
O-OH.
THAT DIDN'T TAKE AS LONG AS I EXPECTED.
HE WENT TO COLLEGE IN TOKYO AND USED TO WORK AS A TEACHER.
HUH.
GOOD. HE SEEMS LIKE AN EXCELLENT CANDIDATE.
ALTHOUGH HE LOOKS SUSPICIOUS.
I'M SURE HE'LL BE ABLE TO KEEP YOU FROM FAILING.

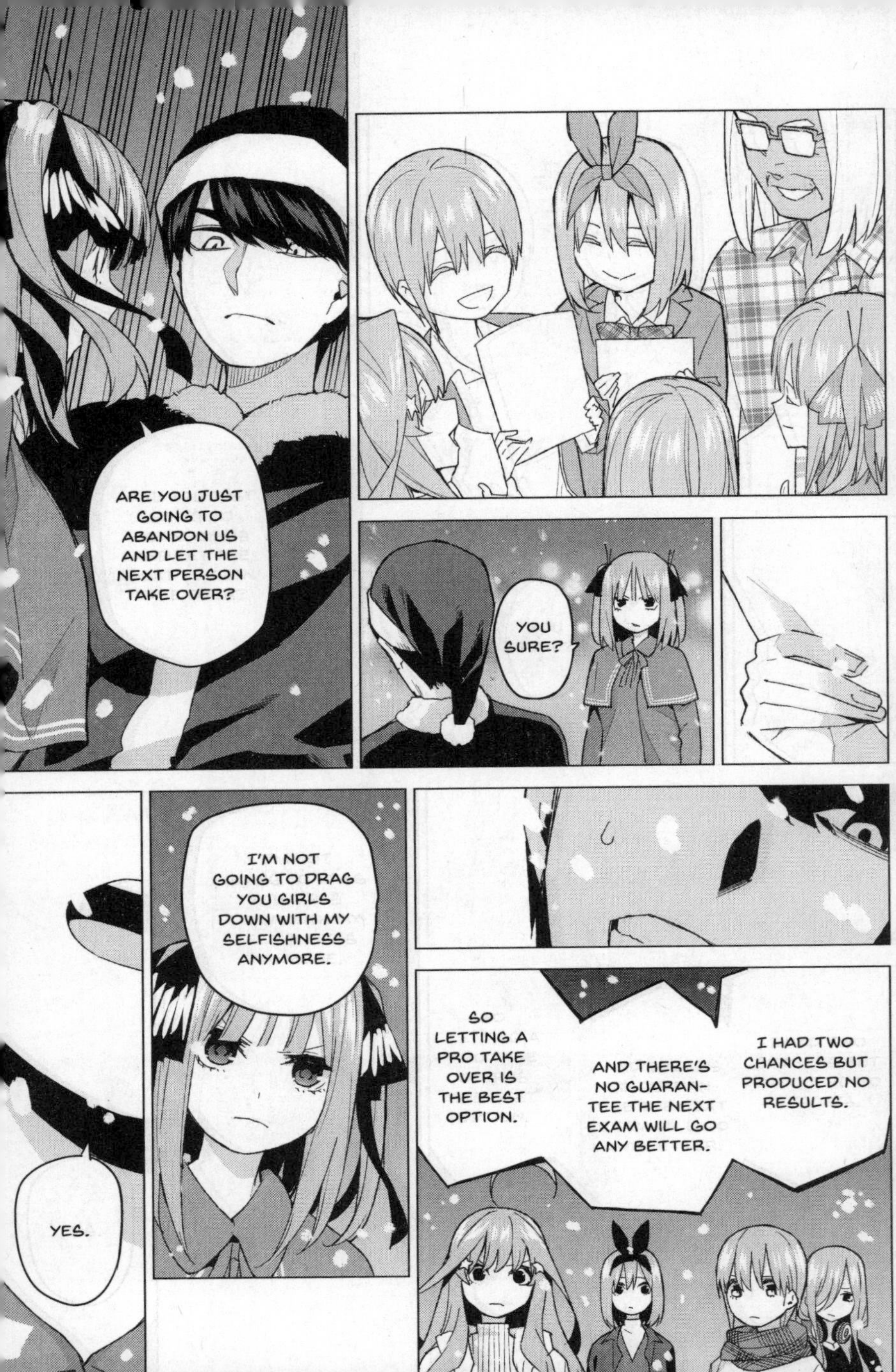
YOU SURE?
ARE YOU JUST GOING TO ABANDON US AND LET THE NEXT PERSON TAKE OVER?
I HAD TWO CHANCES BUT PRODUCED NO RESULTS.
AND THERE'S NO GUARAN-TEE THE NEXT EXAM WILL GO ANY BETTER.
SO LETTING A PRO TAKE OVER IS THE BEST OPTION.
I'M NOT GOING TO DRAG YOU GIRLS DOWN WITH MY SELFISHNESS ANYMORE.
YES.

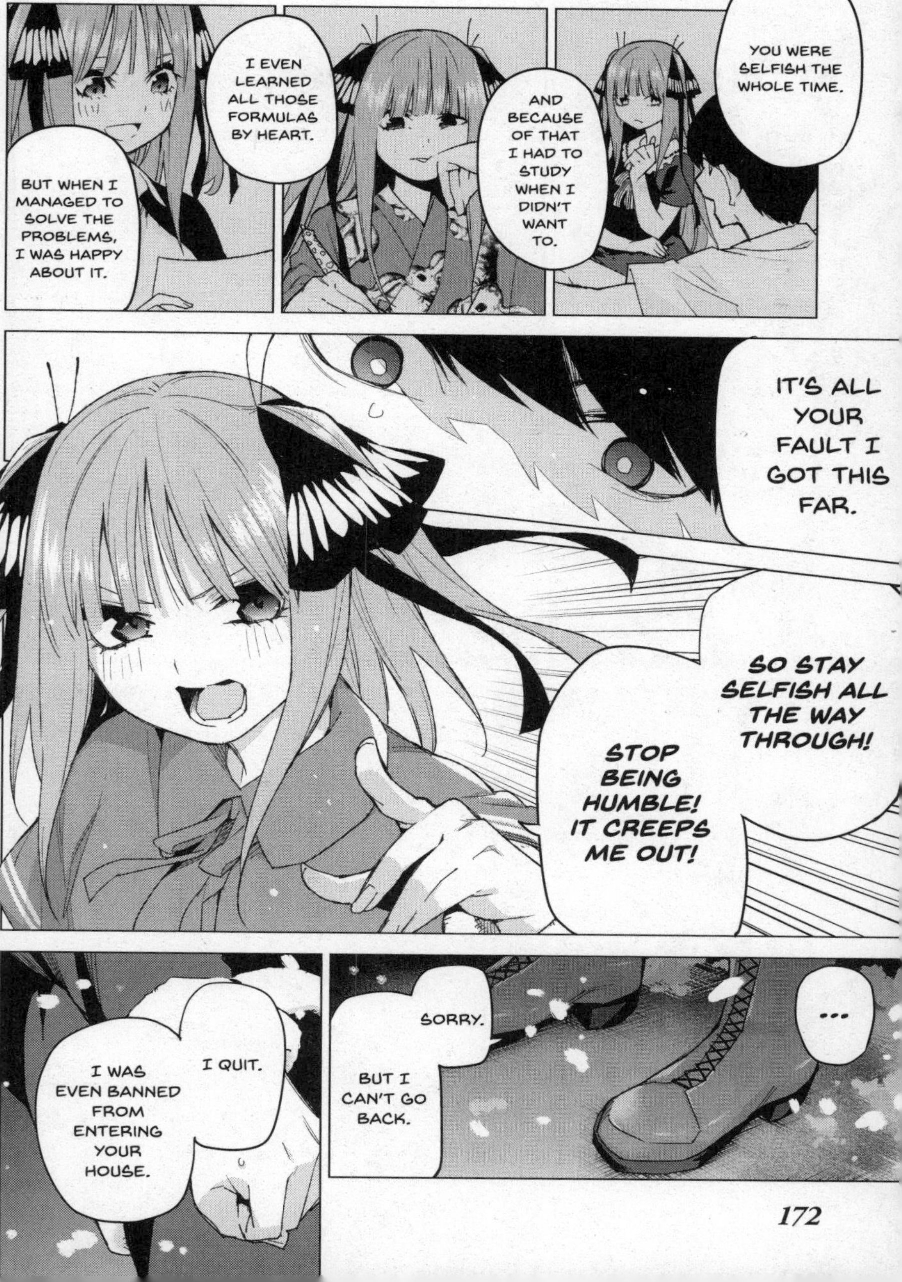
YOU WERE SELFISH THE WHOLE TIME.
AND BECAUSE OF THAT I HAD TO STUDY WHEN I DIDN'T WANT TO.
I EVEN LEARNED ALL THOSE FORMULAS BY HEART.
BUT WHEN I MANAGED TO SOLVE THE PROBLEMS, I WAS HAPPY ABOUT IT.
IT'S ALL YOUR FAULT I GOT THIS FAR.
SO STAY SELFISH ALL THE WAY THROUGH!
STOP BEING HUMBLE! IT CREEPS ME OUT!
...
SORRY.
BUT I CAN'T GO BACK.
I QUIT.
I WAS EVEN BANNED FROM ENTERING YOUR HOUSE.

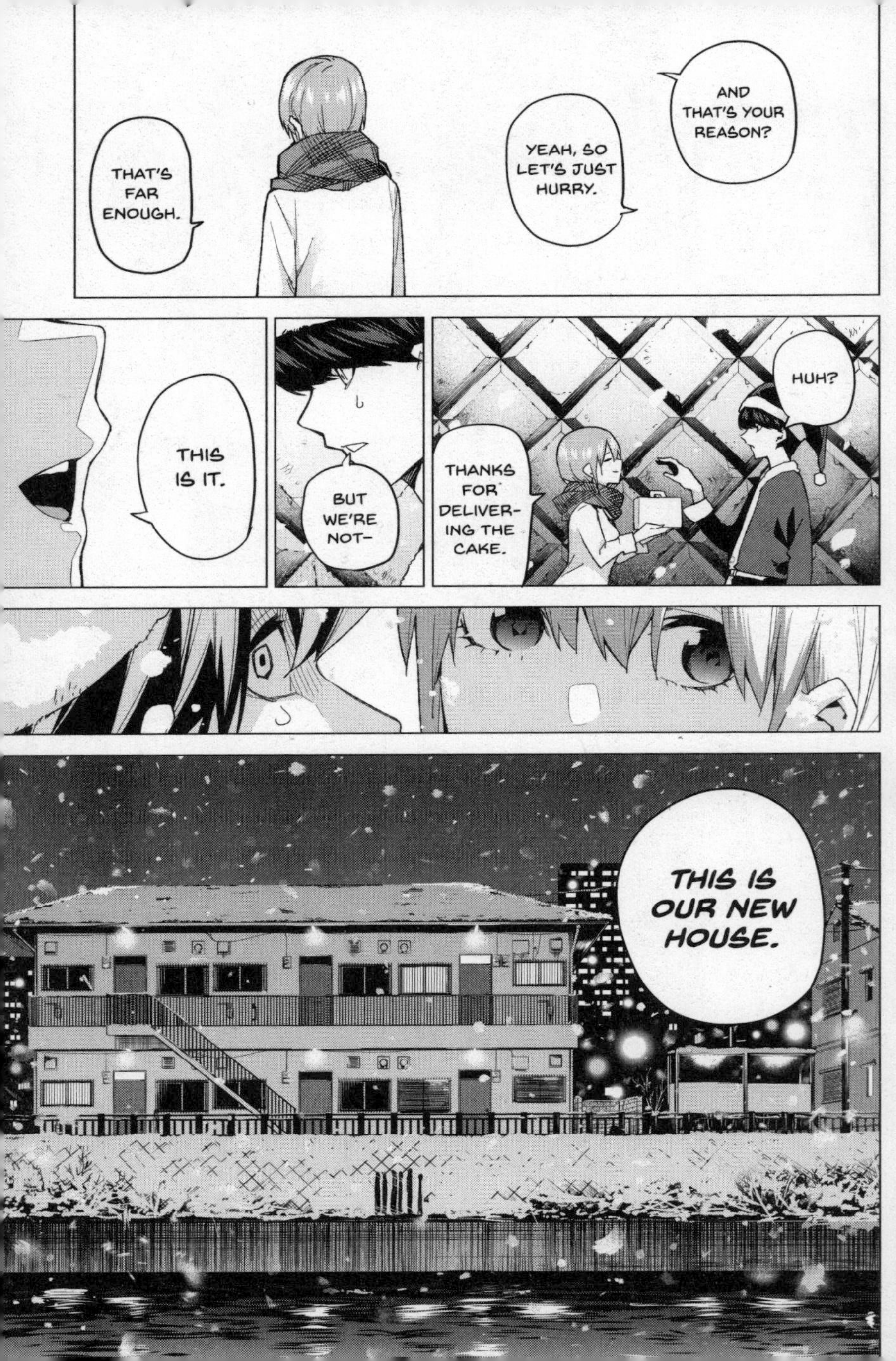
AND THAT'S YOUR REASON?
YEAH, SO LET'S JUST HURRY.
THAT'S FAR ENOUGH.
HUH?
THANKS FOR DELIVER-ING THE CAKE.
BUT WE'RE NOT-
THIS IS IT.
THIS IS OUR NEW HOUSE.

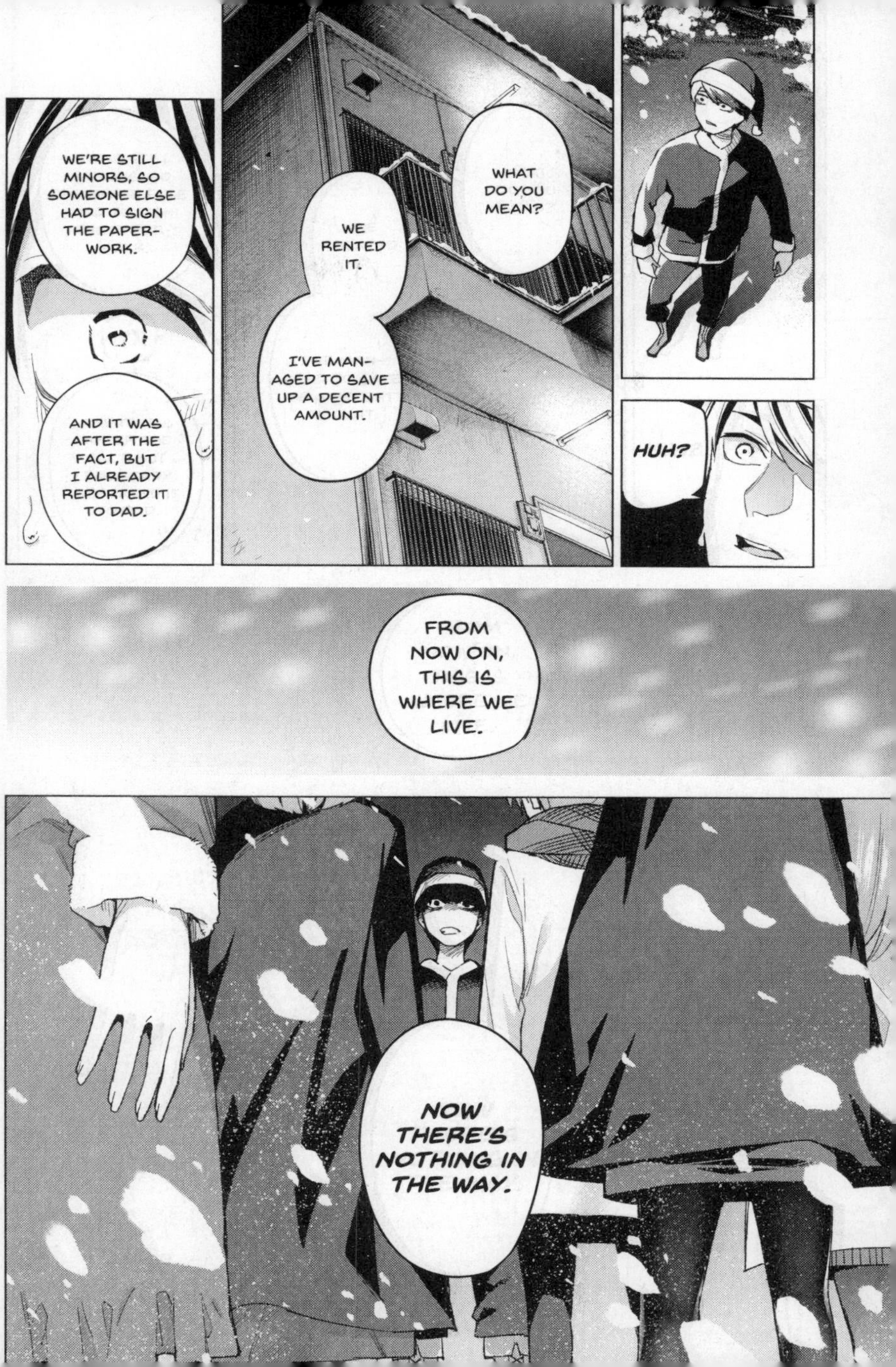
HUH?
WHAT DO YOU MEAN?
WE RENTED IT.
I'VE MAN-AGED TO SAVE UP A DECENT AMOUNT.
WE'RE STILL MINORS, SO SOMEONE ELSE HAD TO SIGN THE PAPER-WORK.
AND IT WAS AFTER THE FACT, BUT I ALREADY REPORTED IT TO DAD.
FROM NOW ON, THIS IS WHERE WE LIVE.
NOW THERE'S NOTHING IN THE WAY.

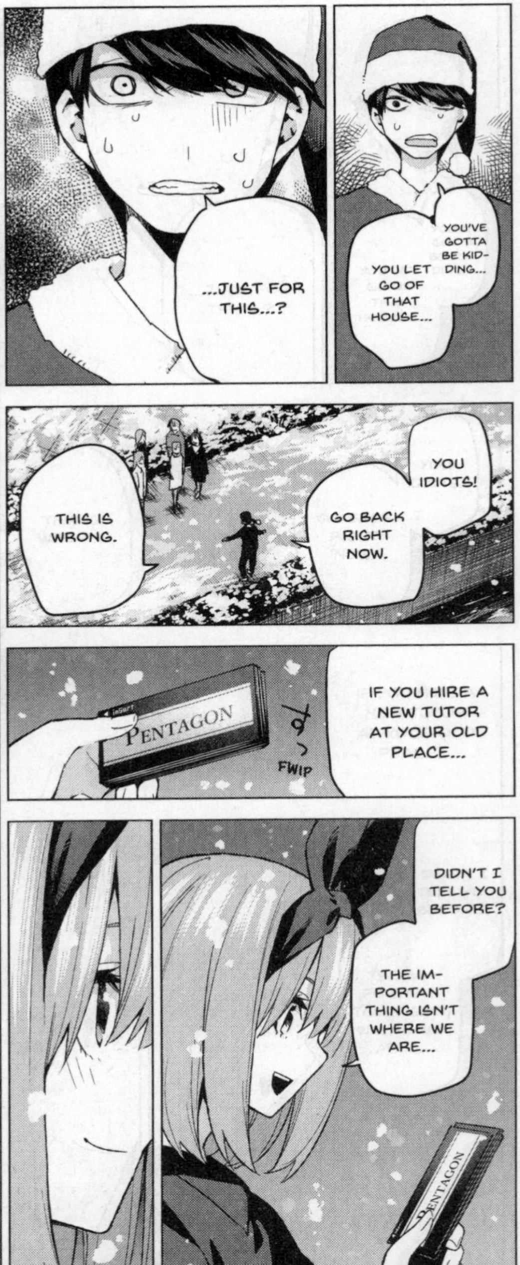
YOU'VE GOTTA BE KID- DING...
YOU LET GO OF THAT HOUSE...
...JUST FOR THIS...?
YOU IDIOTS!
GO BACK RIGHT NOW.
THIS IS WRONG.
IF YOU HIRE A NEW TUTOR AT YOUR OLD PLACE...
FWIP
PENTAGON
DIDN'T I TELL YOU BEFORE?
THE IM- PORTANT THING ISN'T WHERE WE ARE...
PENTAGON
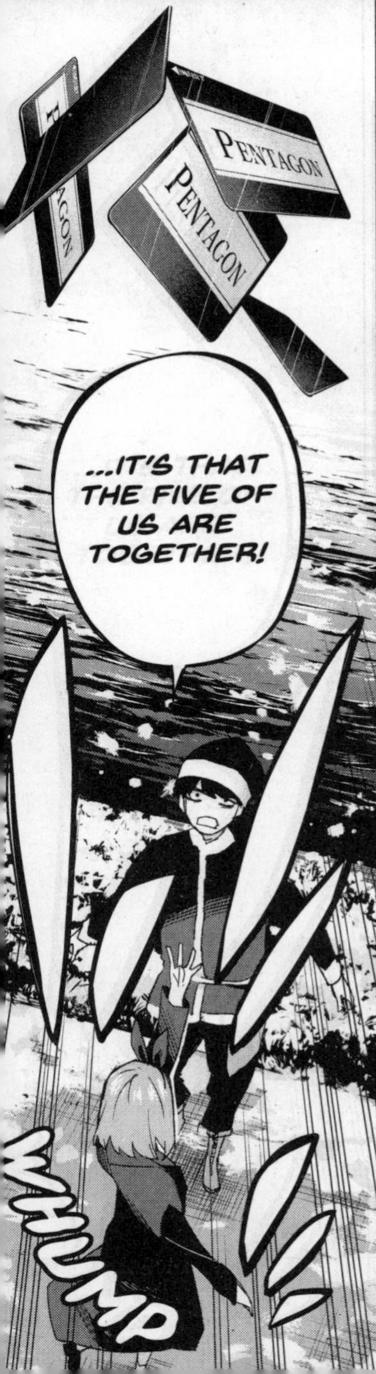
PENTAGON
PENTAGON
...IT'S THAT THE FIVE OF US ARE TOGETHER!
WHUMP

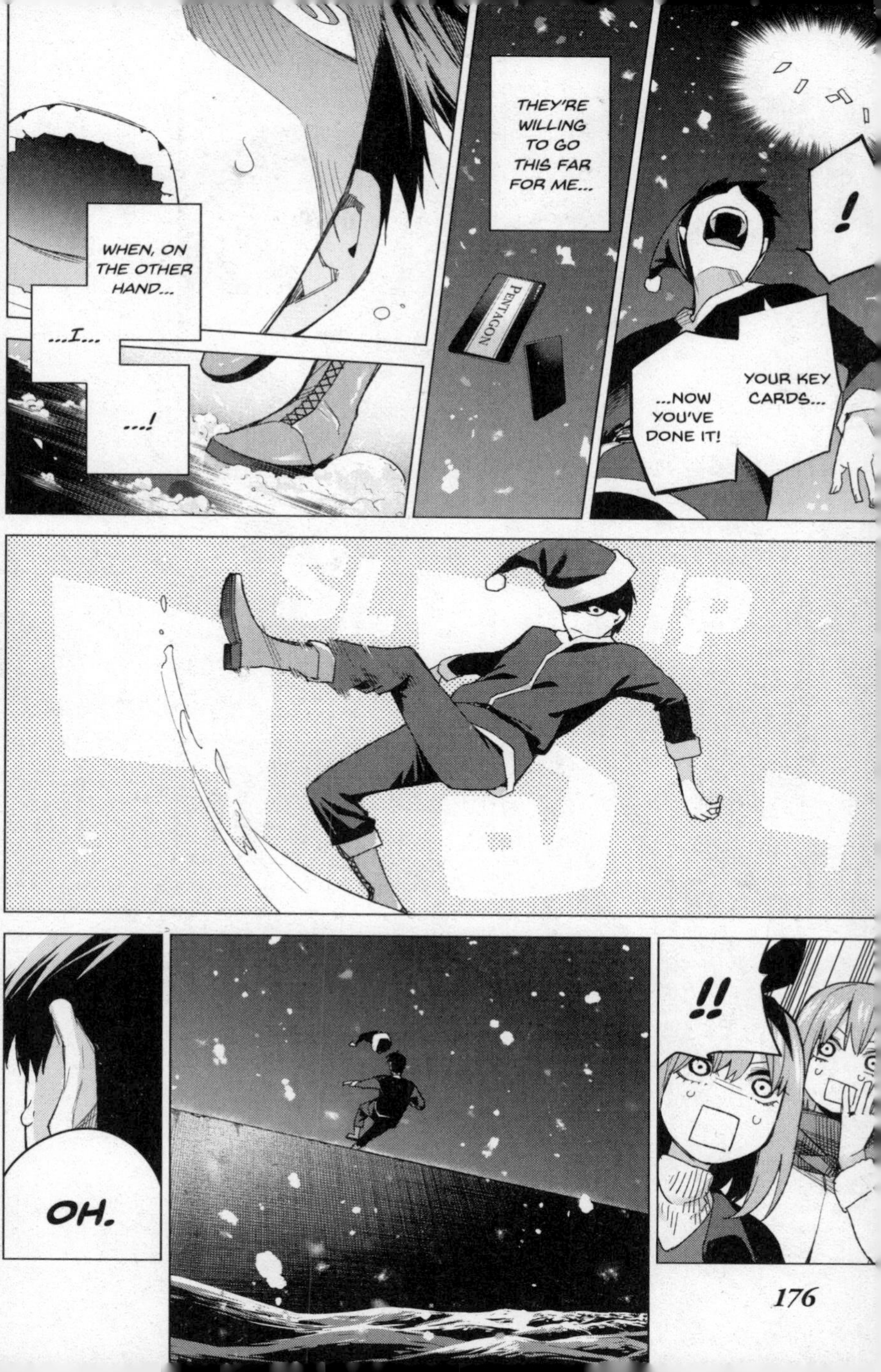
!
YOUR KEY CARDS...
...NOW YOU'VE DONE IT!
THEY'RE WILLING TO GO THIS FAR FOR ME...
PENTAGON
WHEN, ON THE OTHER HAND...
...I...
...!
!!
OH.

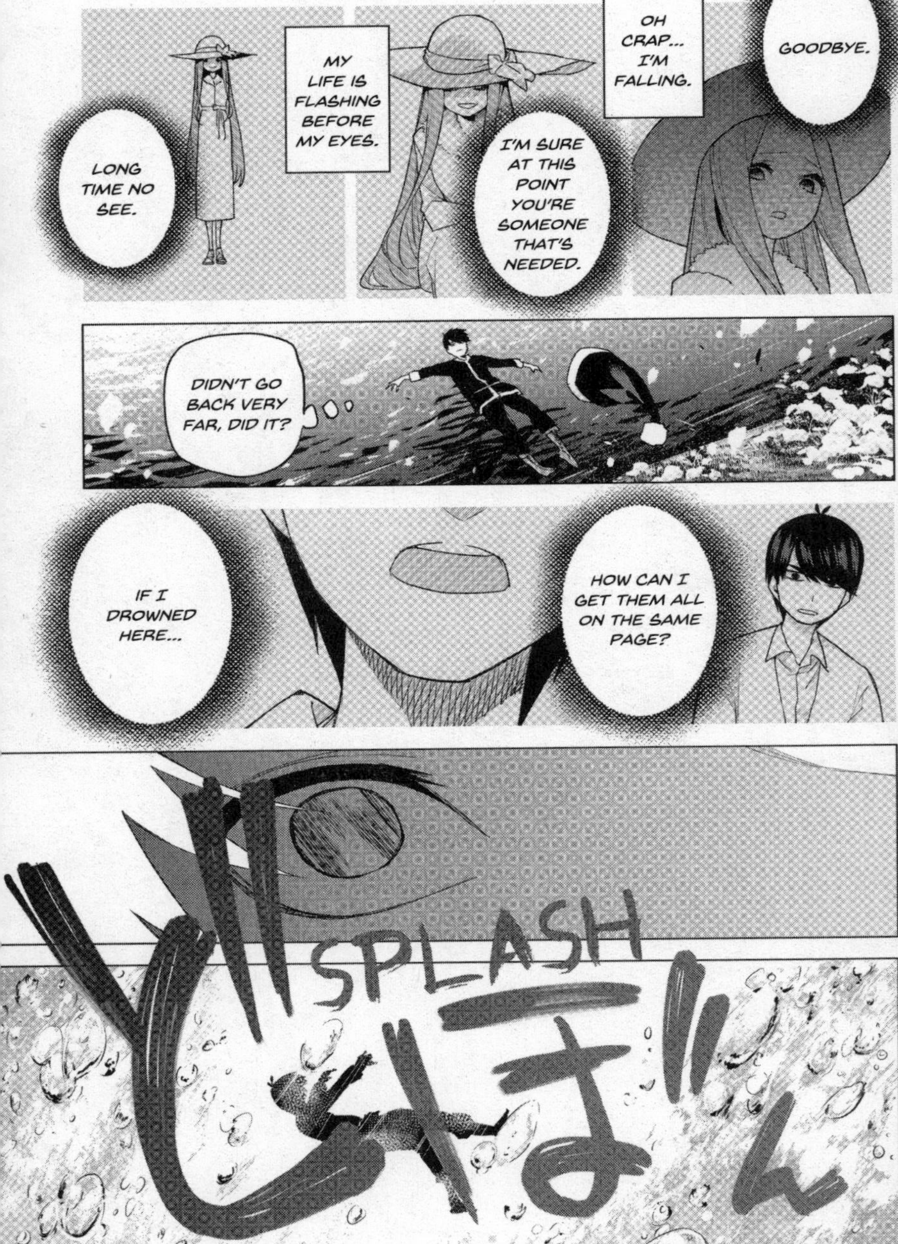
GOODBYE.
OH CRAP... I'M FALLING.
I'M SURE AT THIS POINT YOU'RE SOMEONE THAT'S NEEDED.
MY LIFE IS FLASHING BEFORE MY EYES.
LONG TIME NO SEE.
DIDN'T GO BACK VERY FAR, DID IT?
HOW CAN I GET THEM ALL ON THE SAME PAGE?
IF I DROWNED HERE...
SPLASH

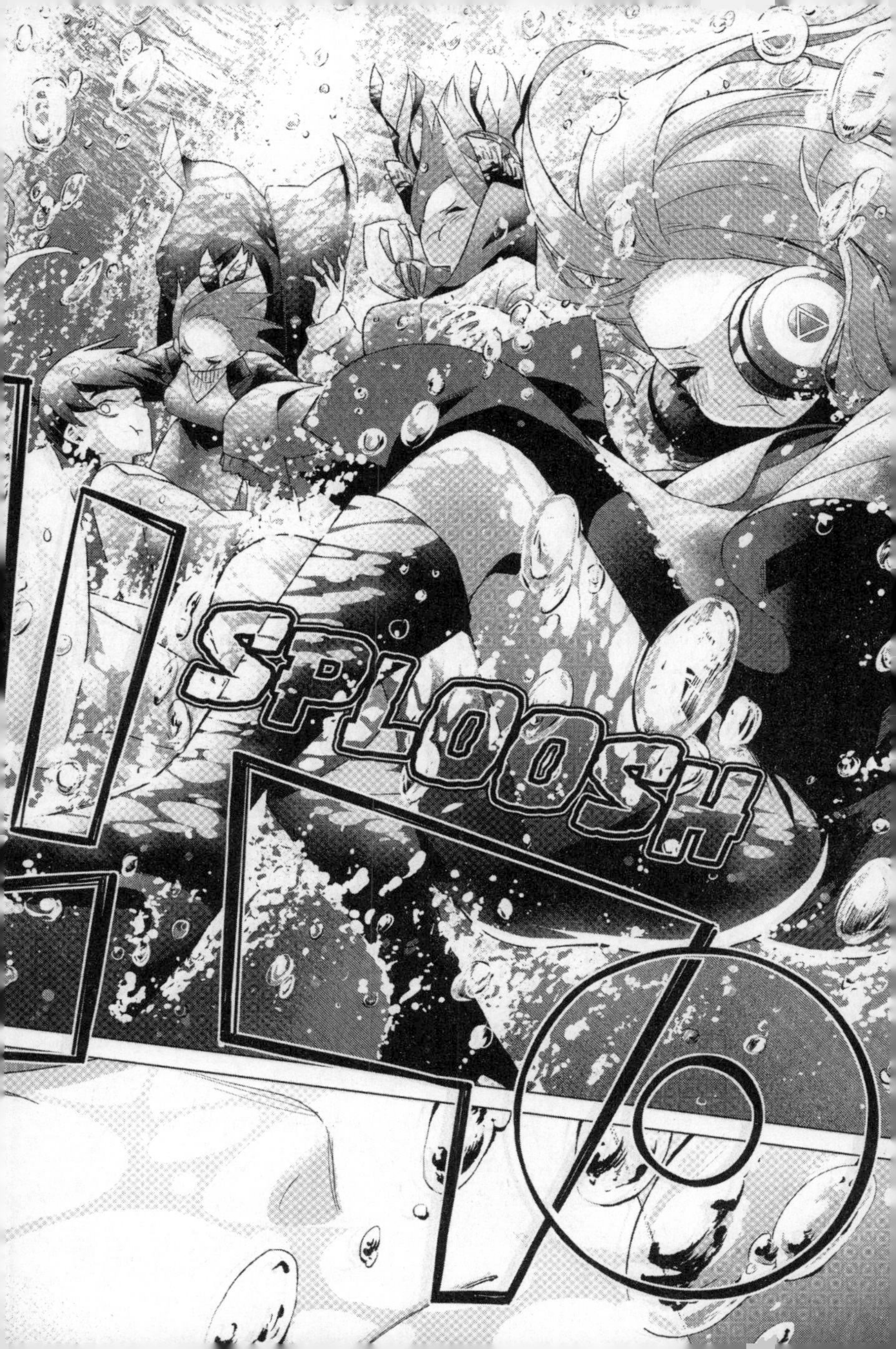
SPLOOSH

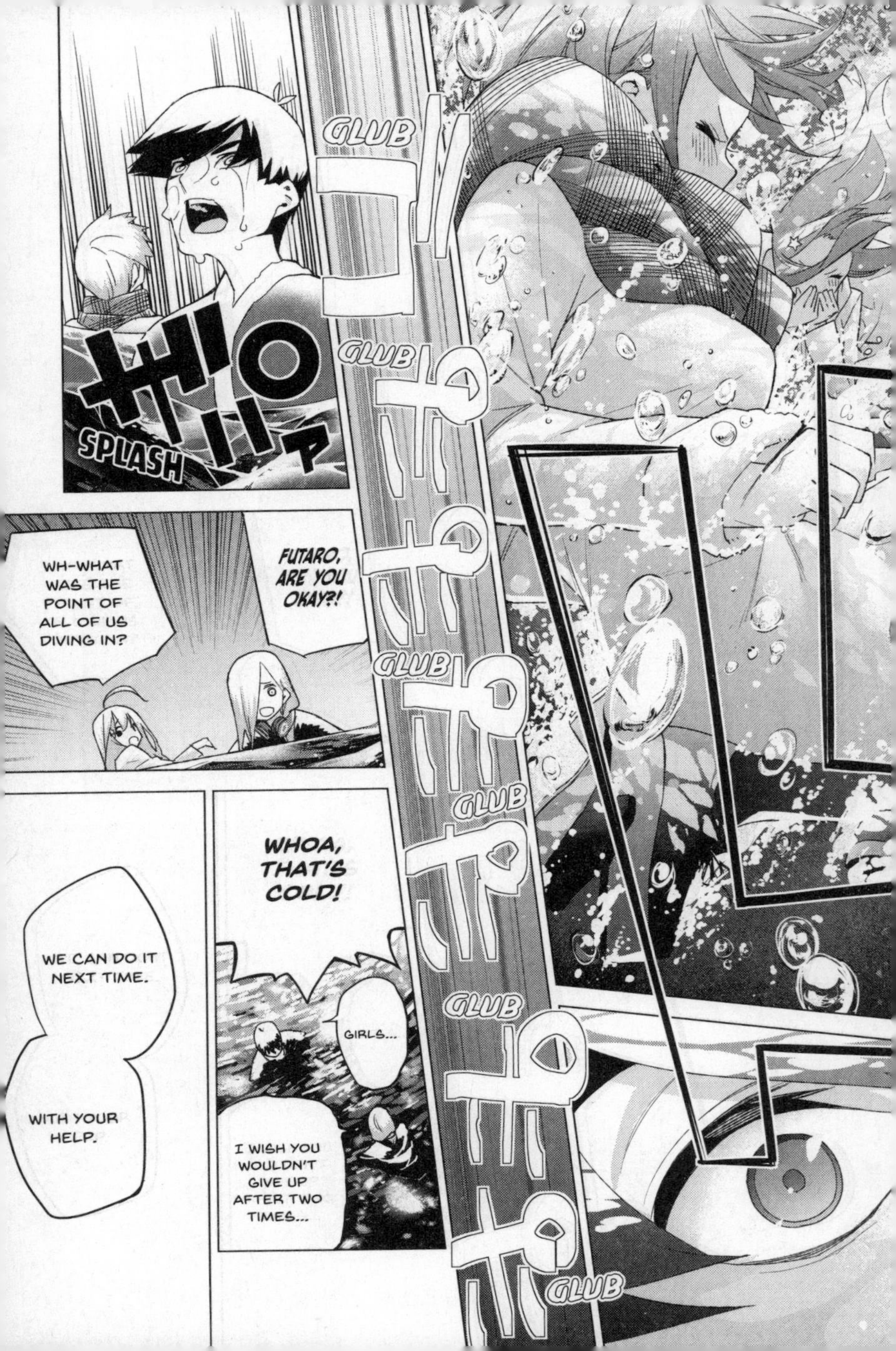
GLUB
GLUB
GLUB
GLUB
GLUB
GLUB
SPLASH
FUTARO, ARE YOU OKAY?!
WH-WHAT WAS THE POINT OF ALL OF US DIVING IN?
WHOA, THAT'S COLD!
GIRLS...
I WISH YOU WOULDN'T GIVE UP AFTER TWO TIMES...
WE CAN DO IT NEXT TIME.
WITH YOUR HELP.

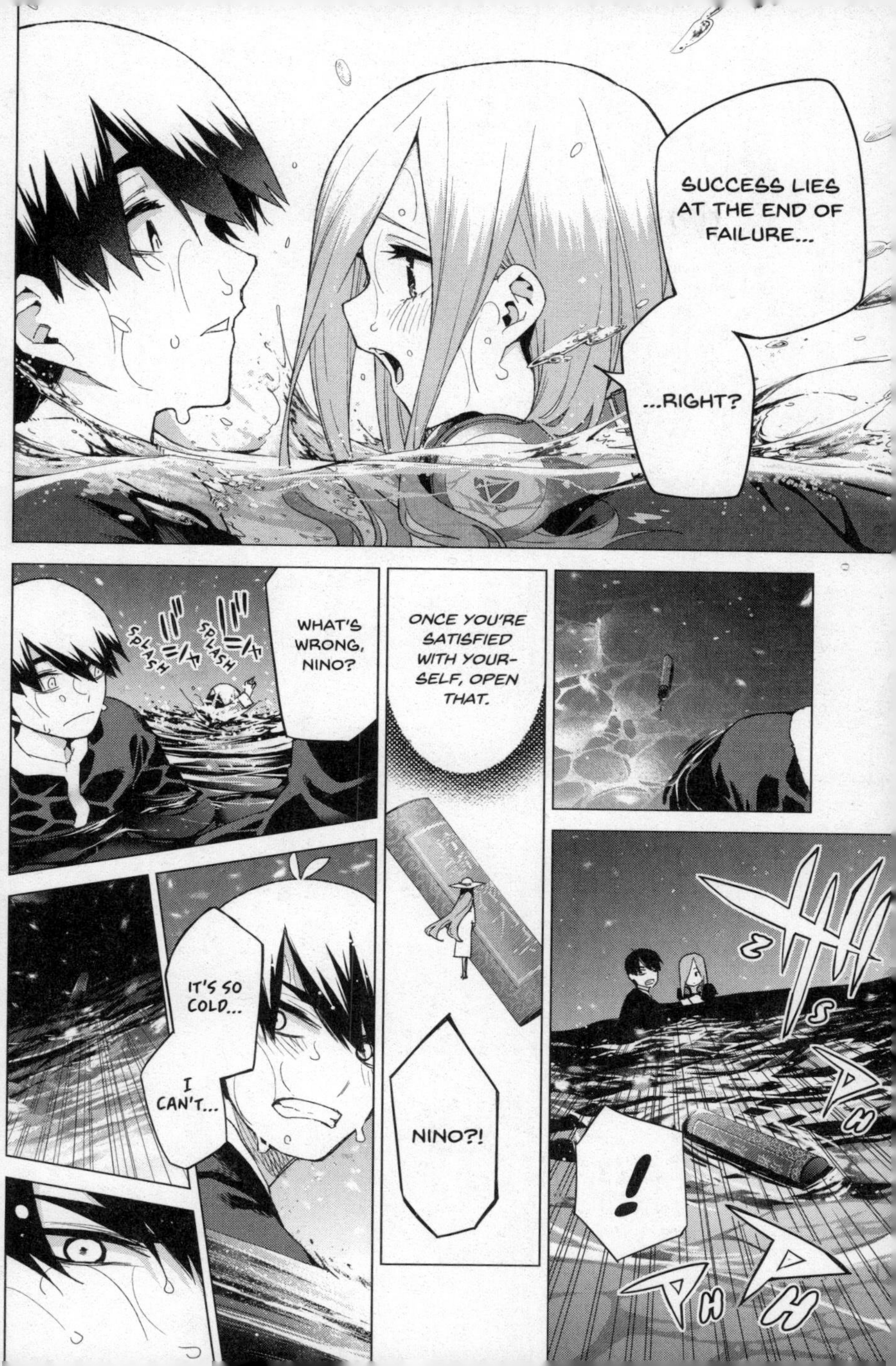
SUCCESS LIES AT THE END OF FAILURE...
...RIGHT?
ONCE YOU'RE SATISFIED WITH YOUR-SELF, OPEN THAT.
WHAT'S WRONG, NINO?
SPLASH SPLASH
!
NINO?!
IT'S SO COLD...
I CAN'T...

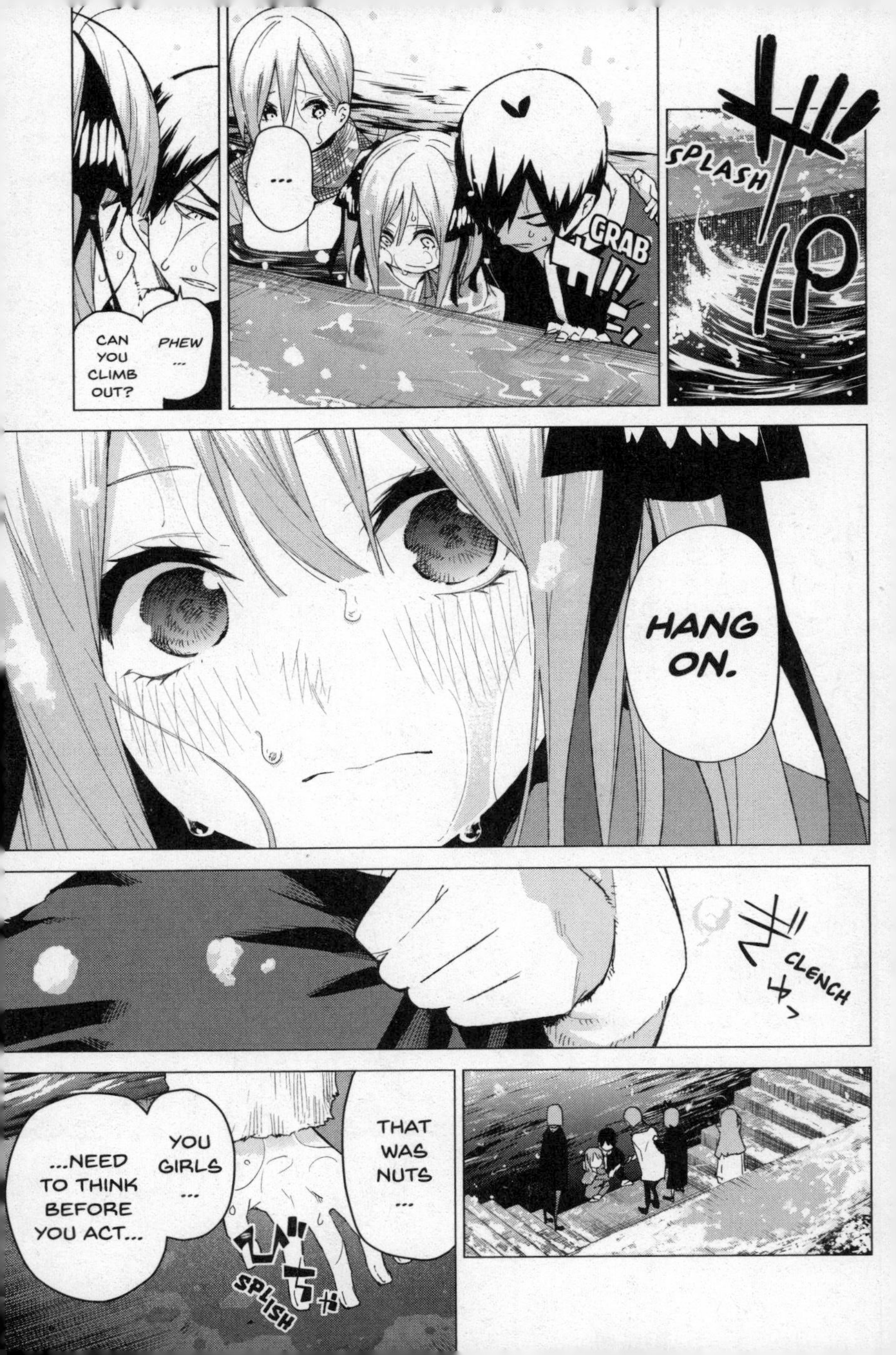
SPLASH
...
GRAB
PHEW ...
CAN YOU CLIMB OUT?
HANG ON.
CLENCH
THAT WAS NUTS ...
YOU GIRLS ...
...NEED TO THINK BEFORE YOU ACT...
SPLISH

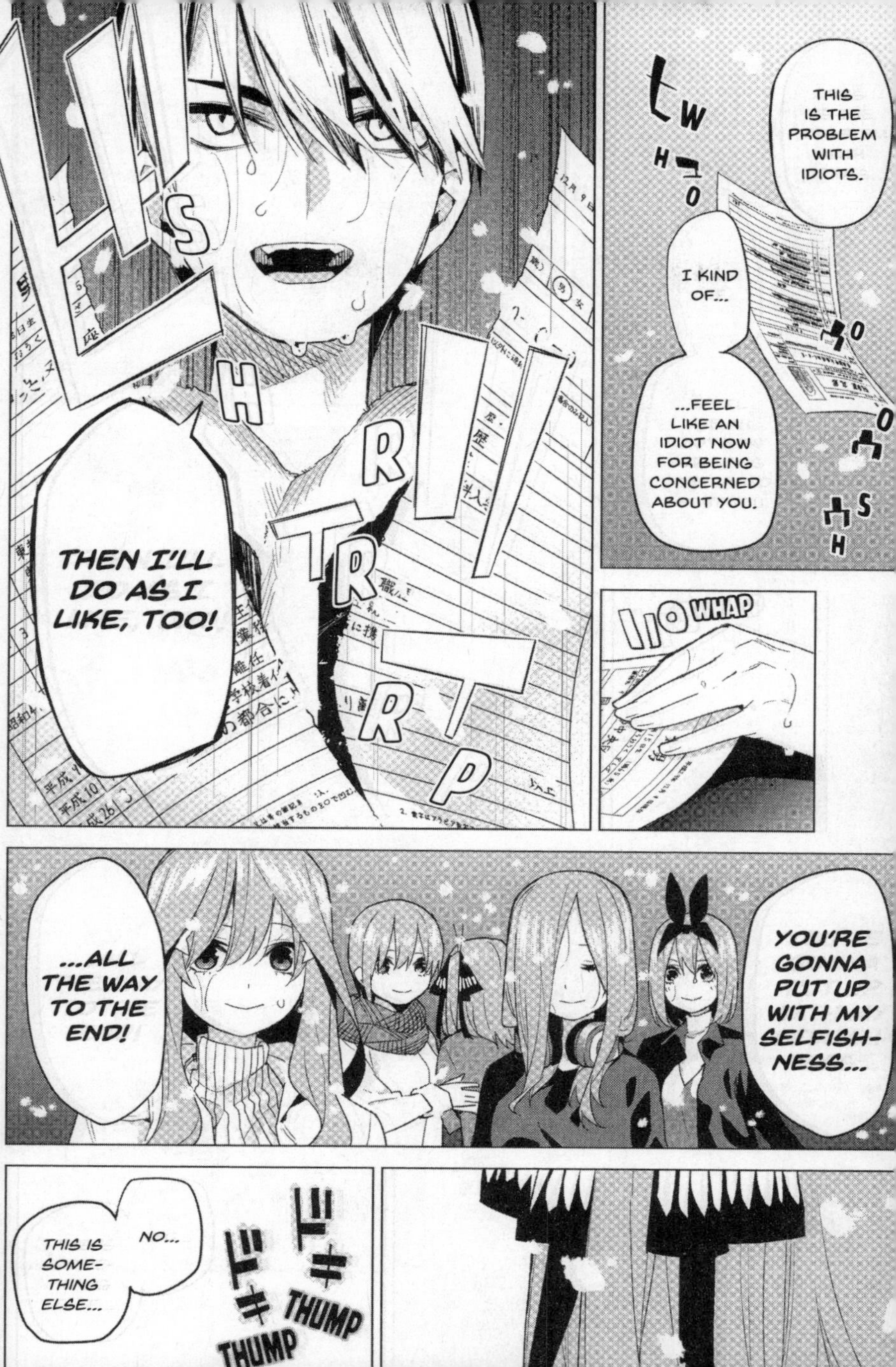
THIS IS THE PROBLEM WITH IDIOTS.
I KIND OF...
...FEEL LIKE AN IDIOT NOW FOR BEING CONCERNED ABOUT YOU.
WHOOSH
WHAP
THEN I'LL DO AS I LIKE, TOO!
YOU'RE GONNA PUT UP WITH MY SELFISH-NESS...
...ALL THE WAY TO THE END!
NO...
THIS IS SOME-THING ELSE...
THUMP
THUMP

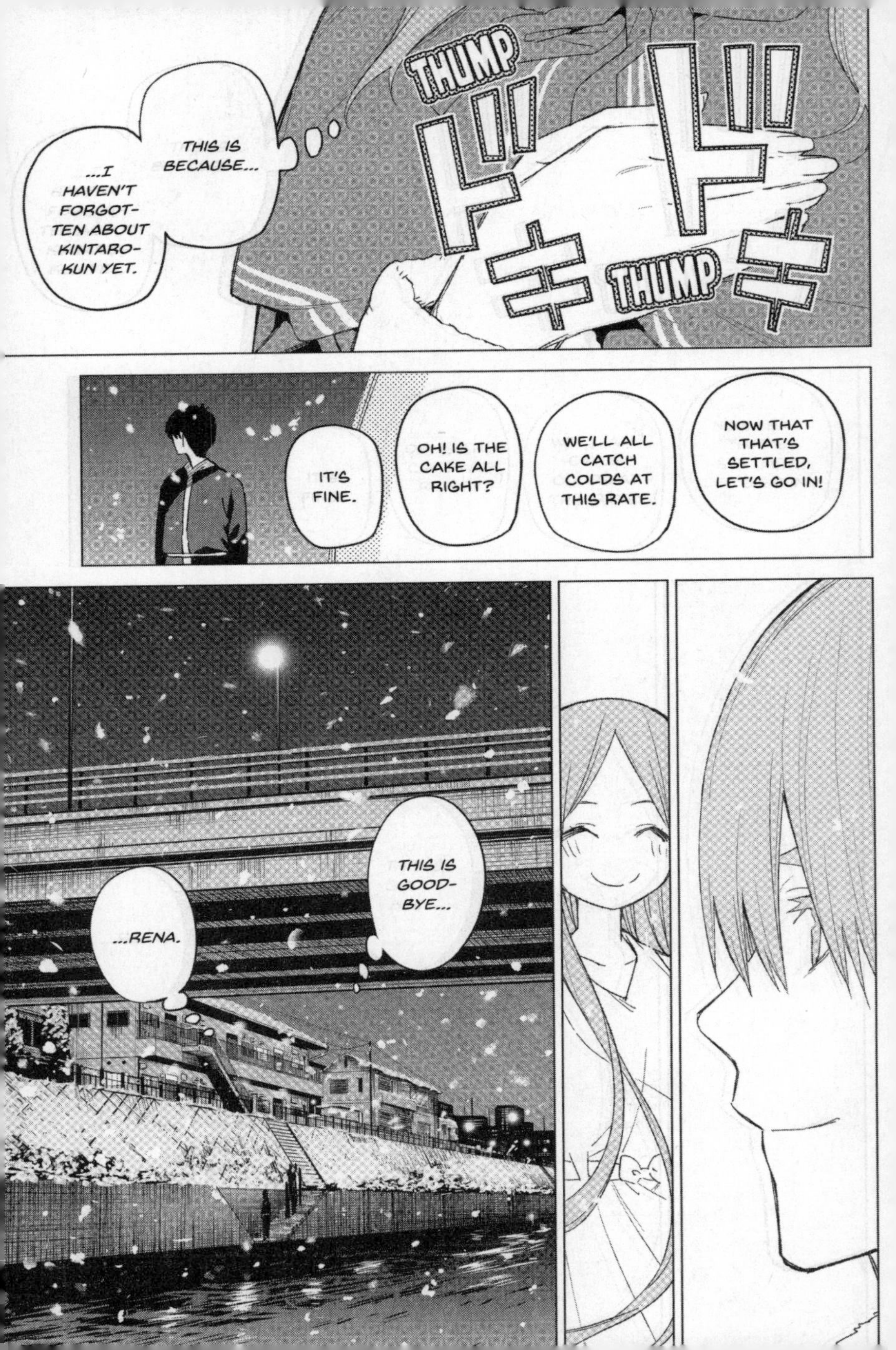
THUMP
THUMP
THIS IS BECAUSE...
...I HAVEN'T FORGOT-TEN ABOUT KINTARO-KUN YET.
NOW THAT THAT'S SETTLED, LET'S GO IN!
WE'LL ALL CATCH COLDS AT THIS RATE.
OH! IS THE CAKE ALL RIGHT?
IT'S FINE.
THIS IS GOOD-BYE...
...RENA.

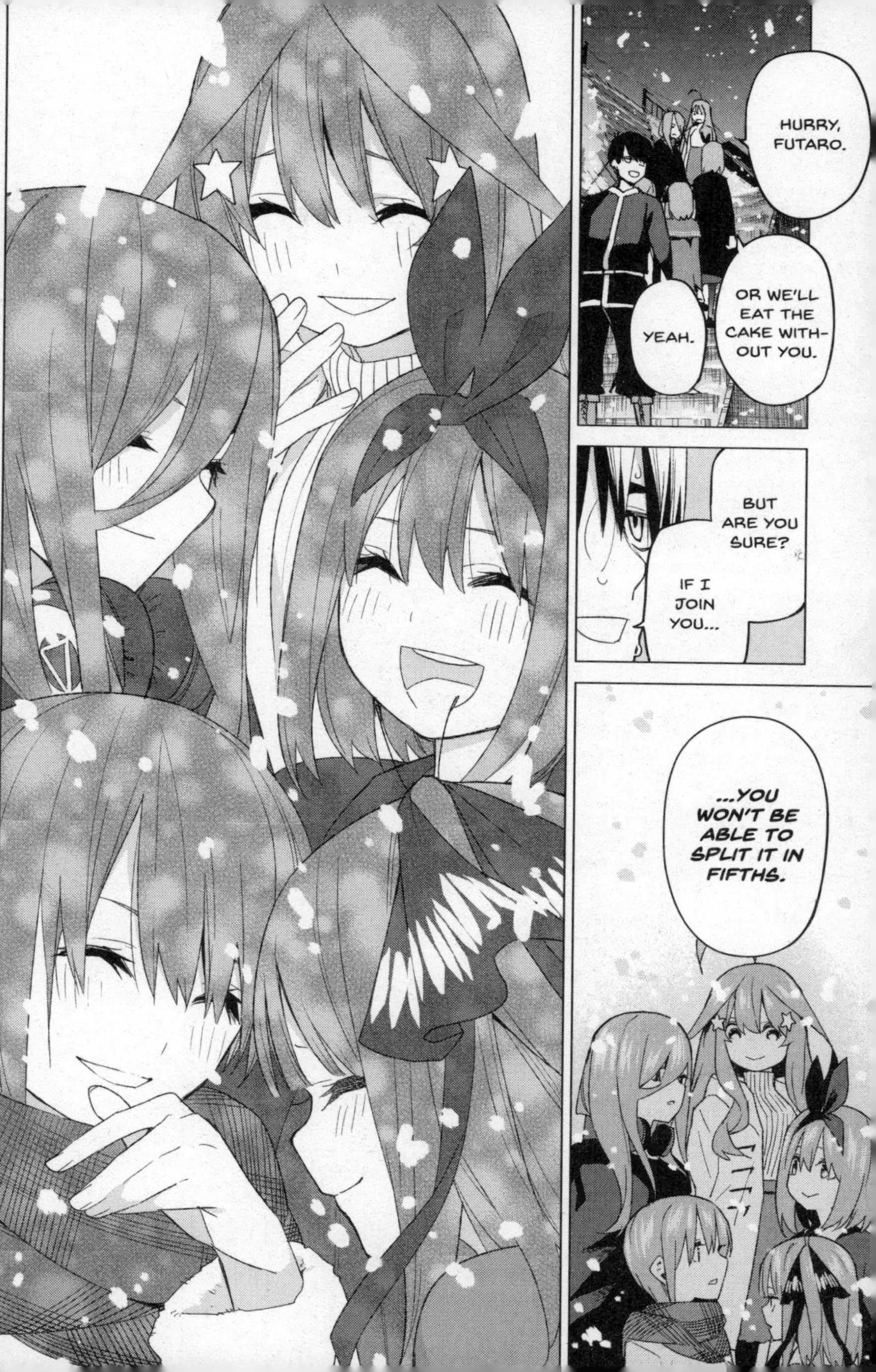
HURRY, FUTARO.
OR WE'LL EAT THE CAKE WITH-OUT YOU.
YEAH.
BUT ARE YOU SURE?
IF I JOIN YOU...
...YOU WON'T BE ABLE TO SPLIT IT IN FIFTHS.

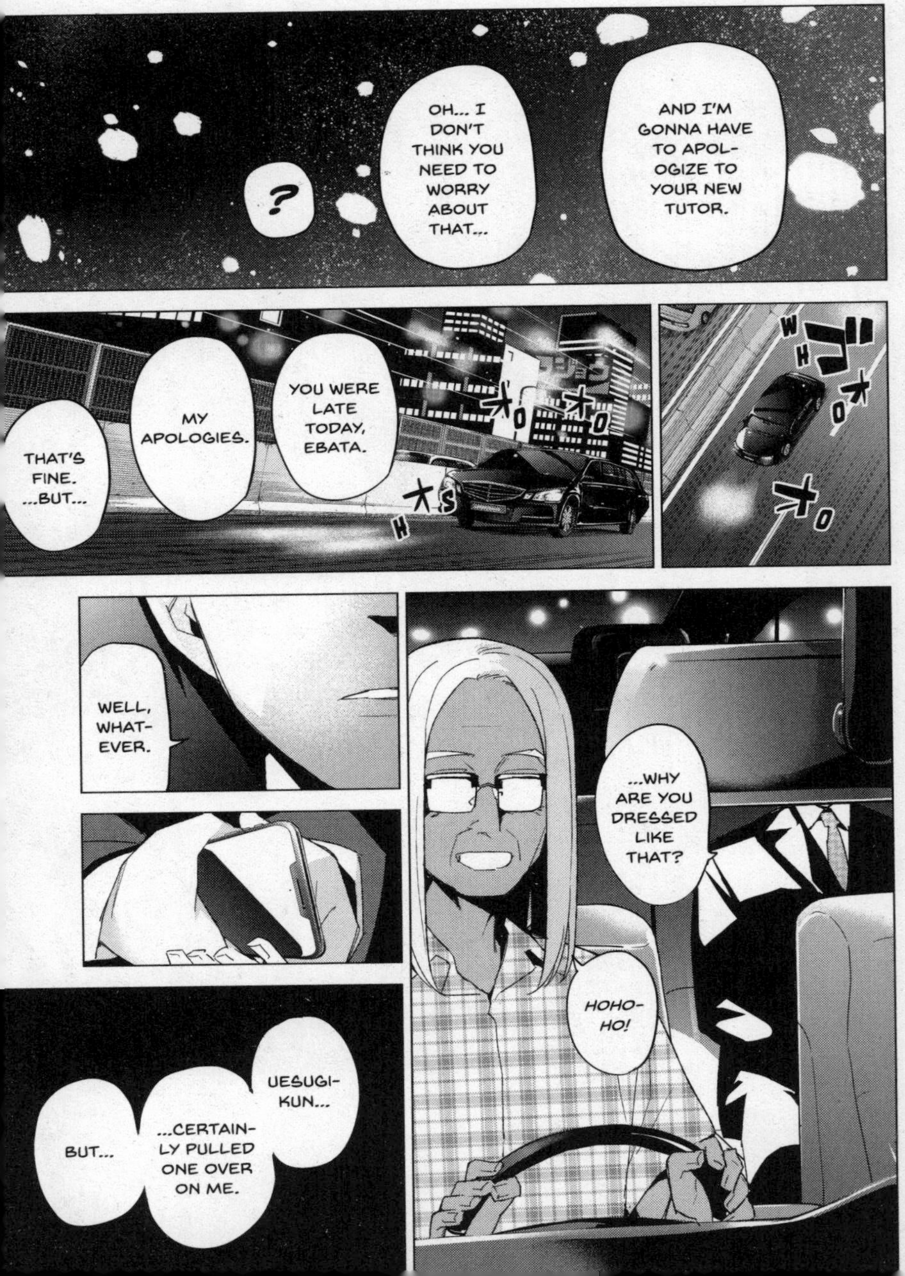
AND I'M GONNA HAVE TO APOLOGIZE TO YOUR NEW TUTOR.
OH... I DON'T THINK YOU NEED TO WORRY ABOUT THAT...
?
YOU WERE LATE TODAY, EBATA.
MY APOLOGIES.
THAT'S FINE. ...BUT...
...WHY ARE YOU DRESSED LIKE THAT?
HOHOHO!
WELL, WHATEVER.
UESUGI-KUN...
...CERTAINLY PULLED ONE OVER ON ME.
BUT...

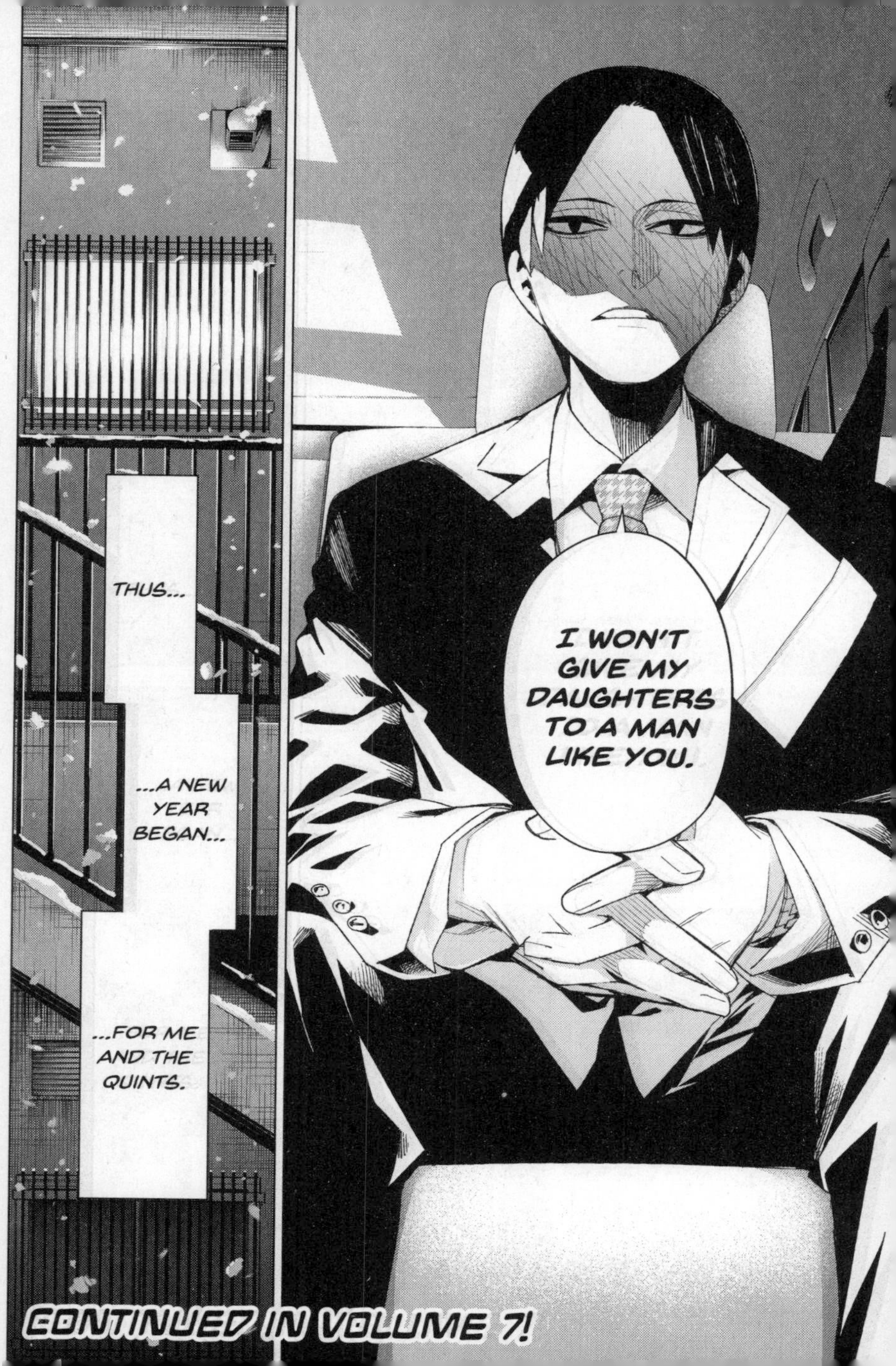
I WON'T GIVE MY DAUGHTERS TO A MAN LIKE YOU.
THUS...
...A NEW YEAR BEGAN...
...FOR ME AND THE QUINTS.
CONTINUED IN VOLUME 7!

Continued in
Volume 7

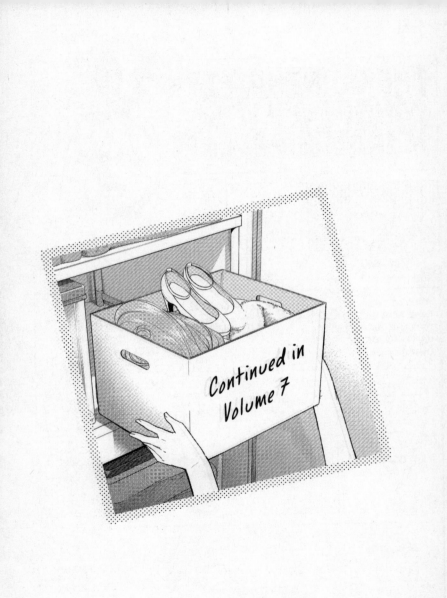

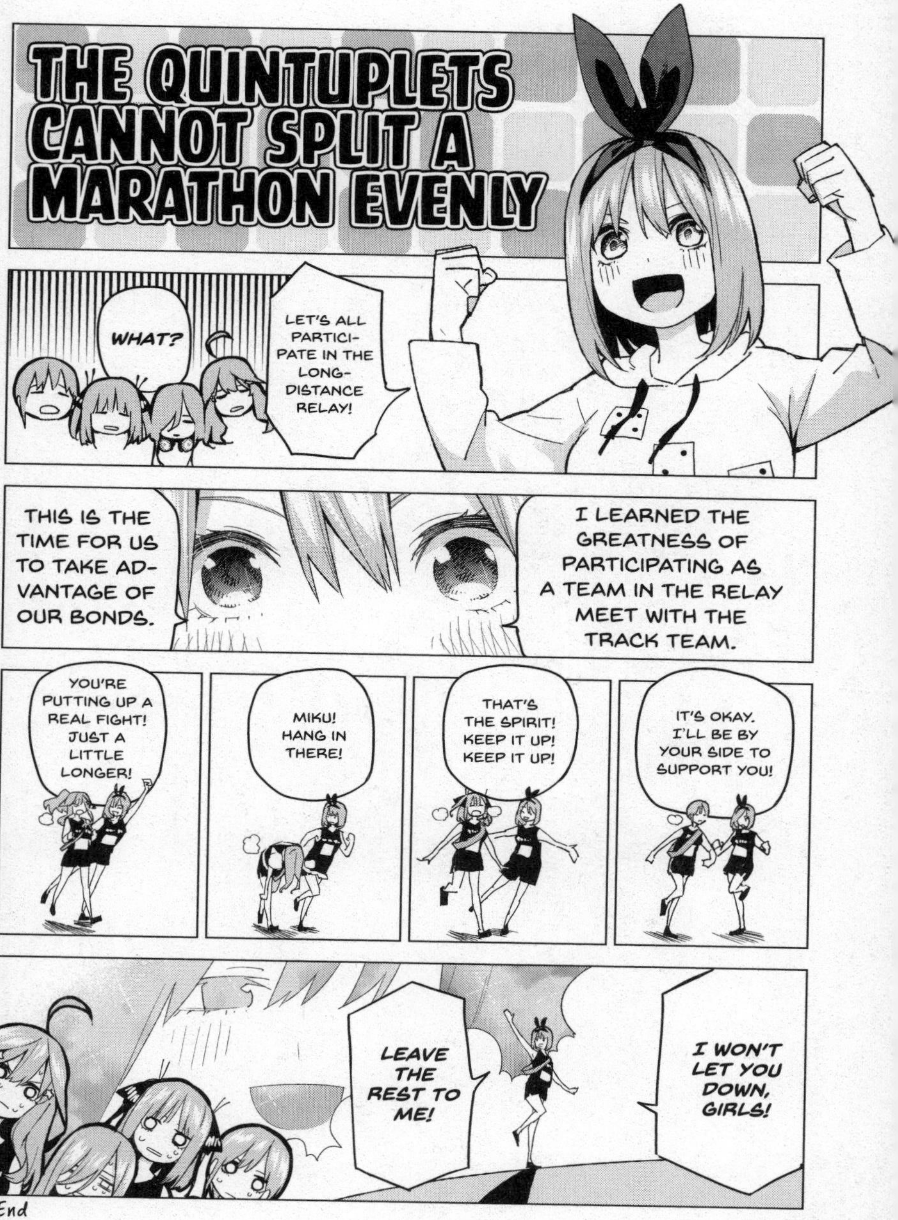
THE QUINTUPLETS CANNOT SPLIT A MARATHON EVENLY
LET'S ALL PARTICIPATE IN THE LONG-DISTANCE RELAY!
WHAT?
I LEARNED THE GREATNESS OF PARTICIPATING AS A TEAM IN THE RELAY MEET WITH THE TRACK TEAM.
THIS IS THE TIME FOR US TO TAKE ADVANTAGE OF OUR BONDS.
IT'S OKAY. I'LL BE BY YOUR SIDE TO SUPPORT YOU!
THAT'S THE SPIRIT! KEEP IT UP! KEEP IT UP!
MIKU! HANG IN THERE!
YOU'RE PUTTING UP A REAL FIGHT! JUST A LITTLE LONGER!
I WON'T LET YOU DOWN, GIRLS!
LEAVE THE REST TO ME!

End

# THE QUINTUPLETS CANNOT SHARE THEIR BUST SIZE EVENLY

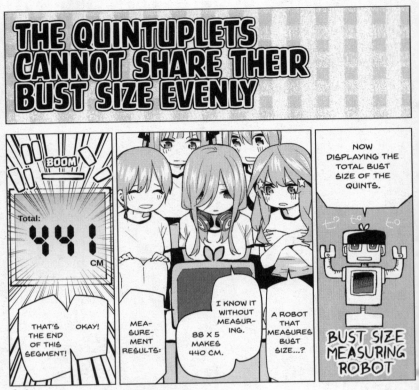

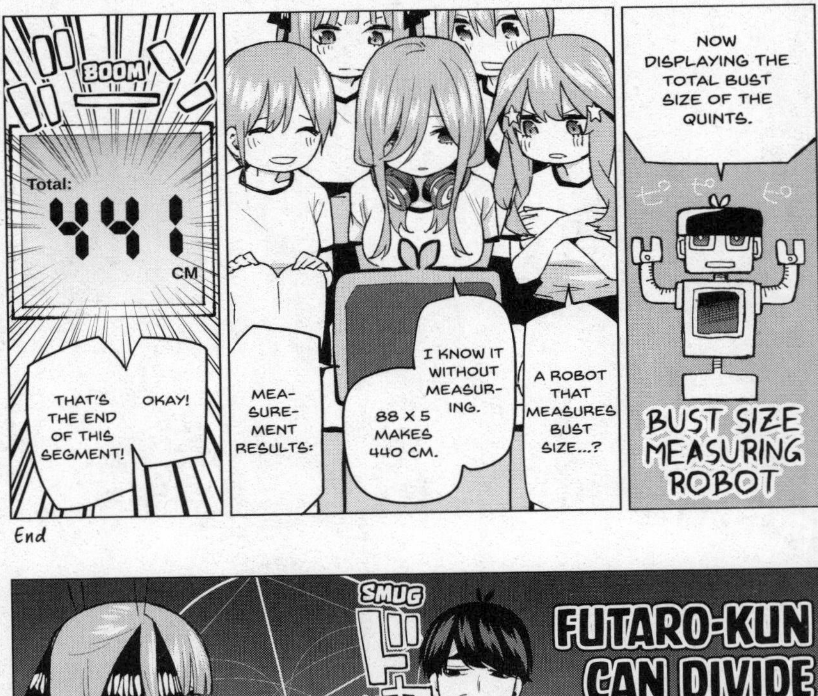
NOW DISPLAYING THE TOTAL BUST SIZE OF THE QUINTS.
BUST SIZE MEASURING ROBOT
A ROBOT THAT MEASURES BUST SIZE...?
I KNOW IT WITHOUT MEASUR-ING.
88 X 5 MAKES 440 CM.
MEA-SURE-MENT RESULTS:
BOOM
Total: 441 CM
OKAY!
THAT'S THE END OF THIS SEGMENT!

End

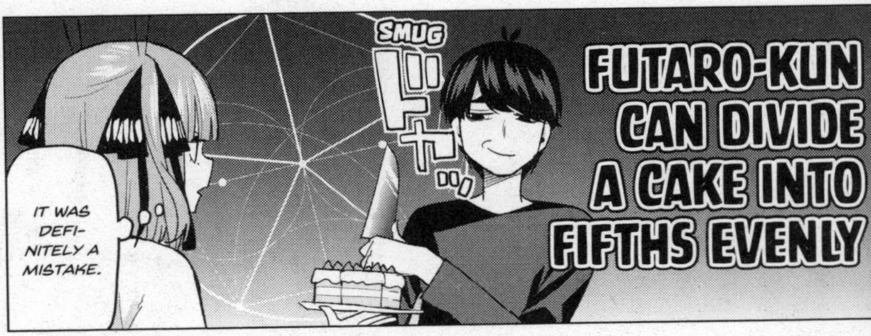
FUTARO-KUN CAN DIVIDE A CAKE INTO FIFTHS EVENLY
SMUG
IT WAS DEFI-NITELY A MISTAKE.

Staff Ueno Hino Cho Erimura

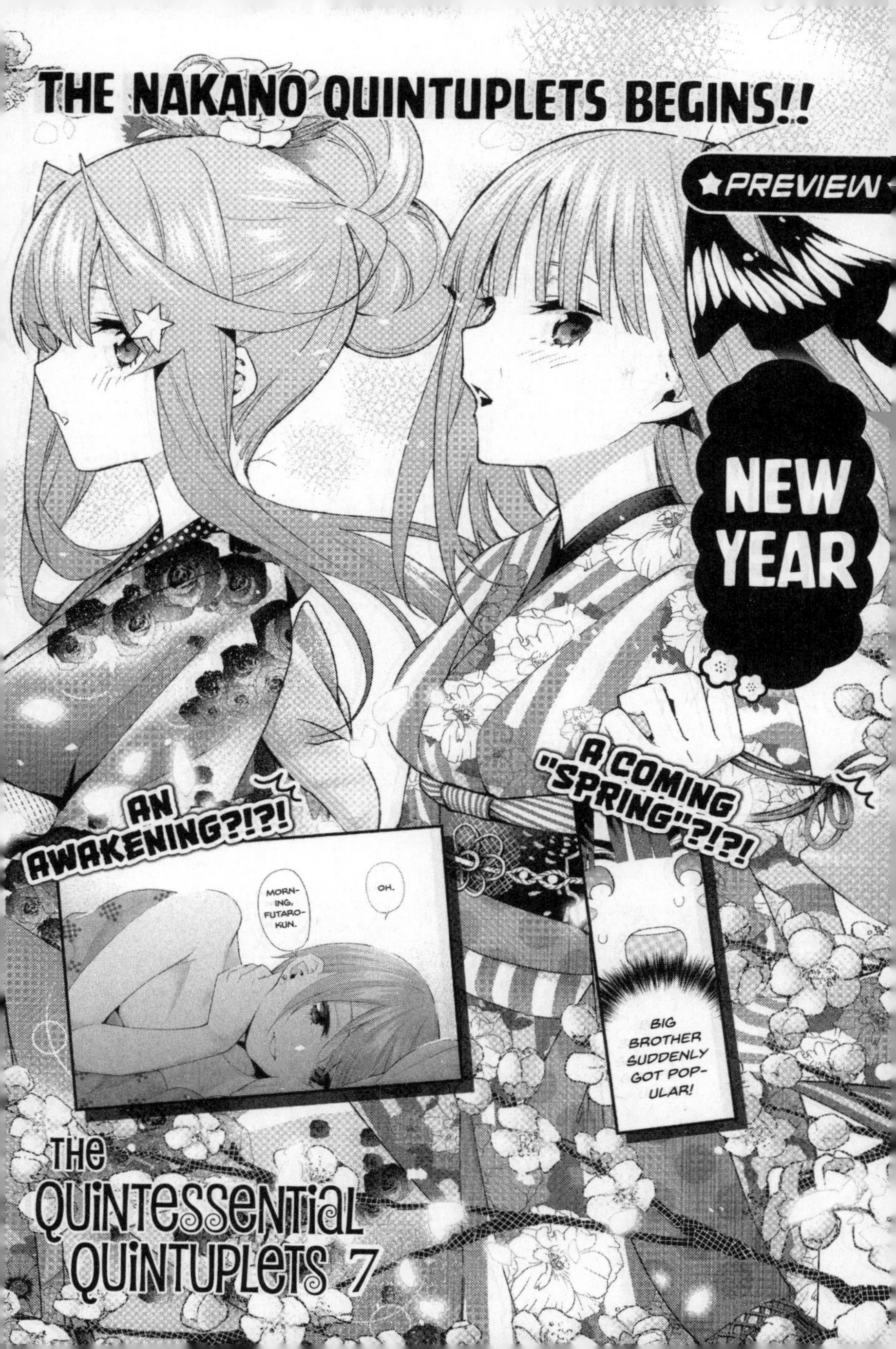
THE NAKANO QUINTUPLETS BEGINS!!
★PREVIEW
NEW YEAR
A COMING "SPRING"?!?!
BIG BROTHER SUDDENLY GOT POP-ULAR!
AN AWAKENING?!?!
OH.
MORN-ING, FUTARO-KUN.
THE QUINTESSENTIAL QUINTUPLETS 7

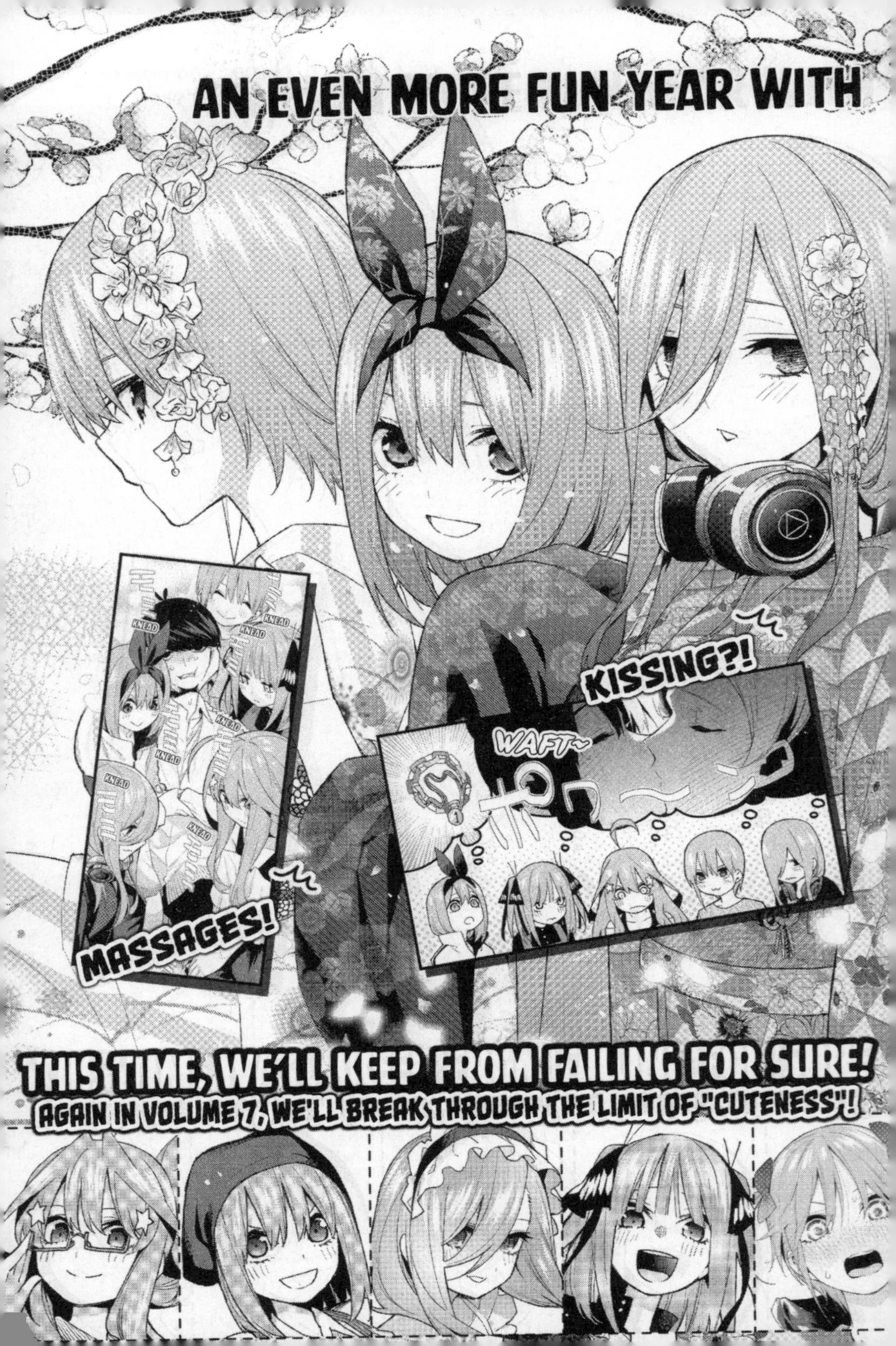
AN EVEN MORE FUN YEAR WITH
KISSING?!
WAFT~
KNEAD
KNEAD
KNEAD
KNEAD
KNEAD
KNEAD
MASSAGES!
THIS TIME, WE'LL KEEP FROM FAILING FOR SURE!
AGAIN IN VOLUME 7, WE'LL BREAK THROUGH THE LIMIT OF "CUTENESS"!

A Kodansha Comics Trade Paperback Original
The Quintessential Quintuplets 6 copyright © 2018 Negi Haruba
English translation copyright © 2019 Negi Haruba

Published in the United States by Kodansha Comics, an imprint of
Kodansha USA Publishing, LLC, New York.

Publication rights for this English edition arranged through
Kodansha Ltd., Tokyo.

First published in Japan in 2018 by Kodansha Ltd., Tokyo
as Gotoubun no Hanayome, volume 6.

ISBN 978-1-63236-855-3

Cover Design: Saya Takai (RedRooster)

Printed in Mexico.

www.kodansha.us

9 8 7 6 5
Translation: Steven LeCroy
Lettering: Jan Lan Ivan Concepcion
Editing: David Yoo, Thalia Sutton
Additional Layout: Belynda Ungurath
Editorial Assistance: YKS Services LLC/SKY Japan, INC.
Kodansha Comics edition cover design by Phil Balsman

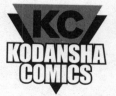

Publisher: Kiichiro Sugawara
Managing editor: Maya Rosewood
Vice president of marketing & publicity: Naho Yamada

Director of publishing services: Ben Applegate
Associate director of operations: Stephen Pakula
Publishing services managing editor: Noelle Webster
Assistant production manager: Emi Lotto